MW01013749

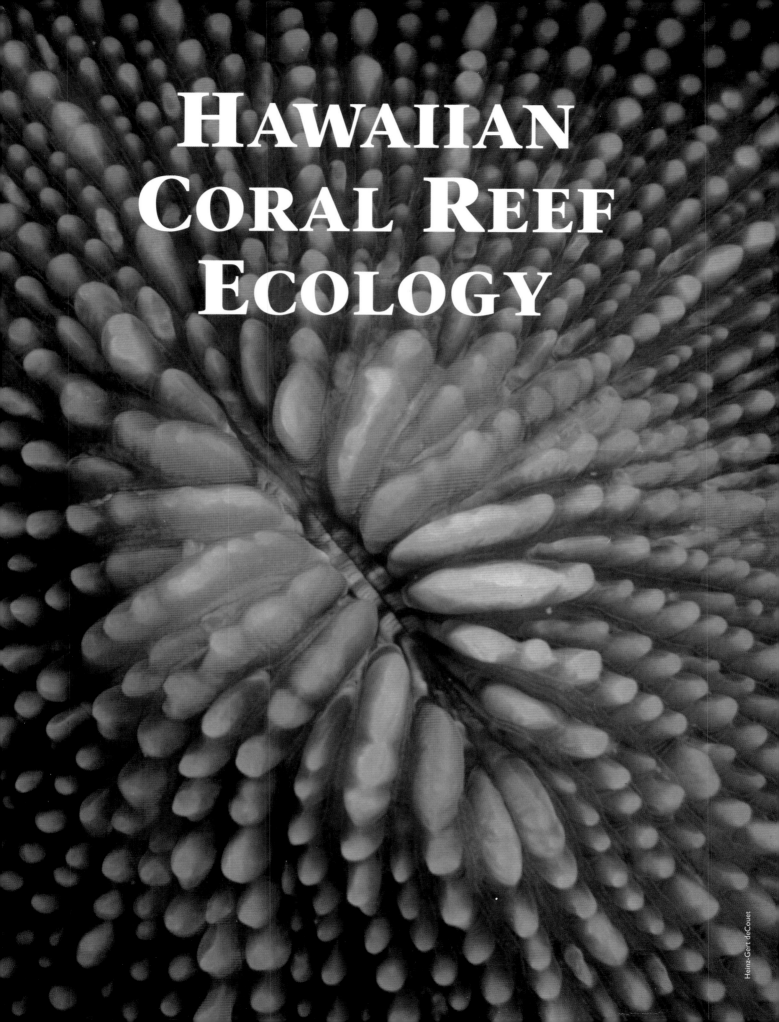

HAWAIIAN
CORAL REEF
ECOLOGY

Heinz-Gert deCouet

For Dr. Nancy Chin, who planted the seed a long, long time ago, to Tina Lau who nourished it and kept it going, and to all the Peter Pans (and a Lorax or two) who helped it to bloom.

Finally, to my mom and dad, who each in their own way, encouraged me to strive to look at the world upside down and sideways, but most importantly, gave me the opportunity to do so.

Copyright © 1998
by Mutual Publishing

No part of this book may be reproduced in any form or by any electronic or mechanical means, including information storage and retrieval devices or systems, without prior written permission from the publisher, except that brief passages may be quoted for reviews.

Cover photo by David Schrichte

All rights reserved
Library of Congress Catalog Card Number: 98-67134

First Printing, April 1999
1 2 3 4 5 6 7 8 9

Casebound
ISBN 1-56647-221-0

Softcover
ISBN 1-56647-234-2

Mutual Publishing
1215 Center Street, Suite 210
Honolulu, Hawaii 96816
Telephone (808) 732-1709
Fax (808) 734-4094
e-mail: mutual@lava.net
url: http://www.pete.com/mutual

Printed in Korea

HAWAIIAN CORAL REEF ECOLOGY

DAVID GULKO

Recommended for use by the Curriculum Research & Development Group (CRDG) of the University of Hawaii as a companion text to their Fluid Earth/Living Ocean Marine Science Program, and with other science courses dealing with marine science in middle schools, high schools, and community colleges.

MUTUAL PUBLISHING

Heinz-Gert deCouet

ACKNOWLEDGEMENTS

This book was only possible because of the help and encouragement of a large number of professional people in both Coral Reef Research and Marine Education. Special thanks go to Mark Heckman, Dr. Carol Hopper, and Dr. Cindy Hunter (Waikiki Aquarium), Drs. Paul Jokiel and Bob Kinzie (Hawai'i Institute of Marine Biology), Dr. Bob Richmond (University of Guam), Dr. Dave Krupp (Windward Community College), John Hoover, and Dr. William Walsh for reviewing the whole or portions of the manuscript. Specific sections were reviewed by: Dr. Greta Aeby (Coral Parasites & Symbiosis); Dr. Deborah Gochfeld (Corallivores); Rich Pyle & Lisa Privatera (Fish Behavior), and Dr. Franklyn Te (Human Impacts). Please note that all of these people are experts in their respective fields, each of them holding a wealth of untapped (ok, I tapped it a little bit...) knowledge; I owe them a huge debt of gratitude. Additional thanks go out to Dr. Roy Bidwell for final editing, Heather Burkett and Jane Hopkins for final layout work.

Anybody can take a good underwater photo, fewer still can take a great photo underwater. Once in a great while you meet someone who can actually compose a picture to show a process or a behavior. Such an artist can take a picture that shows one thing obviously and one or two other things completely different upon closer inspection. I am truly blessed to be associated with a number of these rare type of people. I am indebted to Heinz (Gert) deCouet, Deborah Gochfeld, Paul Jokiel, Sara Peck, Richard Pyle, Marc Rice and Keoki Stender for allowing me to use many of their phenomenal photographs; photographs which have enabled me to show things that others have only been able to talk about. I also wish to thank Greta Aeby, Chris Evans, Richard Grigg, Cindy Hunter, Dave Itano, Ian Johnston, Jean Kenyon, Dave Krupp, Lori Mazzuca, Lisa Privitera, Scott Santos and Yuko Stender for use of their unique photographs on specific subjects, many of which have never before been seen by the general public.

Richard Pyle

TABLE OF CONTENTS

GETTING THE MOST FROM THIS BOOK

This book is designed to be used easily by both novices and experts in reef ecology and corals. Regardless of background, I hope that readers will get a different slant on things each time they go through it. I've tried to make it visually interesting as well as factual so that it can be used as a ready resource. Most importantly, it is hoped that readers will appreciate the complex and intricate behaviors that occur among and between animals found on the reef. We must all work a lot harder to protect the whole resource by supporting it through our friends and community, and by influencing our local, state and federal governments.

A WORD ABOUT THE USE OF SCIENTIFIC TERMINOLOGY

Every effort has been made to represent information in everyday language and still be accurate. Where scientific language is heavily used, drawings are often incorporated to assist in understanding the material. Additionally, there is a full **Glossary (Appendix III)**. Like most scientists, I tend to take terminology too seriously; hopefully, you'll be able to look beyond the names and focus instead on the processes and relationships.

THEORY VS FACT

One of the most interesting things about studying ecology and, to some extent corals, is that so little is set down as fact. Many of the current theories presented in this book have never been extensively tested. Still, introducing you to some of the ongoing research in coral reef ecology should give you a feeling for the complexity of the ecosystem.

In order to minimize confusion, the following (T) symbol is used throughout the book to denote material that comes from untested scientific theories or hypotheses.

LAYOUT OF THE BOOK

There is full use of graphics and drawings throughout, but often minimal text associated with these diagrams. This was done on purpose so readers will become drawn into working their own way through the diagrams. This process allows the wonder of "discovery" which is probably one of the most magical things about science, no matter what your background.

ADDITIONAL FEATURES

Cnidoquestions

These are designed to provoke further thinking and discussion on the topics presented. It is hoped that the reader will delve into the questions in detail as opposed to just looking up the answer in the back of the book. Luckily, some of these questions are open-ended and have no pre-determined answer.

Tidbits & Trivia Pages

Numerous sections of the book present a wide variety of interesting information on a specific topic. Often this information represents recent findings and discoveries in the field of coral reef science; at other times, it's just interesting trivia.

The Big Picture Pages

These bring together and synthesize a lot of related material to show it in a larger setting.

Subject Bibliography

Appendix IV lists related books followed by an additional subject bibliography of scientific papers where one can look for more sources of information on specific subjects of interest.

The Infographic

This concentrated informational graphic is designed to give the reader visual data on symbiotic organisms, reproduction, habitat and predators of the organism(s) being featured. As shown in the example below, each section is labeled and provides specific information. Please refer to the guide below as a key to the different sections.

Predators

These are listed by common name (more information on the coral predators can be found in the section on Corallivores). Please note that common predators are represented, but by no means all the predators associated with many of these reef organisms.

Reproduction

This section primarily shows sexual reproduction (the only asexual reproduction shown is the asexual production and release of planula larvae). It provides information on whether the organism/colony broadcast spawns or broods its larvae. Also whether an organism/colony is hermaphroditic (that is both male and female either simultaneously or sequentially, i.e. starts life as one sex and later changes into the other) or is made up of separate sexes. For many of the organisms featured, the section provides months and moon phases under which spawning/planula release occurs.

Habitat

Light green arrows (as shown) point out where a featured organism is most likely to be found. The graphic is broken up into distinctive regions: Sandy Bay (shallow, sandy bottomed, calm), Calm Bay (relatively shallow [1 - 10 m], calm, may include patch reefs), Reef Flat (very shallow, hard substrate with small sand patches, lots of water movement), Reef Crest (high wave energy, very shallow), Shallow Reef Slope (medium energy, 3 - 15 m), Deep Reef Slope (low energy, 15 - 30 m), Deep (deeper then 30 m), Caves and Ledges (low-light, lots of vertical substrate), Pelagic (open-water, offshore), Rocky Shores (intertidal, basalt substrate, very shallow).

Symbionts

Common symbionts for each organism/colony are shown; these may be commensals, mutualists or parasites. More information on specific symbionts may be found in Section II: Corals as Condominiums, and in Appendix I: Coral Symbionts by Species.

Examples of symbiont symbols:

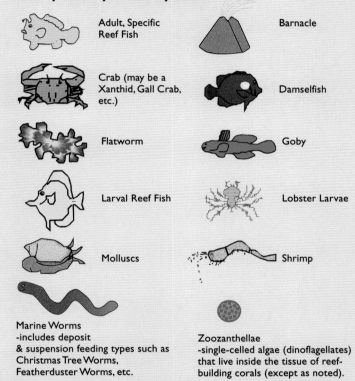

Adult, Specific Reef Fish

Barnacle

Crab (may be a Xanthid, Gall Crab, etc.)

Damselfish

Flatworm

Goby

Larval Reef Fish

Lobster Larvae

Molluscs

Shrimp

Marine Worms
-includes deposit & suspension feeding types such as Christmas Tree Worms, Featherduster Worms, etc.

Zoozanthellae
-single-celled algae (dinoflagellates) that live inside the tissue of reef-building corals (except as noted).

Examples of Reproduction symbols:

Broadcast Spawning

Brood & Release Planula Larvae

Moon Phases

Sequential Hermaphrodites

Simultaneous Hermaphroditic Organisms/Colonies

Separate Male & Female Organisms/Colonies

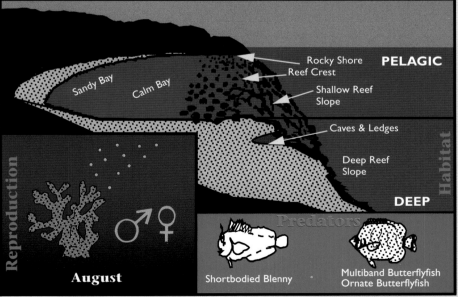

Symbionts

Reproduction

August

PELAGIC

Rocky Shore
Reef Crest

Shallow Reef Slope

Caves & Ledges

Deep Reef Slope

Sandy Bay

Calm Bay

Habitat

DEEP

Predators

Shortbodied Blenny

Multiband Butterflyfish
Ornate Butterflyfish

INTRODUCTION

What's this? A whole book about corals and coral reefs? Where are the fish? Whales? Spectacular underwater scenery? Obviously, this is not a typical "Coffee Table Book" nor is it a "Field Guide." In essence, it's a book for a wide variety of users; from tour boat drivers and dive masters, to teachers and students, to amateur scientists and professional beachcombers.

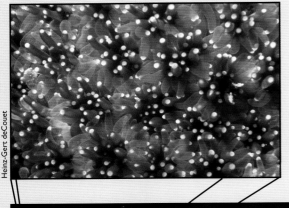

Heinz-Gert deCouet

Heinz-Gert deCouet

THE BOOK ITSELF IS ARRANGED INTO THREE MAJOR SECTIONS:

I. Corals as Organisms

This first section introduces the reader to corals as animals. It looks in detail at the types of individual corals and related organisms; specifically, their behavior, physiology and structure. In essence, it provides a glimpse into the ecology of the coral as an organism.

II. Corals as Condos

This section deals primarily with how individual coral colonies are used as habitat by a wide variety of other organisms. It also examines the ecology of the coral colony.

III. Coral Reefs as Ecosystems

The final section explores the wide variety of interactions and effects on, in, and around coral reefs. It explores the reef as a unique environment made up of a large diversity of organisms dependent upon a concentration of coral colonies and associated structures as a support base. This section also looks at the effect of humans on this ecosystem, and what can be done to better protect it.

WHAT IS THIS THING CALLED ECOLOGY?

Ecology: the study of interactions between an organism and its environment (both physical and biological).

All living organisms interact in some way with their environment.

Interactions may involve members of their own species...

...as well as other species

Within their biological environments, organisms can be organized into distinct groupings:

Species

A natural group of organisms that can interbreed.

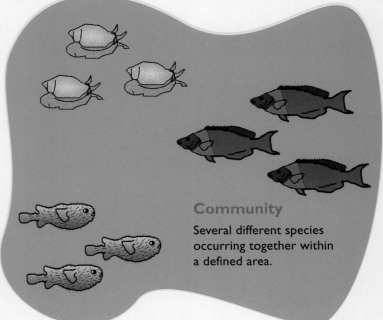

Community

Several different species occurring together within a defined area.

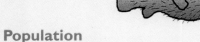

Population

All of the individuals of a species within a defined area.

All of these can live and interact within an ecosystem.

WHAT MAKES UP AN ECOSYSTEM?

ENERGY SOURCE

BIOLOGICAL INTERACTIONS

Predation   Competition
          Symbiosis

CLIMATE

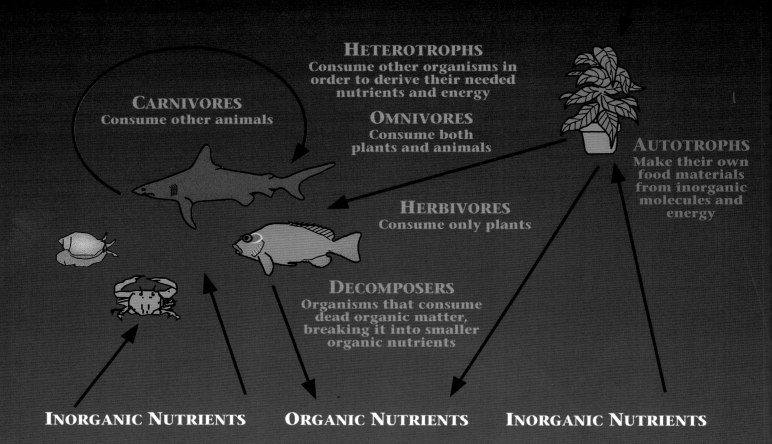

HETEROTROPHS
Consume other organisms in
order to derive their needed
nutrients and energy

CARNIVORES
Consume other animals

OMNIVORES
Consume both
plants and animals

AUTOTROPHS
Make their own
food materials
from inorganic
molecules and
energy

HERBIVORES
Consume only plants

DECOMPOSERS
Organisms that consume
dead organic matter,
breaking it into smaller
organic nutrients

INORGANIC NUTRIENTS   **ORGANIC NUTRIENTS**   **INORGANIC NUTRIENTS**

An **ecological system (ecosystem)** is made up of a variety of different communities and includes both a **biotic** (living or biological) component and an **abiotic** (non-living) component (i.e. climate, physical energy, geological layout). All ecosystems require an ultimate source of energy (usually the sun) which is then transformed into **organic** (biologically-produced) energy by various types of organisms. These are termed **Primary Producers**, usually marine plants, seaweed or phytoplankton in the ocean. This organic energy can then be used by organisms that feed on the primary producers (**Herbivores**) or that feed on their decaying remains after they die (**Decomposers**). Herbivores are in turn preyed upon by organisms that feed only on animals (**Carnivores**). Notice that a cycling occurs in a natural ecosystem of organic nutrients (energy). In addition, inorganic materials such as oxygen, water and minerals are often cycled among and between the abiotic and biotic components of the environment.

Within the biotic component, organisms may interact with each other in a number of ways:

Predation occurs when one organism kills and consumes another organism.

Competition occurs when two or more organisms vie for the same resource which is in limited supply; this could be an abiotic component such as space, or a biotic one such as food or access to a mate.

Symbiosis occurs when two or more different organisms share a close association with each other.

A Quick Note About Systematics:

All living things from the smallest bacteria, to trees, mushrooms and whales can be grouped into five **Kingdoms**. All of the organisms pictured above and to the right are multicellular heterotrophs which belong to the kingdom **Animalia**. A quick look and one can see that there are great differences among many of the animals pictured; we can reduce them down into smaller groupings based on shared characteristics. The largest grouping within a kingdom is called a **Phylum**; each of the animals shown below is in the phylum **Chordata** based on each having a backbone-like structure, a dorsal nerve cord and possessing at some point in its life, pharyngeal gill pouches.

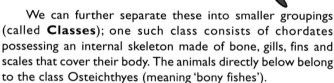

We can further separate these into smaller groupings (called **Classes**); one such class consists of chordates possessing an internal skeleton made of bone, gills, fins and scales that cover their body. The animals directly below belong to the class Osteichthyes (meaning 'bony fishes').

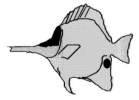

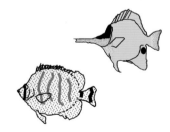

Within the bony fishes are many **families** of fishes. One such family which is very common on Hawaiian coral reefs is the Butterflyfish family (Chaetodontidae) shown on the right.

Unique types of animals within a family can be grouped based upon a two-part scientific name. The first part is called a **Genus** and is always capitalized; the second part is the **species** name and is not capitalized. Such a system of classification becomes very important when trying to talk about organisms to other people, especially those in other areas. For example, the fish shown below on the right is called *Kikakapu* in Hawaiian, but there are other types of fish also called *Kikakapu*. The common English name is the 'Multibanded Butterflyfish' but the same common names are often used elsewhere to describe completely different animals, hence the importance of using scientific names. Think of it like your own name; often your first name is common and shared by many people, but, along with your last name, tends to make you a unique individual who other people can recognize. The fish shown on the right is in the genus *Chaetodon*, in which there are many species of butterflyfish; but it is a unique *Chaetodon* which has been given the species name of *multicinctus*.

KINGDOM	**ANIMALIA**
PHYLUM	**CHORDATA**
CLASS	**OSTEICHTHYES**
FAMILY	**CHAETODONTIDAE**
GENUS	***CHAETODON***
SPECIES	***MULTICINCTUS***

Chaetodon multicinctus

ISLAND FORMATION

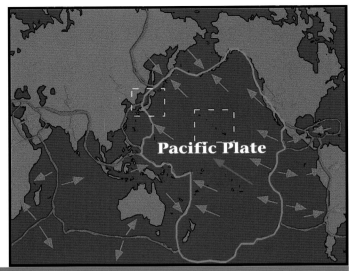

If one were able to view the earth with its oceans drained away, one would see huge mountain ranges spread throughout the lengths of the seafloor. These ranges represent some of the edges of the great crustal plates upon which all the continents and seafloors reside. Crustal (or **lithospheric**) plates are in a constant state of movement (a couple of centimeters per year!). Often in areas where the plates contain continents that moved in opposite or sideways directions, great mountain ranges such as the Himalayas or Andes were formed when the plates collided or rubbed against each other. When contact occurs under ocean areas, often one plate will slide under the other (termed **submergence**). When this occurs (A), friction from one plate sliding under the other melts the crustal material, creating molten rock. This can work its way to the surface of the plate creating a submerged volcano which eventually forms islands such as Japan, the Aleutians, or the

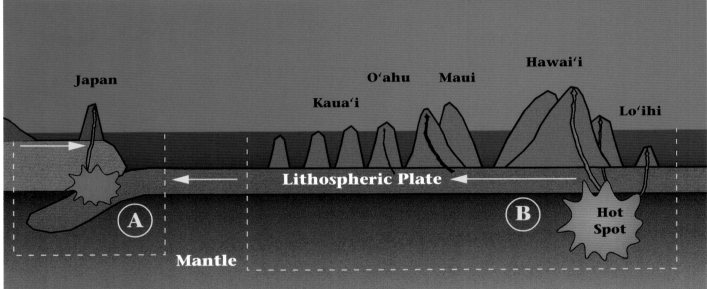

Philippines. These types of islands, often associated with deep trenches immediately offshore (also caused by submergence), are termed **Volcanic Island Arcs**.

Oceanic islands like the Hawaiian Islands (B) are thought to be formed quite differently. As the Pacific Plate moves in a northwesterly direction it passes over a stationary **Hot Spot**, a place where molten rock from the earth's mantle perforates the lithospheric plate. This molten material is very different from the molten rock associated with island arc volcanoes. As long as the plate is roughly over the hot spot, volcanic material can accumulate and add to the emerged island (the island of Hawai'i for example) or eventually form new islands such as Lo'ihi (the still submerged volcano off the southeastern coast of the island of Hawai'i). As the plate continues to move toward the northwest, the emerged islands are eventually cutoff from their lava sources and most volcanic activity ceases. Pools of trapped, insulated lava may eventually be exposed over time due to erosional factors, causing what are termed **post-erosional eruptions** (which formed structures like Diamond Head or Punchbowl on the island of O'ahu).

Islands start to erode from the moment they're born due to factors such as wind, rain and wave action. This is why the Hawaiian Islands become progressively less-pronounced in size and elevation as one moves from the southernmost island (Hawai'i) towards the northwest. These erosional processes are aided by the fact that the islands themselves are basically overweight! Over time the volcanic material that makes up the island (much of which was internal and insulated) will cool and condense. This material is now much heavier than the lighter, expanded material that existed before in its place; it is this increased density from slowly cooling over millions of years that causes the islands to sink. Beyond Kaua'i, the islands practically disappear and sink beneath the surface, leaving atolls (see p. 126) in their place. These too will eventually disappear and one finds submerged islands or seamounts (the Emperor Seamounts extend for quite a distance north of Midway). The Hawaiian Islands serve as both an excellent textbook example and a living laboratory for studying these processes. As we shall see, those tiny colonial animals we call corals play a very important roll in this multi-million year megaprocess.

One of the primary erosional forces on islands is wave action. The beaches that are found throughout Hawai'i are the result of waves eroding away reef, shoreline and mountains; white sand results from eroded reef, black sand from eroded volcanic basalt (lava). Wave action on beaches (*far left*) is very different from wave action on exposed coastlines. If you look at a rocky coastline you'll notice contours and inlets caused by wave action. The erosional force of the wave is often not spent on the innermost spot of the inlet but instead on the sides, eventually causing a sea arch to be formed (*left*); over time the arch will collapse and form a sea stack or small offshore island (*below*).

Waterfalls (primarily caused by rainfall) cut deep valleys into islands (*left*). The windward side of the island will often have steep cliffs (*below*) versus the long valleys and ridges seen on many leeward sides. These cliffs are exposed to the effects of both wind and freshwater runoff in addition to the storm waves that pound into them every winter.

Wave action eroding away the sides of an inlet can often create sea caves such as this massive cave along the north side of Moloka'i (*left*). This cave is large enough to take a small sailboat into. Though it appears calm in this photo, the waves that erode caves such as this expend massive amounts of energy.

Such intense erosional factors may have spectacular results (*left*), such as this massive landslide off the cliffs on the east side of Lana'i.

EVOLUTION OF HAWAIIAN MARINE SPECIES

Due to the highly isolated nature of the Hawaiian Islands, many of the organisms common to reefs throughout the Pacific are rare or absent here. This has created open ecological **niches** (specific roles for distinct species within a community), allowing species that were here to move into them over time. As a result, a limited number of original colonizing species have radiated extensively into unique species found nowhere else in the world.

The following approximate percentages of organisms are **endemic** to the Hawaiian Islands (i.e., found nowhere else in the world except here):

Overall Invertebrates *	**32%**		
Sponges	29%	Marine Snails (Mesogastropods)	21%
Jellyfish (Sea Jellies)	0%	Sea Cucumbers	40%
Reef-Building Corals	18%	Sea Urchins	47%
Non-Reef-Building Corals	49%	Brittlestars	49%
Marine Worms (Polychaetes)	28%	Sea Stars (Starfish)	65%
Overall Reef Fish	**25%**		
Angelfish	57%	Moray Eels	11%
Blennies	62%	Parrotfish	44%
Butterflyfish	14%	Scorpionfish	35%
Cardinalfish	20%	Surgeonfish	0%
Damselfish	44%	Triggerfish	0%
Gobies	40%	Wrasses	39%

* Includes deepwater invertebrates which increases the endemism percentages.

SECTION I:
CORALS AS ORGANISMS

Heinz-Gert deCouet

EVERYTHING YOU EVER WANTED TO KNOW ABOUT CNIDARIANS*
*But were afraid to ask...

Phylum CNIDARIA

Portuguese man-of-war

Hydroids

Upside-down Jellies

Sea Jellies

Box Jellies

Class **Hydrozoa**   Class **Scyphozoa**   Class **Cubozoa**

Anemones

Soft Corals

Sea Fans

Zoanthids

Stony Corals

Precious Corals

Class **Anthozoa**

All of the above organisms belong to the phylum **Cnidaria** (Greek: *knidos* - nettle). A **phylum** is a large grouping of organisms that share basic key characteristics. Cnidarians share the following:

- All contain unique stinging structures called **cnidae** (the most common of which are called **nematocysts**). These stinging cells are one of the defining features of this phylum.
- They are **radially symmetric** (referring to the regular arrangement of body parts around a central axis; imagine a wheel with spokes, any of which can divide the wheel into two equal parts, thus making it radially symmetric).
- Cnidarians are made up of **tissues**, groups of cells specialized for specific functions. They consist of an outer **epidermis**, an inner **gastrodermis** (sometimes referred to as an endodermis) and a middle layer made up of a jelly-like material.
- They have two basic body forms: the **medusa** and the **polyp**.
- They have only one body cavity (the **coelenteron**), with a single opening (i.e., both a mouth and anus) which serves a wide variety of functions (see p. 15).
- They lack a head, a centralized nervous system, and formal excretory, circulatory or respiratory systems.
- They often have a unique larval form called a **planula** larva (see pp. 86-90).

The phylum can be arranged into four discrete classes (a finer grouping of organisms than the level of phylum):

- **Class Hydrozoa**: Hydrozoans consist of the feather-like hydroids often seen on pier pilings, the Portuguese man-of-war, and Fire Corals. They often have both an attached (sessile) and a free-living (medusa) stage.
- **Class Scyphozoa**: Scyphozoans are free-living and often found in open water. These are the Sea Jellies (Jellyfish).
- **Class Cubozoa**: Cubozoans are often mistaken for sea jellies, but differ in a number of important ways.
- **Class Anthozoa**: Anthozoans consist of the anemones, soft corals, sea fans, zoanthids, stony (or reef-building) corals and the precious corals (black coral).

Cnidarian Body Forms

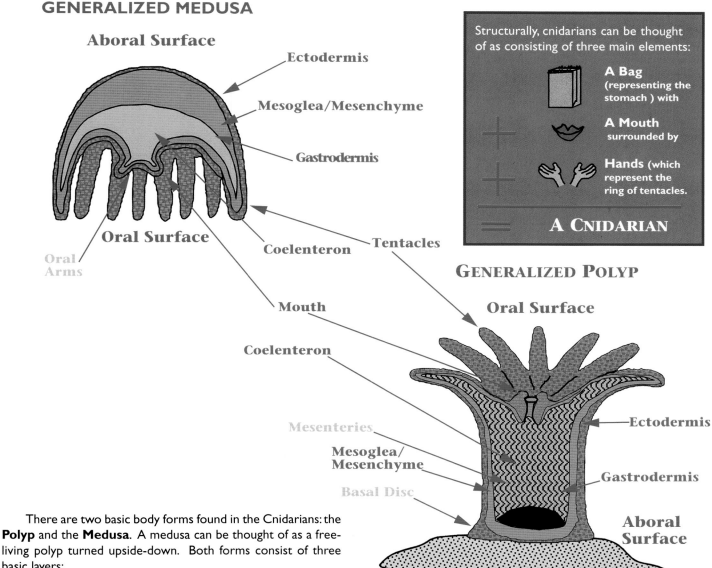

GENERALIZED MEDUSA

Aboral Surface

Ectodermis

Mesoglea/Mesenchyme

Gastrodermis

Oral Surface

Oral Arms

Coelenteron

Tentacles

Mouth

Coelenteron

Mesenteries

Mesoglea/ Mesenchyme

Basal Disc

Structurally, cnidarians can be thought of as consisting of three main elements:

A Bag (representing the stomach) with

A Mouth surrounded by

Hands (which represent the ring of tentacles.

A CNIDARIAN

GENERALIZED POLYP

Oral Surface

Ectodermis

Gastrodermis

Aboral Surface

There are two basic body forms found in the Cnidarians: the **Polyp** and the **Medusa**. A medusa can be thought of as a free-living polyp turned upside-down. Both forms consist of three basic layers:

- the **Ectoderm**, which is the outer-most layer containing cnidocytes (stinging cells), sensory cells, and epitheliomuscular cells.
- the **Endoderm**, which is the inner-most layer. Often referred to as the **Gastrodermis** since it primarily lines the coelenteron (or stomach). It consists of flagellated gastrodermal cells (cells with whip-like tails for moving food and water around) and cells that produce either mucus or digestive enzymes.
- the **Mesenchyme** or **Mesoglea**. This is the jelly-like middle layer of cnidarians; it tends to be relatively thin in Anthozoans and thick in Scyphozoans (hence the name Sea Jellies, though this name can also refer to a variety of other gelatinous creatures such as tunicates or ctenophores).

The medusa is the free-living body form; it contains essentially the same structures as the polyp, lacking primarily just the mesentaries and the basal disc. The medusa form often has manipulative, tentacle-like structures around the the mouth termed **Oral arms**. Scyphozoans spend the majority of their life cycle in this form, while it is totally absent in the Anthozoans.

The polyp is the sessile body form, often being attached to the surface by way of a **Basal** (or Pedal) **Disc**. In Scyphozoans and Hydrozoans this is the asexual stage of the life cycle (the sexual phase occuring in the medusa body form). Anthozoan polyps often contain **mesenteries** which tend to compartmentalize the coelenteron.

A large part of the diversity seen in this phylum is thought to be due to the presence of these two body forms. The sessile polyp and free-living medusa (along with a highly asexual life history) provide a form of plasticity which may have enhanced the exploitation of uniquely different environments.

CNIDARIANS AS CLONAL ORGANISMS

Usually when we think of individuals we imagine each organism existing as a distinctly different being. Each organism is unique due to differences in its genetic make-up. While you and your best friend may both be humans, there are subtle differences (in hair color, eye color, height, etc.) due to very small changes in the genes you both have.

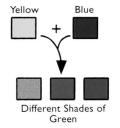

Two Parents produce 3 Offspring
Total of 5 genets

Yellow   Blue

Different Shades of
Green

Sexual Reproduction

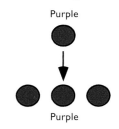

One Parent produces 3 Offspring
Total of 1 genet

Purple

Purple

Asexual Reproduction

Corals and other cnidarians are usually described as **modular** organisms, since they often occur in colonies made up of repeating units. Each unit (polyp) is genetically identical to the rest. Most colonies tend to be physically connected, but genetically identical organisms (or **clones**) can also exist as disconnected organisms or groups. Such **clonal organisms** can originate through a variety of asexual processes (see pp. 78 - 81), and cloning as a process is seen in about 3/4 of all invertebrate phyla.

For sessile organisms (like corals) cloning offers certain distinct advantages:

1) Clonal organisms often have fast growth rates, which allows for rapid exploitation of a habitat.

2) By organizing into modules, a colonial organism can increase in biomass (size) without a corresponding decrease in the surface-to-volume ratio (see below).

3) Cloning may provide the ability to get around the effects of age (senescence); the clone-type lives longer than any single module.

4) Cloning allows the colony's modules to regenerate to replace dead ones (resulting in only partial mortality from the colony's perspective).

5) Spreading the risk of total colony mortality among distant colonies enhances long-term survival of the clone (see right).

If, instead of looking at individual organisms as distinct units, we looked at unique genetic combinations, an "individual" could exist at a number of levels. From this viewpoint, each **genet** would possess a unique genetic component. In the photo of a coral colony shown above, each individual polyp is genetically identical to the next; in such a situation the genet (or "individual") would be the entire coral colony (as opposed to a single coral polyp).

In some cases, colonial organisms may fragment, or release asexually-produced larvae which may disperse and settle some distance from the parent colony, yet remain genetically-identical to that colony. In this case, the genet (or "individual") could actually exist in a number of places at the same time! By now you are probably wondering what, in the world of cnidarians, qualifies as an individual organism? Is it a polyp? A colony? Is it multiple colonies (a sort of super-organism)? Because of the wonders of cloning, the answer is "yes", "yes", and "yes" (I know, looking at the world through the eyes of a genet is often a confusing experience!).

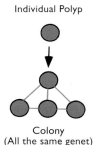

Individual Polyp

Colony
(All the same genet)

The surface area to volume ratio is very important in allowing organisms to exchange materials with their environment. As this ratio decreases, an organism has a more difficult time supplying its cells with nutrients and getting rid of wastes.

Small Organism   vs   Large Organism   vs   Colony of Clones

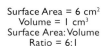

1 cm
1 cm
1 cm

Surface Area = 6 cm^2
Volume = 1 cm^3
Surface Area: Volume
Ratio = 6:1

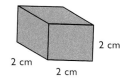

2 cm
2 cm
2 cm

Surface Area = 24 cm^2
Volume = 8 cm^3
Surface Area: Volume
Ratio = 3:1

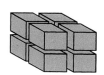

2 cm

Surface Area = 48 cm^2
Volume = 8 cm^3
Surface Area: Volume
Ratio = 6:1

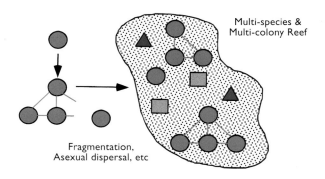

Multi-species &
Multi-colony Reef

Fragmentation,
Asexual dispersal, etc

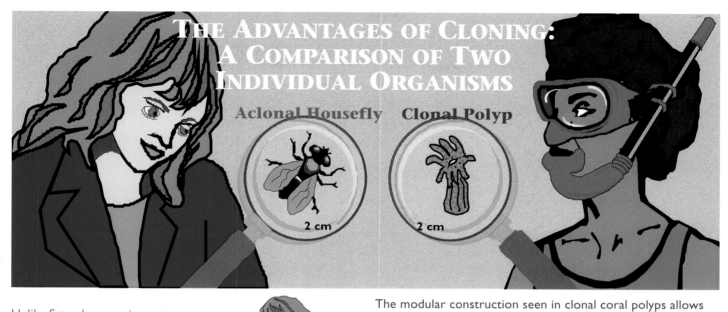

THE ADVANTAGES OF CLONING:
A COMPARISON OF TWO
INDIVIDUAL ORGANISMS

Aclonal Housefly   Clonal Polyp

2 cm   2 cm

Unlike Saturday morning cartoons, aclonal organisms face physiological and biomechanical limits on how large they can grow.

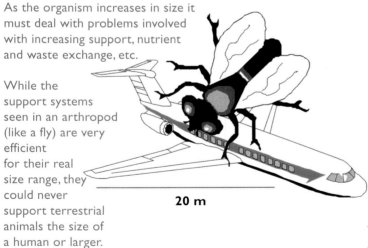

2 m

As the organism increases in size it must deal with problems involved with increasing support, nutrient and waste exchange, etc.

While the support systems seen in an arthropod (like a fly) are very efficient for their real size range, they could never support terrestrial animals the size of a human or larger.

20 m

The modular construction seen in clonal coral polyps allows the genet to escape the constraints on size seen in aclonal animals through asexual cloning of the "individuals" that make-up the genet.

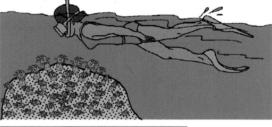

2 m

Because each individual polyp is genetically identical within a colony, the colony (genet) can continue to increase in size simply through asexual reproduction. In other words, the organism remains the same size, but the genet continues to increase.

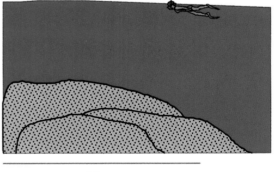

20 m

The colony (or genet) will eventually have its size limited by outside factors such as lack of substrate space or lack of food.

Obviously, the clonal nature of cnidarians has contributed to their plasticity and ability to cover large areas of substrate. Additionally, since each individual is a complete unit with replicative structures, the colony can survive excessive damage through regeneration. Such a situation raises interesting questions concerning the trade-offs that occur (at the level of an individual polyp, colony, or multi-colony genet) in terms of growth, survival and reproduction (both sexual and asexual).

STINGING CELLS

Stinging cells (called **cnidocytes**) are unique to members of the phylum Cnidaria. The actual stinging structures (termed **nematocysts** or **cnidae**) are kept in specialized chambers within the cell (nematocyst capsules). In actuality, one end of the capsule is inverted as a long, coiled hollow thread which, upon release, everts outwards forming the nematocyst. The chamber is kept pressurized by a single covering called an operculum.

Anthozoan cnidocytes lack a cnidocil (trigger mechanism), relying instead on cilia (fine, hair-like structures) to act as a mechanoreceptor. Additionally, the nematocyst chamber is covered by three flaps instead of a single structure.

Each stinging cell is used only once; new cnidocytes are formed by interstitial cells and take approximately 48 hours to replace their fired comrades.

Stinging cells function primarily in capturing prey but may also be used by certain species for defense, movement and/or attachment.

Please note: this diagram is not to scale.

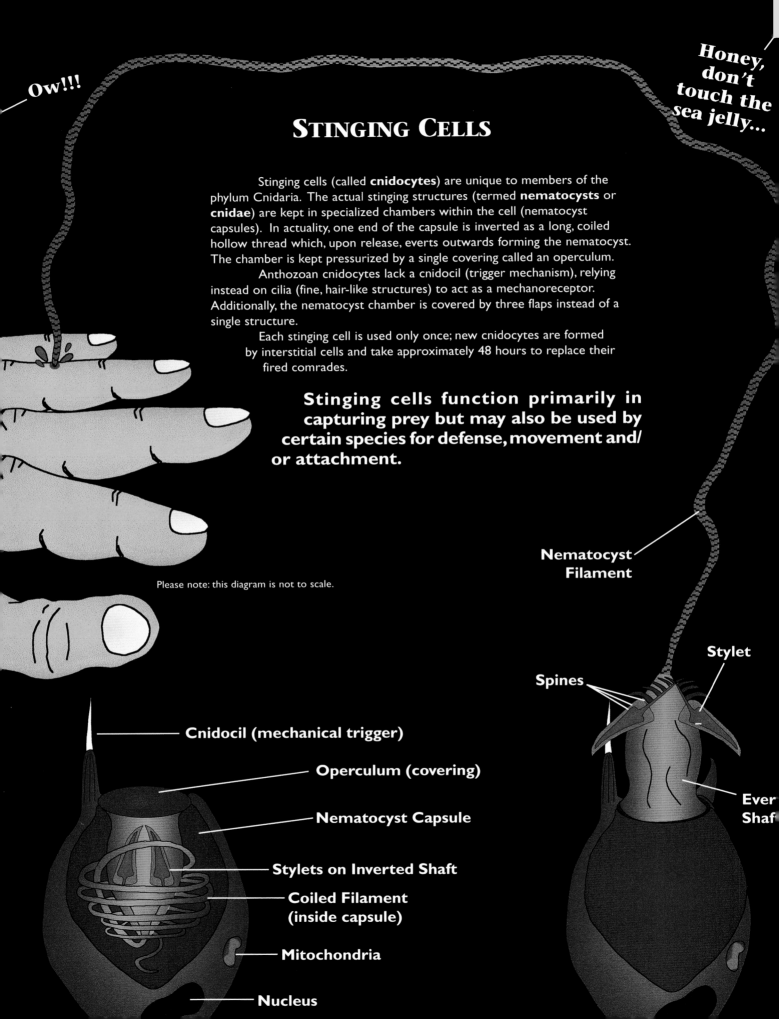

Ow!!!

Honey, don't touch the sea jelly...

Nematocyst Filament

Cnidocil (mechanical trigger)

Operculum (covering)

Nematocyst Capsule

Stylets on Inverted Shaft

Coiled Filament (inside capsule)

Mitochondria

Nucleus

Spines

Stylet

Ever
Shaf

Though the exact mechanism is still not known, here's a hypothesis for how a stinging cell might work:

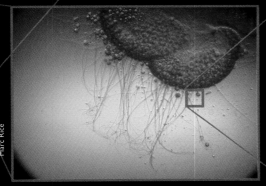

An organism comes in contact **❶** with a stinging cell's mechanical trigger (**cnidocil**) which then causes a break in the pressure-tight seal of the operculum; the resulting pressure change causes the nematocyst to come flying out of the nematocyst chamber with speeds approaching 2 m/second (one of the fastest of all known cellular processes). Another possibility is that the prey's own odor sets off the reaction; such organisms constantly leak waste chemicals into the surrounding water, and it is those chemicals to which the receptor cells respond. By being in close proximity **❷** to the cnidarian, the prey causes a chemical receptor to send a signal **❸** to the stinging cell and adjacent musculo epithelial cells. As a result, the stinging cell starts to take in water **❹** which increases the water pressure inside the nematocyst **❺** chamber; the musculo-epithelial cells start to contract thereby squeezing the cnidocyte. The resulting increased pressure causes the operculum to burst open and, in the matter of a few milliseconds, the nematocyst is forcefully ejected **❻**. Most likely, both mechanical and chemical stimulation occur together.

*ove: A coral colony like this
ght be made up of 100,000
lividual animals, each of which
ight bear 1,000 stinging cells.*

*ne Portugese man-of-war
(bove right) is only about 5 cm
ng. If we look closer at one
ntacle, we can see banks of
ematocyst batteries (above and
ght). When stimulated, these
atteries release scores of
ematocysts (far right).*

Marc Rice

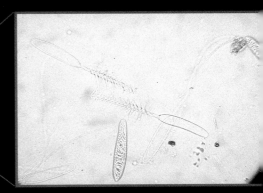

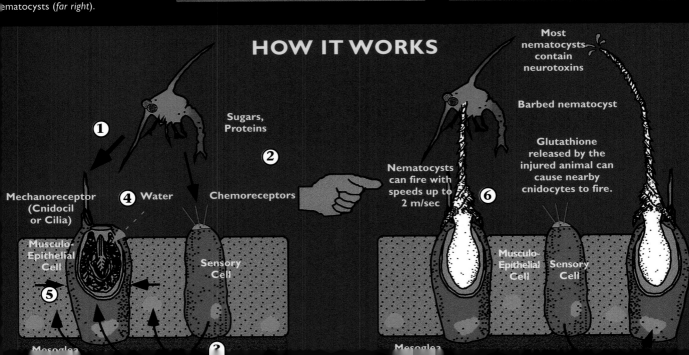

HOW IT WORKS

❶

Mechanoreceptor (Cnidocil or Cilia)

❹ Water

Sugars, Proteins

❷

Chemoreceptors

Musculo-Epithelial Cell

Sensory Cell

❺

Nematocysts can fire with speeds up to 2 m/sec

❻

Most nematocysts contain neurotoxins

Barbed nematocyst

Glutathione released by the injured animal can cause nearby cnidocytes to fire.

Musculo-Epithelial Cell

Sensory Cell

Mesoglea

Mesoglea

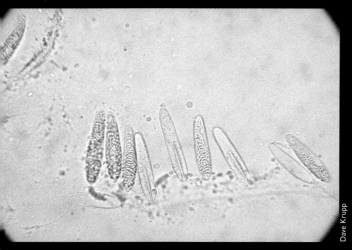

Above: Both fired and unfired nematocysts isolated from Finger Coral (*Porites compressa*).

Dave Krupp

Below: The pelagic nudibranch *Glaucus* feeds preferentially on pelagic hydrozoans (siphonophores) such as the Portuguese man-of-war. This nudibranch swallows and then incorporates the unfired nematocysts into its own tissue for its own defense. The use of a cnidarian prey's unfired nematocysts for a predator's own defense is a form of behavior termed **"kleptocnidae"**, and is seen in aolid nudibranchs, certain ctenophores and a species of freshwater flatworm. Hence, touching one of these nudibranch is likely to produce a sting, just as if you'd touched a Portuguese man-of-war

Cnidocytes tend to be concentrated in the outer tissue (epidermis) around the mouth and tentacle regions; though in some cnidarians they are found in the inner tissue (gastrodermis) that lines the stomach region. Often they are clustered into balls of stinging cells called "nematocyst batteries." Because of their microscopic size (some stinging cells are only 1/1000 mm long!) and close proximity to one another, rarely is only one nematocyst fired; often hundreds to thousands are fired from a single organism.

There are about 30 different kinds of cnidae which can be broken down into three different, basic forms:

True Nematocysts - the hollow nematocyst filament contains a toxin made-up primarily of proteins and phenols. The base of the filament has spines and stylets that aid in nematocyst penetration (as the nematocyst everts out of the nematocyst chamber, the stylets and spines will come in contact first, slicing through to allow penetration of the rest of the filament). Toxin is injected into the unfortunate organism through an opening at the tip of the filament. Most species tend to have toxins that act as neurotoxins; some, such as those of the box jellies and certain hydrozoans, are strong enough to critically injure unprotected humans. In fact, stings from the Sea Wasp (*Chironex* spp.) result in several fatalities every year in the South Pacific. True nematocysts are found in all four classes of cnidarians.

Spirocysts - Lacking toxin and the majority of spines found in true nematocysts, spirocyst filaments are made-up of a sticky form of protein that wraps around and clings to objects. Found only in certain anthozoans.

Ptychocysts - The filament is pleated (instead of coiled)

Some organisms appear to be immune to the effects of a cnidarian's stinging cells. This is self-evident with a heavily-armored crab or shrimp, but how does one explain a soft-bodied animal like a sea slug (nudibranch) or a fish? It seems that a few of these animals have adapted in some way to co-exist or even prey upon cnidarians without being affected by the nematocysts.

Above: Clownfish (*Amphiprion* sp.) are often seen swimming into and among the tentacles of their host anemones. For more on this unique relationship see p. 69.

THE COELENTERON

Look-Down in the water!

Why, it's a digestive organ

It's a defensive device!

Don't look dear!

It's a reproductive organ!

NO, ITS SUPER STOMACH!!

The stomach of a cnidarian (often referred to as a **coelenteron** or gastrovascular cavity) has a variety of functions. In many cnidarians, portions of the body wall extend into the stomach chamber, forming mesenteries. Many anthozoans have extensions of the free end of the mesenteries containing cnidae, cilia and digestive enzyme-producing cells. These structures are called **mesenterial filaments** (*left*); their function is primarily digestion, but as described below, they can also be used for defense and competitive interactions. In anemones, these filaments form long threads which function in both defense and food capture; in some species these threads (called **acontia**) are released through holes in the body wall to protect the exposed sides of the animal (*below*).

A Mixed Bag (Pardon the pun...): Though cnidarians do not have any true respiratory, excretory or circulatory systems, to a limited extent, the coelenteron often functions in these capacities. By having a large internal surface area, the gut wall functions as a gas exchange surface allowing oxygen and carbon dioxide to move into and out of internal cells. Undigested material and cellular wastes can be collected in the stomach and then spit out through the mouth. Extensions of the stomach into the tentacles allow digested food materials to be transported to most of the cells where they are needed.

Hydroskeleton: Although this is most readily seen in the anemones, the shape of most polyps and medusoids is maintained by water pressure (see p. 34). Water is taken in through the mouth, the stomach and, through extensions of the stomach, into the tentacles.

Ptooey!!!

Wheee!!!

Reproduction: The mesenteries of the stomach are responsible for producing the eggs and sperm in anthozoans. In those corals that brood their larvae, fertilization occurs either in the stomach or the planula larvae develop asexually there. Eventually each **planula** larva is released out of the mouth and enters the real world.

Keoki Stender

Defense: The mesenterial filaments or acontia have a much greater reach then the tentacles of the animal. As such, they can provide the animal with a defensive mechanism while maintaining some distance from the threat. The same mechanism can also be used for preventing competitors from over-growing a colony or help a colony overgrow its neighbors.

Doorway for Zooxanthellae: It is thought that corals re-infect their population of endosymbionts with free-swimming (motile) zooxanthellae (single-celled algae that live within certain cells of many corals, see pp. 29 - 32) taken in through their mouths, these plant cells become immobile and eventually end up within cells of the endodermal layer. Likewise, healthy zooxanthellae have been observed being egested (thrown up) by corals; these zooxanthellae may serve as a population for infecting other corals.

BEFORE | AFTER

Cnidoquestion: Can you think of a way that the coelenteron (stomach) could be used for locomotion?

CNIDARIAN RELATIVES
AND IN-LAWS

THE SEA JELLY, *PELAGIA NOTILUCA*, IS RARELY SEEN IN HAWAI'I. THOUGH, LIKE MOST SEA JELLIES, IT TENDS TO BE ENCOUNTERED MORE AFTER STRONG STORMS BRING IT CLOSER TO SHORE. NOTE THE HITCHHIKERS NEAR THE BELL.

CLASS SCYPHOZOA - THE SEA JELLIES

The class Scyphozoa is composed entirely of Sea Jellies (formerly called jellyfish: a term deemed to be politically incorrect and phylogenetically-insensitive). The class consists of about 200 marine species that spend the majority of their lives in the medusa body form. They exist in all of the world's oceans, from tropical to coldwater regions. As free-living organisms, most sea jellies contain sensory organs called **rhopalia**. These organs contain very primitive eye-like structures (called **ocelli**) and balance organs called **statocysts**; the rhopalia functions in allowing the sea jelly to orient its body toward the surface and move towards, or away from, sources of light (a type of response called **phototaxis**). During the short portion of their life cycle when they are sessile (a polyp-like stage called a **scyphistoma**), medusa-like buds (**ephyra**) are produced and shed into the water column (a process called **strobilation**) where they can turn into free-living medusa forms (or what we normally think of as jellyfish (oops, sea jellies)).

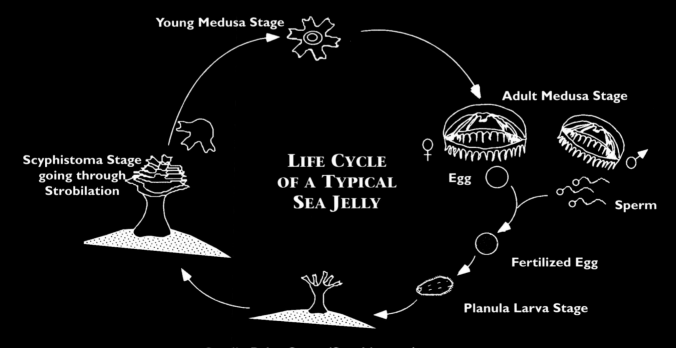

Young Medusa Stage

Adult Medusa Stage

Scyphistoma Stage going through Strobilation

LIFE CYCLE OF A TYPICAL SEA JELLY

Egg

Sperm

Fertilized Egg

Planula Larva Stage

Sessile Polyp Stage (Scyphistoma)

SEA JELLIES IN HAWAII

A variety of sea jellies are found in Hawaiian waters, though most of them are rarely seen on or around coral reefs. Most are pelagic (open-ocean) and are occasionally brought into near-shore waters by storms or unusual wind patterns. Other sea jellies are commonly found around harbors and well-protected bays. One species of tiny sea jelly in Hawai'i (*Kushinouyea hawaiiensis*) has a sessile medusa form which can be found attached to seaweeds in shallow water.

The 'jelly' in sea jellies is actually the **mesoglea**; a middle layer of tissue made up of a matrix of elastic material called collagen. In some pelagic sea jellies the mesoglea is thought to assist in maintaining bouyancy by replacing heavy chemical particles with much lighter ones.

Unlike most sea jellies, the Upside-down Sea Jelly (*Cassiopeia* sp.) spends most of its adult life upside-down pulsating on the bottom of shallow bays. Increasingly large concentrations of these animals have been settling in aquaculture ponds within the State. The color of this animal comes from the high density of symbiotic plants (Zooxanthellae) living within cells of its tissues.

Previous page: The common sea jelly *Aurelia* sp. is a suspension feeder which traps plankton in mucus on its underside. This animal is also known to brood its offspring within its large tentacles (**oral arms**).

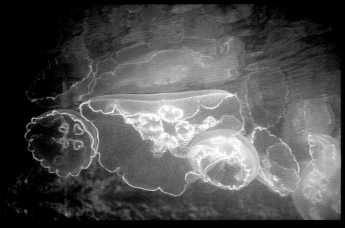

Above: Moon Jellies (*Aurelia* sp.) in the Ala Wai Canal on O'ahu. Note the four reproductive gonads inside the bell and the web-like nerve network imbedded within it. This primitive nervous system allows jellies to coordinate and respond to a free-living existence within a three-dimensional fluid environment.

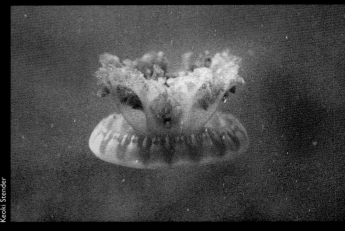

Above: The Upside-down Sea Jelly, or *Cassiopeia* sp. in Kāne'ohe Bay. Like the coral, this sea jelly derives a large proportion of its energy from the symbiotic plants living within its cells (**endosymbionts**).

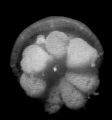

Above: The sea jelly *Mastigias* sp. is sometimes seen in Pearl Harbor and Kāne'ohe Bay.

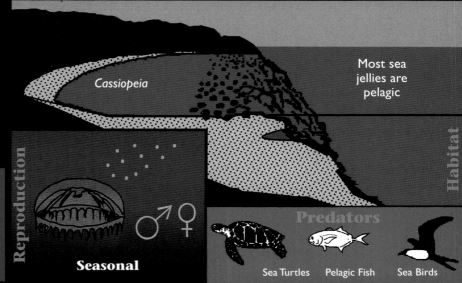

Cassiopeia

Most sea jellies are pelagic

Habitat

Symbionts

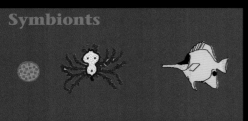

Reproduction

Seasonal

♂♀

Predators

Sea Turtles   Pelagic Fish   Sea Birds

SYMBIOSIS AMONG THE SEA JELLIES

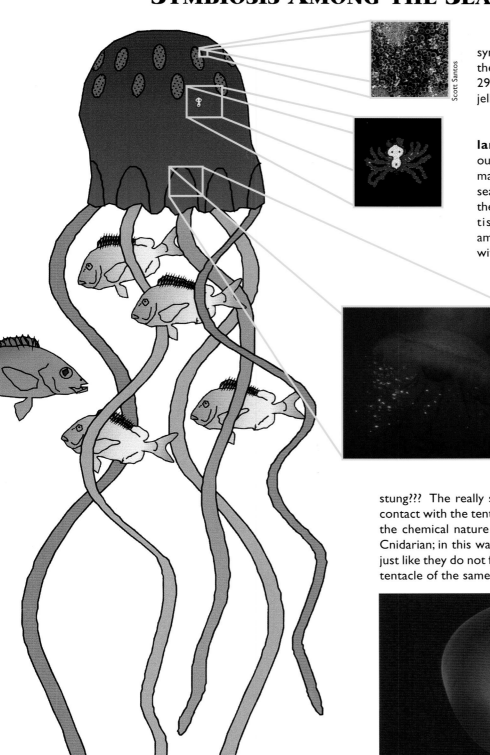

Some sea jellies (*Mastigias, Cassiopeia*) have symbiotic plants (Zooxanthellae) living within their cells. As with other cnidarians (see pp. 29 - 32), the algae provide energy for the sea jelly.

Larval lobsters (called **phyllosoma larvae**) are often found attached to the outside of pelagic sea jellies. The lobster larvae may be deriving protection from living on the sea jelly, though there is some evidence that they are really parasites, feeding on the internal tissues of their host. Small, parasitic amphipods (crab-like animals) frequently live within the bell of certain jellies.

Often times one will find a variety of fish living either within the bell or among the tentacles of a sea jelly. These **consort fish** do not appear to be harmed by the stinging tentacles of the jelly. Sometimes these fish are temporary consorts (such as small jacks), others permanently associate with the jelly or Portuguese man-of-war (the Portuguese man-of-war Fish, for example).

So how come these fish aren't stung??? The really small associated fish probably simply avoid contact with the tentacles. Larger consorts are thought to alter the chemical nature of their own mucus to match that of the Cnidarian; in this way the stinging cells are not induced to fire, just like they do not fire when a tentacle rubs up against another tentacle of the same individual. Ⓣ

A number of species of jacks are known to consort with, or live amongst the tentacles of many pelagic jellies.

CNIDOQUESTION: Given the information shown, what other role might the associated fish play?

SEA JELLIES TIDBITS & TRIVIA

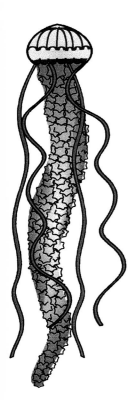

Phylum Cnidaria

Class Scyphozoa (Greek: "cup animals")

>200 species worldwide

Medusa body form dominant

LARGEST SINGLE, NON-COLONIAL CNIDARIAN

The Lion's Mane Sea Jelly (*Cyanea capillata*), found in the North Atlantic, has a floating bell that may have a diameter up to 2.29 m (7.5 ft) with 800 or more tentacles (100-200 ft in length) trailing beneath it.

MIMICRY

Often times small fish will shelter within the tentacles of sea jellies. Some believe that the Threadfin Jack (*left*) is a sea jelly mimic. Perhaps the mimicry functions to lure in small fish for food, or to take advantage of the absence of fast-moving sea jelly predators Perhaps it is both! Ⓣ

Waikiki Aquarium

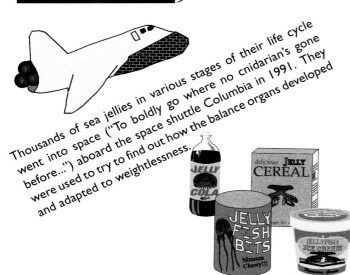

Thousands of sea jellies in various stages of their life cycle went into space ("To boldly go where no cnidarian's gone before...") aboard the space shuttle Columbia in 1991. They were used to try to find out how the balance organs developed and adapted to weightlessness.

Many cultures consider jellyfish a delicacy. Whether it is boiled, steamed, fried or sautéed, it is usually accompanied by a flavorful sauce; perhaps one eats sea jellies for their consistency rather than their flavor.

Jellyfish are not really fish, hence many people instead refer to them as 'Sea Jellies'; both terms emphasize the fact that these animals have a very thick and gel-like middle layer. Don't let this fool you, sea jellies are about 99% water.

A Sea Jelly's body form is called a **medusa** after Medusa, a Greek mythological figure, whose hair was full of snakes... note the resemblance?

Deborah Gochfeld

JELLYFISH LAKE

In Belau, a group of islands in the South Pacific, there are a number of marine lakes which contain huge densities of over 1000/m^3 of the sea jelly *Mastigias*. These jellies have symbiotic plants within their tissues and very few (if any) stinging cells (why?). They vertically migrate from the surface waters into the nutrient-rich anoxic depths of the lake on a daily basis. These vertical migrations are thought to be a trade-off between the need for sunlight and the deeper ammonia-rich layers (which the symbiotic plants use as a nutrient source). As such, their lifestyle differs dramatically from that of most pelagic sea jellies.

BIOLUMINESCENCE

Bioluminescence is common in all cnidarian classes except for the Cubozoans. While bioluminescence is found in other groups of marine animals, it is never found in freshwater organisms due to the requirement of salt for its production.

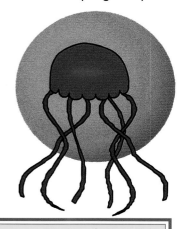

CNIDOQUESTION: Can you think of possible reasons why some sea jellies glow in the dark (are luminescent)?

CLASS CUBOZOA - THE BOX JELLIES

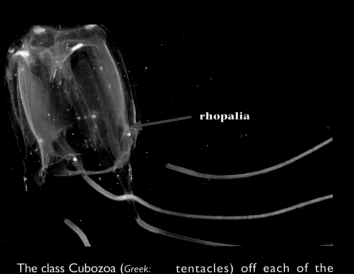

rhopalia

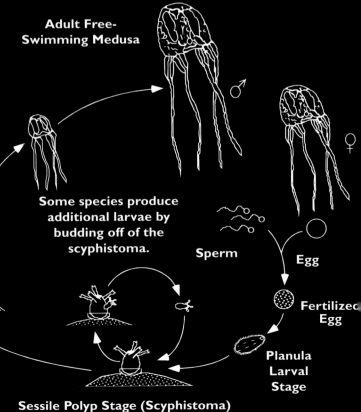

When wind conditions are right, waves of box jellies and/or Portuguese man-of-war come into near-shore waters; this often occurs for Hawaiian Box Jellies 8 - 10 days after the full moon.

The class Cubozoa (*Greek: "cube animal"*), whose members are commonly referred to as "Box Jellies," were formerly considered a subgroup of the class Scyphozoa. Like their cousins the Sea Jellies, Box Jellies spend a small portion of their life cycle in a sessile polyp-like (**scyphistoma**) stage. The adult free-swimming medusa is often mistaken for a sea jelly, but closer inspection reveals a number of key differences between the two groups.

The Box Jellies consist of only 15 marine species that are found only in tropical and semi-tropical regions. The medusa body form is strongly cuboidal (square in cross-section with relatively flat edges) and bears four tentacles (or groups of tentacles) off each of the cuboidal edges. Box jellies have the most advanced sensory structures of any cnidarian; each **rhopalia** contains a **statocyst** for balance regulation and a complex (for a cnidarian) eye-like structure (the **ocellus**) which contains a true lens (cornea) and a multi-layered retina. A single cubozoan eye is made-up of up to 11,000 sensory cells! These "eyes" allow small box jellies to orient and swim quickly toward light sources (suggesting that they may use this ability to feed at night on luminescent plankton). Often, the rhopalium is located between the tentacles (see above).

In Hawai'i, two species of box jellies are found:

Carybdea alata
and *Carybdea rastoni.*

The deadly Sea Wasp (*Chironex fleckeri*) is a species known from the Australia-Malaysia region and is not found in Hawai'i.

LIFE CYCLE OF A HYPOTHETICAL BOX JELLY

Adult Free-Swimming Medusa

Some species produce additional larvae by budding off of the scyphistoma.

Sperm

Egg

Fertilized Egg

Planula Larval Stage

Unlike the sea jellies, the box jelly scyphistoma develops directly into a single medusa.

Sessile Polyp Stage (Scyphistoma)

CLASS HYDROZOA - THE HYDROIDS

Two nudibranchs feeding on a colonial hydroid off the Great Barrier Reef in Australia.

Feather hydroids such as *Pennaria disticha* are the most commonly seen type of hydroids in Hawai'i, often on pier pilings, in caves, and underneath overhangs; occasionally they are seen out in the open on reefs. Note the hydropolyps with banks of stinging cells; like their Portuguese man-of-war cousins, these cells can cause discomfort to the unwary snorkeler or diver who happens to brush up against them.

Keoki Stender

The class Hydrozoa includes a wide variety of organisms which are often mistaken for other types of animals or plants. This mistake can be regretted quickly by the unaware diver since many hydroids release one of the most painful stings with even the slightest contact. Hydroids differ from other cnidarians in that they lack well-defined cells within their mesoglea (that thin jelly-like middle layer), their gastrodermis (or inner layer) lacks cnidocytes, and their gonads (sperm and eggs) develop in the epidermis (outer layer).

Yet another characteristic of hydroids is their **polymorphism**, the retention of structurally-distinct organisms (frequently having unique functions) within a colony. Most hydroid species are **dimorphic**, containing two different types of individuals: the **Gastrozooid** (whose primary function is feeding, but may also be involved in prey capture and colony defense) and the **Gonozooid** (which functions almost exclusively in producing free-living sexual medusae). The gonozooids often lack mouths and tentacles. Hydroids can be either hermaphroditic or dioecious (separate sexes), though the medusa phase is always dioecious and reproduces sexually. In general coral reefs do not contain large, obvious hydroids instead most members of this class that are commonly found on reefs are **cryptic** (hidden) or **epizoitic** (growing atop other organisms). Unlike the scyphozoans which spend large portions of their lives as medusae, or the anthozoans which spend their entire adult life as polyps, hydrozoans often spend significant portions of their lives as both medusae and polyps:

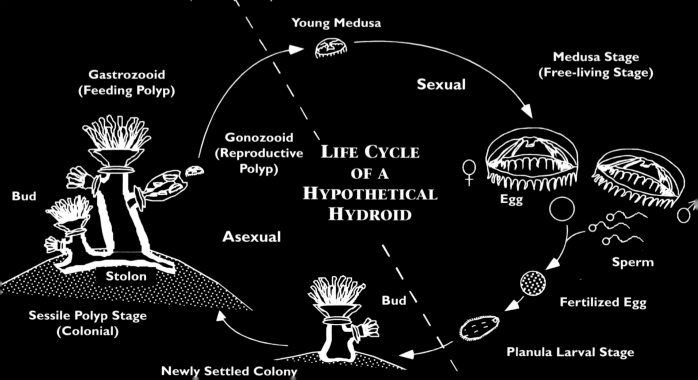

LIFE CYCLE OF A HYPOTHETICAL HYDROID

Young Medusa

Sexual

Medusa Stage (Free-living Stage)

Gastrozooid (Feeding Polyp)

Gonozooid (Reproductive Polyp)

Egg

Bud

Asexual

Sperm

Stolon

Bud

Fertilized Egg

Sessile Polyp Stage (Colonial)

Planula Larval Stage

Newly Settled Colony

HYDROZOANS:
HYDROCORALS & SEA FAN HYDROIDS

ydrocorals are hydrozoans hich form colonies pos-essing calcareous (lime-one) exoskeletons. Two milies (Milleporidae and tylasteridae) make-up the ydrocorals, though neither found in Hawai'i. Prob-ly the best known of the ydrocorals are those ermed 'Fire Coral' Millepora sp.); often con-sed for a true stony coral, ese hydrozoans have sym-iotic zooxanthellae which low them to create large, lcareous skeletons. Like nany hydrozoans, the sting f a Fire Coral's nemato-ysts can be very powerful nd painful (hence the ame...).

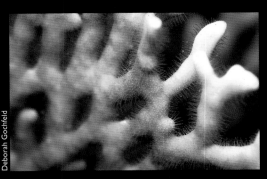

Deborah Gochfeld

Above: Fire Coral (*Millepora* sp.) can grow as massive, encrusting or branching colonies. Color tends to range from white to pale yellow. From a distance, the colony looks smooth, but close inspection shows the surface to be covered with small pores through which the hydropolyps emerge.

Though common elsewhere in the Pacific, members of the family Stylasteridae (*above*) are not found in Hawai'i. The delicate branching and colors make this hydrocoral a favorite with both the aquarium and ornamental trades.

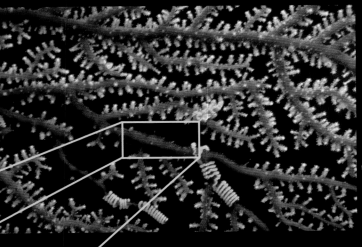

Left: Sea Fan Hydroids (family Solanderiidae) are relatively rare in Hawai'i. Colonies of *Solanderia* sp. are either male or female and may have reproductive gonophores visibly present. Superficially, this hydroid closely resembles a sea fan (gorgonian). Polyps are whitish on a reddish-brown chitin-like exoskeleton composed of gorgonin. The spiral tan structures are the egg cases laid by a predatory nudibranch.

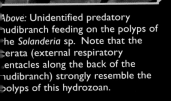

Above: Unidentified predatory nudibranch feeding on the polyps of the *Solanderia* sp. Note that the cerata (external respiratory tentacles along the back of the nudibranch) strongly resemble the polyps of this hydrozoan.

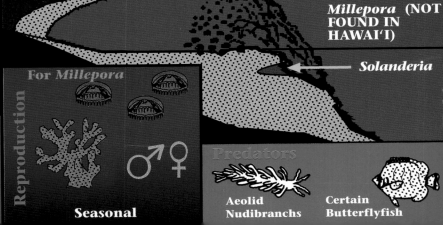

Millepora (NOT FOUND IN HAWAI'I)

Solanderia

Habitat

Symbionts
For *Millepora*

Reproduction

For *Millepora*

♂ ♀

Seasonal

Predators

Aeolid Nudibranchs

Certain Butterflyfish

HYDROZOANS:
PELAGIC HYDROZOANS -
THE SIPHONOPHORES & THE CHONDROPHORES

Pelagic hydrozoans are found near the surface of the ocean, often using modified floats or sails to assist in moving about with the aid of winds and currents. Siphonophores are hydrozoans which form free-floating colonies whose members frequently have different functions and structures. The colonies often consist of both polyp and medusa forms; the medusa members are usually responsible for locomotion and reproduction, while the polyps function primarily in feeding and colony defense. The Portuguese man-of-war (*Physalia physalis*) is the most commonly seen siphonophore in Hawai'i.

Chondrophores differ primarily in the disk shape of the colony, underneath which sits a single feeding polyp form (the gastrozooid).

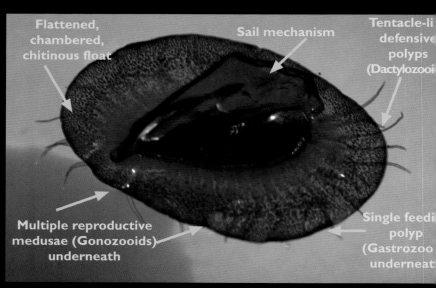

Flattened, chambered, chitinous float

Sail mechanism

Tentacle-li defensive polyps (Dactylozooi

Multiple reproductive medusae (Gonozooids) underneath

Single feedi polyp (Gastrozoo underneat

Above: The Chondrophore By-The-Wind-Sailer (*Velella velella*) is closely related to the Portuguese man-of-war (Hey, I didn't make-up these names) but differs primarily in the construction of the triangular, sail-like mechanism in the center with only a single gastrozooid underneath it.

Left Like most hydrozoans, siphonophores are capable of delivering very painful welts from batteries of stinging cells located along their tentacles. Even washed-up, dead-appearing ones on the beach can deliver painful stings if handled.

Marc Rice

Above: The Portuguese man-of-war (*Physalia physalis*) seen from underneath the surface. Can you pick out the various organisms that make-up this colony? ...It's ok to look at the next page and cheat if you have to...

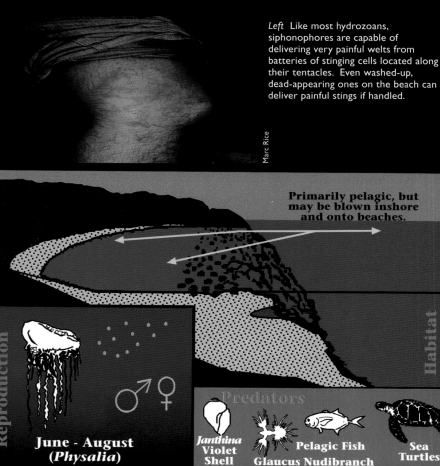

Primarily pelagic, but may be blown inshore and onto beaches.

Habitat

Symbionts

Nomeus sp.

Reproduction

June - August
(*Physalia*)

♂ ♀

Predators

Janthina Violet Shell

Glaucus Nudibranch

Pelagic Fish

Sea Turtles

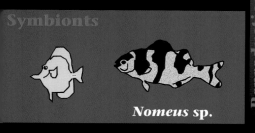

PORTUGUESE MAN-OF-WAR
PHYSALIA PHYSALIS
(Greek: *physa* - an air bubble)

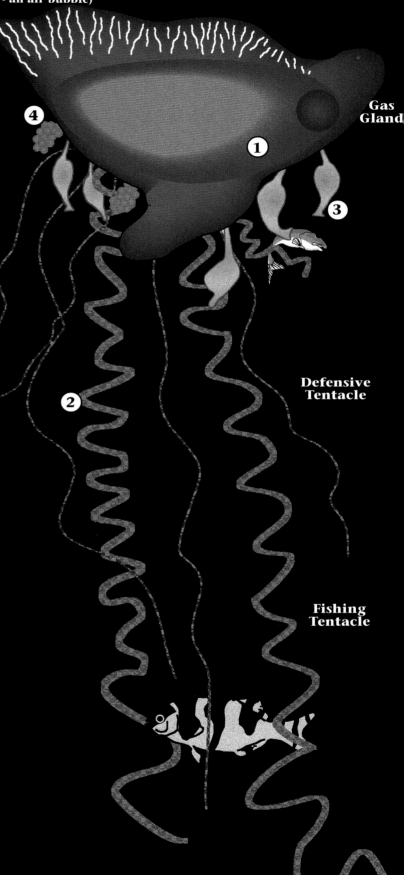

Gas Gland

Defensive Tentacle

Fishing Tentacle

Probably the most well-known of the pelagic hydrozoans, the Portuguese man-of-war is often mistakenly described as a jellyfish. Even more surprising to most people is the realization that the Portuguese man-of-war represents not a single organism but a highly complex colony of different individual organisms (both polyp and medusa forms), each of which plays a key role in the survival of the colony.

(1) **Pneumatophore** This gas-filled float is derived from the larval stage and serves as both a floatation device and a sailing mechanism (man-of-war can use the wind to move along the surface of the ocean). It is essentially a highly modified, inflated polyp which is kept inflated through the addition of gas (primarily carbon monoxide) into the double-walled, chitin-lined chamber from a gas-producing gland. The float (or sail), which in some Atlantic Portuguese men-of-war can reach up to 30 cm in length, from time to time will dip to one side in order to moisten the walls of the float which assists in maintaining inflation.

(2) **Dactylozooids** are non-feeding individuals with each one having one very long, unbranched tentacle. In some individuals, these tentacles can reach 10 m in length. The dactylozooid's role in the colony is defense and immobilization of prey.

(3) **Gastrozooids** have a large mouth and a single, long hollow tentacle with many branches. The mouth fastens onto prey items and the digested material is passed (via a series of internal canals) to the rest of the colony.

(4) **Gonozooids** The reproductive members of the colony, gonozooids are either male or female. They produce eggs and sperm which are released to fertilize with gametes from other colonies.

The strong patterning in the body coloration of the Portuguese man-of-war Fish (*Nomeus* sp.) is believed to allow the fish to act as a decoy to lure prey for the man-of-war to feed on. The adult fish is only found associated with its host.

HYDROID TIDBITS & TRIVIA

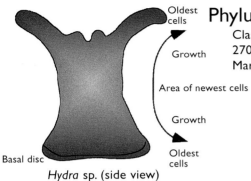

Oldest cells
Growth
Area of newest cells
Growth
Oldest cells
Basal disc

Hydra sp. (side view)

Phylum Cnidaria

Class Hydrozoa (Hydroids, Portuguese man-of-war, Fire Corals)
2700 species worldwide
Marine & Freshwater

Order Hydroida (~ 30 species in Hawai'i) -
   Feather hydroids & the Sea Fan Hydroid *Solanderia*.

Order Milleporina - Fire Corals (DO NOT OCCUR IN HAWAI'I).
   Solid, calcareous skeleton; zooxanthellae.

Order Stylasterina - *Stylaster* (DO NOT OCCUR IN HAWAI'I).
   Solid, calcareous skeleton.

Order Siphonophora - Portuguese man-of-war. Pelagic, colonial.

Order Chondrophora - Blue Buttons, By-The-Wind Sailors. Pelagic, colonial.

A HYDROID FOUNTAIN OF YOUTH

One the most common of all hydrozoans is the freshwater hydra, a very simple animal shown here in its polyp form. Like most sessile hydropolyps, the hydra cells move outward as the animal grows, so that the cells nearest the tips and the basal disc are the oldest, and this is where the majority of cell death occurs. The center region contains the area of highest cell formation. Someday when you have the time, watch a hydra and you'll see that all of the cells in an individual's body are completely replaced within a couple weeks...under such circumstances a hydra might never grow old!

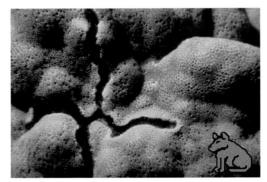

A HYDROID AS WATCHDOG

A number of massive and encrusting corals in Hawai'i are inhabited by a type of alpheid shrimp that creates grooves (such as the one shown above), the shrimp uses these grooves not only as a living space, but also as a place to grow a variety of algae and cyanobacteria upon which it feeds. Characteristic of these grooves are species of fine hydroids (*Rhizogeton* sp.) which line the openings and may serve to protect the "farm" from potential grazers...

FIRE CORALS

Fire corals are the only major member of coral reefs that produce free-swimming medusae.

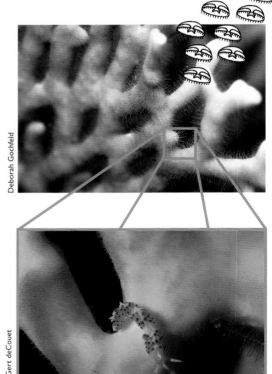

Deborah Gochfeld

Heinz-Gert deCouet

...And speaking of nudibranchs, this little guy makes a living out of feeding specifically on the polyps of Fire Coral.

Heinz-Gert deCouet

Cerata

The aeolid nudibranch *Pteraeolidia ianthina* (left) feeds on a variety of local hydroids, absorbing their stinging cells without firing them, and placing them in its cerata for its own defense. The color of the nudibranch is strongly affected by the amount of zooxanthellae (a symbiotic algae) that inhabits its tissues. The squiggly white stuff in the photo is the egg mass being laid by the nudibranch.

SECTION I: CORALS AS ORGANISMS

INTRODUCTION TO THE CORALS

Heinz-G[illegible]eCouet

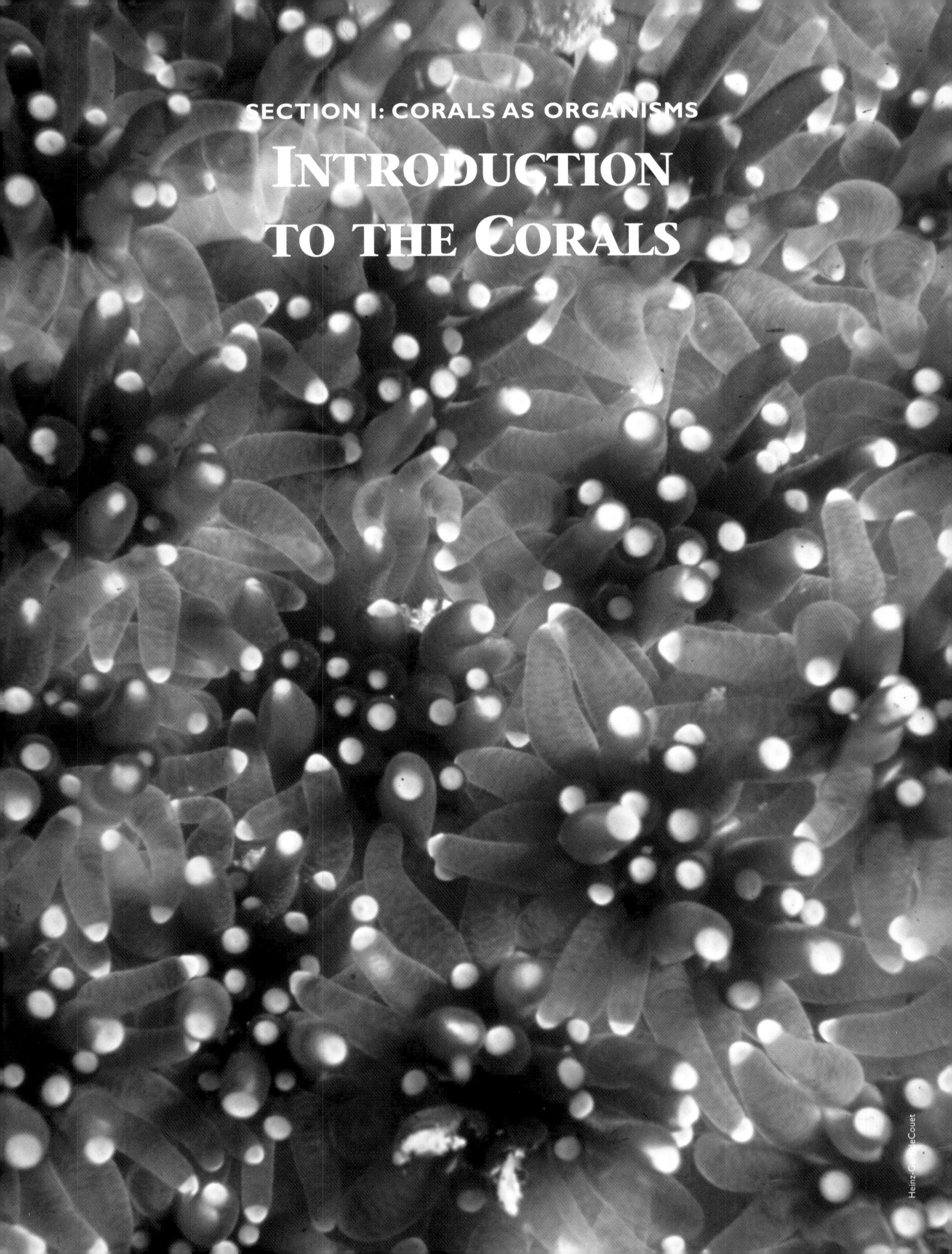

ANIMAL?
VEGETABLE?
MINERAL?

Heinz-Gert deCouet

Corals are strange little beasts. Geologically they are much like a rock: hard, solid, full of minerals. At the same time, they resemble plants in that one can measure photosynthesis within them. During the Renaissance, the most eminent scholars of the day classified corals as plants; yet in the late 1600's they were viewed as members of the mineral kingdom. The name 'Lithophyta' was coined in 1704 to describe them as "stone plants". It wasn't until the 1730's that the scientific community accepted them as animals. Yet, what kind of animal were they? As the 1800's came around, scientists lumped them in with the sponges, and it wasn't until around the turn of the century that the world recognized the existence of a phylum called Coelenterata which was made up of two groups: the Cnidarians, which possessed nematocyst- filled stinging cells, and the Ctenophores (or Comb Jellies) which lacked nematocysts but had adhesive structures called **colloblasts**. Only relatively recently have the Cnidarians been recognized as their own unique phylum within the kingdom Animalia; it is within this group that the corals reside.

Like sea jellies, the comb jellies are radially symmetrical and gelatinous, but lack cnidocytes for capturing prey. Instead, comb jellies have adhesive structures called **colloblasts** which are released from long paired tentacles coming off of the main body. Characteristic of this group are the presence of eight equally-spaced rows of **comb plates** (the phylum name Ctenophora means *comb-bearing*) on which beating cilia propel the organism through the water column. Primarily pelagic, they can often be seen in the water column offshore (next time you're doing a safety stop after diving look for them amongst the plankton that drifts by you). A small, benthic, crawling ctenophore can also sometimes be seen attached to seaweeds (such as *Halimeda, Sargassum,* etc.).

ZOOXANTHELLAE

(Symbiodinium, sp.)

Imagine that you and your best friend were going to run a race until one of you dropped. Now further imagine that you and your friend were genetically identical in every way. Who would win the race? Being genetically identical, you should both drop at the same time. Now, imagine what would happen if you cheated: you've got an endless supply of candy bars in your pocket. Everything else being equal, you've got a source of energy that isn't available to your friend; you should out-compete her everytime. Corals exist in a highly competitive, low nutrient world where space is at a premium. But some corals cheat. They've got the equivalent of candy bars in their pockets. These corals (and certain other cnidarians, sponges and molluscs) have, living inside their tissues, a type of single-celled alga (called a **Dinoflagellate**) that photosynthesizes and provides the coral with energy.

Dinoflagellates are characterized by the presence of two **flagella** (whip-like locomotory structures). Some dinoflagellates contain toxins and can occasionally occur in large blooms (called "Red Tides"). Others, termed **Zooxanthellae**, go through a non-motile symbiotic stage where they reside inside the tissues of their host.

The zooxanthellae in cnidarians (the most common species is called *Symbiodinium microadriatiicum*) live primarily inside the endodermis or epidermis (in corals they are most often found within the endoderm). A single zooxanthellae is about 10 microns (roughly 1/10 the diameter of a human hair), yet it is the zooxanthellae (in densities of up to a million/cm^2!) that often provide the host coral with its characteristic coloration (usually

Transmission into Corals:

Symbiotic Stage

Asexual Reproduction in the Coral:
Fragmentation, Budding or Fission

Non-Direct Transmission:
Non-Zooxanthellate Coral Eggs

Non-Zooxanthellate Coral Planula Larva

Direct Transmission:
Zooxanthellate Coral Planula Larva

Coral Sperm

Coral Planula Picks Up Zooxanthellae

Free-Living Stage

When certain corallivores such as pufferfish feed on corals, the zooxanthellae pass intact through their digestive systems.

Zooxanthellate Coral Eggs

Settlement

New Coral Colony Picks Up Zooxanthellae

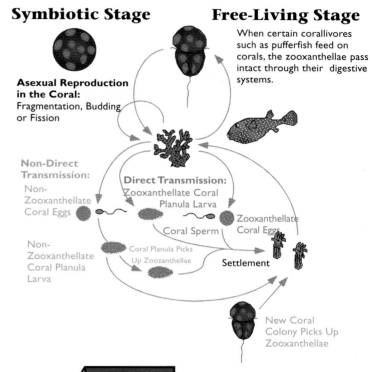

Zooxanthellae

The Chloroplast: The functional organ where photosynthesis primarily occurs.

brown to yellowish, though the coloration may be affected by the coral's accessory pigments). Corals that contain zooxanthellae (termed zooxanthellate corals) are often the primary reef-building corals (termed **Hermatypic Corals**).

Muscatine *et al.* (1984) calculated that in the stony coral *Stylophora pistillata*, less than 5% of the photosynthetically-produced carbon (sugar) is used by the zooxanthellae themselves. The rest is translocated (transferred) to the host coral. This large amount of photosynthate provides enough energy for the coral's metabolism and then some, making *Stylophora,* and other corals like it, functional autotrophs (in terms of energy and carbon). Obviously, the amount of photosynthate is going to vary with the species of coral, geographic location, water conditions and depth.

Other studies have shown that the presence of the zooxanthellae within a coral's tissues greatly enhances the coral's ability to produce a hard, calcium carbonate skeleton.

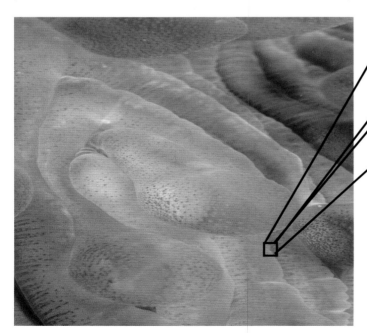

Above: Zooxanthellae within the tissue of the Mushroom Coral, *Fungia scutaria.* Zooxanthellae concentrations in some coral hosts can reach densities of up to 30,000 algal cells per mm^3 of coral tissue.

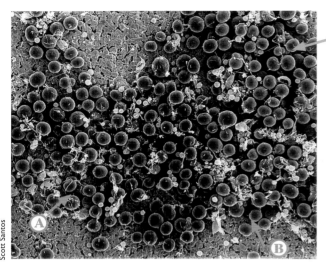

Above: A concentration of zooxanthellae isolated from the anemone *Aiptasia pulchella*. Note both the free-living, swimming form with flagella (**A**) and the non-motile, endosymbiotic form (**B**) are present.

The process of photosynthesis takes inorganic sunlight and uses it to fix carbon as a sugar (organic energy).

Reefs often fix carbon at rates of 2500 grams (that's roughly 5 1/2 lbs!) of carbon per square meter per year, yet when one looks around most reefs it's difficult to spot many plants that could produce such high levels of organically-bound energy. The secret is that many of the plants are microscopic and live primarily inside the innermost layer of the coral tissue. Inside the corals the zooxanthellae find a safe environment with high light levels and plenty of nutrients (keep in mind that this is occurring in a ocean environment that is often characterized as being nutrient-poor).

Ⓣ One hypothesis concerning nutrient enrichment of reefs (from coastal run-off, sewage, etc.) is that the increase in nutrients leads to an explosion of zooxanthellae growth inside the corals. This could have the effect of unbalancing the delicate symbiotic relationship between the two organisms and causing collapse of the system.

Another hypothesis is that corals under extreme stress expel their populations of zooxanthellae (bleaching events, see p. 182). One thought is that this may allow the corals to re-infect themselves with strains of zooxanthellae better adapted to the prevailing environmental conditions.

Below: Though rare in most corals, some species actually place zooxanthellae within their unfertilized eggs as they initially form within the ovaries.

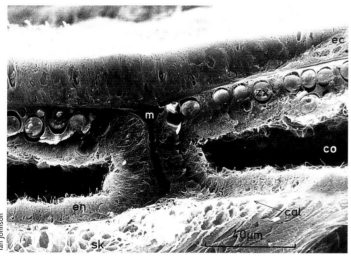

Zooxanthellae reside primarily inside the uppermost section of the innermost (endodermal) tissue layer. The size of these algal cells is about 10 micrometers (roughly 1/10 the diameter of a human hair); and often one finds densities of a million zooxanthellae cells per square centimeter of living coral tissue. *Above:* Zooxanthellae within Lace Coral, *Pocillopora damicornis*. *Below:* Zooxanthellae within a plate form of Rice Coral, *Montipora capitata*. Key to letters in electron micrographs: **ec** = ectodermal tissue, **zx** = zooxanthellae, **en** = endodermal (or gastrodermal) tissue, **co** = coelenteron, **cal** = calyx (or carbonate skeleton).

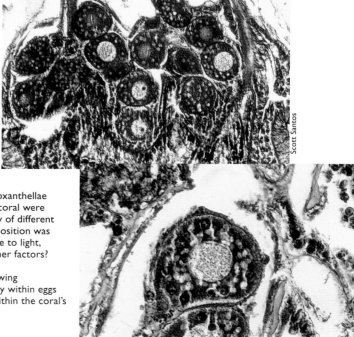

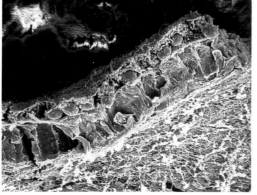

Left: What if the zooxanthellae within a single host coral were actually a community of different species whose composition was regulated in response to light, temperature and other factors?

Right: Close-up showing zooxanthellae already within eggs (oocytes) forming within the coral's ovaries.

CORAL - ALGAL SYMBIOSIS
WHAT DOES EACH OF THEM GET OUT OF THE RELATIONSHIP?

Light Energy (Visible & UV)

Light is necessary for photosynthesis to occur; but certain wavelengths of light (such as UV) can be harmful.

Some corals have pigments which absorb UV light exciting certain molecules which in turn emit lower frequencies of visible light. Such fluorescence might be used for photosynthesis, in addition to protecting both coral and zooxanthellae from the harmful effects of UV.

Harmful UV light can be filtered by coral pigments or special UV-absorbing chemicals (Mycosporine-like Amino Acids or MAAs).

Corals provide protection for their endosymbionts through their hard skeletons stinging cells.

The excess organic energy translocated to the coral host is rich in carbohydrate but low in nitrogen compounds (important building blocks for proteins); most corals supplement this food source by actively feeding on zooplankton or dissolved organic nitrogen (DON).

The symbiotic algae also act like a "kidney" for the coral, removing waste materials which are then used to assist the algae in conducting photosynthesis

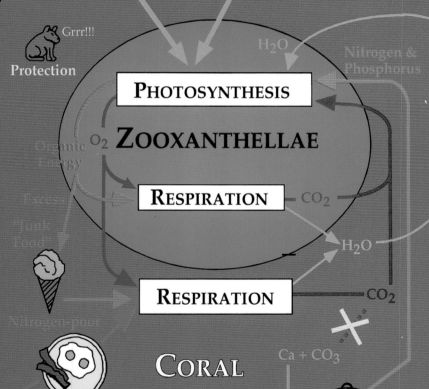

Giant clams formerly were found throughout much of the tropical Pacific (though not in Hawai'i), but have become increasingly rare with over-collection. *Tridacna gigas* (*below*) is the largest of the six species of giant clams, attaining lengths over 1.5 m in older individuals. Like the corals, the size of these clams is thought to be related to the symbiotic relationship with their zooxanthellae:

- The zooxanthellae provide the clam with additional energy which can be used for growth.
- The zooxanthellae are thought to assist directly with the formation of the clam's calcium carbonate skeleton.

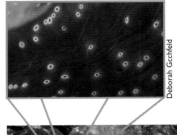

Deborah Gcchfeld

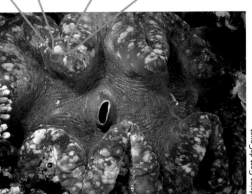

Heinz-Gert deCouet

The brilliant colors seen in the mantle tissue (*left*) of many giant clams is thought to be due to UV-filtering pigments.

Heinz-Gert de Couet

Certain octocorals are thought to be so dependent on their **endosymbiotic** (living inside the tissue of a host) plants that they are not able to functionally feed (they lack the highly-formed digestive mesenteries seen in other anthozoans and have minimal, if any, nematocysts for food capture in their tentacles).

A wide variety of cnidarians, including stony corals, soft corals, anemones and zoanthids (*below center*), hydroids and sea jellies have endosymbiotic zooxanthellae. Additionally, certain bivalves, nudibranchs (*below right*), sponges and worms may have unicellular algal cells living inside their tissues.

Richard Pyle

(T) Some animals do not have single-celled plants living in their tissues, but instead make use of the intact chloroplasts (photosynthetic sites) from the algae they feed on. One group of molluscs, the Saccoglossans (*above*) places the intact chloroplasts (after digestion of the algae) in the tissue on their backs. The assumption is that photosynthesis occurs, with the animal deriving some benefit from the chloroplasts. Being an animal (as opposed to a plant), it cannot maintain the

Marc Rice

chloroplasts for long; eventually they break down and require the animal to replace them after its next vegetarian meal. *Haminoea* sp. (*left*) is another mollusc that is thought to temporarily make use of the chloroplasts from its food.

Heinz-Gert deCouet

CNIDOQUESTION: Obviously endosymbiotic zooxanthellae/ host relationships have evolved separately in a number of phyla. Given the examples shown and what you know about these organisms (the coral polyp and the zooxanthellae), how might this symbiosis have originally arisen?

SKELETON FORMATION

Light

The skeleton provides the coral animal with a protective cup which is almost impossible to remove once the polyp retracts into it. The skeleton is thought to be secreted by the basal epidermis in such a way that, as the coral secretes new skeletal cups, it closes off the old cup chambers (See p. 41). This creates spaces for cryptic and burrowing organisms to live in. This "habitat" within the reef framework has not been well-studied.

Different types of corals lay down skeleton at different rates; massive corals like *Porites lobata* (Lobe Coral) grow at rates of 0.3 - 2 cm/yr, while branching corals like *Pocillopora meandrina* (Cauliflower Coral) can grow at rates up to 10 cm/yr.

There's still a lot we don't understand about skeleton formation in hermatypic corals; we know that the symbiotic zooxanthellae are involved, but we still don't know the exact mechanism.

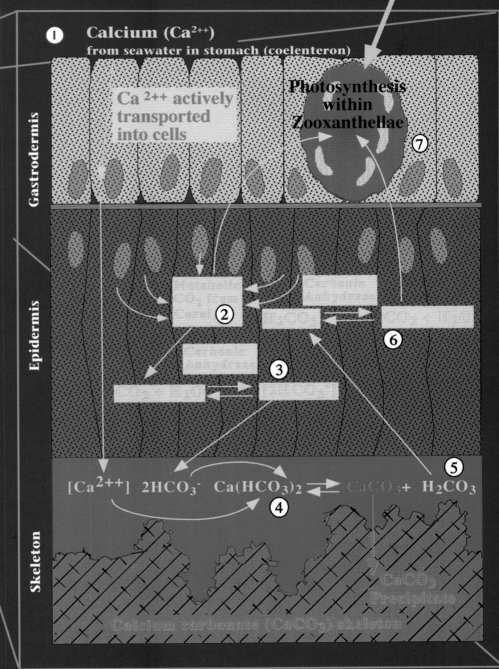

① **Calcium (Ca^{2++})**
from seawater in stomach (coelenteron)

Ca^{2++} actively transported into cells

Photosynthesis within Zooxanthellae ⑦

Gastrodermis

Epidermis

Metabolic CO_2 from Coral ②

Carbonic Anhydrase

H_2CO_3 ⑥ $CO_2 + H_2O$

Carbonic Anhydrase

$CO_2 + H_2O$ ③ $2HCO_3^-$

Skeleton

$[Ca^{2++}]$ $2HCO_3^-$ $Ca(HCO_3)_2 \rightleftharpoons CaCO_3 + H_2CO_3$ ⑤

④

$CaCO_3$ Precipitate

Calcium carbonate ($CaCO_3$) skeleton

Richard Grigg

Above: Cross section through a *Porites lobata* skeleton showing annual banding patterns. Why should such patterns exist?

Diagram of Hypothesized Skeletal Formation in a Hermatypic Coral

① Calcium ions (Ca^{2++}) are taken up by the coral from seawater. ② Carbon dioxide (CO_2) from coral respiration chemically combines with water to form carbonate ions (HCO_3^-). ③ Calcium and carbonate ions combine to form calcium bicarbonate; this unstable form breaks down into: ④ **Calcium carbonate ($CaCO_3$)** which is deposited as skeleton and ⑤ carbonic acid (H_2CO_3), which can itself be broken down ⑥ into carbon dioxide and water. The ability of zooxanthellae to use the CO_2 ⑦ allows this process to continue without building-up dangerous levels of CO_2.

(Modified after Goreau (1959), in 'Invertebrates', R.C. Brusca & G.J. Brusca, 1990. Printed with permission from Sinauer Associates, Inc.)

WHAT MAINTAINS THESE POLYPS' SHAPES?

For many colonial cnidarians the calcareous skeleton maintains the shape of the colony, but what maintains the shape of a polyp or even a tentacle on a polyp? Many marine invertebrates make use of water pressure to maintain their shapes; such **hydroskeletons** are commonly seen in such animals as seastars, sea cucumbers, tunicates, a wide range of worms, and of course, cnidarians. Cnidarians make use of water pressure (**hydrostatic pressure**) to not only maintain their polyp shape, but in conjunction with their muscles, use it to move both their tentacles and the main body of the polyp.

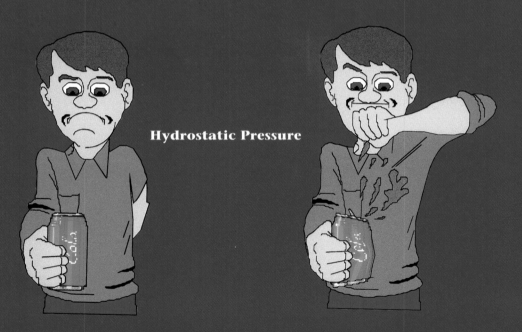

Hydrostatic Pressure

A sealed can of soda is practically impossible to crush by hand by non-bodybuilder-types out to hurt themselves. This is due to the fluid inside the sealed can being kept under pressure. Such hydrostatic pressure pushes against the wall of the can maintaining its shape (or that of a tentacle or polyp, or even the shape of a sea cucumber).

When the pressure is released (by pulling the pull tab to open the can), the thin aluminum shell can now be easily crushed, even with the fluid inside. Often people don't realize that they can severely damage a cnidarian or an echinoderm by momentarily lifting them out of the water, in part because of the dramatic change in external pressure.

CORAL SLIME

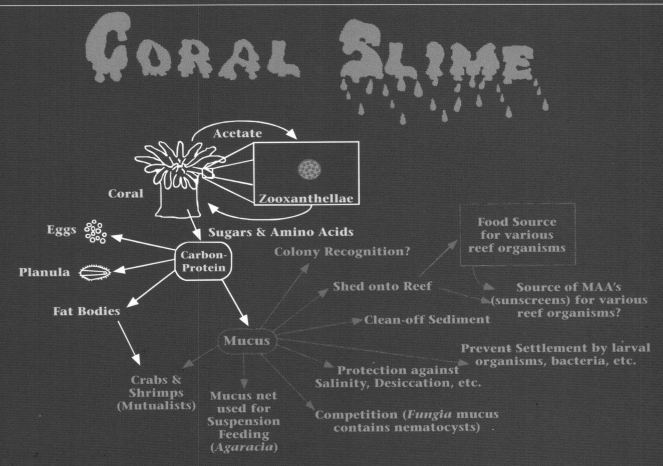

Acetate

Coral

Zooxanthellae

Eggs

Sugars & Amino Acids

Planula

Carbon-Protein

Colony Recognition?

Food Source for various reef organisms

Fat Bodies

Shed onto Reef

Source of MAA's (sunscreens) for various reef organisms?

Clean-off Sediment

Mucus

Prevent Settlement by larval organisms, bacteria, etc.

Crabs & Shrimps (Mutualists)

Mucus net used for Suspension Feeding (*Agaracia*)

Protection against Salinity, Desiccation, etc.

Competition (*Fungia* mucus contains nematocysts)

As stated earlier, the endosymbiotic zooxanthellae produce a huge amount of photosynthate (sugar-like compounds) which is translocated to the host coral as carbohydrate and amino acids. This, in turn, can be used by the coral to produce complex carbon-protein materials and eventually mucus (a thick, gooey, slime-like substance). Mucus is secreted from gland cells located in the epidermis. So, why produce mucus? Some think that this may be done primarily as a way of efficiently getting rid of huge quantities of excess organic carbon; in fact, it is estimated that between 10-30% of the total photosynthate produced by the zooxanthellae within a coral is excreted by the coral as either mucus or as Dissolved Organic Material (DOM). While this might be the case, a wide variety of other uses for mucus have been found in many different cnidarians.

Being made up of organic carbon, mucus may serve as a food source for a diversity of reef organisms; it is an important food source for marine bacteria and micro-zooplankton, which in turn serve as fodder for other reef organisms. Mucus may also be directly consumed by planktonic and benthic filter-feeders, and suspension-feeders. Most interesting, perhaps, is the idea that currents may carry large amounts of mucus offshore and into oceanic waters where it could serve as an initial food source for many larval fish in the plankton; presumably, this would increase survival of these organisms and result in more of them reaching adulthood and recruiting into nearshore waters.

Other suggested uses for mucus include it being a food source for symbiotic crabs and shrimp that inhabit certain branching species of coral (p.112); as a way to clean sediments off of a colony or solitary coral (Not bad for an organism with no arms, huh?); as a way of preventing the settlement and

successful attachment of larval invertebrates; and, in many shallow species, as a preventive stress response to extreme environmental change such as desiccation, temperature or salinity changes.

Certain species of coral (*Agaracia* sp.) actually use mucus to form mucus nets to trap organic particles; after which, the net is then hauled back into the mouth and stomach cavity for digestion. Mushroom coral (*Fungia scutaria*) have been shown to secrete mucus-containing nematocysts which come in contact with adjacent coral colonies and may help to prevent competition for space. It's also been suggested that some cnidarians use the chemical make-up of their mucus as a way of discerning "self" from "non-self" (in other words, as a way of preventing firing of nematocysts when a tentacle rubs up against another part of the same colony versus part of another colony or organism). As you can see, coral slime has a lot more uses then just something gross to rub on your dive buddy.

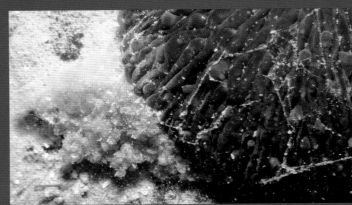

HAWAIIAN CORALS
REEF-BUILDING CORALS

THE UNIQUENESS OF HAWAIIAN CORAL REEFS

A "typical" view of a coral reef off of Australia

At first, this might seem to make Hawaiian reefs rather "bland", "boring", "depauperate"... but 'au contraire', it's what often makes Hawaiian reefs unique. It's thought to account for the exceptionally high amount of endemic Hawaiian marine species; and is believed by many to account for why certain species of fish and invertebrates look and act radically different than similar members of the same species found in other parts of the South Pacific.

Throughout the tropical Pacific, the make-up of many reefs are often similar, with the coral *Acropora* comprising the majority of the bottom cover. Many species of *Acropora* form densely-branching or "Tabletop" colonies which provide large amounts of "protected" three-dimensional space for a wide variety of fish and invertebrates. One result of this is that South Pacific reefs are frequently characterized by very complex assemblages of corals (frequently over 20 species) and reef fish (frequently over 100 species).

Hawaiian reefs do not (with very few exceptions) contain the dominant form of coral (*Acropora*) found throughout the rest of the tropical Pacific. This has resulted (along with the highly isolated nature of the Hawaiian Islands themselves) in coral reefs that are made-up of relatively few species of corals which often have limited branching (and therefore limited "protected" three-dimensional space).

An example of a monospecific reef. This type of reef has the lowest diversities of species, and often characterizes extreme habitats.

Another aspect of Hawaiian reefs is their very close proximity to major urban centers. This has resulted in Hawaiian reefs being impacted by a much wider assortment of human-related activities then many reefs elsewhere in the Pacific. It has also led to their being amongst the most studied of coral reef ecosystems. Finally, it's often easier to observe interactions between corals (or fish) within lower diversity reefs where the effects of individual species can be teased out of the interaction. What this means to the average diver is that he or she is more likely to actually observe behaviors in such an environment where one can easily focus on individual organisms.

A "typical" view of a Hawaiian coral reef.

HAWAIIAN CORAL ZONATION

Though each island varies, and major differences are seen between reefs on the leeward versus the windward sides, one can very broadly describe habitat zones that are seen on many Hawaiian reefs. Because of the dominance of a few corals in Hawai'i, whole sections (sometimes whole reefs!) can be characterized by a single species of coral. Often a wide variety of encrusting corals can be found in association with the dominant coral. While all the zones shown below rarely occur in the same area, a hypothetical Hawaiian reef might look like this:

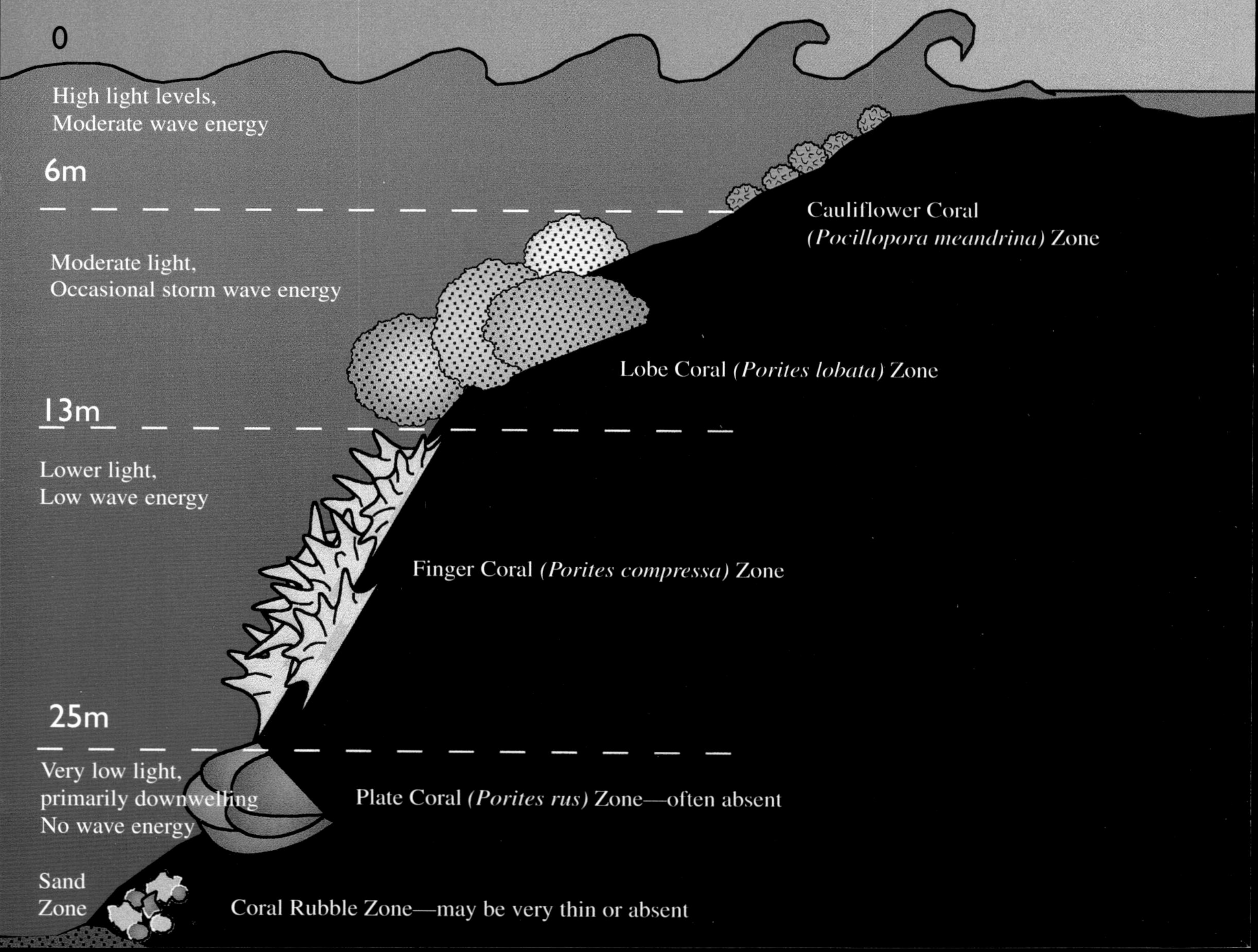

0

High light levels,
Moderate wave energy

6m

Moderate light,
Occasional storm wave energy

Cauliflower Coral
(*Pocillopora meandrina*) Zone

Lobe Coral (*Porites lobata*) Zone

13m

Lower light,
Low wave energy

Finger Coral (*Porites compressa*) Zone

25m

Very low light,
primarily downwelling
No wave energy

Plate Coral (*Porites rus*) Zone—often absent

Sand
Zone

Coral Rubble Zone—may be very thin or absent

A LAYPERSON'S GUIDE TO IDENTIFYING CORAL GROWTH FORMS

The shape of a colony tends to be based on three major factors: **Wave Action, Light Level, and Genetics.** The forms of many coral colonies are pre-programmed genetically and then acted upon and shaped by physical factors.

Massive

Coral colonies found in areas of high wave action tend to be solidly constructed, with the colony tending to have a similar shape in all directions, often forming a large, mound-like structure. Examples of this massive form includes Lobe coral (*Porites lobata*).

Branching

Coral colonies found in very calm, shallow areas tend to be branched; once again, maximizing the available surface area. Examples of branching include Lace coral (*Pocillopora damicornis*), & Elkhorn coral (*Pocillopora eydouxi*). Cauliflower coral (*Pocillopora meandrina*) is an example of a branched coral adapted for higher energy environments.

Plate-like (Laminar)

Deep on the reef slope, where wave action has little effect and where light levels are diminished and primarily downwelling, one may find plate corals. Such a growth form maximizes exposure to downwelling light while minimizing the amount of skeletal structure (since light levels are low, this minimizes the amount of energy available for heavy skeletons). An example of a coral with this growth form is *Porites rus*.

Rubble

These are not live coral but their skeletal remains. Parts of colonies often break loose, some are reattached to the substrate and become new colonies while others die and become rubble, often serving as a new substrate for a wide variety of other organisms to live upon, such that, even in death, the colony serves as a habitat.

Finger-like (Columnar)

In calmer or deeper waters, beneath the reach of normal wave action, a colony's growth form seems to be a response to maximizing the available light. The colony needs to maximize its surface area such that large numbers of its symbiotic zooxanthellae are exposed to light in order to provide the colony with energy. In waters less then 30 - 40 meters, a lot of light is refracted, allowing even vertical polyps' zooxanthellae to photosynthesize. An example of this form in Hawai'i is seen in colonies of Finger coral (*Porites compressa*).

Encrusting

In areas of very high-energy or very low-light, coral colonies tend to have a flat, spread out growth form. These encrusting colonies often grow over other growth forms of coral.

An Impostor!

Though this looks like a coral, it's actually a calcareous alga (note the lack of polyps) whose growth form is under many of the same influences as the coral it competes with for space.

Free-Living

A few corals have evolved to NOT live attached to the substrate. This allows them to exist in areas where most coral colonies (and other sessile organisms such as calcareous algae, bryozoans and sponges) cannot. An example of a free-living coral (as an adult) is the Mushroom Coral (*Fungia scutaria*).

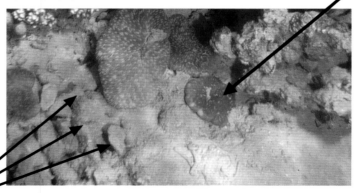

CORAL HYDROMECHANICS: SHAPELY CORALS

The shape of a coral may also be a product of millions of years of evolution acting to form a physical structure that is highly adapted to take advantage of its physical environment.

Coral colonies are thought to use their shapes to assist in sediment shedding, protection from predation and to compete with adjacent neighbors. Another intriguing idea is that the shape of some corals may increase the residence time of the water passing directly adjacent to the coral colony. This would allow increased time for suspension feeding as portions of passing water spend longer amounts of time in contact with specific sections of coral tissue. Another view would be that by breaking up a colony's surface into branches, corals are maximizing the amount of surface area exposed to the flow of water (and therefore suspended food).

WHOOSH!

WATER FLOW

THE TOPSY-TURVY WORLD OF SOLITARY CORALS

The shapes of many solitary, free-living corals such as *Fungia* or *Cycloseris* make it difficult for them to be flipped over except under extreme conditions of water motion. Once this occurs, the shapes of these corals facilitate their becoming righted again through the shape of their skeletons...

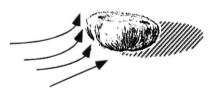

Strong water motion and the unstable nature of the convex shape serves to tilt the skeleton upwards.

Once the skeleton is upright, it presents a much greater cross-section to the prevailing water currents which facilitate it being turned over the rest of the way.

Once righted, the coral's upright shape is very stable. The septa (skeletal ridges) on the skeleton may serve to slow down water passing over the skeleton. The water is then channeled by the septa towards the center and the polyp's mouth, assisting in feeding.

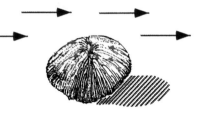

(Diagram modified and reprinted with permission from *Nature* (262: 212-213). Copyright 1976, Macmillan Magazines Limited.)

SKELETAL CHARACTERISTICS USED IN IDENTIFYING CORALS

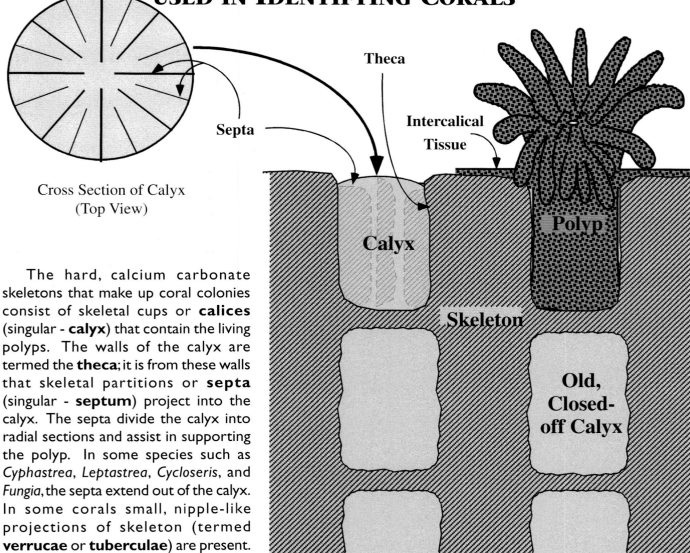

Cross Section of Calyx
(Top View)

Cross Section of Colony Skeleton (Side View)

The hard, calcium carbonate skeletons that make up coral colonies consist of skeletal cups or **calices** (singular - **calyx**) that contain the living polyps. The walls of the calyx are termed the **theca**; it is from these walls that skeletal partitions or **septa** (singular - **septum**) project into the calyx. The septa divide the calyx into radial sections and assist in supporting the polyp. In some species such as *Cyphastrea*, *Leptastrea*, *Cycloseris*, and *Fungia*, the septa extend out of the calyx. In some corals small, nipple-like projections of skeleton (termed **verrucae** or **tuberculae**) are present.

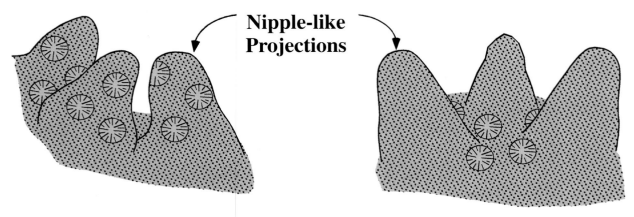

Nipple-like Projections

Coral with Calices on the verrucae
(ex. *Pocillopora*)

Coral with Calices between the tuberculae
(ex. *Montipora*)

Family *Acroporidae*

TABLE CORAL
Acropora cytheria
(Greek: *Akron* - summit or tip, Latin: *porus* - pore)

Acroporid corals are the most common corals found on Pacific reefs, numbering over 350 species. Until recently this type of coral was not thought to occur in the Hawaiian Islands (although fossilized species have been found at a number of sites on the island of O'ahu). We now know that three species of *Acropora* (*A. cytheria, A. valida,* and *A. humilis*) can be found in the Northwest Hawaiian Islands, primarily around French Frigate Shoals. Other than a couple of colonies of *Acropora cytheria* off the island of Kaua'i, none of these species are found in the main Hawaiian Islands. While extremely rare in Hawai'i, *Acropora* is a dominant coral at Johnston Atoll, only 720 km away.

All three species are primarily found on steeply sloping or vertical reef faces. All three species characteristically have numerous narrow branches containing large numbers of raised tube-like calices with a single, larger tube-like calyx at the tip. *A. cytheria* typically grows outward as a table form, while the other two species resemble branching, bush-like forms. Though

Above: A rare Table Coral colony found off of French Frigate Shoals, Northwest Hawaiian Islands. Note the shading effect of the colony's growth form on adjacent coral species competing for the same available space.

similar in appearance, *A humilis* has much thicker branches than *A. valida.* Colony color ranges from pale cream to brown, with paler-colored branch tips (*A. valida* occasionally has purplish branch tips).

While all three of these species release egg-sperm bundles during the summer months, each of them appears to spawn on a different moon phase. This is in contrast with other parts of the Pacific where the same species synchronize their spawning with other corals into mass spawning events.

Since these corals are sexually active and occur in Hawai'i, an interesting question to mull over is why *Acropora* is not more prevalent throughout the main Hawaiian Islands?

A primary predator on this coral, the Chevron Butterflyfish (*Chaetodon trifascialis*) is only found as an adult in the Northwest Hawaiian Islands where its only food source (*Acropora*) is found. Elsewhere in the Pacific, *Acropora* is one of the preferred foods of the Crown-of-Thorns Seastar (*Acanthaster planci*).

Above: A number of colonies of *A. valida* off French Frigate Shoals.

Above: The high branching nature of this species provides large amounts of cover for larval fishes.

Symbionts

Reproduction

June – July

Habitat

Predators

Chevron Butterflyfish

RICE CORAL
Montipora capitata
(Latin: *mons* - mountain, *porus* - pore)

Rice coral (*Montipora capitata*) in Hawai'i was previously called *Montipora verrucosa*. The Hawaiian version varied substantially from *Montipora verrucosa* seen elsewhere in the Pacific; as such, a number of authors have classified this coral as *Montipora capitata*. It occurs in a wide variety of growth forms, each of which bears the characteristic tuberculae adjacent to the calices in which the polyps sit.

The same colony of Rice coral can often show finger-like branching, encrusting and plate-like growth forms. This coral, along with Finger coral (*Porites compressa*), appears to be highly resistant to stresses such as sedimentation and salinity changes based upon studies done in Kāne'ohe Bay where it is commonly found. Color is usually tan to brown with white edges.

Montipora capitata releases egg-sperm bundles whose eggs contain zooxanthellae which are thought to provide the developing planula larvae with energy while they are in the plankton.

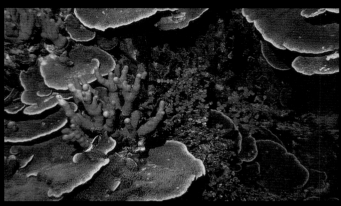

Keoki Stender

Above: Plate-like forms of Rice coral surrounding a head of Finger coral The white edges represent the growing edge of the colony.

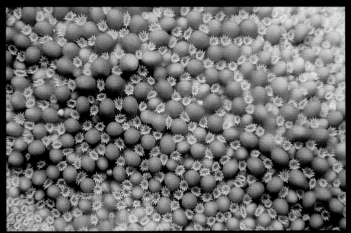

Keoki Stender

Members of the genus *Montipora* frequently have characteristic star-shaped cups (or calices), often adjacent to nipple-like skeletal projections called tuberculae.

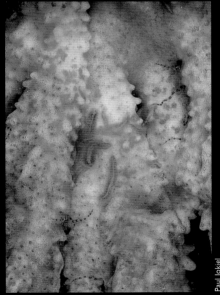

Paul Jokiel

Above: The parasitic flatworm, *Prosthiostomum montiporae* feeds specifically on the living tissue of this coral.

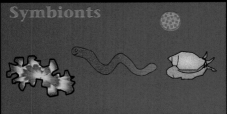

Symbionts

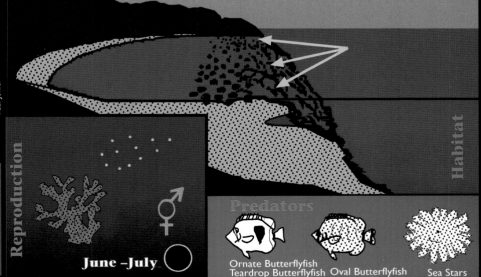

Reproduction

June –July

Habitat

Predators

Ornate Butterflyfish
Teardrop Butterflyfish Oval Butterflyfish   Sea Stars

BLUE RICE CORAL
Montipora flabellata and *Montipora patula*
(Latin: *mons* - mountain, *porus* - pore)

Both *Montipora patula* and *Montipora flabellata* can occur here from tidepools or the intertidal zone down past , but are most frequently found high on the reef slope or in ow bays with moderate wave action. Both species tend to as encrusting forms; often growing around or over older, lished colonies of other species. *Montipora flabellata* has ense blue color; *Montipora patula*'s color varies as the tissue een the polyps (the intercalical tissue) can range between o brown; the polyps tend to be bluish in color (but can also n, giving the colony more of a tan coloration as a whole). tula is relatively rare compared to *M. flabellata*.

Recently the suggestion has been put forward that the blue in these two corals results from a pigment that fluoresces e presence of ultraviolet radiation. Such UV, once fluoresced visible light, could then be used by the symbiotic algae for osynthesis. Ⓣ

Above: The bluish color of *Montipora flabellata* is hard to miss in the field. This coral is endemic to Hawai'i

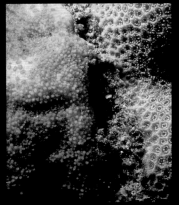

Above: Both *Montipora patula* (*left*) and *Montipora flabellata* (*right*) are characteristic in being sucessionist species, often growing over colonizing species such as lobe coral (*Porites lobata*) or cauliflower coral (*Pocillopora meandrina*).

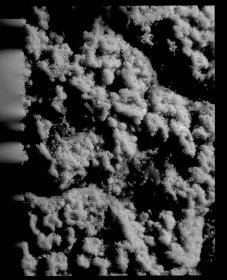

ve: *Montipora flabellata* 's tuberculae are often ed together to form wave-like ridges around calices . It is often found in shallower, higher e energy environments than *M. patula*.

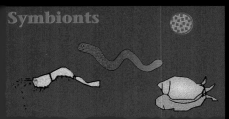

Symbionts

Reproduction

Summer – Fall

Predators

Teardrop Butterflyfish

Sea Stars

Habitat

FLAT LOBE CORAL
Pavona duerdeni
(Latin: *pavo* - peacock)

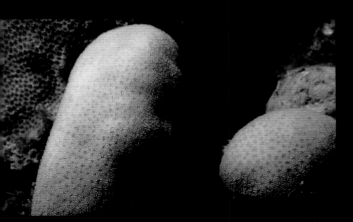

Flat lobe coral (*Pavona duerdeni*) is easily identified in olde colonies by the characteristic upright, flat, ridge-like lobes; thes discs can become quite thick. Young colonies are encrusting Like other species of *Pavona* in Hawai'i, *Pavona duerdeni* tends t occur in the shallower reef environments; it can occur anywher exposed to moderate to strong wave action, but is most frequentl found high on the reef slope or the reef crest on offshore reef. Color ranges from a light gray to a brownish gray.

bove: Flat Lobe coral colony in the field off Puako, Hawai'i. Note the disc-ke shape of the older colony on the left.

bove: Moderate to high wave energy environments like the edge of the barrier reef off Kāne'ohe Bay, O'ahu are excellent places to look for *Pavona* colonies.

The calices (skeletal cups) in this coral have a unique star like shape (*above*), which makes this one of the more beautifu corals to look at close-up.

Like most members of this family (Agariciidae), very little is known about the reproductive life history or specific predators on Flat Lobe coral. This is especially true in Hawai'i where this coral is rarely a dominant component of the coral fauna on a reef.

Symbionts

Reproduction

Unknown ?

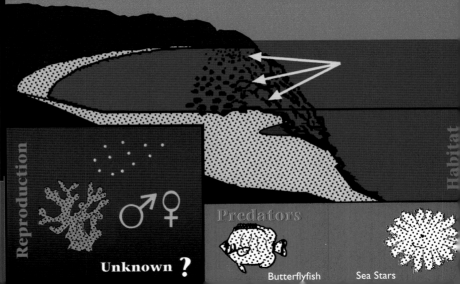

Predators

Butterflyfish   Sea Stars

Habitat

CORRUGATED CORAL
Pavona varians
(Latin: *pavo* - peacock)

Corrugated coral (*Pavona varians*) is so named due to the curling ridges and valleys making up the calices, which some say esemble the corrugations in a cross-section of cardboard (isn't his an excellent argument against the heavy use of common ames???). These narrow, curling ridges are the prime identifying haracteristic of this encrusting species. Like other species of *avona* in Hawai'i, it tends to occur in the shallower reef nvironments, though it can occur down to depths of 25 m or hore. Like *Pavona duerdeni*, *P. varians* tends to occur in areas xposed to moderate to strong wave action, most frequently eing found on the reef slope or the reef crest of offshore eefs. Color ranges from tan to brown.

The calices (skeletal cups) in this coral (*right*) have long, heandering ridges, which upon close inspection makes it very asy to identify in the field. *Pavona varians* is an excellent coral look for intratentacular budding (see pg. 78) occurring within he grooves.

Above: Pavona varians coral colony off Kapoho, Hawai'i. This species is the most commonly encountered form of *Pavona* in waters around the main Hawaiian islands.

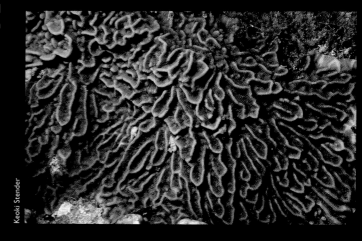

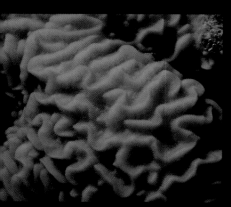

There is some question as to whether he Hawai'i form is a separate (endemic) ecies from forms of *Pavona varians* ported from elsewhere in the Pacific.

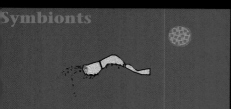

Symbionts

Reproduction

June-July

Habitat

Predators

Butterflyfish Sea Stars

CRUST CORAL
Leptastrea purpurea
(Greek: *leptos* - slender, *aster* - star)

A close relative of the Brain Coral (which does not occur ■ Hawai'i), *Leptastrea purpurea* is one of only three members f this family (Faviidae) found in Hawai'i. An encrusting coral ■at does well in a wide range of environments (from shallow ■gh energy to deep reefs), this coral nevertheless is not a ■ommon representative of Hawaiian reefs. Color ranges ■nywhere from a light brown to green or even purple. Often ■e oral disc is lighter colored then the sides (*bottom right*).

A symbiotic crab (*Troglocarcinus* sp.) can sometimes be found ■habiting deep pits like the one shown here.

The calices (skeletal cups) in this coral are relatively large, ■rongly angular and often adjacent to one another (*below*). A ■milar, though rarer species, *L. bottae* has calices which are slightly ■ised and are separated from one another.

Unlike some members of this family (Faviidae), very little is ■nown about the reproductive life history or specific predators ■ *Leptastrea*. This is especially true in Hawai'i where this coral ■ rarely a dominant component of the coral fauna on a reef.

Above: Unusually large encrusting colony of *Leptastrea purpurea* off of the island of Moloka'i.

Deborah Gochfeld

■bove: Close-up showing skeleton with retracted ■lyps.

Symbionts

Reproduction

Unknown ?

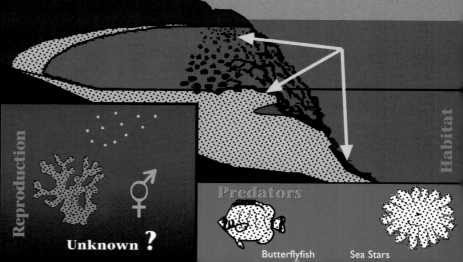

Predators

Butterflyfish   Sea Stars

Habitat

OCELLATED CORAL
Cyphastrea ocellina
(Greek: *kyphos* - humped, *aster* - star)

Like other members of the family Faviidae, *Cyphastrea ellina* has large calices (though not as large as *Leptastrea* which also found here). An encrusting form, it is usually found earshore in shallow water, frequently in areas that have oderate wave action. Color ranges anywhere from tan to eddish brown.

A tiny symbiotic crab (*Troglocarcinus minutus*) can ometimes be found inhabiting pits between the calices.

The calices (skeletal cups) in this coral are round, large and elatively deep; the walls of which tend to rise well above the urface of the colony. Unlike *Leptastrea*, the areas between the alices have sharp skeletal plates and points. Often the different alices, while crowded together, will point in different directions.

Unlike most corals, *C. ocellina* release planula more or less n a monthly basis, though it tends to concentrate its release etween April and June. It is still not clear whether this species sexually produces its planula or broods the fertilized eggs within s coelenteron until planula are formed.

Above: Encrusting colonies of *Cyphastrea ocellina* on a ledge off of Lana'i Lookout, O'ahu.

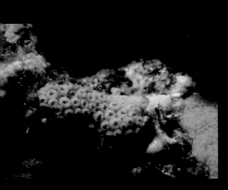

bove: Close-up showing skeleton ith retracted polyps.

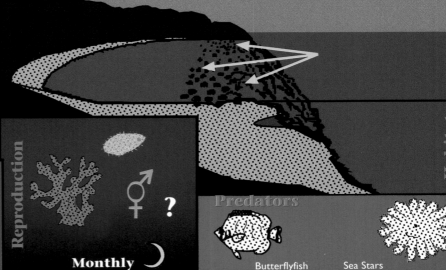

Symbionts

Reproduction

Monthly

Predators

Butterflyfish   Sea Stars

Habitat

HUMPBACK CORAL
Cycloseris vaughani
(Greek: *kyklos* - circle, *seris*- lettuce)

Humpback corals (*Cycloseris vaughani*) are often mistaken r Mushroom corals (*Fungia scutaria*). Both are free-living, olitary, roughly circular corals that tend to be found living mongst the coarse rubble at the base of reefs. *Cycloseris* is ore circular in shape and usually occurs deeper than *Fungia* ometimes below 40 m). An easy way to tell the two apart is looking at the aboral side; *Fungia* have small, nipple-like rojections arising off the underside while *Cycloseris* is smooth. vaughani is characterized by a raised, mound-like skeleton. A elated species, *Cycloseris hexagonalis* is much rarer, has a strongly eometrical shape, and is often found deeper than *C. vaughani*.

Very little is known about the ecology of these corals. They e not common, and tend to occur in areas not frequented by ost divers.

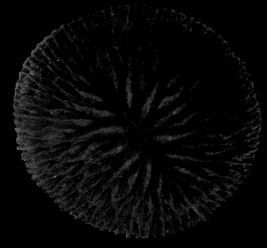

Above: Humpback coral removed from the top of the barrier reef off Kane'ohe Bay, O'ahu. Compare this photo with the one to the lower left showing the same animal with its coelenteron inflated.

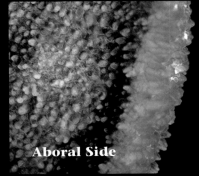

Aboral Side

Deborah Gochfeld

Above: Close-up shot showing the underside (aboral side) of a mushroom coral which is covered with many small, nipple-like projections. *Cycloseris* o the other hand, has a smooth aboral surface.

bove: *Cycloseris* and small *Fungia* have the ility to move about through inflation of eir coelenteron and secretion of mucus. he circular, white shape in the center is the keleton. If these animals happen to verturn (not an uncommon occurrence on oft substrates exposed to occasional storm urges), they can right themselves through e use of their tentacles and coelenteron.

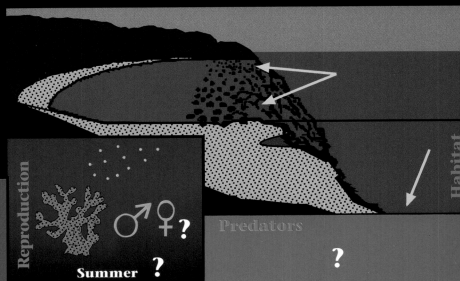

Symbionts

?

Reproduction

♂♀?

Summer ?

Predators

Habitat

?

MUSHROOM CORAL
Fungia scutaria
(Latin: *fungus* - mushroom)

Mushroom (or Razor) coral (*Fungia scutaria*) is one of the
solitary, free-living Hawaiian corals. In essence, it is one
antic coral polyp with a dense, unattached skeleton.
shroom corals are typically commonly found at the base of,
in-between coral heads, often on reef flats where they are
tected from heavy wave action. Adult individuals range in
e from 5 to 20 cm. Often confused with *Cycloseris vaughani*,
y can be differentiated by looking at the aboral side.
shroom corals have a rough aboral side with many small
nes, whereas *Cycloseris'* aboral side is much smoother.
owth forms typically assume circular or oblong shapes. The
or typically ranges from pale to dark-brown, occasionally with
ple or green tentacles.

Mushroom corals were one of the few corals commonly
d by the ancient Hawaiians (who called it *ko'a-kohe*) and used
s an abrasive for polishing canoes or rubbing the bristles off
igs before they were cooked.

Being a free-living coral, *Fungia scutaria* has adapted in a
mber of ways to the stresses of living on loose substrate (see
40). Its shape serves to hydrodynamically prevent it from
ng flipped over by surge. By being specialized to live as a
oxanthellate coral unattached to the substrate, *Fungia* avoids
mpeting for the precious little open settlement space that
sts on the reef.

Below: Mushroom corals get their name from the stalking growth form of
asexually-produced offspring. These stalks are usually attached to the reef
substrate (often old or dead *Fungia*) and are thought to break off due to the
effects of increased weight (due to growth), boring sponges and wave action.
Once this occurs, the individual coral leads a free living existence, often at
the base of the reef it arose on. Also note the large amount of mucus being
given off by the top coral; mucus serves a number of roles in these corals
(see p. 35).

Keoki Stender

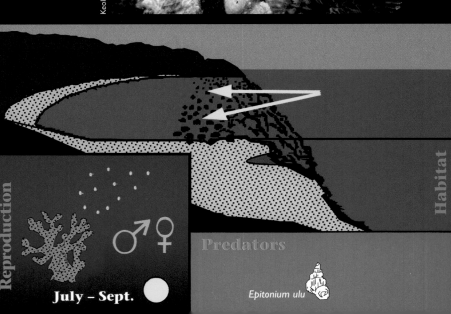

Symbionts

Reproduction

July – Sept.

Predators

Epitonium ulu

Habitat

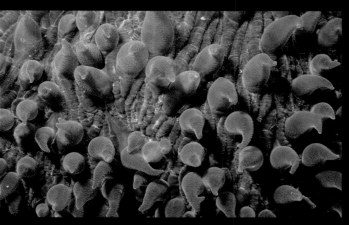

Above: Mushroom corals tend to have a large number of tentacles surrounding their centralized mouth. The tentacles are most prominent at night and contain high concentrations of nematocysts (note the small white dots massed over each tentacle).

Above: Adapted to live on loose substrate, yet still maintaining symbiotic zooxanthellae; Mushroom corals avoid the heavy competition that occurs for open hard substrate on coral reefs.

Above: The parasitic snail, *Epitonium ulu*, feeds by sucking the tissue of the host Mushroom coral. These snails are usually found near the base of the solitary coral and will often lay their eggs on the underside of the *Fungia* they are feeding on.

One of the more interesting symbiotic relationships seen with some Mushroom corals is the presence of a mutualistic bivalve (similar to a clam or mussel) called *Fungiacava* sp. that lives entirely within the coelenteron (stomach cavity) of the host coral. Its incurrent siphon extends into the coral's stomach along with the mollusc's foot which serves to act like a tongue to help it select assorted plankton (much of which may be too small for the coral itself to feed on) brought into the cavity by the coral and upon which the mollusc feeds. Additionally, *Fungiacava* may feed on excess zooxanthellae and mucus released by the coral. Waste products from the mollusc may then in turn be used by the zooxanthellae within the coral's tissues for the process of photosynthesis. *Fungiacava* has not been found in Hawai'i.

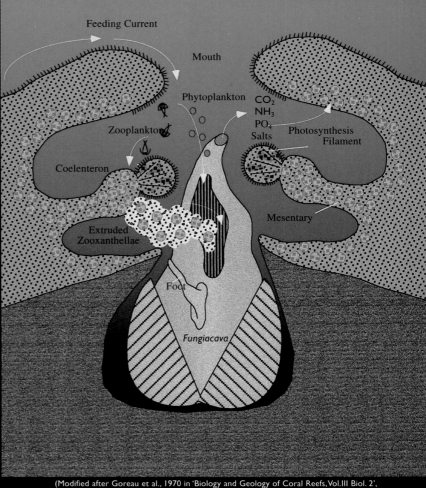

Feeding Current

Mouth

Phytoplankton

CO_2
NH_3
PO_4
Salts

Photosynthesis
Filament

Zooplankton

Coelenteron

Mesentary

Extruded
Zooxanthellae

Foot

Fungiacava

(Modified after Goreau et al., 1970 in 'Biology and Geology of Coral Reefs, Vol.III Biol. 2', O.A. Jones & R. Edean, eds. Printed with permission from Academic Press, Inc.)

Family *Pocilloporidae*

LACE CORAL
Pocillopora damicornis
(Latin: *pocillum* - cup, *porus* - pore)

Lace Corals (*Pocillopora damicornis*) tend to occur in shallow depths, often in protected bays or on top of inner reef flats where they are protected from heavy wave action. *Pocillopora damicornis* distribution may also be limited from reef slopes not only by wave action, but also by feeding preferences and foraging behaviors of corallivores like butterflyfish (see pp. 97, 158). Adult colonies tend to have a generalized bushy form, though in Hawai'i a large number of different morphological varieties have been noted. Interestingly, many of these varieties have different monthly planula larvae release times, raising interesting questions about the possibilities of sub-species occurring here. Close inspections of colonies representing these different varieties will reveal distinct color and branch growth forms. The colony color can range from pale yellow to dark brown. Unlike most corals, *P. damicornis* releases planulae more or less on a monthly basis, though different morphological forms will release planula on different moon phases. In Hawai'i it is thought that this species asexually produces its planulae, which develop in the coelenteron and then are released through the mouth (see p. 80). In other parts of the Pacific, *P. damicornis* reproduces only sexually in the late spring/early summer (Western Australia) or not at all (Panama), lending weight to the idea that regional environmental effects play a strong role in spawning behaviors in corals. The monthly release of offspring results in Hawaiian Lace Corals releasing between 25 - 50% of their biomass per year as planulae!

Deborah Gochfeld

Heinz-Gert deCouet

Above: Lace corals are often loaded with a wide variety of invertebrate symbionts.

Above: Extended polyps and planula larva *of P. damicornis*

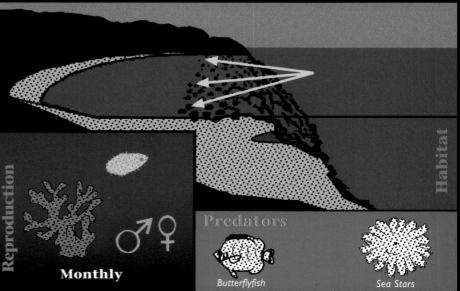

Symbionts

Reproduction

Monthly ♂♀

Habitat

Predators

Butterflyfish   *Sea Stars*

ANTLER CORAL
Pocillopora eydouxi
(Latin: *pocillum* - cup, *porus* - pore)

Antler Coral is the largest and most heavily branched of the pocilloporid corals in Hawai'i, reaching colony heights in deeper water of over 92 cm (over 3')! Such a large three-dimensional object in a reef environment attracts a wide variety of shelter-seeking animals. Often associated with these colonies is a variety of reef fish, with schools of *Dascyllus* Damselfish being a common occurrence. Where *P. eydouxi* and *P. meandrina* (Cauliflower Coral, next page) tend to overlap in their distributions, they often can be difficult to tell apart as their colony forms will tend to look similar; the major difference will be in *P. eydouxi*'s well-developed septa which will fuse towards the center of each calyx forming a column-like structure termed a columella.

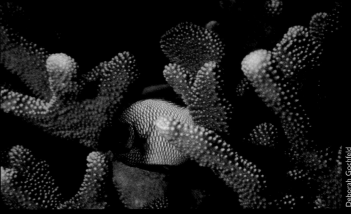

Above: Plankton-feeding *Dascyllus* Damselfish venture only a little distance from the safety of *P. eydouxi*'s branches in their quest for food.

Above: The Blue-Eyed Damselfish specializes in feeding on pocilloporid corals and are almost always found associated with this coral. Males will often guard nest territories around the bases of *P. eydouxi*.

Calm, deep bays

Habitat

Symbionts

Reproduction

Summer? ❓

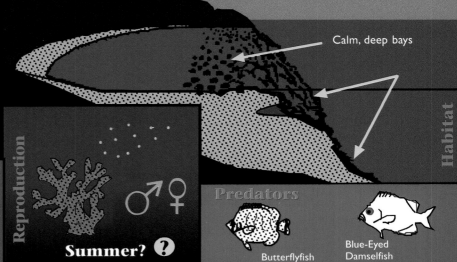

Predators

Butterflyfish   Blue-Eyed Damselfish

Family *Pocilloporidae*

CAULIFLOWER CORAL
Pocillopora meandrina
(Latin: *pocillum* - cup, *porus* - pore)

Lisa Privitera

One of the most common corals in shallow, high-energy environments, *Pocillopora meandrina* is a colonizing species (see pp. 132 - 135) that is often the first coral to establish on recent lava flows. The distinctive bush-like cauliflower shape provides relative stability in the face of seasonal swell and intense wave energy. With increasing depth this coral is often replaced by other corals (notably *Porites*), except in strong current-swept areas where *P. meandrina* may dominate. Colonies may reach diameters of up to 60 cm (roughly 2 ft) and range in color from brown to tan to pink. Branches are often flat and thick, with calices atop, and between, the verrucae (*below left*). Unlike *Porites* or many *Montipora* species, *Pocillopora* species seem to be not as tolerant of sediment-laden waters and are often absent from calm bay areas such as Kāne'ohe Bay; perhaps this is due to the branching colony shape, which would serve to trap much of the sediment amongst the polyps.

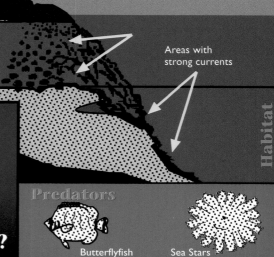

Deborah Gochfeld

Above: The Arc-Eye Hawkfish is only one of a number of fish species that make use of this species of coral as either a substrate to hunt from, or as a shelter.

Above: *P. meandrina* is sometimes referred to as "Rose Coral" due to some shallower water colonies having a brilliant rose color. The color comes not from the zooxanthellae-filled polyps but from pigments in the coral tissue connecting the polyps. One theory behind this coloration phenomena is that this may be an adaptation to high UV environments (see p. 202), where pigments in the tissue alter ultraviolet radiation into the visible range. The resulting fluorescence we see as a bright rose-color; but more importantly, it allows both protection of the coral and zooxanthellae from the harmful effects of UV, while providing additional usable light for photosynthesis (and therefore more energy for the coral).

Areas with strong currents

Habitat

Symbionts

Reproduction

♂ ♀

May - June?   ◯ **?**

Predators

Butterflyfish   Sea Stars

FINGER CORAL
Porites compressa
(Latin: *porus* - pore)

Finger coral (*Porites compressa*) is the most common
awaiian coral in wave-protected reef environments (calm bays
d reef slopes, often on the leeward sides of islands). It is even
ore interesting when one considers that this very common
d successful Hawaiian coral is probably endemic. Its dominance
Hawaiian reefs may be due to its fast growth rate, relative
sistance to non-physical environmental stress, and upright
owth form (which may limit some competitive and predatory
eractions). Growth forms can vary, but typically assume an
right, finger-like branching. Color ranges from a yellow to
ayish-tan to light brown.

Above: As one of the most common corals in Hawai'i, *Porites compressa*
frequently dominates Hawaiian reefs, and will occasionally form
monospecific reefs in areas under low-disturbance regimes (see pp. 132 -
135).

Deborah Gochfeld

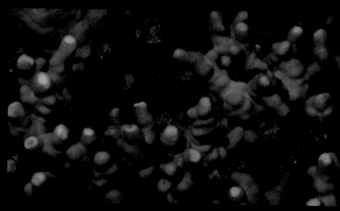

nt: Often the branch tips are most exposed to predation and show the
st evidence of having been nibbled on; additionally, the tips are the most
ve-growing regions of the colony. By the way, notice anything interesting
king use of this habitat?

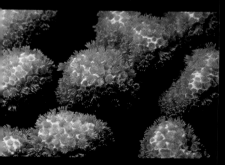

ove: As with most *Porites*, Finger Coral is
aracterized by very small polyps.

Symbionts

Reproduction

June - August

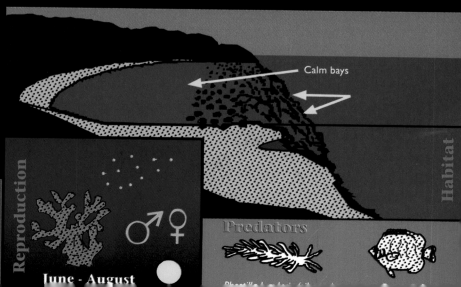

Calm bays

Habitat

Predators

Lobe Coral
Porites lobata
(Latin: *porus* - pore)

Lobe coral (*Porites lobata*) is the most widespread and
mmon of the Hawaiian corals. It can occur anywhere from
intertidal zone down to below 40 m, but is most frequently
nd high on the reef slope just below the area of highest wave
on. Growth forms vary, but typically assume massive or
crusting forms; with the encrusting forms usually occurring
he most exposed areas. Dome-like massive forms may reach
ghts of several meters and can represent colonies that are
ndreds of years old. Deep forms may resemble lobate Finger
al. Color ranges from a yellowish olive-green to brown.

Above: Massive Lobe coral colony off of Barber's Point, O'ahu.

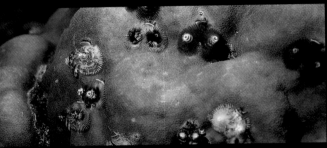

ove: Note the diversity of Christmas tree worms and vermitid molluscs
e p. 117) present; only the feeding structures of these organisms are
ible, the animals are safely burrowed within the dead skeleton of the
al colony.

Massive colonies are often home to a great variety of
mbionts such as the brightly colored Christmas tree worms.
hese worms are thought to gain a foothold as larvae by settling
op damaged polyps (possibly due to fish predation). Long,
rrow cracks (*below*) represent the home of a commensal
pheid shrimp which uses the crevices as a safe place to do
me gardening; the shrimp raises filamentous and blue green
gae upon which it feeds (see p. 26).

Like most members of the family Poritidae, Lobe coral has the characterist.
snowflake-shaped cup (or calyx) in which the individual coral polyps live.

Symbionts

Reproduction

♂ ♀

July - August

Predators

Shortbodied Blenny

Multiband Butterflyfish
Ornate Butterflyfish

Habitat

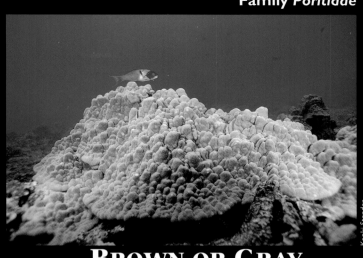

PLATE CORAL
Porites rus

BROWN OR GRAY
LOBE CORAL
Porites evermanni

Above: Healthy Plate Coral assemblage in Kealakekua Bay, Hawai'i. At this depth, light is primarily downwelling resulting in plate-like forms to maximize surface area capture of light by the zooxanthellae and minimize skeletal construction. As such, these formations are very fragile and easily broken by careless divers (or snorkelors who break off shallower corals creating a landslide effect). The slightly irregular surface may well function in allowing mucus to help shed settled sediments off the colony.

Most frequently referred to as Plate Coral, *Porites rus* actually can occur in a number of growth forms (*below*) at deeper depths where it is primarily affected by light levels and competition for space.

Looking very much like *Porites lobata*, *P. evermanni* can be distinguished by its irregular lobes and very shallow calices (*right*) which give it a smoother appearance than *P. lobata*. Additionally, it is often found on shallow reef crests and reef flats, and often will have a rich brown, gray or grayish-purple coloration.

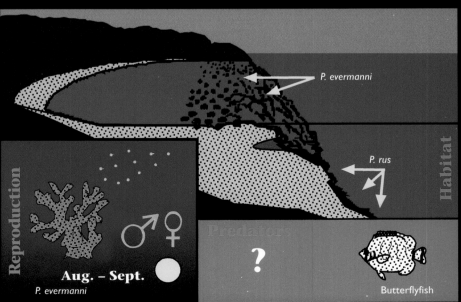

P. evermanni

P. rus

Habitat

Symbionts

?

Reproduction

♂ ♀

Aug. – Sept.
P. evermanni

Predators

?

Butterflyfish

SECTION I: CORALS AS ORGANISMS

NON-REEF BUILDING CORALS & CORAL RELATIVES

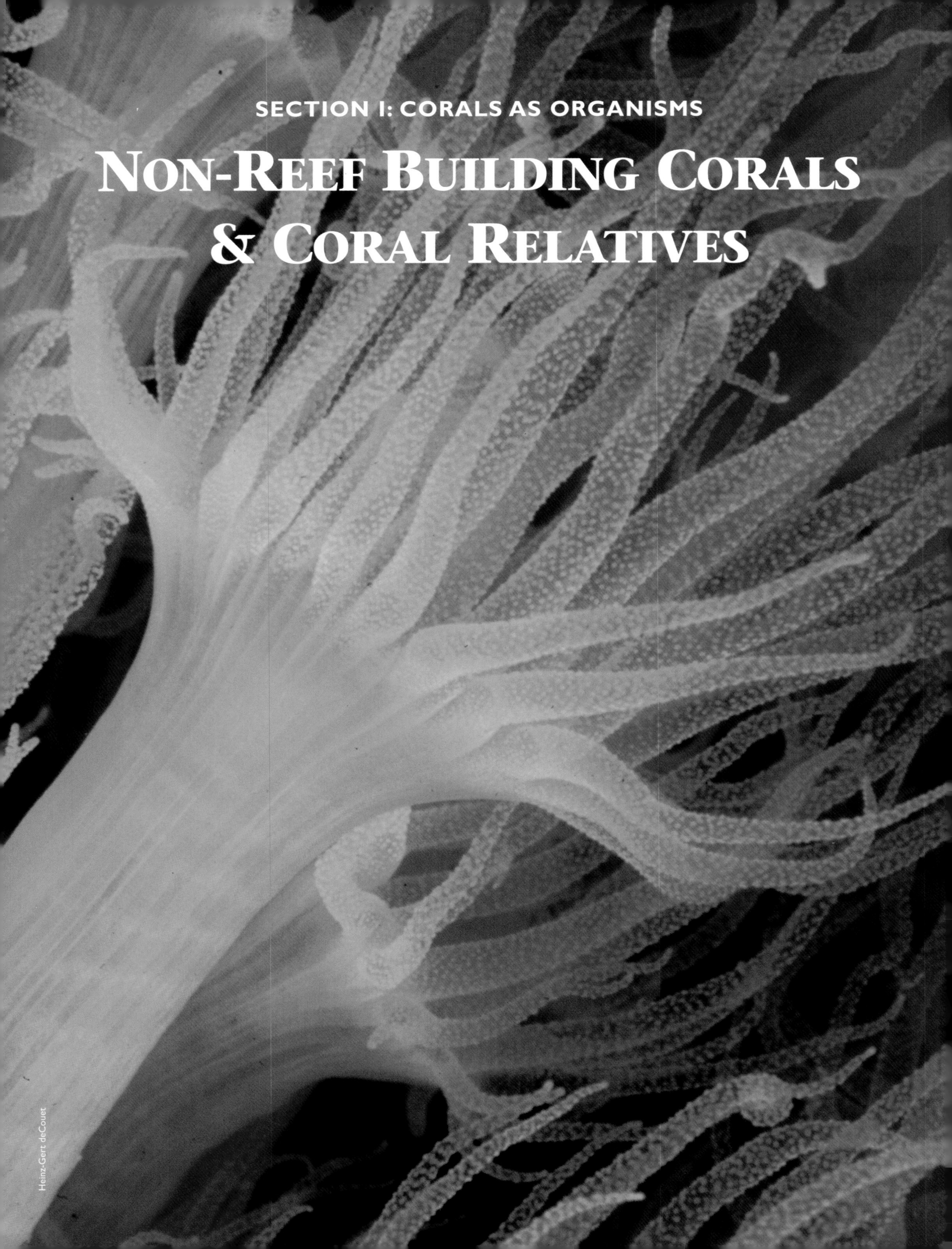

Heinz-Gert deCouet

ORANGE CUP CORAL
Tubastraea coccinea
(Latin: *tubus* - tube, Greek: *aster* - star)

Probably the most frequently seen of the **ahermatypic** corals (those corals that exist without symbiotic algae), Orange Cup Coral (*Tubastraea coccinea*) is commonly found in areas where **hermatypic** corals are rare; caves, overhangs and deep, vertical faces. Occurring in shaded environments in very shallow water, *Tubastraea* can also be found below 40 m (120 ft) growing out in the open on very steep-reef slopes. Growth forms characteristically resemble clusters of polyps; which, when extended, are large and fleshy. Color ranges from orange to pink to black (though some scientists think these represent three distinctly different species).

Above:Tubastraea coccinea is common in caves and overhangs in shallow water and along vertical walls in deeper waters. Note the male and female Potter's Angelfish (*Centropyge potteri*), these fish often make their nests at the base of such vertical walls.

Colonies of *Tubastraea* are sometimes home to species of symbiotic shrimp that live among the polyps but are rarely seen due to their highly cryptic nature. These shrimp are similar to the shrimp seen on seastars and sea urchins.

Tubastraea may be one of the few corals in Hawaiian water that has internal fertilization. The resulting planula larvae are brooded (develop) within the coelenteron before they are released.

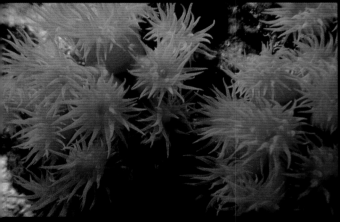

Above: Lacking symbiotic zooxanthellae, *Tubastraea* are highly modified for effectively capturing and consuming zooplankton in the waters surrounding the colonies. Note the elongated tentacles (the small yellowish dots are cnidocyte clusters), elongated bodies and enlarged mouth. *Tubastraea* tend to feed primarily at night when plankton are more plentiful in coastal waters.

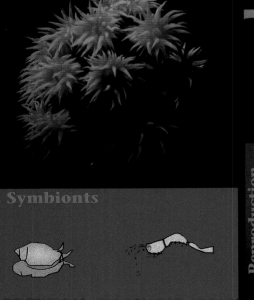

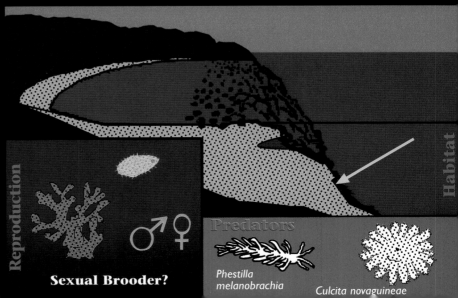

Symbionts

Reproduction

Sexual Brooder?

Predators

Phestilla melanobrachia

Culcita novaguineae

Habitat

Space in low light environments near or on reefs is often just as much in demand as space on the reef itself; it's just that the prospective home buyers are different. Often *Tubastraea* has to compete against sponges (*left*), and bryozoans for settlement space.

Tubastraea is commonly found on both Pacific and Atlantic reefs. In some places outside of Hawai'i, a dark green branching form called *Tubastraea micranthea* (*right*) occurs; this species actually grows out in the open, competing with hermatypic corals in areas where currents are brisk insuring a plentiful supply of zooplankton.

Heinz-Gert deCouet

Left: The black form of *Tubastraea coccinea* with the polyps completely retracted into the calices. Some scientists think this may be a different species. Note the predatory nudibranch *Phestilla melanobrachia* making a beeline directly towards its next meal. Usually these nudibranchs are bright orange but this one has been feeding on the black form and has adopted its coloration.

OTHER DENDROPHYLLIDS:

Tubastraea belongs to a group of corals within the family Dendrophylliidae. Other members of this family are rather rare in coastal waters in Hawai'i; but when present, are frequently mistaken as *Tubastraea* (though close inspection will often reveal distinct differences).

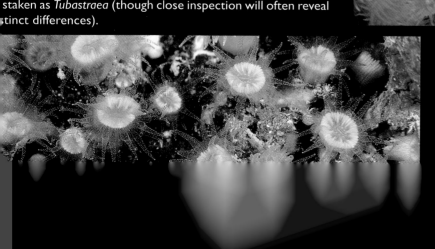

Above: Dendrophyllia sp. is very rare in shallow waters in Hawai'i. This large colony was found covering the inside of a very large sea cave on the windward side of O'ahu.

Left: Balanophyllia affinis is usually found only in caves or overhangs. It tends to be solitary while *Tubastraea* often occurs in clumps. The shape of the calyx is also more elliptical than that of *Tubastraea*. If you look closely at this photo you can spot examples of feeding behavior.

WIRE CORAL
Cirrhipathes anguina
(Latin: *cirratus*- curled, Greek: *pathos*- evil)

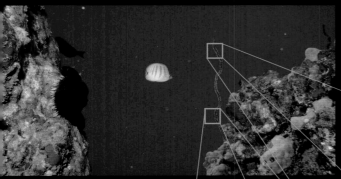

Wire coral (*Cirrhipathes anguina*) is the most common the Hawaiian antipatharian corals, a group that also includes t black corals (see next page). It tends to occur in medium high-current waters, anywhere from low-light, vertical surface below the low tide level (usually caves & inverted ledges) down below 100 m (300 ft). Other forms of wire cor (*C. spiralis*, *Stichopathes* sp.) are commonly found in dept exceeding 300 m (900 ft). The growth form is long, unbranche whip-like colonies. The lengths of colonies vary, in some are wire corals may reach over 2 m (6 ft)!

Color is green to brown in living colonies.

bove: Wire coral colony off of Lana'i Lookout, O'ahu. Though in shallower ater than where this species is usually found, this colony has minimized ompetition from hermatypic corals by growing from a vertical face where oth light conditions and topography work against the successful olonization by reef-building corals.

Close inspection of wire oral colonies will often reveal he presence of symbiotic airs of shrimp and/or gobies hat inhabit the outer surface f the colony. The shrimp eeds on mucus & organic etritus. The goby feeds on lankton. Most gobies cannot ed on midwater plankton nce they lack swim bladders nd are poor swimmers. By ving on the wire coral, the onge's Goby is able to exploit his food resource (midwater lankton), while still retaining ubstrate shelter.

Heinz-Gert deCouet

Above: Close-up shot showing the Wire Coral's polyps. Close inspection reveals the symbiotic shrimp *Dasycaris*sp.

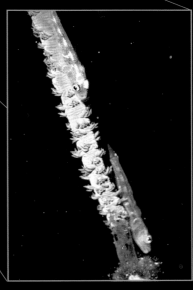

Right: Close-up shot showing a pair of Yonge's Goby (*Bryaninops yongei*). Note the goby's egg mass laid on the tip of the coral colony where they first cleared away coral tissue to create a nest area. The color of the eggs is indicative of their age.

Much is still not known bout the ecology of wire orals; for instance, we have ery little data about natural redators or reproductive trategies. We do know that his ahermatypic coral can be ery abundant in exposed, teep-sloped, deeper reef reas.

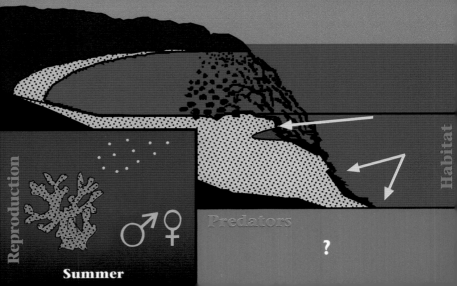

Symbionts

Reproduction

♂ ♀

Summer

Predators

?

Habitat

BLACK CORAL
Antipathes sp.
(Greek: *Anti* - against, *pathos*- disease)

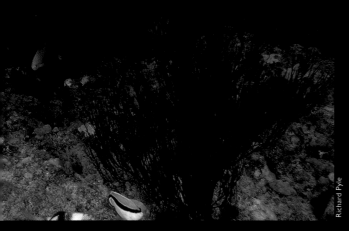

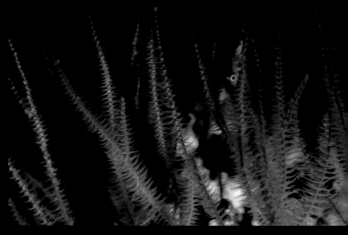

Richard Pyle

ove: Large black coral trees in depths less than 60 m (180 ft) are a rare ght in Hawai'i. The large three-dimensional structure of black coral trees ovides lots of shelter space for a diverse assemblage of organisms, thus eating a unique deep-water ecosystem.

Black Coral gets its name from the color of its skeleton, which ffers from that of reef-building corals in being made-up of a dense, orny material. The polyps and external tissue can range in color om brown, to red, to even white. Black corals occur primarily n the deep reef, past 40 m (120 ft); some large trees have been en by scientists in research submersibles below 400 m (1200 ft)! rowth forms typically assume a tree or bush-like shape, with some olonies reaching heights of over 2 m (6 ft). Some big trees are ought to be over 100 years old.

Above: Close-up showing polyps in *Antipathes dichotoma*. Lacking well-developed calices, the polyps are non-retractable and surround the skeleton on all sides. Like the Wire Coral, Black Corals derive all of their nutrition from captured zooplankton; most colonies tend to be situated in areas with reasonable current flow. Note the symbiotic Black Coral Goby (*Bryaninops tigris*) that lives atop the branches.

Because of their highly three-dimensional shapes, black corals tend to have a large number of sheltering fish and invertebrates. Overcollection of these corals within recreational diving depths, primarily by recreational divers, has decreased the available habitat for these symbionts; obligate symbionts such as the goby literally have nowhere else to live.

Black coral is the official Hawai'i state gem.

Richard Pyle

ove: The Longnose Hawkfish (*Oxycirrhites typus*) is en found associated with large, branching black ral trees. The body pattern of the fish allows it blend perfectly with the branching pattern of the lony.

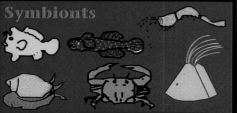

Symbionts

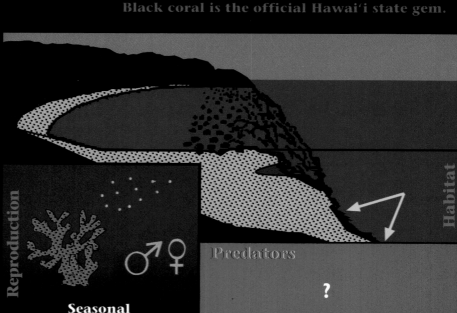

Reproduction

Seasonal

Habitat

Predators

?

OCTOCORALS: SEA FANS, SOFT CORALS & SNOWFLAKE CORALS

Octocorals are a subclass of anthozoans which are easily recognized by the presence of eight branched tentacles surrounding the mouth. Consisting of both hard and soft forms; the skeleton, when present, is composed of fused skeletal fragments (called **sclerites**). There are six orders, of which five are found in Hawai'i; of these, the Stolonifera and the Pennatulacea (Sea Pens) are found only in very deep water. The remaining three orders: the Alcyonacea (Soft Corals), the Telestacea (Snowflake Corals) and the Gorgonacea (Sea Fans) can be found within SCUBA depths but are by no means abundant in Hawaiian waters. The Blue Coral, *Heliopora*, which belongs to the order Coenothecalia is not found in Hawai'i.

Though common elsewhere in the Pacific, only one shallow species of sea fan, *Acabaria bicolor*, (*below*) is found in Hawai'i. Its skeleton is composed of two parts: an outer section made up of loose sclerites, and an inner section formed of a horn-like substance called **gorgonin**.

Above: Soft Corals are often a dominant feature on reef flats and shallow reef slopes surrounding many tropical Pacific islands (but not in Hawai'i). Many soft corals use chemical defenses such as distasteful and toxic compounds to limit competitive and predatory interactions.

Sara Peck

Above: Snowflake Corals (*Carijoa riisei*) are believed to have been introduced to Hawai'i sometime after 1970. They have become quite common on vertical faces exposed to currents around the island of O'ahu. Interestingly, one can often identify a terminal polyp surrounded by daughter polyps.

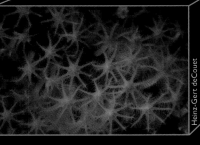

Heinz-Gert deCouet

Above: Up close it is easy to see the eight, branched tentacles that make-up each polyp. Note that the polyp body is reddish with white tentacles. The stems of this octocoral are frequently covered with epiphytes.

Symbionts

Reproduction

♂ ♀

Seasonal

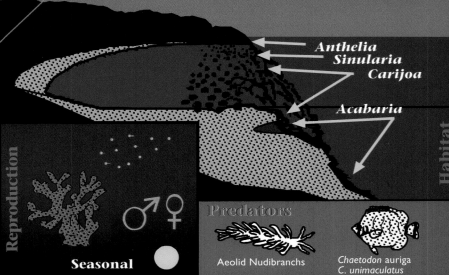

Anthelia
Sinularia
Carijoa

Acabaria

Habitat

Predators

Aeolid Nudibranchs

Chaetodon auriga
C. unimaculatus

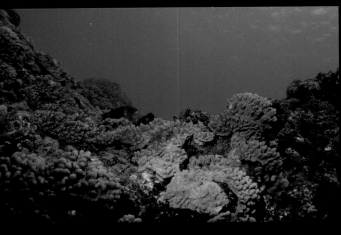

Above: A large colony of Soft Finger Coral (*Sinularia abrupta*) off of the Halona Blow Hole, O'ahu. Large colonies like this tend to be found in areas where there is strong current flow near shore. If you look closely you might notice a large benthic invertebrate rummaging amongst the *Sinularia* for small invertebrates seeking shelter there.

Soft Corals have only recently been described from Hawaiian waters. Leather Coral (*Sinularia abrupta*) is found primarily around O'ahu. It closely resembles Finger coral (*Porites compressa*), but lacks the rigid skeleton; relying instead on a skeleton composed of semi-fused skeletal fragments (called **sclerites**) made of **calcite** (most stony coral skeletons are made of another calcareous material called **aragonite**). In the field it often appears gray, though it may range from brown to green in color. The very rare and endemic *Sinularia molokaiensis* has only been found off of the island of Moloka'i.

Endemic to the Hawaiian Islands, Blue Octocoral (*Anthelia edmondsoni*) is found primarily in shallow water. The tentacles appear light blue to purple in color (the body of the polyp may be clear to tan); though most colonies are small, this bluish color tends to make them stand out in the shallow environments in which they are found. Though not responsible for its characteristic color, zooxanthellae are found in this species. Truly a "soft coral", *Anthelia edmondsoni* have no sclerites in their tissues, each polyp being connected to the next by an expansion of tissue along the bottom (termed a **stolon**).

Above: Leather Coral (*Sinularia abrupta*) colony off of the Halona Blow Hole, O'ahu. Note the Longnose Butterflyfish (*Forcipiger flavissimus*) removing small prey invertebrates hiding among "the fingers". Predators on *Sinularia* are rare, presumably due to the chemical defenses produced by the soft coral which act as a feeding deterrent; though the Teardrop Butterflyfish (*Chaetodon unimaculatus*) is known to feed on *Sinularia* sp. elsewhere.

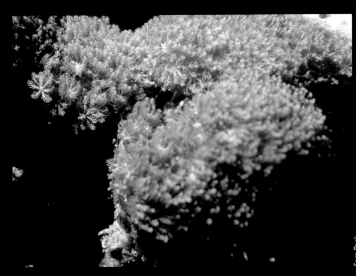

Sara Peck

Above: Close-up of Blue Octocoral (*Anthelia edmondsoni*). Note the eight "feathery" tentacles surrounding each mouth, such **pinnate** (or branched) tentacles are characteristic of the octacorals .

Above: Close-up of Soft Finger Coral (*Sinularia abrupta*) showing the polyps.

Above: Blue Octocoral (*Anthelia edmondsoni*) in the rocky subtidal region, Pūpūkea, O'ahu.

OCTOCORAL TIDBITS & TRIVIA

Phylum Cnidaria
CLASS ANTHOZOA
SUBCLASS OCTOCORALLIA

Polyp form with eight, branched tentacles. Colonial.

Order Alcyonacea - Soft corals (*Sinularia, Anthelia*)

Order Coenothecalia - Blue Coral, *Heliopora* (NOT found in Hawai'i).

Order Gorgonacea - Sea Fans (*Acabaria*); Pink Corals, *Corallium* (found only in deep water).

Order Pennatulacea - Sea Pens (found only in deep water in Hawai'i).

Order Telestacea - Snowflake Corals (*Carijoa*).

Though uncommon and very small in Hawai'i, some sea fans in the South Pacific are huge, measuring meters across.

SEA FANS AS BIRTH CONTROL???

Scientists in the Caribbean have been looking into using hormone derivatives from sea fans in the production of birth control pills.

VEGETARIAN CORALS

Recently a number of soft corals and sea fans have been found to be facultative herbivores, feeding selectively on phytoplankton (microscopic plants that live in the water column). Look at the Spicule Coral (*Dendronephthya* sp.) below; the branching, closely spaced tentacles function as a sieve for suspension feeding. *Acabaria bicolor* (found in Hawai'i) also is thought to function as an herbivore.

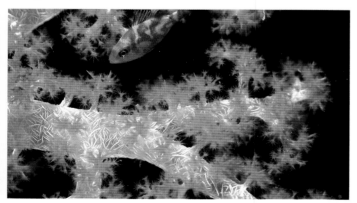

Dendronephthya sp. was not thought to occur in Hawai'i until a couple years ago when a Remotely Operated Vehicle (ROV) videotaped one growing on the side of a sewage outfall off of O'ahu in several hundred feet of water. This probably represents an accidental introduction.

SEA PENS

One of the few cnidarians adapted to live on soft substrates, sea pens (*above*) are often luminescent. It is thought that such luminescence may serve to attract plankton into the stinging tentacles. Like many cnidarians sea pens have their own symbionts (*right*).

ZOANTHIDS:
"The Flower Animals...er, Animal Flowers?"

This order of anthozoans look like clusters of sea anemones yet differ in a number of ways. Entirely tropical, zoanthids are usually colonial and often form dense mats in very shallow, nearshore waters (reef flats, back reefs, shallow lagoons, intertidal) or along rocky coasts. Often they are short and button-like in appearance, having a broad oral disc with short tentacles. Like anemones they do not secrete a hard skeleton, though they do have a thickened cuticle around each polyp's column and between polyps in the colony; often these are embedded with sand particles. Most of them have zooxanthellae. A number of species in Hawai'i have a brilliant coloration associated with the oral disc (Why? And what might be the function of those sand particles? For an out-of-this-world hypothesis (pardon the pun...) see p. 202).

Above: A mat of zoanthids with an anemone. Though both lack calcareous skeletons, many differences exist.

Above: The most commonly seen zoanthid on Hawaiian coral reefs is Pillow "Coral" (*Palythoa caesia,* used to be called *Palythoa tuberculosa*). This zoanthid often appears as an encrusting mat near the reef crest or right along rocky shorelines. Its color is characteristically tan or gray.

Above: Species identification of zoanthids is difficult in the field. Certain endemic zoanthids such as *Palythoa toxica* and *Zoanthus kealakekuaensis* are known for the strong toxins found in their mucus secretions; as such, one should avoid handling zoanthids.

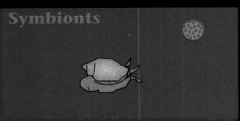

Above: Close-up of Pillow "Coral". Due to a lack of calcareous skeleton, this zoanthid is cushiony to the touch (hence the name...). Note that like the stony corals, Pillow "Coral" zoanthids can go through bleaching episodes (see p.182) involving loss of its symbiotic zooxanthellae (upper right corner of photo).

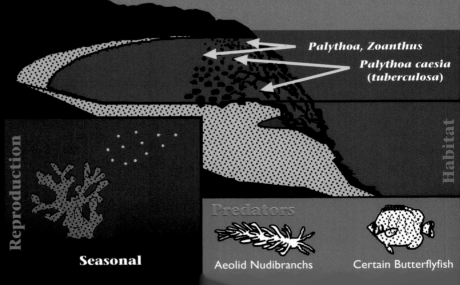

Palythoa, Zoanthus

Palythoa caesia (tuberculosa)

Habitat

Symbionts

Reproduction

Seasonal

Predators

Aeolid Nudibranchs

Certain Butterflyfish

SEA ANEMONES IN HAWAI'I

A variety of sea anemones are found in Hawaiian waters, though most of them are either cryptic or found in very shallow water. A few are specialized to live atop other organisms ranging from seaweeds and sea grasses to various crabs.

Anemones are characterized as solitary organisms lacking a calcareous skeleton. Reproductively, they have as wide a range of sexual and asexual strategies as those seen with the corals; some species such as *Aiptasia pulchella* are **viviparous**, brooding the fertilized eggs internally and releasing them as young polyps which can then quickly settle near the adults. Depending upon the species, an anemone's diet might include small fish, echinoderms, crustaceans, plankton and possibly the excrement from associated, symbiotic fishes. Some species maintain relationships with zooxanthellae in the same way corals do, deriving energy from their symbiotic algae.

Unlike most sea anemones, *Boloceroides mcmurrichi* (*below right*) actively swims by pulsating through the water. This anemone will shed moving tentacles to distract potential predators while the anemone makes its escape; the lost tentacles will later be regenerated. Close inspection, and lots of patience in counting, will reveal up to 400 tentacles on a single Swimming Anemone.

Above: The color in the common sea anemone *Aiptasia pulchella* comes from its symbiotic zooxanthellae, just as it does in corals. This species has been frequently used in research since it is easy to rear in a lab and can serve as a ready source of zooxanthellae cultures for studies.

Keoki Stender

Above: The Sand Anemone (*Heteractis malu*) is one of the largest anemones in Hawai'i reaching a diameter up to 15 cm (~6"); these anemones have become rare in Kāne'ohe Bay due to over-collection for the aquarium trade.

Sand Anemones may have about 384 tentacles and occasionally be slightly iridescent; such iridescence might be a defense against high levels of UV radiation on the exposed, shallow reef flat.

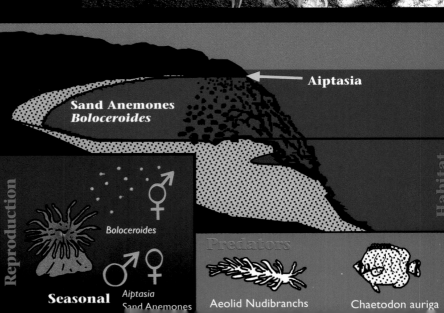

Aiptasia

Sand Anemones
Boloceroides

Habitat

Symbionts

Boloceroides Aiptasia

Sand Anemones

Reproduction

Boloceroides

Seasonal *Aiptasia*
Sand Anemones

Predators

Aeolid Nudibranchs

Chaetodon auriga

ANEMONE SYMBIOSIS

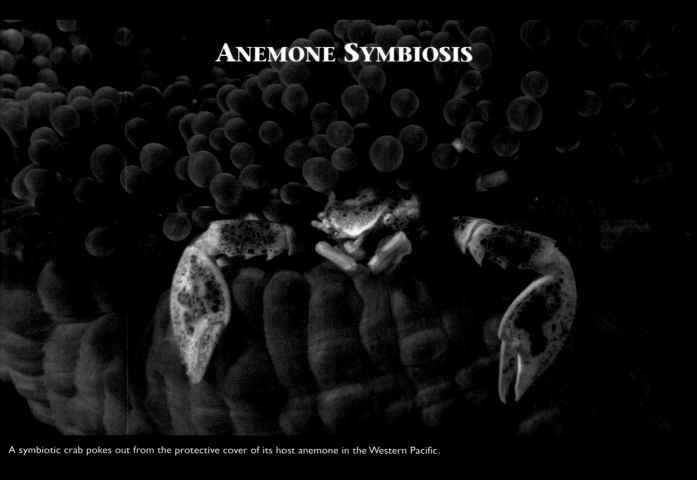

A symbiotic crab pokes out from the protective cover of its host anemone in the Western Pacific.

A great variety of symbioses exist between anemones and other marine organisms.

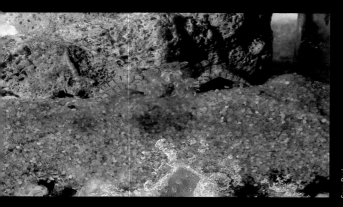

Sara Peck

The 'Pom-Pom' Crab (*Lybia edmondsoni*) carries a set of anemones (*Triactis producta*) on the ends of its claws. Originally thought to be used for defense, observations have shown that the crab also actively uses the anemones like a mop as it drags its claws along the bottom, under the rubble in which it lives. Detritus and small organisms are swept up and adhere to the anemone's tentacles, from which a portion of the food is removed and consumed by the crab.

The Anemone Hermit Crab (*Dardanus* sp.) is known for carrying one or more anemones (*Calliactis polypus*) atop the mollusc shell in which it lives. This symbiosis is so strong that when the crab gets to be too large for its shell and moves to another one, it will gently lift and transfer its anemones from the old to the new shell! This interesting symbiosis is actually more complex than first meets the eye; at the entrance to the shell is often found a second species of anemone (*Anthothoe* sp. shown in the photo), and inside the shell a polychaete worm or a flatworm. Can you think of how these organisms might benefit or harm the host crab?

Cnidoquestion: What could the anemone and crab possibly get out of this relationship?

Richard Pyle

(T) One of the best known of all marine symbioses is the relationship between the anemonefish and its host anemone. There are 28 species of anemonefish (all but one belonging to the genus *Amphiprion*) and 10 species of host anemones. None of these fish are naturally found in Hawaiian waters, though one of the host anemone species (*Heteractis malu* or the Sand Anemone) is found in Hawai'i and sometimes has juvenile Hawaiian Domino Damselfish (*Dascyllus albisella*) associated with it. These damselfish are not considered to be a true anemonefish because they are not dependent on the anemone for their survival.

Originally, many people thought that only the anemonefish benefitted from the relationship, but actually this complex symbiosis benefits both parties. The fish gains protection from predation and a safe nest site for its eggs; the anemone gains removal of parasites (such as small invertebrates), removal of wastes and sediment via water currents generated by the fish as it swims through the anemone's tentacles or when it is fanning it's eggs, and protection from certain predators. This last point is thought to occur because anemonefish, like most damselfish, are fiercely protective of their territories; in this case it's thought that the anemonefish would drive off fish such as butterflyfish that might otherwise nibble on the anemone's tentacles.

Exactly how anemonefish acclimate to living amongst the tentacles of their host without being stung is still a subject of debate, but one current hypothesis suggests that the fish possess a protective mucus coating such that the anemone's stinging cells are not triggered to fire in their presence. Whether this mucus coating is rubbed off of the anemone and onto the fish, or is produced by the fish itself, has still not been determined.

Richard Pyle

Anemonefish are considered to be obligate symbionts since they depend upon this relationship with the anemone for their survival.

Anemonefish are one of the only marine fish known to start off life as a male and sex change into a female as an adult (often referred to as **Protandrous hermaphrodites**). Additionally, some species of anemonefish live in "nursery" anemones which contain only juveniles and no adults. Look at the section on sex change in reef fish (pp. 159 - 160) and try to explain why these two observations might be so...(hey, did you think it was just going to be all pretty pictures?).

Heinz-Gert deCouet

Often close inspection of these large anemones will turn up other symbionts...

Heinz-Gert deCouet

Certain other species of fish have been known to also acclimate to anemones. A close relative of the anemonefish, the Domino Damselfish (*Dascyllus trimaculatus*) is shown here also sheltering in the tentacles of the anemone.

ANEMONE LOCOMOTION

Keoki Stender

Most anemones are relatively sessile for the majority of their lives...though a few, when the moment is right, can display awe-inspiring bursts of movement that would make even a snail blush:

A number of anemones remain sessile and still are able to move about by using a hermit crab's shell as a substrate (a type of symbiosis called **Phoresis** meaning, "to carry").

Current

Many anemones move by releasing their pedal disc and sliding about on a thin layer of slime.

Some, such as the swimming anemone Boloceroides (see p.67), swim in the water column by rapid flexing of their column and thrashing of their tentacles.

Some anemones can secrete gas into their coelenterons (stomachs) while closing off their mouths. This has the effect of turning them into a pseudo-balloon or a SCUBA buoyancy compensator, which allows them to float in the water column after releasing their hold on the bottom substrate.

This often has the effect of breaking off small pieces of the anemone which then, in turn, grow into whole new anemones (a form of asexual reproduction termed 'fragmentation', see p. 72).

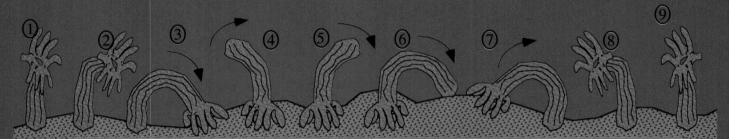

Some anemones can actually move about the bottom through a complex series of somersaults ① - ⑨. This involves contracting certain longitudinal muscles on one side of the animal which causes the animal to bend in a set direction ② - ③. Adhesive cnidae in the tentacles are then used to temporarily hold the animal to the substrate ④. At the same time the pedal disc is released and longitudinal muscles on the other side of the animal contract causing it to "flip over" ⑤ - ⑥. The anemone then re-attaches to the bottom with its pedal disc, having moved a couple body lengths from its original position. Other anemones modify this and "walk" by using their tentacles!

Because of their relatively thick and heavy calcareous skeletons, combined with the constraints of living as a colony, only a few coral species are actually capable of movement as adults:

AND WHAT OF THE CORALS???

SOME SMALL CORAL COLONIES MAY RAFT

(see p. 89)

Rafting may serve as a dispersal agent for certain species.

SOME SMALL SOLITARY CORALS MAY BE ABLE TO MOVE ABOUT BY ALTERING THEIR BUOYANCY

Ⓣ Some species of *Cycloseris* and small individual *Fungia scutaria* show a behavior of swelling up by inflating their coelenterons (stomachs) while closing off their mouths. The photo to the right shows two individual *Cycloseris vaughani*, the one on the left is indicative of how one usually finds them during the day; the one on the right shows the nighttime behavior of swelling its coelenteron (the bright white object inside is the skeleton). Careful inspection shows that this animal has moved (slid), possibly on mucus (note the trail behind it). One possible function for this swelled coelenteron behavior may be to alter the coral's density and allow it to move about. Such a mechanism probably would not work for large individuals due to the mass of their skeleton.

OTHERS ARE DRAGGED ABOUT:

This living Murex mollusc (*Murex elongatus*) has had its shell overgrown by a settled *Montipora* coral (*right*). This coral, that started out as a hitchhiker, has grown to a point where the Murex can no longer move the coral skeleton's weight around.

Sara Peck

In some areas of the South Pacific, the small solitary coral (*Heteropsammia michelini*) is dragged around by the sipunculid worm (*Pspidsiphon corallcola*) attached to its base. The worm initally inhabits an empty mollusc shell onto which the coral planula settles; eventually the coral grows over the shell resulting in a symbiosis where the worm gains protective shelter and the coral gains transport and avoidance of being covered by sediment.

ANEMONE BEHAVIOR

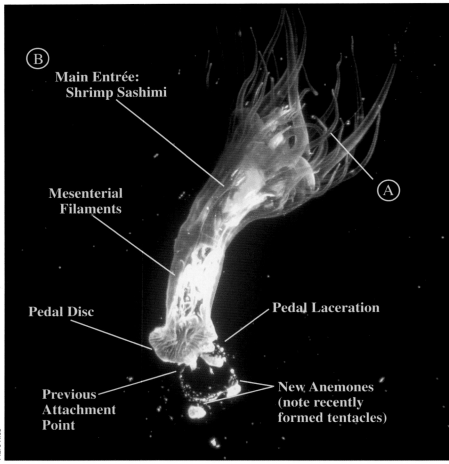

B Main Entrée:
Shrimp Sashimi

A

Mesenterial
Filaments

Pedal Disc

Pedal Laceration

Previous
Attachment
Point

New Anemones
(note recently
formed tentacles)

Marc Rice

C Digested
Remnants
of
Shrimp

New Anemones

Movement over time

Marc Rice

In some respects one can look at an anemone as a super-sized model of a coral polyp (without the calcareous skeleton). Take the way it feeds for example: after capturing the prey with stinging cells located on its tentacles, it manipulates the captured prey into its mouth (A). Once inside the coelenteron, mesenterial filaments secreting digestive enzymes start the job of digesting the prey organism (B). After some time has passed, the digested nutrients (C) can then be passed around to the other cells that make up the body.

That is not to say that in many ways anemones are not unique among Cnidarians. Anemones are one of the few polyp forms capable of movement on a regular basis. Primarily due to the lack of a heavy, stationary, calcareous skeleton; anemones can move about through use of a variety of mechanisms (see Anemone Locomotion, pp. 70 - 71). The two photos on this page depict an anemone on a glass plate; you can see where the anemone is attached by its pedal disc (*left*), note the previous attachment point). The anemone moves by sliding along the surface on a trail of mucus; periodically re-attaching itself in selected spots (*left*).

Solitary anemones such as *Aiptasia pulchella* (*left*) can go through a form of asexual reproduction much like fragmentation seen in coral colonies. Termed **Pedal Laceration**, the anemone breaks off pieces of its pedal disc which quickly develop small tentacles and a mouth, each becoming a miniature version of the parent anemone (Quick Crude Analogy: Imagine clipping a toenail and having it turn into a whole new you!).

Hawaiian Coral Tidbits & Trivia

Phylum Cnidaria
CLASS ANTHOZOA
ORDER SCLERACTINIA

~ Over 150 species in Hawai'i, of which roughly 45 species are reef-building corals.

~ 18% endemic, one of the highest endemism rates in the world for corals.

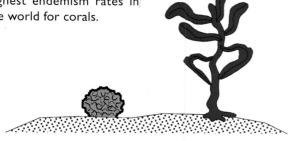

AN ANIMAL AS A PLANT OVERACHIEVER???

Because of its endosymbiotic zooxanthellae, Hawaiian Lace Coral (*Pocillopora damicornis*) can actually out-photosynthesize most marine plants, fixing up to 29 grams of carbon per square meter per day (one of the highest primary production rates ever recorded within any ecosystem!).

A FIRM FOUNDATION FOR THE FUTURE...

The city of Honolulu (*above*) is built upon the skeletal remains of a Finger Coral reef that stretched from Diamond Head past the Honolulu airport. Interestingly, portions of the fossilized remains of this reef became limestone caverns over thousands of years as freshwater eroded its way through the reef. These caverns (or grottos) had a number of surface entrances that were used by the ancient Hawaiians as both water sources and religious sites. In fact, a number of important areas in Honolulu (Kawaiaha'o Church, 'Iolani Palace) are located precisely where they are due to originally being access points to these underground caverns.

WHAT'S A NICE CORAL LIKE YOU DOIN' IN A PLACE LIKE THIS?

One of the deepest of all known reef corals is the endemic *Leptoseris hawaiiensis*. This coral, which often is found shallower than 100 m, has been found as deep as 165 m (~ 540 feet).

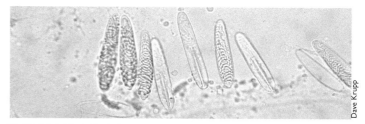

Dave Krupp

INDUCIBLE DEFENSES...

Some recent work by scientists at the Hawai'i Institute of Marine Biology suggests that some coral colonies may enhance their defenses against predation as a result of partial predation against the colony, similar to the inducible defenses against herbivory seen in many plants. This often may take the form of increased batteries of nematocysts (*above*), change in growth form, or possibly the production of chemical compounds to discourage predation.

THE CREATOR OF FREE-LIVING CORALS: A SEA TURTLE???

Sea turtles in Kāne'ohe Bay will often rest on the patch reefs within resting holes that they have carved out of depressions among the corals. Frequently they dislodge and break-off sections of coral colonies which fall to the base of their sleeping areas. The turbulence caused by each visit of the turtle rotates the fragments about, allowing polyps to form on all sides of the small, non-attached colony. As a result of the sleeping habits of a reptile, **coralliths** (free-living colonies of a normally sessile coral) are formed!

SECTION I:
CORAL ECOLOGY

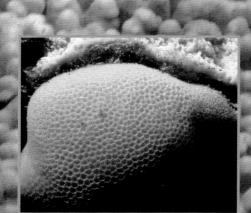

CORAL COMPETITION

REPRODUCTION AND LARVAE

PREDATORS ON CORALS

Deborah Gochfeld

GENERAL ECOLOGICAL INTERACTIONS IN CORALS

Corals are constantly interacting with other organisms around them; how successful a coral (or coral colony) is, often depends on how successful the coral is in dealing with many of the interactions depicted below.

PREDATION

Predation can occur by organisms which will feed on any sessile organism (Generalists); often these are limited by the coral's (or colony's) defenses. Specialists are those organisms which are adapted to minimize the effects of the coral's defenses; this results in the specialists being able to feed on a food resource unavailable to most other animals.

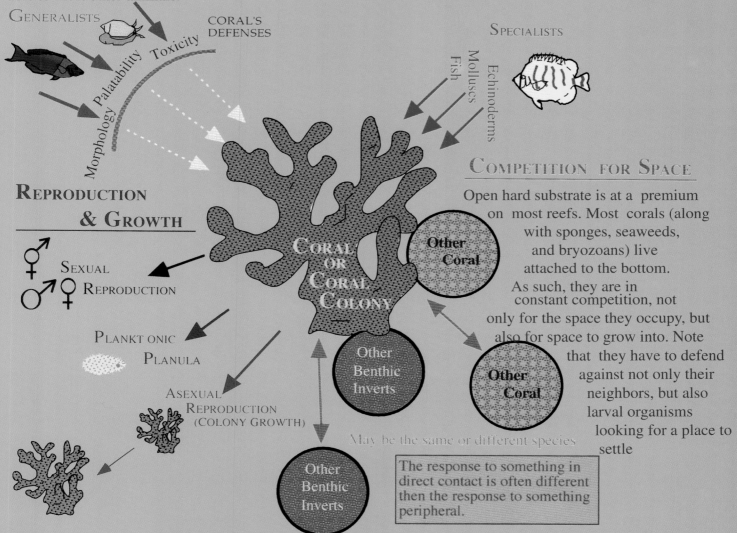

GENERALISTS

CORAL'S DEFENSES

Palatability Toxicity Morphology

SPECIALISTS

Echinoderms Molluscs Fish

REPRODUCTION & GROWTH

SEXUAL REPRODUCTION

PLANKTONIC PLANULA

ASEXUAL REPRODUCTION (COLONY GROWTH)

CORAL OR CORAL COLONY

Other Coral

Other Benthic Inverts

Other Coral

Other Benthic Inverts

May be the same or different species

COMPETITION FOR SPACE

Open hard substrate is at a premium on most reefs. Most corals (along with sponges, seaweeds, and bryozoans) live attached to the bottom. As such, they are in constant competition, not only for the space they occupy, but also for space to grow into. Note that they have to defend against not only their neighbors, but also larval organisms looking for a place to settle

The response to something in direct contact is often different then the response to something peripheral.

(After Coll and Sammarco, 1986)

These are some of the major factors that corals have to allocate energy to in order to survive in their respective habitats - can you think of others? Can you apply this basic scheme to other sessile marine invertebrates? Marine plants? How about fish or sea turtles? Remember that most corals are attached to the substrate and cannot move around in order to deal with the above situations - imagine yourself 'Super Glued to your chair while you read this, how might that affect your interaction with others, your ability to get food, mate or do your job?

FOOD CAPTURE

The majority of reef-building corals, and all ahermatypic corals, feed on small planktonic organisms or dissolved organic matter (DOM) in the water. For corals whose symbiotic plants are busy conducting photosynthesis during the day, most prey capture occurs at night (though a few may also feed actively during the day).

Above: A polyp in a *Porites compressa* colony has captured a larval crab in preparation for dinner.

Three Different Methods

I. Most corals capture prey by use of nematocysts on their tentacles (steps ① – ③).

II. Some corals (in the Agaricid family) act as suspension feeders, using mucus nets or filaments to trap organic particles and small organisms. The mucus is then withdrawn back into the mouth and the material captured is digested.

III. Some species feed by use of mesenterial filaments.

① Tentacles capture and move prey towards the mouth.

② Digestive chemicals (enzymes) secreted by cells lining the stomach (coelenteron) break down prey into small chunks, these can then be absorbed by other cells lining the stomach.

③ Any undigested material is often burped back out through the mouth.

CORAL REPRODUCTION

Corals lead very prolific lives; colonies are often in a constant state of asexual reproduction intermixed with occasional sex. The next couple of pages explore the diversity of ways that corals reproduce and discusses how such strategies may benefit the corals involved.

Asexual Reproduction:

ASEXUAL BUDDING AND FISSION

Growth of a coral colony involves the production of both new skeleton and new polyps. These polyps are produced asexually through either the process of fission or budding. In **fission**, the new polyp is formed by the oral disc (mouth) invaginating to produce a new mouth within the original ring of parental tentacles (**Intratentacular Reproduction**). **Budding** occurs when the new mouth is formed outside the original ring of parental tentacles (**Extratentacular Reproduction**).

Close inspection of almost any coral colony will show the presence of asexual production of new polyps (can you spot it occurring in the photo at the bottom of the page?). Perhaps the easiest coral on which to observe this process occurring is the Orange Flower Coral (*Tubastraea coccinea*) where small polyps can be seen budding from the sides of larger ones (*right*).

Above: A patch reef in Kāneʻohe Bay, Oʻahu. Many of these colonies started out as single polyps that asexually reproduced themselves (budding and fission). New colonies eventually arose as pieces of established colonies broke-off and reattached to the substrate (fragmentation).

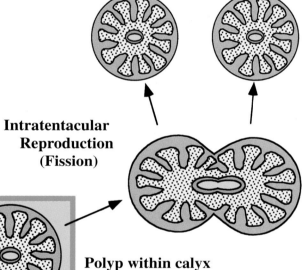

Intratentacular Reproduction (Fission)

Polyp within calyx

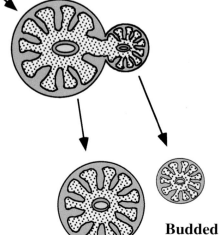

Extratentacular Reproduction (Budding)

Parent Polyp

Budded Polyp

Asexual Reproduction:

ASEXUAL FRAGMENTATION

One of the most common forms of asexual reproduction is breakage of one or several smaller sections of a coral colony. These sections are genetically identical to the parent colony and are composed of living groups of polyps which over time can grow over the substrate on which they've settled, creating new colonies, often in close proximity to the parent colony. The initial cause of the breakage is frequently due to physical forces such as wave or storm action (though sometimes biological activity may bring about fragmentation).

 Certain coral forms are more prone to fragmentation than others, specifically branching and upright forms

② Strong wave action (or storm surge) causes a breaking off of external branches which fall onto the nearby substrate.

③ Over time, these fragments attach to the substrate and grow into full branching colonies, possibly assisted by the proximity of genetically identical larger colonies nearby (thereby limiting the effects of competition for space from other colonies or species of coral).

Above: On a reef flat like this, many of the coral colonies seen resulted from fragments of surrounding colonies or pieces washed up onto the flat during storms.

Above: Careful inspection of Lobe Coral (*Porites lobata*) colonies shown above reveals that many of these colonies appear similar to other colonies nearby, while some adjacent colonies look distinctly different. Genetic studies have shown that situations like this usually consist of fragments of various (genetically different) colonies which are actively fighting each other for space (**Intraspecific competition**). Often the fragments that are genetically identical (i.e., the ones that came from the same parent colony) will either fuse together or stop growing along their adjacent borders.

Above: A fragment of a single septum (small skeletal element) from a *Fungia scutaria* that has formed into a complete juvenile polyp - perhaps the ultimate in fragmentation!

CNIDOQUESTION: Can you think of at least four different biological sources of fragmentation?

Asexual Reproduction:

ASEXUAL PRODUCTION OF PLANULA LARVAE

A number of corals appear to asexually produce planulae within their coelenterons (termed 'asexual brooding'). Often it is hard to tell whether brooded planula larvae were formed asexually by a polyp or were formed through **sexual brooding** (a process of taking in sperm through the mouth of the polyp, fertilizing the egg and maintaining it within the coelenteron until a competent larval form emerges). By looking at the genetic similarity to the parent polyp, one can determine whether a planula was produced sexually or asexually. Studies have shown that certain species of *Acropora* and *Seriatopora* sexually brood their larvae; while other studies have shown that *Pocillopora damicornis* in Hawai'i produce larvae that are genetically identical to the parent colony, suggesting that these are asexually-brooded planulae.

In Hawai'i, *Pocillopora damicornis* releases asexually-brooded planulae on a monthly basis; studies of reef habitats have suggested that a large number of the colonies were produced through this form of planulation, making this the dominant form of colony reproduction for this species.

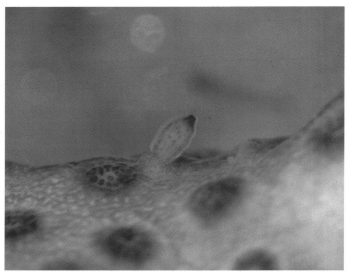

Above: A planula larval form being "spit out" through the mouth of the parent polyp in a colony of *Pocillopora damicornis*. Note the coloration of the planula is identical to that of the polyp; the planula emerges already infected with symbiotic zooxanthellae which can provide it with nourishment while it is in the plankton. *P. damicornis* planulae have among the longest recorded survival times in the plankton, presumably due to their pre-existing zooxanthellae.

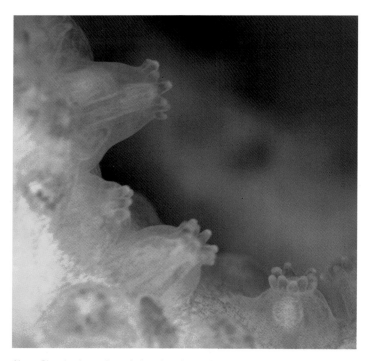

Above: Planulae being brooded within the coelentera of a number of polyps within a colony of *Pocillopora damicornis*.

Ⓣ

Above: Pocillopora damicornis polyps with a recently released *P. damicornis* planula. The white bulges at the tips of the polyps' tentacles are fat bodies; congregations of stored lipids which form from lipid bodies in the polyp's pharynx. Some scientists have suggested that asexually-produced larvae originate by budding off of these pharyngeal lipid bodies, while other scientists think that they are formed through internal parthenogenetic development of the egg (parthenogenesis is the development of the egg into a larval form without being fertilized by a sperm). As with many aspects of coral biology, the jury's still out on this one...

Asexual Reproduction:

POLYP BAIL-OUT

A very interesting and unique form of asexual reproduction has been observed in *Seriatopora hystrix*, a stony coral from the Great Barrier Reef. Under conditions of environmental stress, the polyps in this coral will break their tissue connections with each other (termed **intercalical tissue**). They then emerge independently from their calices, float off into the water column and resettle onto the substrate as independent polyps. Soon they're re-initiating skeleton formation and asexually budding; producing new, independent colonies. This unique behavior of emerging out of their skeletal shelter and leaving behind the old colony has been termed 'Polyp Bail-out' and has recently been observed in *Pocillopora damicornis* colonies in Hawai'i.

Why should individual coral polyps adapt such a strategy? Some researchers have suggested that under conditions of extreme environmental stress (and given the presence of zooxanthellae within the coral), it might be more advantageous to "pack-up and leave" (leaving behind the old skeleton home, so to speak...) and take one's chances elsewhere where environmental conditions might not be as severe. Such a strategy would seem to work best for those corals adapted for rapid colonization; in fact, it has been suggested that such a mechanism as polyp bailout might help to account for the large success these two corals share in colonizing certain environments. Ⓣ

Above: Polyp bail-out occurring in *Pocillopora damicornis*. Note how the polyps have broken the tissue connection between polyps and then lift-up out of their calices (skeletal cups).

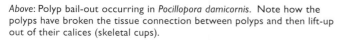

SEXUAL REPRODUCTION

Many of the Hawaiian corals reproduce sexually during specific times over the summer. What makes this interesting and different from many other places in the Pacific is that the corals here spawn at different times for different species. Many of the *Montipora* species spawn a couple days after the new moon in the mid-evening (around 9 P.M., or so). *Porites compressa* and *Fungia scutaria* both spawn a couple days after the full moon; though *Fungia* shoots-off in the early evening (around 6 P.M.), while *Porites* is a night owl, getting romantic around midnight or so.

So by now you've got to be asking yourself "how do they 'do it'?" Imagine for the moment that you're in a very romantic mood but you find yourself superglued to your chair...and your husband across the room is in the same predicament. Such is the problem facing most sessile marine organisms; how they get around this is through a process called **Broadcast Spawning**. The gametes are released from the corals where they mingle in the water column, with fertilization taking place externally. Under such circumstances synchronization becomes critical. If you spit out your eggs (did I mention that like many other processes, gamete formation takes place in the stomach (coelenteron) with release occurring through the polyp's mouth...) but nobody releases any sperm, you've not only wasted a large amount of energy investment in gamete production, but also blown your one big

chance to sexually reproduce (many corals only have sex once or twice a year!). One way to get around this problem is to produce both eggs and sperm (i.e. being **simultaneous hermaphrodites**); in this way you're assured that any member of your species in close proximity that also spawns will be able to fertilize your eggs and vice-versa. Hermaphroditic coral colonies often release **gamete bundles** made up of eggs and sperm. The sperm hitch a free ride to the surface aboard the buoyant, fatty egg; after a short period of time the sperm are released from the bundle and start to swim. The eggs become viable a short time later and are then receptive to becoming fertilized; such a mechanism prevents self-fertilization. Many of the *Montipora* species are hermaphroditic in Hawai'i. Those corals that are **gonochoric** (producing separate sperm and eggs) are primarily represented by *Porites* and *Fungia* in Hawai'i. For both hermaphroditic and gonochoric corals, synchronization involves a seasonal component (temperature) and a monthly or daily component (day length, tidal factors, amount of nocturnal moonlight). As you can imagine, once the gametes are released they will quickly become diluted and remain viable for only a limited amount of time (those little sperm don't have enough energy to swim about forever). Obviously, synchronized spawning (especially at times of low water movement) along with production of huge amounts of sperm and/or eggs helps to maximize fertilization success.

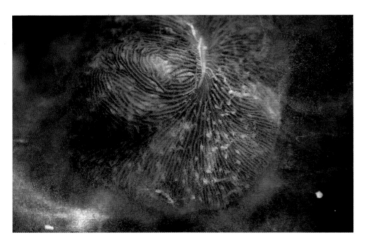

Solitary female *Fungia scutaria* releasing eggs a couple of days after the full moon. Synchronized spawning with male individuals maximizes the chances of fertilization and minimizes wastage of energy investment.

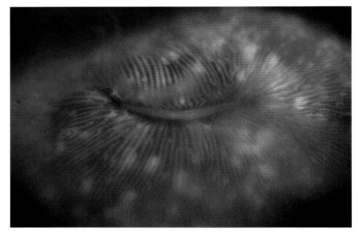

Solitary male *Fungia scutaria* unloading a huge amount of sperm around the same time as the female. Scientists still aren't sure if the corals are using **pheromones** to synchronize their spawnings and perhaps attract/guide the sperm towards the egg.

Sex and the Single Polyp

REPRODUCTION AMONG THE CORALS

So why should corals try to propel their gametes up and away from the reef? The reef itself is full of a wide variety of filter-feeding organisms (including corals) and planktivorous fishes, which together form a "Wall of Mouths". Such an environment is not very conducive to successful fertilization and development.

CNIDOQUESTION:
Why do most corals spawn at night?

By being in a egg-sperm bundle, the sperm actually hitch a ride to the surface, saving them precious energy required for swimming and finding eggs to fertilize.

Fertilization!!

High lipid (fat) content causes gametes to float to the surface.

Some eggs contain zooxanthellae.

Egg-sperm bundle

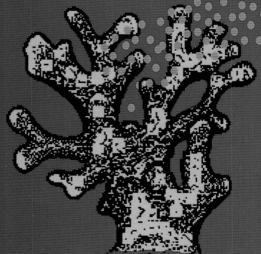

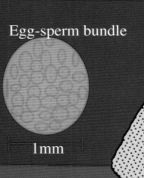

1mm

Hermaphroditic (both sexes together)
Montipora capitata June & July

Gonochoric (separate sexes)
Porites compressa June - August
Porites lobata   July - August
Fungia scutaria   July - September

The majority of species in the Pacific that have been examined are hermaphroditic, though that's not the case in Hawaii.

As you can see, even sexual reproduction is highly variable amongst the different corals and involves a number of different strategies.

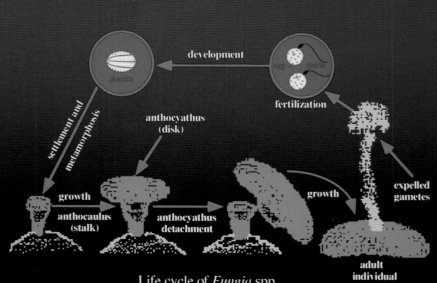

Life cycle of *Fungia* spp.
(adapted by Krupp, 1995 and expanded upon from Pearse et al., 1987)

SEX IN THE SEA: A VOYEUR'S VIEW OF MONTIPORA CAPITATA

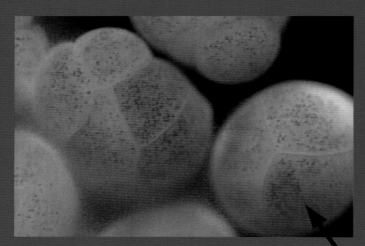

Recently released egg-sperm bundles from the hermaphroditic coral *Montipora capitata*. The bundles are made up of groups of eggs surrounded by transparent masses of sperm. The dark brown spots represent zooxanthellae that have been incorporated into the eggs before release (*Montipora* is unusual amongst spawning corals in possessing zooxanthellae within its gametes).

Montipora capitata releasing egg-sperm bundles during a spawning event in Kāneʻohe Bay, Oʻahu.

Zooxanthellae incorporated into eggs

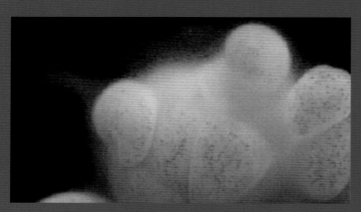

After twenty minutes to an hour (depending on turbulence) of floating near the surface, the bundle start to break apart.

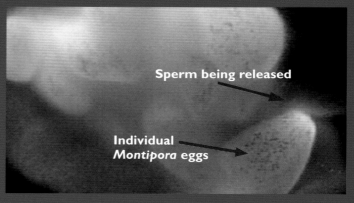

Sperm being released

Individual *Montipora* eggs

As the bundles comes apart, sperm clouds are released. The sperm will intermix with released eggs from other colonies leading to fertilization.

THE INBREEDING PARADOX

In nature, most organisms have evolved mechanisms to avoid mating with closely related members of their population. Such matings tend to lead to a situation termed **inbreeding** where genetic diversity decreases due to the close-relatedness of the individuals. Questions arise as to how hermaphroditic corals avoid self-fertilization either within a gamete bundle or between bundles from the same colony. The jury's still out on this one, but there is some evidence that certain species avoid this problem through sperm being released prior to the egg becoming susceptible to fertilization. Other species are thought to be genetically encoded to discourage self-fertilization either through chemical attractants or specific reception sites.

Even so, it's interesting that studies done in Guam have shown that 6 hours after sperm release the probability of self-fertilization increases. In such a situation, the lack of fertilization and length of time might lead to a breakdown in the mechanisms listed above; a sort-of "use it or lose it strategy".

MASS SPAWNING EVENTS

A mass spawning of *Acropora* coral in Papua New Guinea.

Deborah Gochfeld

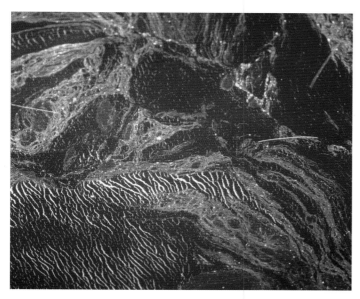

Spawning slicks such as this one are a common site after mass spawning events.

Killer Spawn!!!

In 1989 a mass spawning event occurred in an isolated bay in the north-western region of Australia. Unusual tides and currents caused the spawning slick to remain within the bay without dispersing. The millions and millions of floating gametes quickly used up most of the oxygen, first through respiration and later as they decayed. Within a few days over a million dead reef fish washed ashore; later surveys showed that a large portion of the corals in the bay had also died. (T)

Whoops...

The ultimate in synchronized spawning events are the mass spawning phenomena where multiple species all release their gametes on the same night, in the same area. Millions and millions of gametes from a variety of different coral species all intermingle at the surface in a massive fertilization soup. The ensuing slick of gametes the next morning can extend for miles and is often mistaken for an oil spill by the uninformed reef visitor. Why should this occur? Wouldn't this be maladaptive in terms of wastage of gametes and increased chances of producing non-viable hybrids? Some scientists feel that even with these costs, environmental constraints may force coral species to limit their spawning times to a few short windows of opportunity. Other scientists feel that this has evolved as a way of minimizing predation on the gametes (or possibly the ensuing planula larvae); the idea here is that by everyone releasing at once, they flood the market (so to speak) and thereby decrease the proportion of each of their potential offspring that would be eaten (the "Dilution Effect").

Mass spawning events have been mostly studied on Australia's Great Barrier Reef; but have also been observed on other reefs in Australia, the Philippines, Okinawa, Palau, Fiji and Papua New Guinea.

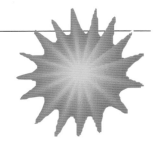

LIFE AS A CORAL LARVAL FORM
(OR "I WAS A TEENAGE PLANULA")

After a planula larva is produced, it has to survive for a period of time in a pelagic world far different from the sessile, colonial one of its parents.

Planula larvae may be widely dispersed away from the parent colony by currents and tidal conditions.

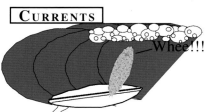

CURRENTS

Whee!!!

DISPERSAL

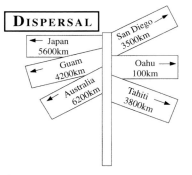

Japan 5600km
Guam 4200km
Australia 6200km
San Diego 3500km
Oahu 100km
Tahiti 3800km
?

SEX?

Sorry kid. You're too young.

The planula larval stage is primarily non-reproductive.

SETTLEMENT CUES

When it comes time to settle, many species have distinct chemical and/or light cues that they use to find appropriate substrates.

Unlike its parents, which may be tens of meters underwater, most planular stages exist in the upper few meters where they may be exposed to high levels of ultraviolet radiation. It's been discovered that organisms with a long planular larval stage often have large amounts of u.v. absorbing chemicals incorporated into their tissues.

UV EFFECTS

FOOD

While in the plankton, planulae from different species may use one of a number of feeding strategies:

"The Bag Lunch"
Zooxanthellae provided by parents, symbiosis produces energy for the planula.

"The Fast Food Approach"
Zooxanthellae taken up while in the plankton, symbiosis produces energy for the planula..

Yum!

"The Snack on the Job Approach"
Planulae feed on smaller forms of plankton.

"The Diet & Settle Fast Approach"
Non-feeding; Planula lives on energy reserves from egg. Settles quickly.

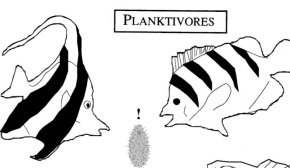

PLANKTIVORES

!

In its larval stage the coral is part of the zooplankton. As such, it is exposed to both selective and non-selective plankton-feeders. Note: this may include filter-feeders such as other coral colonies.

Pocillopora damicornis planula larvae.

LARVAL DISPERSAL

Planulae that are produced by corals on one reef have the potential to reach and seed reefs far, far away. Often, the **dispersal** of such planktonic larvae away from source reefs is dependent not only on tidal currents, but on regional and global surface currents.

Near the Hawaiian Islands, the summer regional currents create a series of **gyres**, or circular currents, which may serve to keep planktonic larvae near the islands. Such a mechanism may be very important in isolating Hawaiian species and resulting in the high amount of endemism seen in Hawaiian corals.

Pacific surface currents showing dispersal routes for planktonic larvae. Note that planula larvae produced off of Australia, Indonesia, or the Philippines (areas of high species diversity) would be shunted by surface currents either north or south into colder waters before traveling towards Hawai'i. As such, species of coral in Hawai'i are more similar to species assemblages from the Eastern Pacific, than they are to assemblages from the South Pacific.

Most coral planulae spend only a short time as part of the zooplankton (the cave-dwelling *Balanophyllia elegans* broods planula that crawl away from the parents, in essence spending no time in the plankton). Some, such as those from *Pocillopora damicornis* (*above*), are adapted for long-distance dispersal. They contain stored energy reserves and zooxanthellae which presumably provide the planula larvae with nourishment.

CORALS WITH LONG-LIVED LARVAE:

Species	Max. recorded larval period
Galaxea aspera	49 days
Cyphastrea ocellina (Hawai'i)	60 days
Acropora sp.	91 days
Pocillopora damicornis (Hawai'i)	103 days

So how did corals get to Hawai'i???

One way that short-lived planulae might reach isolated islands such as Hawai'i is through "Island Stepping Stones". In such a case, larvae travel through regional currents to nearby islands where they settle and form adult colonies that release new planulae into the ocean. This process continues, forming a series of intermediate stepping-stones for the expansion of a species.

Still, the closest island to the Hawaiian Islands is Johnston Atoll, 720 km to the southwest. *P. damicornis* with a competency period (the length of time that the larval form can successfully exist as part of the plankton) of 103 days could presumably reach Hawai'i in the 50 or so days that it would take to travel given today's current patterns. But what about other species of corals that have much shorter competency periods yet are also found in Hawai'i?

CORAL RAFTING AS A MEANS FOR DISPERSAL

One of the most difficult things for marine biologists to explain is how many of the invertebrates (including sessile corals) and fish reached the highly isolated Hawaiian Islands? As stated earlier, larval dispersal may account for some of these colonizations, but the majority of inverts and reef fish spend only a few weeks as planktonic larvae (far too short a period to reach Hawai'i in the prevailing currents). Rafting of organisms on/or associated with floating objects may provide an answer to this riddle.

Corals have been found floating on driftwood and pumice (lava rock that floats due to its highly porous nature). Colonies can grow and may even reach a size where sexual reproduction can occur. The drifting object may eventually come into nearshore waters where surf abrasion can knock loose fragments of the coral; these in turn may then be able to attach and colonize new reef areas.

A very young and healthy colony of *Pocillopora damicornis* growing atop a floating beer bottle. Numerous calcareous algae and bryozoans are also present.

HOW CORALS GAIN FOOTHOLD IN NEW ENVIRONMENTS

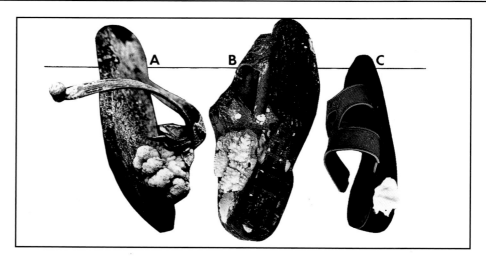

The floating objects (**A** thong found floating in Chunda Bay, Cape Cleveland, Australia by A. Watt in 1985 with attached *Pocillopora*, algae and barnacles; **B** thong collected at Pago Bay, Guam in 1988 by S. Amesbury and R. Richmond, with a large colony of *Pocillopora* having a long axis measuring 7 cm and a colony of *Porites* having a long axis measuring 3.5 cm; **C** thong with abraded *Pocillopora* colony collected at Lizard Island, Australia by E. Cox and F. Stanton in 1988) appear to support the hypothesis that rafting is the "**sole**" means of long range dispersal. This idea was **kicked** around at the turn of the century, and surfaced again recently (Jokiel 1990a, 1990b). For eons, corals have colonized natural flotsam such as pumice, drift wood, charcoal, coconuts and seeds (Jokiel 1990a). The contemporary problem of discarded footwear in the marine environment (Venrick et al. 1973, Gregory 1990) has provided corals with a modern means of literally "**walking on water**". The thongs from the Southern Hemisphere are for the right foot, while the thong from the Northern Hemisphere is for the left foot. It would be premature at this time to implicate the Coriolis effect. A more attractive hypothesis is that the thongs from the Great Barrier Reef may represent evidence of research on long range dispersal starting off on the **right foot** (e.g. Jokiel 1990b).

P. Jokiel (1992) *Coral Reefs* 11(4): 192. Copyright Springer-Verlag. Modified and reprinted with permission.   See original for references.

CORAL LARVAL SETTLEMENT AND RECRUITMENT

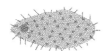

A variety of cues are thought to be involved in causing the planula larvae to settle and metamorphose into a polyp. Light, surface structure, and the presence of other organisms all may play a role. Often these sites are **cryptic**, being underneath natural surfaces where the emerging colony can eventually grow outwards and into the open.

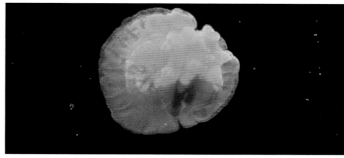

Recently settled and metamorphosed *Tubastraea coccinea* polyp. Note the formation of tentacle buds signifying this to be a juvenile polyp. Soon it will bud-off sister polyps creating a new colony.

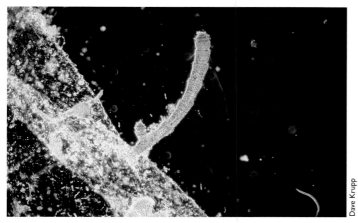

Dave Krupp

There's some evidence that planula larvae respond to settlement cues given off by the presence of microscopic algae. Such algae would presumably be among the first to settle open clear areas.

Certain soft corals (such as *Sinularia* and *Sarcophyta*) have been shown to produce toxic secretions which inhibit the successful settlement of stony coral planulae.

◄ *Pocillopora meandrina* colony and a young *Porites* colony (both less than 3 months after settlement); note the bright fluorescent coloration present on both colonies. ►

Yuko Stender

Skeleton record showing how the present-day polyps all arose from a single ancestor.

Many massive coral colonies, consisting of thousands and thousands of polyps, arose from a single planula larva which successfully settled.

Settling Planula Larva

Founder Polyp

Because successfully settled (attached) planula larvae are almost impossible to observe in the wild, scientists often refer to corals as having undergone "successful recruitment" when they are large enough to be observed attached onto a substrate with the unaided eye.

Some coral larvae have been observed to clump together upon settlement, often fusing to form aggregated colonies. Such clumping may allow new colonies to reach a size refuge at which size-related mortality is greatly reduced.

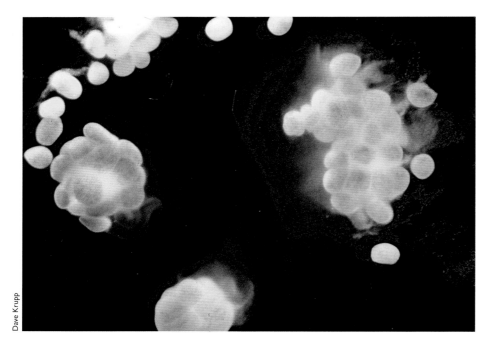

Once attached to the substrate, juvenile polyps will start to lay down the foundations of a skeletal calyx.

Reversible Metamorphosis

An unusual twist on metamorphosis and settlement has been observed in *Pocillopora damicornis*. Under conditions where recently settled polyps experience extreme stress, polyps can retract from recently-formed skeletal calices, and form a motile planula-like form. In this state the polyp can re-enter the plankton, in essence becoming a "planktonic polyp", which can both feed (through use of its tentacles) and make use of its symbiotic zooxanthellae. These "secondary planulae" can then search for a better substrate to settle on and re-metamorphose into a polyp again.

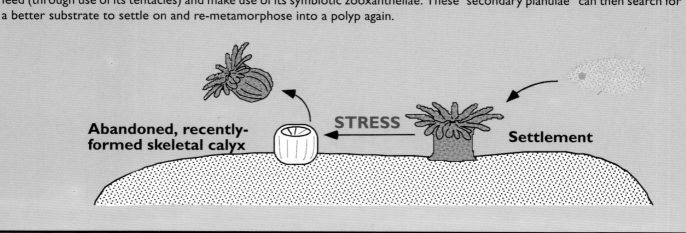

Abandoned, recently-formed skeletal calyx   STRESS   Settlement

CORAL WARS

CORALS CAN COMPETE FOR SPACE IN A NUMBER OF WAYS:

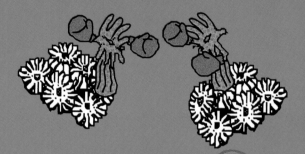

DIRECT TENTACULAR COMPETITION

- Colonies sting adjacent colonies using concentrations of nematocysts, tentacles, polyps or differences in nematocyst toxins.

Mesenterial filament

MESENTERIAL / DIGESTIVE FILAMENTS

- Mesenterial (or digestive) filaments arise in the coelenteron (sac-like gut), and are much longer than the polyp's own tentacles, allowing a longer reach in those species that use this method. The advantage is the ability to attack more distant colonies without exposing the attacking colony to direct counter-attack by the other colony's tentacles.

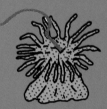

BULLDOZING

- A zone of skeleton and/or dead tissue is pushed in front of the zone of active coral growth; in essence, plowing over the colony in front of it and killing it.

SHADING

- By growing up and spreading out, the colony will create a shaded zone directly beneath it. Most potential competitors would have to first enter the zone of reduced light beneath the colony (reduced light would presumably mean less energy to the coral from its zooxanthellae, and therefore less energy available for competition) in order to interact with the "Table" coral. Often seen with *Acropora*, but may also occur with some plate corals.

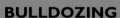

Direction of colony growth

Coral competition can be either **Interspecific** (between different species) or **Intraspecific** (between genetically-different colonies of the same species).

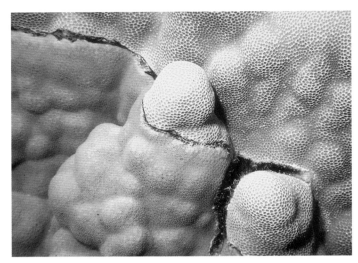

Intraspecific competition between a two genetically different colonies of *Porites lobata*.

Interspecific competition between *Porites compressa* and *Montipora capitata*.

Left: Interspecific competition between a form of Purple coral (*Montipora patula*) and Lobe coral (*Porites lobata*). Note the characteristic pink stress response seen in *Porites* corals near the edge of "No Man's Land" between the two competing colonies.

OTHER FORMS OF COMPETING FOR SPACE INCLUDE:

- some corals produce long tentacles (called **sweeper tentacles**) which sway back and forth, preventing encroachment by adjacent colonies.

- chemical substrate zones produced by, and surrounding colonies of *Cyphastrea*. These zones effectively prevent both encroachment by other corals and settlement of larvae.

- occurring within the territory of certain damselfish (see p. 157)

- colony defense by symbionts (see p. 112)

Space can be at such a premium that corals will settle out almost anywhere. Here a colony of *Pocillopora meandrina* has started to grow on a dead wire coral. The colony is now at such a state that it is weighing down the dead wire coral skeleton.

Above: Corals also compete against a wide variety of non-coral, sessile organisms for space. The colonies of Lobe coral (*Porites lobata*) above are competing with calcareous red algae; at this depth the amount of light available may play a key role in the outcome of such competition.

PREDATORS ON CORALS

Richard Pyle

MAJOR PREDATORS ON REEF CORALS IN HAWAI'I

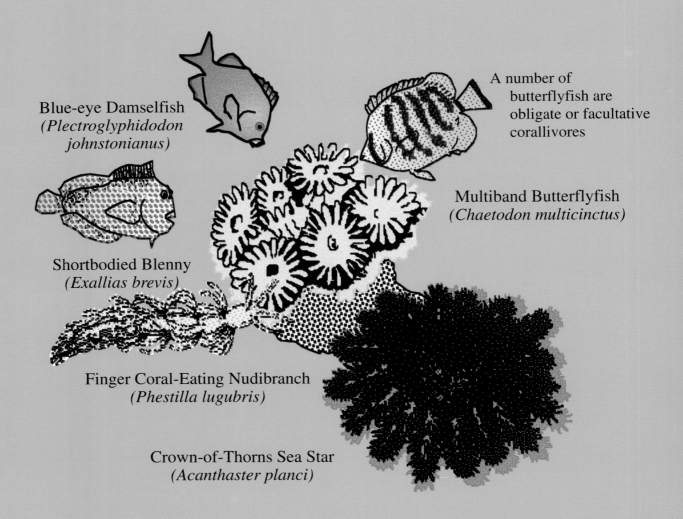

Blue-eye Damselfish
(Plectroglyphidodon johnstonianus)

A number of butterflyfish are obligate or facultative corallivores

Multiband Butterflyfish
(Chaetodon multicinctus)

Shortbodied Blenny
(Exallias brevis)

Finger Coral-Eating Nudibranch
(Phestilla lugubris)

Crown-of-Thorns Sea Star
(Acanthaster planci)

A **corallivore** is an animal that specializes in feeding on corals. Often times these animals are fish, seastars or molluscs. There are two types of corallivores:

Obligate Corallivores are highly specialized to feed only on corals; usually these animals will prefer only certain prey species, though there also are some generalist species that will feed on a wide variety of corals.

Facultative Corallivores are species that will feed on corals in addition to a number of other prey species. A good example of a facultative corallivore in Hawai'i is the Spotted Pufferfish (*Arothron meleagris*) which feeds on corals in addition to algae, sponges, bryozoans and molluscs. Some species are **opportunistic omnivores**, which will feed on both invertebrates and algae in proportion to their abundance on the reef.

THE CORALLIVORES:
THE SHORTBODIED BLENNY
(*EXALLIAS BREVIS*)

Phylum Chordata, Class Osteichthyes, Family Blennidae

Richard Pyle

DESCRIPTION:

One of the larger blennies seen in Hawai'i, the Shortbodied (or Leopard) Blenny is covered with clusters of spots. These spots tend to be reddish in males and yellow to brown in females. Under natural light, the clusters of spots on this animal often mimics the calices and lobes seen on many *Porites* colonies. Highly territorial around *Porites* colonies, males will often clear a space amongst the substrate upon which the female will lay her eggs. The nest of eggs will appear bright yellow at first; this color will fade as the batch of eggs develops. The male guards the nest until hatching.

LIKES:

An obligate specialist on *Porites* corals such as Lobe Coral (*Porites lobata*) and Finger Coral (*Porites compressa*), Shortbodied Blennies seem to be primarily found around well-established colonies of *Porites lobata*. This may have to do more with the shape of the colony facilitating feeding than any large difference between species of *Porites*.

DISLIKES:

This fish is rarely seen outside of the vicinity of *Porites* colonies. Though specialist predators on *Exallias* are unknown, the spotted pattern of the fish itself (which blends in amazingly well with *Porites lobata*) might make it difficult for a daytime predator to see.

MODUS-OPERANDI:

The Shortbodied Blenny maintains small territories surrounding colonies of *Porites*. Most of the time this species is inactive as compared to *Chaetodon multicinctus*, another obligate specialist on coral, which spends most of its time foraging and feeding. Characteristic of these blennies are small circular bites they take out of the coral colonies they feed on. Fresh bites have a whitish appearance; over time, the colony regenerates the lost polyps and the bite mark fades as the new polyps grow into its place. Since the blenny takes only small bites over a wide range on the colony, it usually has a minimal impact on the health and well-being of colony that it feeds on.

Above: Male Shortbodied Blenny (*Exallias brevis*) guarding a patch of eggs within its territory. Hanauma Bay, O'ahu. Females spawn every 3 -4 days; usually silver in color 2 days prior to hatching, eggs will vary in color as they age in the nest (average 8 days). Note the bite marks of varying age on the corals surrounding the blenny and its nest.

THE CORALLIVORES:
CORAL-FEEDING BUTTERFLYFISH
(CHAETODON SP.)

Deborah Gochfeld

Above: Butterflyfish species will often show distinct preferences for certain species of coral, ignoring more abundant species surrounding it.

Phylum Chordata, Class Osteichthyes, Family Chaetodontidae

DESCRIPTION:

Butterflyfish come in a wide variety of colors and shapes, though they tend to share the following characteristics: disk-shaped bodies, often with yellow coloration, and a long, terminal mouth with highly modified teeth (the family name 'Chaetodontidae' refers to their brush-like teeth).

Perhaps more interesting is the relationship between sexual behavior and food in these fish. Butterflyfish can be divided into three basic feeding guilds: Corallivores, Benthic Invertebrate Feeders (which may occasionally feed on coral) and Planktivores (which primarily feed on microscopic animals living in the water column). Those butterflyfish that are obligate corallivores tend to be **monogamous** (they remain with the same mate year after year). Benthic invertebrate-feeding butterflyfish tend to be **polygamous** (they form mating pairs, but partners may vary with each mating); while planktivorous butterflyfish are considered to be **promiscuous** (often found living in schools, they can randomly mate with any member of the opposite sex within the school)!

"Why should a corallivore prefer certain species of coral over others, aren't they pretty much all the same to a fish?"

Actually, corals vary in a variety of macro- and microscopic ways:

- The growth pattern of the coral colony.
- The caloric (energy) content of tissue.
- The amount of mucus production.
- The amount of accessible tissue (some corals have a lot of their tissue deep within the skeleton (termed **Perforate** corals) versus some that have most of it on the surface of the skeleton (termed **Non-perforate** corals)).
- The size, number and distribution of nematocysts.

Some, or all of these may have contributed to the lack of general reef fish that feed on coral relative to the amount of coral coverage on a reef. In fact, some scientists have theorized that many coral colonies' irregular surfaces are a result of evolution to discourage predation by generalists. Likewise, it's thought that butterflyfish corallivores have evolved small, protruding mouth parts to feed within the crevices caused by such irregular growth (Motta, 1980).

BUTTERFLYFISH: A ROGUES GALLERY

LIKES:

Dependent on species (see below):

Richard Pyle

Chaetodon auriga
(Threadfin Butterflyfish)

Opportunistic omnivore; tears its food. Prefers soft corals, worms, sea anemones, stony corals and algae.

Deborah Gochfeld

Chaetodon ephippium
(Saddleback Butterflyfish)

Opportunistic omnivore. Feeds on a variety of stony corals and algae.

Chaetodon multicinctus
(Multiband Butterflyfish)

Obligate generalist corallivore. Endemic. Feeds on a variety of stony corals, but prefers *Pocillopora meandrina*; takes very small bites (a 'polyp picker').

Deborah Gochfeld

Chaetodon ornatissimus
(Ornate Butterflyfish)

Browsing obligate corallivore; takes large bites. Prefers *Acropora, Montipora, Pocillopora* and *Porites* species. Feeds on coral species in proportion to their abundance.

Debborah Gochfeld

Chaetodon quadrimaculatus
(Fourspot Butterflyfish)

Generalist obligate corallivore. Prefers *Pocillopora meandrina* but will also feed on *Porites, Montipora* or *Pavona varians*.

Chaetodon trifascialis
(Chevron Butterflyfish)

Specialist corallivore. Prefers *Acropora*. Seen primarily in the Northwest Hawaiian Islands.

Deborah Gochfeld

Chaetodon lunulatus (trifasciatus)
(Oval Butterflyfish)

Browsing obligate generalist corallivore. Feeds on a variety of coral species in proportion to their abundance.

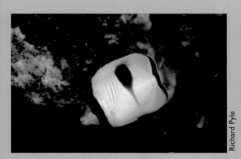

Richard Pyle

Chaetodon unimaculatus
(Teardrop Butterflyfish)

Grazing opportunistic omnivore with a large blunt mouth. Prefers large-polyp corals such as *Leptastrea purpurea, Montipora patula* and *Montipora capitata* and soft corals. Avoids *Porites* species. Juveniles often feed on corals.

Richard Pyle

Chaetodon tinkeri
(Tinker's Butterflyfish)

Grazing opportunistic omnivore. Feeds on a wide variety of algae and invertebrates, including some deep-water corals.

THE CORALLIVORES:
THE BLUE-EYE DAMSELFISH
(*PLECTROGLYPHIDODON JOHNSTONIANUS*)

Phylum Chordata, Class Osteichthyes, Family Pomacentridae

DESCRIPTION:

A medium sized damselfish, gray to yellowish gray in color with distinctive bright blue eyes and a bluish tinge along the margin of the dorsal fin.

LIKES:

Obligate specialist on *Pocillopora* (Antler Coral, Cauliflower Coral or Lace Coral), but will also feed on Finger Coral (*Porites compressa*) or Lobe Coral (*Porites lobata*). Often seen around Antler Coral heads (*Pocillopora eydouxi*).

DISLIKES:

Tends to avoid encrusting corals but this may have as much to do with lack of protective cover as food preference.

Deborah Gochfeld

MODUS-OPERANDI:

Strongly site specific, Blue-Eyed Damselfish will often be associated with single large coral heads, groups of coral heads, or irregular areas of the reef with lots of sheltering space. They are most often found at sites deeper on the reef slope. As with many damselfish, the males defend the nest site and adjacent area.

Deborah Gochfeld

Large Antler Coral (*Pocillopora eydouxi*) heads like the one above often serve as both hotel and restaurant for the Blue-Eyed Damselfish. Two such fish can be seen in the above photo, can you spot them???

A juvenile Blue-Eyed Damselfish sheltering amongst the Bubble Algae and rubble at the base of a coral head.

THE CORALLIVORES:
THE FINGER CORAL-EATING NUDIBRANCH
(PHESTILLA LUGUBRIS)

Phylum Mollusca, Class Gastropoda, Order Nudibranchia, family Cuthonidae

DESCRIPTION:

An Aeolid Nudibranch (a suborder of the nudibranchs characterized by lacking true gills, instead having a series of long, frilly projections (called **cerata**) all along their backs. Most aeolids feed on cnidarians of some sort), 10 - 30 mm long, that has a coloration pattern that mimics the coral it feeds on. Unlike other aeolid nudibranchs, *Phestilla* does not incorporate the unfired nematocysts of its prey into its cerata for its own defense; instead it seems to rely on being well-camouflaged, concealed and perhaps nocturnal. Like most nudibranchs, it is hermaphroditic.

LIKES:

Tends to feed exclusively on members of the genus *Porites*, primarily Finger Coral (*Porites compressa*). A similar species, *Phestilla melanobrachia*, feeds exclusively on Orange Flower Coral (*Tubastraea coccinea*); the color of this nudibranch is orange, pinkish or black, depending on the form of *Tubastraea* that it has been feeding upon. Though rarely found in the field, *Phestilla lugubris* is occasionally spotted around *Porites* rubble.

DISLIKES:

Tends to not be found associated with any coral other than *Porites*.
Predators: Invertebrate-feeding fishes such as wrasses and certain butterflyfish. Recent work suggests that *Phestilla* is preyed upon by symbiotic crabs found associated with colonies of *Porites*.

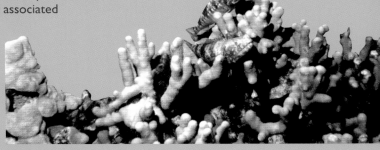

MODUS-OPERANDI:

Planktonic larvae of *Phestilla* preferentially settle out of the plankton in the presence of their prey coral, presumably this is initiated by the presence of a chemical given off by the *Porites* colony. Adults readily feed on the living polyps of the coral colony leaving behind an empty skeleton. *Phestilla* will often lay its egg masses on the dead coral it has been feeding on.

Above: The unsuspecting prey...(the coral, not the pair of lizardfish).
Below: The predator at work.

Adult *Phestilla lugubris* with egg masses laid on dead *Porites compressa* colony.

Deborah Gochfeld

THE CORALLIVORES:
THE STRIPEBELLY PUFFER
(AROTHRON HISPIDUS)

**Phylum Chordata,
Class Osteichthyes,
Family Tetraodontidae**

DESCRIPTION:

Pufferfish derive their name from their ability to inflate their bodies with water. Many people think that this response is used to frighten potential predators or to make them difficult to consume, but careful observation of their behavior on the reef shows that these animals use their ability (like many other types of reef fish) to lodge themselves within cracks and crevices on the reef when threatened. The Stripebelly Puffer is the largest of the nearshore Hawaiian puffers and is commonly found in estuaries, bays, and along reefs. Its close relative, the Spotted Puffer (*Arothron meleagris*), is primarily associated with coral reefs.

LIKES:

The Stripebelly Puffer is a facultative omnivore that will feed on a wide variety of algae and invertebrates (including both soft and stony corals). *Arothron meleagris* feeds more exclusively on invertebrates (with a large portion of its diet being reef corals).

DISLIKES:

Have a very variable diet; specific coral species preferences are unknown.

PREDATORS:

As stated earlier, these animals have the ability to inflate their bodies with water in order to lodge themselves within a hole or crevice (similar to a triggerfish erecting its dorsal spine); they also are one of the few reef fish to have tissue relatively toxic to humans.

MODUS-OPERANDI:

Puffers feed through the use of a beak-like structure made-up of fused teeth. This allows them to take-up chunks of substrate, which is then pulverized by the flat plate-like teeth fused in behind the beak. Such an adaptation allows pufferfish to effectively feed on a wide range of hardened organisms (including calcareous algae and stony corals).

Above: An inflated Spotted Puffer (*Arothron meleagris*). Note the fused teeth that form a crunching beak.

Above: An inflated Spiny Puffer or Porcupinefish (*Diodon hystrix*) in its natural form. By inflating itself within a crevice the fish effectively wedges itself such that a predator cannot remove it.

THE CORALLIVORES:
THE CROWN-OF-THORNS SEA STAR
(ACANTHASTER PLANCI)

Phylum Echinodermata, Class Asteroidea Family Acanthasteridae

DESCRIPTION:

Large, cryptically-colored sea stars having between 9 and 23 arms covered with brittle, venom-covered spines; adults range from 25 - 35 cm (but may be as large as 60 cm) in diameter. They have separate sexes, and spawn in Hawai'i from May to August. Synchronized spawning is thought to occur through the use of a pheromone which produces spawning aggregations; this same pheromone may be used to form feeding aggregations.

LIKES:

Tends to favor the faster growing coral species such as *Montipora* (Rice Coral) or *Pocillopora* (Lace Corals or small Cauliflower Corals). *Acropora*, which is only rarely found in Hawai'i, is among its noted favorites; as this genus is considered to be the dominant coral in the Pacific, this might help explain the lack of large *Acanthaster* outbreaks in Hawai'i. *Acanthaster* preferentially attacks damaged corals.

DISLIKES:

Tends to avoid corals such as *Porites* (Finger Coral, Lobe Coral) or those protected by symbiotic crabs and shrimps (see pp. 112, 117).

PREDATORS:

Protective structures include cryptic coloration and toxin-filled spines which can inject would-be harrassers. In addition, few fish feed on *Acanthaster*, possibly due to the high amount of saponins in their tissues. *Acanthaster* eggs and larvae are preyed upon by stony corals themselves (remember, corals feed on plankton); the eggs have also been found within the stomachs of the Sergeant Major (*Abudefduf* sp.). Larvae are thought to settle out of the plankton on coral rubble and coralline algae (*Lithophyllum*) at the base of reef slopes. Such a habitat provides a refuge from predation; juveniles feed exclusively on coralline algae until they are large enough to undergo metamorphosis to an adult that feeds on corals. While juveniles, they are preyed upon by Xanthid crabs and the Stripebelly Pufferfish (*Arothron hispidus*).

Adults are preyed upon by the Triton's Trumpet (*Charonia tritonis*), Helmet Shells (*Cassis cornuta*), Harlequin Shrimp (*Hymenocera picta*), the Stripebelly Pufferfish (*Arothron hispidus*) and the larval stage of a predatory worm (*Pherecardia striata*).

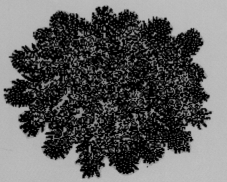

The Harlequin Shrimp (*Below*) rarely kills an *Acanthaster*, it acts more like a parasite since it is far too small to consume more then a small part of the arm. It is through the act of feeding on the sea star that the little shrimp creates open wounds through which the larval Lined-Fireworm (*Pherecardia striata*) can enter the sea star's body cavity. The predatory worm reproduces and feeds inside of its food; it's offspring will eventually kill the sea star from the inside-out. This form of predation in which the Harlequin Shrimp paves the way for the involvement of the worm has been termed 'Facilitated Predation'.

Above: The most common adult predator on *Acanthaster* is the Triton's Trumpet which cuts through the sea star's body wall with its radula (modified teeth) and inserts its proboscis (feeding tube) into the arms, sucking-up gonads and digestive glands.

Chris Evans

Marine Option Program

MODUS-OPERANDI:

The Crown-of-Thorns Sea Star feeds by everting its stomach through its mouth and digesting the coral tissue externally. Such a form of feeding can be very effective; one *Acanthaster* may consume up to 6 m² of coral tissue/yr! Large concentrations (outbreaks) of these animals can be devastating (one "outbreak" in the Ryukus resulted in 13 million sea stars being killed by human controls!), making them the most serious biological threat to coral reefs in many areas where they occur.

Deborah Gochfield

Deborah Gochfield

Above: Everted stomach of an *Acanthaster* exposed during feeding.

Control of these organisms has been difficult; the eggs and larvae of *Acanthaster* have been found to contain large amounts of saponins, toxins that serve to detract fish from feeding on the pelagic stages. These same saponins may serve to limit fish predation on the adults and possibly warn coral symbionts of the sea star's approach (see p. 112). As with most sea stars, *Acanthaster planci* have amazing powers of regeneration. Because of this, and the fact that they are a large sea star, few predators can effectively consume them.

Right: All that remains after the *Acanthaster* has finished feeding. Note that the surrounding *Porites* colonies have been left untouched, suggesting strong prey preferences by this sea star.

Human control programs have involved the following:

-   Paying fishermen a bounty for each seastar (quickly realized that by cutting them up, they would regenerate, providing an easily replenishable income source for the fishermen but only increasing the problem...).
-   Injecting each sea star with a solution like copper sulfate (very cost prohibitive, and once they die, the copper sulfate leaches out onto the reef where it could kill other invertebrates including the corals!)
-   Collecting the sea stars and placing them on land to dry out (smelly and very expensive).

Most control programs worldwide have proven to be unsuccessful.

Acanthaster occur only in the Indo-Pacific and occasionally have occurred in large outbreaks which have caused significant damage to the associated reefs. Major outbreaks have occurred on the Great Barrier Reef, in Micronesia, the Ryukus, Samoa,

and the Society Islands. In some of these areas the coral cover went from 78% to 2% in less than 6 months!!! In Hawai'i, an abnormally concentrated population of *Acanthaster* was found off of southern Moloka'i in 1969 (160 sea stars on one isolated coral mound). A later survey (1970) estimated about 20,000 sea stars were present. Based on problems reported elsewhere in the Pacific, an eradication program was initiated and 26,000 *Acanthaster* were destroyed using injections of ammonium hydroxide (which, like copper sulfate, will kill other invertebrates if it leaches out of the dead sea stars).

The cause of these "outbreaks" has been extensively argued over the last twenty years. It breaks up into two basic camps: those that favor **natural causes** and believe that these "outbreaks" may occur in cycles; and those that believe that this is only a recent phenomena that has been brought about due to **human causes** (examples include removal of predators like the Triton's Trumpet, increased pollution and sedimentation caused by coastal development and deforestation).

As a large animal with a plate-like covering, *Acanthaster* have thin, tentacle-like skin gills to aid in respiration; these extend out of the skin between the spines (*Left*).

Being so large and possessing protective spines makes the Crown-of-Thorns Sea Star an excellent recruitment device for certain fish larvae. Because small fish (*Left*, look closely) and invertebrates (The symbiotic shrimp *Periclimenes* sp. is often found on sea stars) can live atop the animal, *Acanthaster* have specialized protective pinchers called **pedicellaria** (can you spot them?) to protect their skin gills.

Sara Peck

CNIDOQUESTION:
BITE MARKS
CAN YOU MATCH THE CORALLIVORE BELOW
WITH ITS DISTINCTIVE FEEDING SCAR ?

Each of these marks is descriptive of the fish that feeds on that coral. When you see these marks in the field keep a sharp lookout as you're probably within that corallivore's feeding territory.

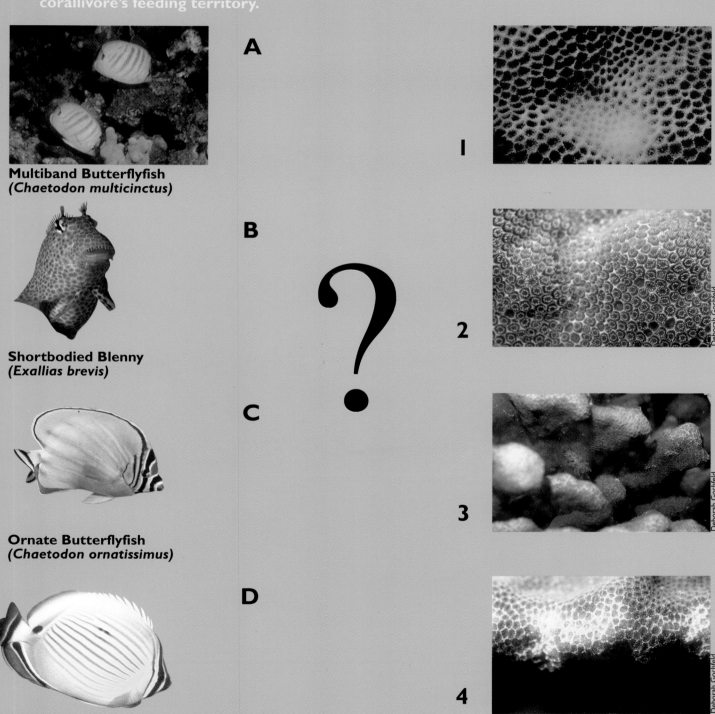

A

1

Multiband Butterflyfish
(Chaetodon multicinctus)

B

2

Shortbodied Blenny
(Exallias brevis)

C

3

Ornate Butterflyfish
(Chaetodon ornatissimus)

D

4

Oval Butterflyfish
(Chaetodon lunulatus)

CORALS AS CONDOMINIUMS

Heinz-Gert deCouet

LIVING CORAL COLONIES ARE USED AS HOMES, RESTAURANTS AND WORK PLACES BY A WIDE VARIETY OF ORGANISMS

SECTION II: CORALS AS CONDOMINIUMS
CORALS AS CONDOS

On the reef, many organisms maintain **symbiotic** (an association between two or more organisms) relationships with their coral hosts. These relationships are of three major forms:

Host   Symbiont

Associations where the (usually) smaller organism [Symbiont] benefits as does the (usually) larger organism [Host]
= **MUTUALISM**

Associations where the symbiont benefits but the host neither benefits nor is harmed by the relationship
= **COMMENSALISM**

Associations where the symbiont benefits and the host is harmed by the relationship
= **PARASITISM**

In addition, we can define relationships based on the type of association:
- Associations for protection (**Aegism**), such as those involving camouflage with, residence within or upon host organisms.
- Associations for sharing of food resources (this is true commensalism - which means "at the table together").
- Associations for transport.
- Associations for substrate/settlement space.

Corals act as hosts for a wide variety of symbionts. Some of these are **obligate** associations, meaning the organisms can't live without the association. Examples include the endosymbiotic zooxanthellae that live within the tissue of the coral; others are purely opportunistic or **facultative**, such as larval fish settling out of the plankton and on to a head of coral. Because of the large three-dimensional area that they cover, corals can provide a large surface area and shelter among the colony's branches from numerous reef predators. Tissue, mucus and associated detritus can serve as a food source; while a colony's hard skeleton provides a habitat for burrowers and gall-forming crabs. Nematocysts and mesenterial filaments, while serving as a defense for the colony, may also protect those animals sheltering among the colony's branches.

Corals can sustain a large number of symbionts, primarily because:

1) Due to their symbiotic zooxanthellae, they function as primary producers (high source of organic carbon).

2) They grow by asexual reproduction allowing them to regenerate a large amount of the damage done by symbionts and predators.

3) Excess energy from the zooxanthellae may be shed by the coral as mucus thus providing a low cost energy source for commensals and free-living organisms closely associated with the colony.

4) Of their ability to produce calcareous skeletons, which along with the associated energy mentioned above, provides a number of niches for a wide number of symbionts and coral reef inhabitants.

The number of symbiotic relationships that one can see on a coral reef are staggering, perhaps the greatest concentration of symbioses within any one single habitat on the planet. Examples other then those directly associated with corals include: sea turtle cleaning behavior by surgeonfish; cleaner wrasses and cleaning stations; cleaner shrimps and cleaning stations; alpheid shrimps & gobies; goatfish & jacks; trumpetfish & schools of herbivorous fishes; parasites on a wide variety of coral reef fish & invertebrates; larval fish & obligate symbionts living amongst the spines of sea urchins and *Acanthaster planci*; sponge, decorator & anemone crabs; crabs and shrimp (*Periclimenes* sp.) living atop and inside sea cucumbers, sea stars and sea urchins, to name a few (whew!)...

Heinz - Gert deCouet

THE BIG PICTURE:
ROLES OF CORAL COLONIES AS HOSTS

WHY SHOULD SUCH A GREAT DIVERSITY OF ORGANISMS ASSOCIATE DIRECTLY WITH CORAL COLONIES?

(Modified after W. Deas (1976)).

Utilization of a Coral Colony by Coral-Associated Animals

POSSIBLE BENEFITS TO ANIMAL FROM ASSOCIATING WITH THE CORAL COLONY

CORAL ASSOCIATE	Primary Benefits	Secondary Benefits
(A) Longnose Butterflyfish	Food-Other coral-associated organisms	
(B) Xanthid Crabs	Shelter	Food-Coral tissue, mucus?
(C) Xmas Tree Worms	Shelter	
(D) Domino Damselfish	Shelter	Food (plankton) collected from water near host
(E) Parrotfish	Food-Zooxanthellae, algae growing on dead skeleton.	
(F) Gall Crab	Shelter/Reproduction	Food (plankton) collected from water near host
(G) Marine Snails	Food-Coral tissue	Substrate for eggs
(H) Butterflyfish	Food-Coral tissue	
(I) Coral Goby	Shelter	
(J) Juvenile Fish	Shelter/Recruitment	
(K) *Phestilla* Nudibranch	Food-Coral Tissue	
(L) Ambush Predators	Background Camouflage	Food-Sheltering fish
(M) Sea Urchin	Shelter	
(N) Trapezid Crabs	Shelter/Food-Coral mucus, fat bodies	
(O) Boring Sponge	Shelter/Substrate	Food (plankton) collected from water near host
(P) Hawaiian Sergeant	Shelter/Nest	Food (plankton) collected from water near host
(Q) Barnacles & Bivalves	Shelter	Food (plankton) collected from water near host
(R) Flatworms	Food-Coral Tissue	
(S) Alpheid Shrimp	Shelter/Food-Coral mucus, fat bodies	
(T) Hawkfish	Shelter/Reproduction	Background Camouflage

A coral colony may interact with the organisms around it in a number of ways. Its nematocysts can protect associated animals from predators, but may also kill these animals or their larvae as they attempt to settle. Its tissue may serve as a food source, yet it is low in calories and contains enzymes (in the mesenterial filaments) that can harm potential gourmets. Its mucus can likewise be eaten, or serve as a slimy-substance to entangle and snare the larval stages of associated animals. Its hearty skeleton can serve as a solid substrate to grow on and shelter under, yet the same symbiont that settles on it may be overgrown and killed by the colony itself. In essence, the coral colony and all of its symbionts live in a dynamic world of change, where each event can serve as an opportunity for some and a detriment for others.

A Generalized Coral Colony and Representative Organisms Associated with it.

THE FOLLOWING PHOTOS REPRESENT A VARIETY OF TYPES OF
CAN YOU MATCH THE PHOTO WITH THE

1) A Hawaiian Cleaner Wrasse cleaning a Papio (Jack). One of the most well-known examples of symbiosis, but actually there's more to this behavior than meets the eye (see pp. 164 - 165). ▶

2) The anemone hermit crab will carefully transfer its anemones to its new shell when it outgrows the old one. ▼

Keoki Stender

4) The Sponge Crab (*Dromia dormia*) holds onto a trimmed piece of sponge using specially modified legs. ▼

Keoki Stender

5) The Hawaiian Shrimp Goby (*Psilogobius mainlandi*) lives in burrows dug by snapping shrimp. The shrimp (*Alpheus* sp.) has very poor eyesight and relies on the goby to guard the entrance to their burrow in exchange for sharing it with them. ▶

Richard Pyle

6) The Bumble Bee Shrimp feeds on the tube feet of echinoderms such as sea cucumbers. ▶

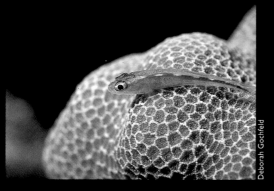

Deborah Gochfeld

8) Rarely seen in shallow water, the Coral Goby (*Pleurosicya micheli*) lives atop large coral colonies of *Porites* and *Montipora*.

Richard Pyle

9) No, this is not a cleaner wrasse but a mimic that preys on confused fish that make the same mistake that most readers do who see this photo.

SYMBIOSES OCCURRING ON HAWAIIAN CORAL REEFS:
TYPE(S) OF SYMBIOSIS SHOWN?

Sara Peck

◄ 3) The shrimpfish tends to live amongst the spines of the long-spined sea urchin.

(A) Mutualism

Both organisms benefit.

(B) Commensalism

Share food or where the symbiont benefits but the host neither benefits nor is greatly harmed by the relationship.

(C) Parasitism

The symbiont benefits while the host is harmed by the relationship.

(D) Aegism

An association for protection.

(E) Inquilism

(Latin: *Incolinus* - who lives within) Where one organism shelters on or within another organism.

(F) Endoecism

Where one organism shelters in the burrow or defensive shelter of another organism.

(G) Phoresis

(Greek: *Pherein* - to carry) Where one organism uses another for transportation.

(H) Epizoism

Where a sessile organism lives atop another organism.

7) Often times you will see jacks and goatfish swimming together, with the jack following the goatfish taking advantage of any small fish that are spooked out of the rubble by the goatfish's probings for small invertebrates. ►

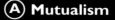

Keoki Stender

◄ 10) Yes, that's the same crab in both photos... but how many of you realized that in the photo on the left the crab is coming out of the anus of the sea cucumber where it makes its home?!! I introduced this crab to the "Red Hot Dog" Sea Cucumber pictured (*left*) so that it could be easily seen. Normally this species of crab (*Lissocarcinus orbicularis*) is seen on a variety of sea cucumbers that tend to be covered with grains of sand, often having it adhere to their surfaces; it's probably no surprise then that the color of the crab matches this situation (*right*). It's thought that the crab emerges from its anal home to roam the external surface of its host, feeding on attached parasites (such as the parasitic snail *Balcis* sp.; there's one in this photo - can you find it?). If it seems strange to you for a crab to live in the anus (scientists use a nicer sounding word - 'cloacal cavity'), ponder this: the gills of the sea cucumber are also located in this cavity - why?

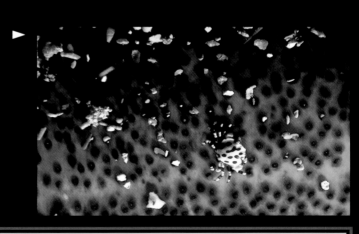

CNIDOQUESTION: There are at least 15 other distinct examples of symbiosis pictured in this book...can you find them and describe the type of symbiosis shown? Some of them are already labeled, others are not. Remember, count only the ones actually pictured or photographed.

**Animals Associated with
Corals or Coral Colonies:**

CRABS

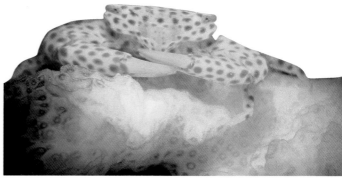

Crabs are one of the most common and overlooked of the creatures found inhabiting in, on, and around coral colonies. Often hidden among the branches of a coral, near the base, or under the rubble exist a wide variety of species, some of which maintain strong associations with specific species of corals.

Above: Trapezid crabs like this fellow (*Trapezia intermedia*) are among the most common of the coral-associated crabs.
Trapezia intermedia is usually found on *Pocillopora meandrina* and occasionally on other *Pocillopora* species. It usually occurs in pairs.

Marc Rice

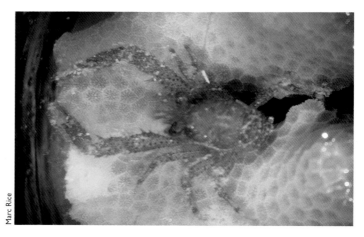

Marc Rice

Above: Because of their hard exoskeleton, crabs are well-adapted to roaming around atop the coral colony free from most of the effects of the coral's stinging cells. This allows many larval crabs to recruit in and around colonies where small nooks and crannies can be used for shelter. Often, even the rubble (*below*) at the base of coral heads has a number of species of crabs roaming around in it. These crabs feed primarily on the myriad of small invertebrates (worms, molluscs, and other crustaceans) that live within the rubble.

Above: Some crabs are adapted to live among the branches of Finger Coral (*Porites compressa*). The long claws allow the crabs to remain safely among the branches while capturing and manipulating its food.

CNIDOQUESTION:

Why should this Trapezid crab (top photo) have dark red spots?
"Aw, come on, you can come up with a more detailed answer than 'camouflage' can't you?"

Left: This is a settled Pebble Crab (*Carpilius convexus*). Crab larvae that settle out of the plankton and onto coral colonies may be preyed upon by resident crabs, shrimp or fish. Many presumably are; but if they can find a place to hide and grow, they may reach a size refuge where they can exist within the boundaries of the coral colony. In the case of the Pebble crab, eventually it will reach a size where it will have to shelter outside of the coral head upon which it now rests, instead using whole groups of coral colonies and large outcroppings for cover.

Right: This is not a live crab (nor a dead one either), but a discarded exoskeleton (**molt**). Because their skeleton is on the outside of the body, crabs (and other crustaceans) must occasionally discard their old skeleton in order to grow. Imagine your kid trying to wear the same clothes at six years of age that (s)he did when (s)he was four. The crab faces the same problem but solves it in an amazing way: first, it reabsorbs and softens some of its skeleton; then, through a slit near where the abdomen meets the carapace, it pulls its entire body out of the skeleton. At this point the crab is very vulnerable to predation and often shelters deep within the cracks and crevices of the reef. The crabs bloats itself with water and then secretes a new exoskeleton around its inflated body. After the new skeleton hardens, the crab will release the water from its body. The end result is a new skeleton with plenty of room to grow into (imagine having your four year old kid wearing a six year old's clothes until she grows into them...).

Right: Sandwiched-in among the cracks and crevices, within the ledges found in the rocky intertidal, and along shallow reef slopes are the Flat Rock Crabs (*Percnon planissimum*). Another crab occasionally found in this same habitat is the Hawaiian Swimming Crab (*Charybdis hawaiiensis*). Swimming crabs can be easily distinguished by the presence of a modified, paddle-shaped fifth pair of legs and long, lacerating claws.

**Animals Associated with
Corals or Coral Colonies:**

DEFENSE OF CORALS BY CRUSTACEAN SYMBIONTS

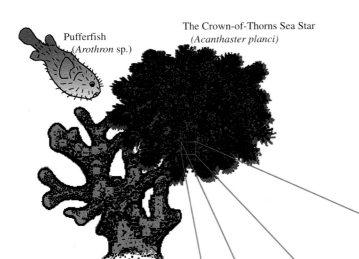

Pufferfish
(*Arothron* sp.)

The Crown-of-Thorns Sea Star
(*Acanthaster planci*)

Some corals are rarely preyed on by the Crown-of-Thorns Sea Star, even though preference studies show these corals to be among its favorite foods. Behavioral observations in the field have shown that in some areas this species of coral (*Pocillopora*) has both symbiotic crabs and shrimp that live within the branches. At the approach of a Crown-of-Thorns (the sea star puts out a chemical cue that the coral's defenders can detect), the crab and shrimp emerge onto the tips of the coral branches and go through a series of agonistic displays to try and harass the sea star. If the sea star persists, these behaviors change into a direct harassment of the animal with the crabs and shrimp using their pinchers to attack and break off spines and tube feet of the sea star. In most cases the sea star is driven away from the colony without the benefit of a good meal.

Benefits to Symbionts:

- Physical Shelter
- Predator Protection
    Via Nematocysts
- Food (Coral Mucus)
- High Energy Food (Fat
    Bodies)
[Found only in those corals
with protective symbionts]

Alpheid Shrimp & Trapezid Crab on
Pocillopora Coral

Do Corals Bribe Their
Ⓣ Symbionts?

In tropical rainforests, Acacia trees produce swollen portions full of nutrients or nectars which their symbiotic ants feed on; in return, the ants defend their food resource (the tree) against most herbivores. Perhaps there is a similar mechanism operating here; if the crabs and shrimp were only on the coral for shelter, then the dead skeleton should suffice - why risk their lives battling a Crown-of-Thorns if the sea star isn't going to destroy your shelter (remember, the seastar just eats the animal tissue and leaves behind the intact skeleton)? It has been shown that on those colonies that harbor these crabs and shrimp the corals tend to concentrate photosynthate (translocated from their zooxanthellae) as fat bodies located in the tips of their tentacles. The crabs and shrimps, on the other hand, seem to have specialized claws that not only aid them in defending the coral, but also allow them to snip off the ends of the tentacles and feed on the fat bodies. If, however, the Crown-of-Thorns kills the coral then their food source is gone; hence, as is seen with the ants and the acacia, the crabs and shrimp will stubbornly defend their host coral.

> CNIDOQUESTION: What might be the advantage to a Crown-of-Thorns Sea Star in chemically advertising its presence to corals that might contain crab and shrimp defenders?

Microscope photo of tips of *Pocillopora* tentacles containing fat bodies stored there by the coral.

> CNIDOQUESTION: Do you think this type of defense would be effective against a corallivore like a fish? Why or why not?

**Animals Associated with
Corals or Coral Colonies:**

GALL CRABS AND CORAL GALLS

Some symbiotic crabs have the ability to radically alter the morphology of the coral colonies that they inhabit. Many of these crabs form permanent chambers (called **galls**) within the coral skeleton. These **gall crabs** tend to spend their entire adult life associated with one small part of a single coral colony; one often can find between 10 - 50 galls on a single coral head. The gall crab *Hapalocarcinus marsupialis* tends to form galls in Pocilloporid corals (primarily Lace Coral, *Pocillopora damicornis*). The process starts with the growing tip of a colony of Lace Coral (*Pocillopora damicornis*), as the tip starts to divide and a branch starts to form

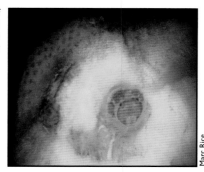

Right: Close-up of an unidentified species of gall crab inhabiting a colony of *Porites*.

(Steps 1 - 2 in the diagram below) a small female gall crab, fresh out of the plankton, settles at the developing fork (Step 3). The small crab creates feeding currents with its claws which help to cause the coral colony to grow up and around it (Step 4), thereby modifying the skeleton and creating the gall chamber itself. As this continues a second chamber will form above the first (Step 5). Eventually, the now adult female will settle in the larger chamber; the smaller chamber starts to fill in with debris. At this point, the colony has pretty much entombed the soft-shelled, female crab, creating the gall in which she lives (Step 6). She is too large to leave the gall but the male of the species is much smaller and can easily slip through the small openings in the gall to inseminate the female (Step 6). Once fertilized, the eggs will be carried by the female under her abdomen until they hatch. The young larval crabs slip out through the openings in the gall and enter the plankton (Step 7); the female, trapped in her gall, eventually dies and is entombed within the coral skeleton.

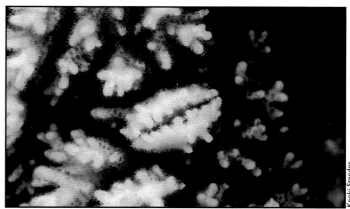

Above: P. damicornis in the field. If you look carefully you can discern a fully-developed crab gall; note how the gall itself contains living coral polyps.

female crab

Above Left: Close-up of a *P. damicornis* colony showing an opened-up gall. Note the size of the two chambers and the small female crab.
Above Right: Extreme close-up of the same *Hapalocarcinus* crab bearing eggs.

> **CNIDOQUESTION:** Why do you find only female crabs living within the galls?

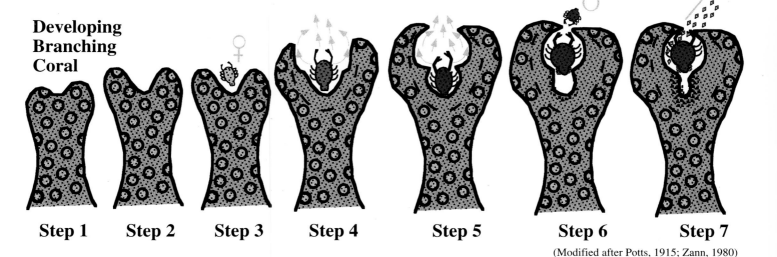

**Developing
Branching
Coral**

Step 1   Step 2   Step 3   Step 4   Step 5   Step 6   Step 7

(Modified after Potts, 1915; Zann, 1980)

**Animals Associated with
Corals or Coral Colonies:**

SHRIMPS

▲ Ahh, what's this? A reef shrimp cleverly disguised as an Antarctic Krill...no one would suspect an innocent-looking member of the colder water plankton, an animal that usually serves as an appetizer for whales and other hungry members of the food chain. Wait a minute - that is a krill. How'd that get in here? This is supposed to be shrimp associated with coral reefs.

▲ Er, that's not a shrimp either. That's a Red Reef Lobster (*Enoplometopus occidentalis*); it's actually a relative of the Maine lobster; but don't feel too bad, shrimps and lobsters are very closely related and have many similar characteristics. You're really having difficulty with the concept of a shrimp, huh? Let's look at some of the basics: shrimps, lobsters and crabs are all **decapods**; possessing ten legs, a fused cephalothorax, and an abdomen encased by an exoskeleton.

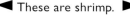 ◄ These are shrimp. ►

Many of the shrimps observed on coral reefs are either commensal or mutual symbionts.

Harlequin Shrimp (*Hymenocera picta*) are specialized to feed on sea stars; their front claws act like fine scissors to snip off bite-size bits of their prey. This shrimp is becoming increasingly hard to find in the wild due to heavy collection for the aquarium trade; because of its specialized diet, many don't survive in captivity.

The Candy Cane Shrimp (*Parhippolyte uveae*), like many shrimps, is usually only seen at night when it emerges to scavenge for food. Their eyes, like many crustaceans, are extremely reflective and are easily observed with a light while night diving.

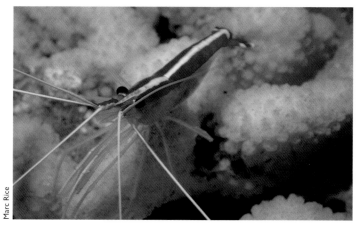

Both the Barber Pole Shrimp (*Stenopus hispidus*) and the Scarlet Cleaner Shrimp (*Lysmata amboinesis*) act as cleaners, setting-up cleaning stations on the reef.

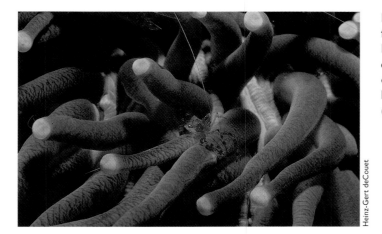

In parts of the Pacific where large anemones are common, one frequently finds a symbiotic shrimp living amongst the tentacles. In Hawai'i, an analogous situation occurs with *Stegopontonia commensalis* and other shrimps that live among the primary spines of various long-spined venomous sea urchins such as the Salt & Pepper Urchin (*Echinothrix calamaris*) or the Black Spiny Urchin (*Echinothrix diadema*).

Close inspection of most seastars will often be rewarded with the discovery of various species of little symbiotic shrimp called *Periclimenes*. Other closely-related shrimp commonly inhabit Spanish Dancer nudibranchs, sponges, corals and bivalves. As shown below, these animals are often difficult to see on their hosts due either to their translucent nature or color patterning.

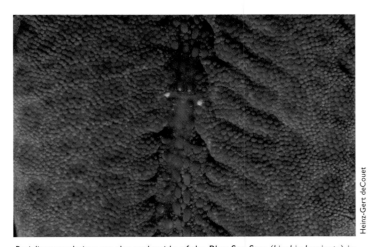

Periclimenes shrimp on the underside of the Blue Sea Star (*Linckia laevigata*) in Australia.

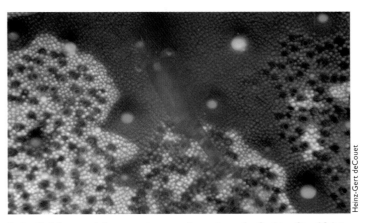

A tiny *Periclimenes* shrimp roaming over the surface of a Cushion Star (*Culcita novaeguineae*). Often a large Cushion Star will have 6 - 10 such shrimp making it their home.

And what of the reef shrimp of which most divers have heard (that is, if they listened carefully)? The Snapping Shrimp are certainly among the most numerous of the reef shrimp, inhabiting a wide range of substrates. Characteristic of these tiny shrimp (most are less than a couple centimeters in length) is their single enlarged snapping claw which is constantly making a loud snapping sound. Most divers become quickly acclimated to the noise, not even realizing that they are being serenaded by an orchestra of thousands.

Snap!
Snap!

Pop Quiz: Can You Spot the Parasite???

(Answer on p. 238)

**Animals Associated with
Corals or Coral Colonies:**

WORMS, WORMS,

FREE-LIVING CARNIVORES

Above: The Fireworm is one of the dominant predators within the framework of the coral colony and surrounding rubble. It derives its name from the unpleasant feeling people get upon touching the worm, whose loose bristles stick into the skin providing an irritating sensation similar to that of fiberglass fibers.

Coral reefs are often full of worms; beautiful crawly ones, magnificent stationary ones with colorful feeding plumes, or ones with crawling, iridescent tentacles. In fact, it's usually very difficult to see most worms on a reef since the main body of the worm tends to be safely buried in a tube, often within a coral colony or the rubble at the base of a coral head. What one tends to observe is the modified feeding tentacles which are often extended out during the day. On the other hand, the majority of the free-living worms are primarily active at night, venturing forth in search of prey which they hunt down and consume. As nocturnal predators, these worms have advanced sensory systems such as eyes and probing tentacles (**cirri**). Such structures are greatly reduced in the stationary worms.

LIVE! NAKED WORMS!!!

(well, at least this is what they look like out of their tubes)

Featherduster Worm   Spaghetti Worm
(*Sabellastarte sanctijosephi*)   (*Lanice conchilega*)

SUSPENSION FEEDERS

Suspension feeders like the Featherduster Worm and the Xmas Tree Worm use their feather-like tentacle plumes to filter food particles out of the water column. The Featherduster Worm (*Sabellastarte sanctijosephi*) is now being heavily collected for the aquarium trade.

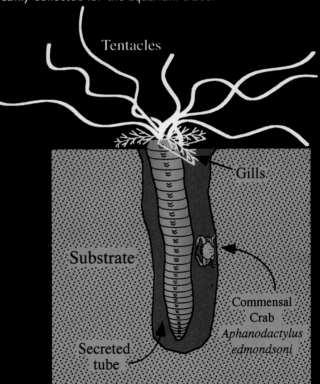

Tentacles

Gills

Substrate

Commensal
Crab
*Aphanodactylus
edmondsoni*

Secreted
tube

DEPOSIT FEEDERS

The Spaghetti Worm is commonly seen in the rubble at the base of many coral heads and in tidepools. The long, whitish tentacles are the only part of the worm visible, the remainder being safely sheltered within a secreted tube buried in the rubble. This worm has recently been studied for its medicinal properties.

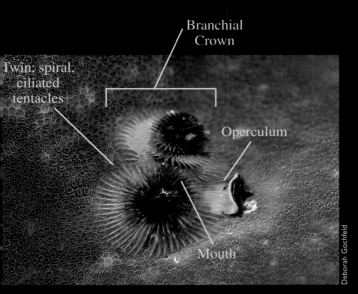

Twin: spiral, ciliated tentacles

Branchial Crown

Operculum

Mouth

Deborah Gochfeld

The branchial crown on Christmas Tree Worms (*above*) are actually spiral plumes of highly modified, ciliated tentacles. These tentacles are used for both respiration and filter feeding.

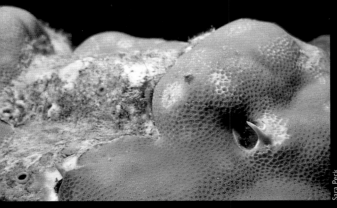

Sara Peck

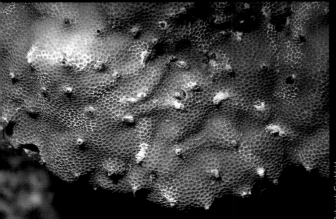

Deborah Gochfeld

Above: Spirorbid worm tubes on a colony of *Porites*. It may be advantageous for the coral to have high densities of worms like this within the colony; the

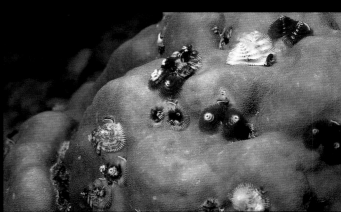

Some evidence from Australia suggests that polyps adjacent to Christmas Tree Worms (*Spirobranchus giganteus*, *above*) on a colony of *Porites* often survive predation by the Crown-of-Thorns Sea Star (*Acanthaster planci*). These remnant polyps can then asexually regenerate and recolonize the skeletal coral head after the seastar has moved on. Studies have shown that irritation of the seastar's tube feet and everted stomach discourages active feeding. In the presence of Crown-of-Thorns, Christmas Tree Worms will often re-emerge, causing their operculum and branchial crown to push against the tube feet and stomach of the Crown-of-Thorns, often causing it to leave that area of the colony. In addition, many *Spirobranchus* tubes are protected by a sharp horn (*left*), which, in concert with the other actions of the worm, could result in a ripping effect on the Crown-of-Thorns' exposed stomach, further discouraging contact. ⓣ

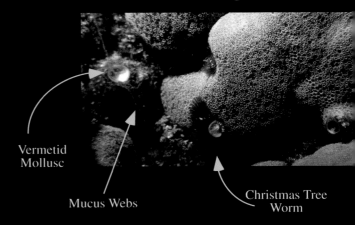

Vermetid Mollusc

Mucus Webs

Christmas Tree Worm

Though often mistaken for a worm, the Vermetid Mollusc (sometimes called a 'Cookie-Cutter Worm' for the cookie-cutter-like holes that the opening of the shell makes in unwary wader's hands and feet) is a form of solitary snail living inside the coral colony and whose shell emerges slightly above the level of the polyps. The shells of these mollusc's can also be observed growing on a variety of hard substrates in shallow water. Vermetids put out mucus webs which trap organic matter

CORAL AS A RECRUITING GROUND

I WANT YOU!

Reef Recruiting Station

Above: While in the plankton, many larval fish are transparent, soon after settling on the reef these animals start to acquire pigment.

Above: A recently recruited, larval Convex Pebble crab takes shelter among the rubble at the base of a coral head.

Because of their three-dimensional shapes, coral colonies can serve as important refuges for juvenile, mobile reef organisms such as fish, crustaceans and molluscs. Many of these animals begin their lives living a pelagic existence in the plankton. Based on settlement cues that are still not fully understood, they leave the plankton and settle (**recruit**) on the reef, often within the branches of a coral colony, or the rubble and shelter provided at its base. Given that such animals would be quickly preyed upon if they were out in the open, the shelter of the coral colony allows these organisms a refuge until they reach a size where they can roam around the reef with minimum risk of predation.

Such recruitment strategies raises interesting questions about what factors control the distribution and make-up of fish (and presumably mobile invertebrates) that are found on reefs...

Two major theories have been proposed to account for the make-up of fish on reefs. The 'Order Hypothesis' proposes that fish assemblages are stable over time, recruitment being controlled by factors present within the reef ecosystem itself. Based on this theory, the types and numbers of fish recruiting onto a reef should be highly ordered and stable over time. The 'Chaos Hypothesis' states that there is an overabundance of larval fish in the plankton; whichever ones recruit onto a particular coral head is purely chance (a "lottery"). This theory suggests that on the small scale, fish assemblages on reefs are

Above: Schools of juvenile fish often shelter among corals; measurements have shown that the amount of nutrients (ammonium, particulate nitrate and phosphate) excreted by the fish into the water is similar to the amounts from other sources. The structure of the coral colony's branches may impede the water flow long enough for the polyps to take up some of these

**Animals Associated with
Corals or Coral Colonies:**

CORAL ZITS!!!

What causes those small, round pink pimples seen occasionally on Finger Coral? It's actually a fish parasite...

Because of the altered polyps within a colony, the parasite gives the coral the appearance of having acne, hence the name "Coral Zits".

Preferentially feeds on infected colonies

Final Fish Host
example: *Chaetodon multicinctus*

Fecal transfer of parasite offspring

LIFE CYCLE OF THE PARASITIC TREMATODE
PODOCOTYLOIDES STENOMETRA

Initial Snail Host

The flatworm acts as a parasite on the snail (well, actually it castrates the snail).

"Yeah, I'd say that's a parasite..."

Podocotyloides stenometra (hmmm, perhaps 'coral zits' isn't such a bad name after all...) is thought to infect corals by chewing its way into coral polyps, where it encysts, living off its energy reserves. In such a state, infected coral colonies can experience up to a 50% decrease in colony growth!

Ⓣ

Intermediate Coral Host
Porites compressa

Often times infestations of *Porites* colonies are confused with other problems affecting corals (such as tumors, necrosis, etc.) since a common response of coral colonies to stress is the characteristic "pink" coloration seen in affected tissues.

(After Aeby, 1992)

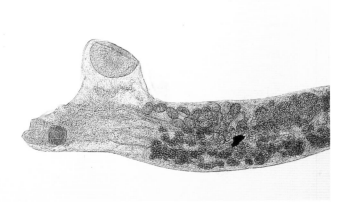

Greta Aeby

Above: Microscopic view of the digenetic trematode (fancy lingo meaning flatworm) parasite within its final host. Note the protruding ventral sucker adapted for holding onto the insides of a fish's intestinal tract, and the mass of eggs which will start the cycle all over again.

The parasite alters a colony's appearance by inducing swelling of polyp tissue, bleaching, and appearance of characteristic pink polyp coloration. Swelling prevents the polyp from easily retracting into its protective skeletal cup.

It's thought that this alteration of the intermediate coral-host facilitates transfer to the final corallivorous fish-host. Once the fish has selectively consumed the infected polyps, the colony will regenerate new uninfected polyps in their place, resulting in minimal long-term effect on the colony.

Trematodes are a member of the phylum Platyhelminthes (often called flatworms).

The colorful flatworms that you see out on top of reef flats are *Podocotyloides'* non-parasitic, free-living cousins.

SECTION III:

CORALS REEFS AS ECOSYSTEMS

Lisa Privitera

CORAL REEF TYPES

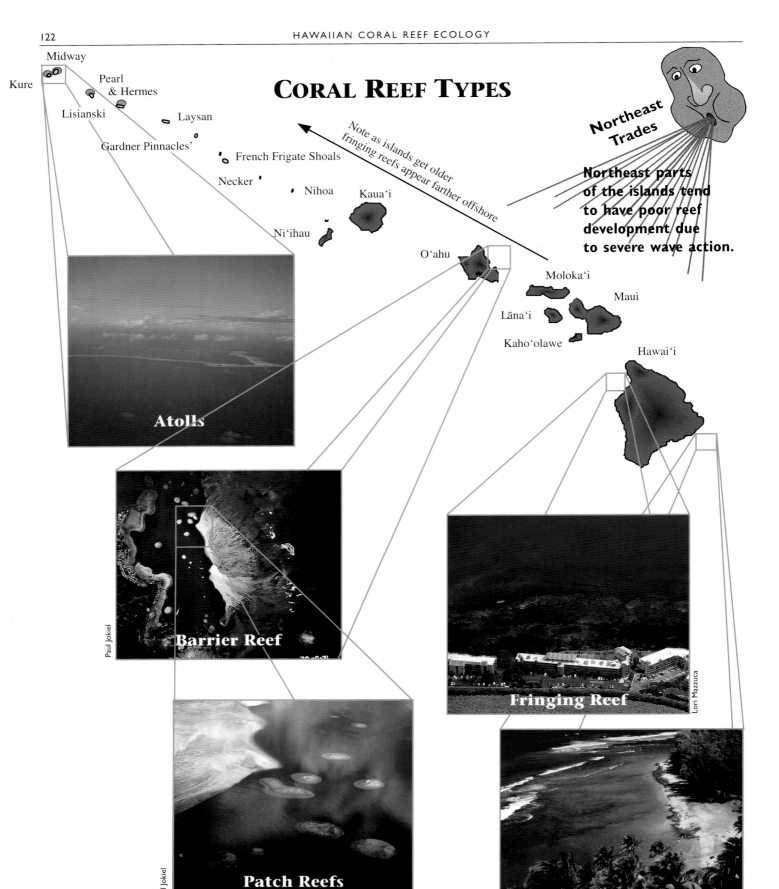

Note as islands get older fringing reefs appear farther offshore

Northeast Trades

Northeast parts of the islands tend to have poor reef development due to severe wave action.

Midway
Kure
Pearl & Hermes
Lisianski
Laysan
Gardner Pinnacles'
French Frigate Shoals
Necker
Nihoa
Kaua'i
Ni'ihau
O'ahu
Moloka'i
Maui
Lāna'i
Kaho'olawe
Hawai'i

Atolls

Barrier Reef

Paul Jokiel

Patch Reefs

Paul Jokiel

Fringing Reef

Lori Mazzuca

Reef Communities

Coral reefs can be classified into one of a number of discrete types, all of which occur within the Hawaiian Islands.

Reef Communities

A reef community is a non-structural reef composed of an assemblage (community) of non-connected, loose coral colonies. A **reef community** often represents the beginnings of a true coral reef or a habitat under intense disturbance where an actual fringing reef cannot develop.

Below: Reef communities can be seen in one form or another on nearly all of the main Hawaiian Islands, most often on highly exposed coastlines affected by constant disturbance. Additionally, reef communities are common on the youngest island: the Big Island (Hawai'i). In isolated areas, such communities may serve as the only refuge for a large number of different organisms; this community within a community is extremely fragile and very prone to disturbance by man.

Above: A small reef community in the South Pacific.

Over time, a reef community may cement itself together, growing upward and outward from the submerged slope of the island; eventually forming a fringing reef and reef flat...

Fringing Reefs

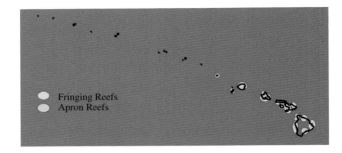

As coral colonies continue to grow and interact with other sessile organisms, a structural reef will appear directly offshore of sections of the island. Such a **fringing reef** includes an outwardly growing reef slope, a reef flat and may have channels cutting through it. Juvenile fringing reefs are often termed **apron reefs**; eventually a number of apron reefs grow together and form fringing reefs.

Fringing reefs are the most common type of reef seen in the Hawaiian Islands, being present on most of the main islands. The Big Island (Hawai'i) because of its relatively young age has very few fringing reefs, but a large assortment of apron reefs, especially along the Kona Coast. Well developed fringing reefs can be seen along the entire southern side of Moloka'i, parts of O'ahu, Kaua'i and Maui.

Most fringing reefs are made up of a reef slope (this is often where the highest amount of coral exists), a reef crest (where the highest energy zone is) and a reef flat (this area often has the lowest coral diversity and is usually the area most heavily impacted by runoff from the adjacent shoreline).

◄ Unlike many places in the Pacific, most of the reefs in Hawai'i are directly adjacent to shore; which along with our high population (roughly 1.4 million people; the highest in the Pacific next to Papua New Guinea) and limited land area, create situations where activities on shore can have tremendous impacts on the reef.

Paul Jokiel

Lori Mazzuca

Anatomy of a Fringing Reef:

A- Beach
B- Reef Flat
C- Reef Crest
D- Reef Slope
E- Sediment/Rubble
    Zone at Base
F- Calcareous
    Substrate
G- Original Volcanic
    Island Substrate

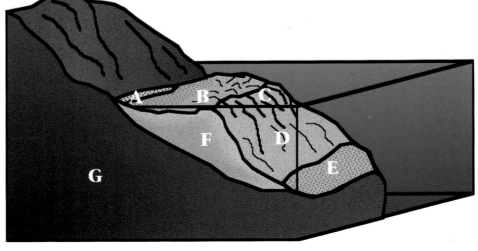

Barrier Reefs

As an island continues to erode away and sink, the fringing reefs will appear to move farther and farther offshore. Eventually a barrier reef will be formed, separating a relatively large body of water (a **lagoon**) from the offshore circulation.

Kāne'ohe Bay, O'ahu is one of the few places in the United States where one can see three different types of reef at one place. ▶

▼ The back and fore reef areas of a barrier reef.

Back Reef

Fore Reef

Paul Jokiel

Anatomy of a
Barrier Reef:

A- Back Reef
B- Fore Reef
C- Cay or Motu
   (rubble island)
D- Spur & Groove
E- Lagoon
F- Secondary Fringing
   Reef
G- Channel
H. Patch Reefs
I. Reef Slope
J. Calcareous Substrate
K. Original Volcanic
   Island Substrate

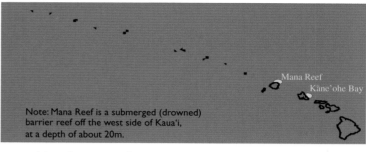

Note: Mana Reef is a submerged (drowned) barrier reef off the west side of Kaua'i, at a depth of about 20m.

Mana Reef
Kāne'ohe Bay

Most barrier reefs are formed as fringing reefs continue to grow while the adjacent shoreline erodes away. As such, barrier reefs lie along shorelines, just farther offshore than fringing reefs (some are more than 100 km (60 miles) from the shoreline!). The largest barrier reef in the world, the Great Barrier Reef off Australia, is more than 2000 km (1200 miles) long! Other major barrier reefs occur off of Belize (in the Caribbean), Fiji and New Caledonia.

In Hawai'i we have two known barrier reefs. The one off of Kāne'ohe Bay is not a true barrier reef in terms of how it was formed, but fits the bill in terms of its function. The barrier reef in Kāne'ohe Bay was formed back in the Holocene (more than 10,000 years ago) when a series of massive landslides removed a large part of the Ko'olau volcano into the sea. The exposed floor of the crater was colonized by corals and an emerging reef was born. As with barrier reefs seen elsewhere, secondary fringing reefs are found along the shorelines fronting Kāne'ohe Bay and patch reefs have formed within the lagoon (bay). Passes or channels are usually formed in the barrier reef that allow water to be exchanged between the lagoon and open ocean; Kāne'ohe Bay has two such channels.

Paul Jokiel

In general, barrier reefs tend to have much higher species diversity than fringing reefs. This may be due to the greater variation in habitat (channels, fore reef, back reef, lagoon, etc.), and a greater separation from the influences of adjacent land masses.

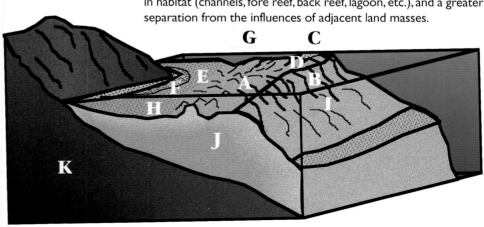

Atolls

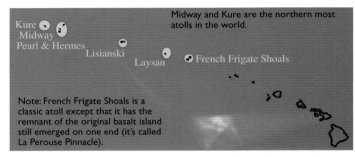

Midway and Kure are the northern most atolls in the world.

Kure
Midway
Pearl & Hermes Lisianski
Laysan French Frigate Shoals

Note: French Frigate Shoals is a classic atoll except that it has the remnant of the original basalt island still emerged on one end (it's called La Perouse Pinnacle).

If the coral reef surrounding the island grows at a rate equal to, or faster than, the sinking rate of the island - an atoll will be formed as the volcanic island sinks beneath the sea.

An **atoll** is a ring or horseshoe-shaped reef surrounding an isolated body of water, the **lagoon**. Of the 330 known atolls, all but 9 of them are in the Pacific and Indian Oceans. Atolls can range in size from over 2400 km² (that's roughly 1400 square miles for you non-metric types) for Kwajalein Atoll in the Marshall islands to less than a couple km² for a number of atolls in the Central Pacific.

Over time, storms will dislodge large chunks ▶ of reef substrate and wash them up onto the reef flat. Wave action will erode these into coarse calcareous sediments which will accumulate and form non-volcanic, flat islands called **Cays** or **Motus**.
As time progresses, vegetation may appear through transport by currents or birds. Highly-vegetated terrestrial ecosystems may appear over time. ▼

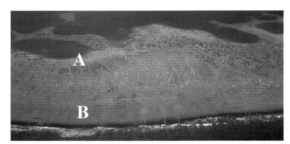

The outer edge of an atoll often consists of a well defined reef face, a reef flat and a back reef. Where trade winds are prevalent, one often sees distinct differences in both the width and species composition of these three areas. Windward sides, with their heavier wave action, tend to have more massive corals, often in well-developed spur-and-groove formations. The windward reef flat is frequently covered with a variety of coralline algae. The leeward sides of atolls are often more sheltered and thus tend to not have spur-and-groove formations making up the reef face; the reef flat tends to have fewer coralline algae and more corals then its windward counterpart.

Atolls often offer some of the most pristine of coral reef habitats; this is due primarily to the lack of land (and its associated impacts) near most of these structures. Major impacts on atolls include increasing human populations and the potential effects of a rising sea level.

Due to their low elevation, motus and cays are easily impacted by waves caused by storms and hurricanes. Associated with this is the concern of many island countries as to the effects of major industrial countries on global warming. Increased global temperatures could cause the partial melting of the polar ice caps resulting in increased sea level which would cause low elevation atoll nations, such as The Marshall Islands, to cease to exist.

Anatomy of an Atol:

A- Back Reef
B- Fore Reef
C- Cay or Motu (rubble island)
D- Vegetated Motu
E- Lagoon
F- Patch Reefs
G- Reef Slope
H. Calcareous Substrate
I. Original Volcanic Island Substrate

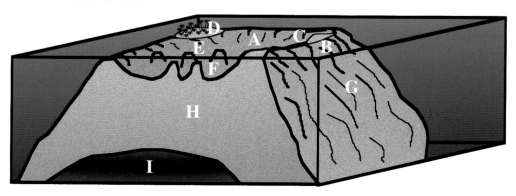

HAWAIIAN CORAL TIDBITS & TRIVIA

Coral Reefs:

- Cover 600,000 square kilometers (roughly 370,000 square miles) of the earth's surface.
- Comprise roughly 0.2% of the world's ocean, but provide 11% of the the world's fish harvest.
- Consist of four basic "types":
  - Patch Reefs - small, isolated coral reef formations
  - Fringing Reefs - large coral reef formations closely bordering a shoreline.
  - Barrier Reefs - a coral reef formation separated from the shore by a lagoon.
  - Atolls - a roughly ring-shaped group of coral reefs without volcanic islands.

LARGEST CORAL REEF

The Great Barrier Reef in Australia is roughly 2,300 kilometers long, making it the largest single biological feature on earth.

Richard Grigg

PRODUCTIVITY

Coral reefs are among the most productive ecosystems on the planet. Compared to open ocean in tropical waters, coral reefs are up to 100 times more productive (as in the production of organic carbon compounds, the basis for most life forms). Such high production rates allow coral reefs to support the great diversity of organisms that are found there. Some reefs may support a greater variety of organisms then the densest rainforest.

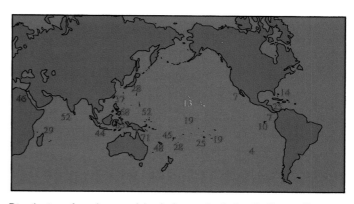

Distribution of coral genera (plural of genus, i.e. *Porites, Pocillopora, Montipora,* etc.) throughout the Indo-Pacific and Caribbean. Note how the diversity of coral genera decreases away from the center of diversity in the Southeast Asian-Northern Australian region (after Wood, 1983).

"CORAL" REEFS?

Most coral reefs are an assemblage of benthic organisms of which corals sometimes make-up a small fraction. Calcareous algae such as *Porolithon* serve to cement together much of the reeftop. Bryozoans and sponges fill cryptic and other spaces. As with corals, all serve as habitat for a wide range of organisms.

CORAL REEFS PAST AND PRESENT

Of the 7500 known species of coral, about 5000 species are extinct. Fossil coral reefs have been found in such unlikely places as the tops of mountain ranges and areas on the European continent. Often important hydrocarbon deposits (that's oil to you and me) are found adjacent to fossil reefs.

OLD: GEEZERS

Current evidence suggests that some massive coral colonies are over four hundred years old. Given the highly clonal nature of these corals, some scientists think such colonies may be functionally immortal.

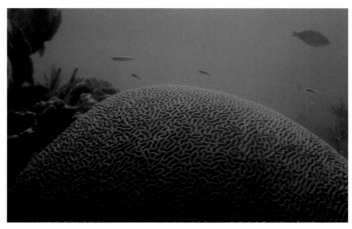

MAJOR FACTORS LIMITING THE OCCURRENCE

The need for light for their symbiotic plants is thought to limit reef-building corals to shallow, clear water.

LIGHT

If you look at the map above, you can see that coral reefs only occur between certain latitudes, and then only within certain areas. What major factors limit where coral reefs can be found?

Since most corals are sessile organisms, they require a hard substrate to attach to. Soft substrates such as sandy or muddy bottoms cannot support coral reefs.

Most of the world's oceans lie in relatively deep water, where light levels are too low for zooxanthellae photosynthesis.

TEMPERATURE

The above map shows that coral reefs are limited to areas within 20° north or south of the equator, within which temperatures rarely go below 18°C. Studies have shown that most reefs tend to grow well between temperatures of 23 - 25°C. Note that even within the 20° latitudes, reefs are absent off the coast of South America where upwelling and cold currents moving northward are a constant feature.

OF CORAL REEFS GLOBALLY

SALINITY

Areas such as the Persian Gulf have coral reefs existing in salinities as high as 42 parts per thousand.

The majority of coral reefs are found in areas with salinities between 32 - 35 parts per thousand. Areas with river mouths, such as the Mississippi Delta or Amazon Delta, are devoid of coral reefs due to the huge volumes of fresh water and sediments discharged.

OUTCOMPETED BY OTHER SESSILE INVERTEBRATES

Areas of high nutrients, etc. allow other sessile organisms such as macroalgae or sponges to outcompete corals for space.

SEDIMENTS

Sediments tend to smother corals and clog their feeding structures; they also serve to reduce the light available for the symbiotic zooxanthellae.

Too Cold!!!

Too Cold!!!

70
60
50
40
30
20
10
0
10
20
30
40
50
60

KEY
 Major river mouths
Areas with major coral reefs
- - - Limits of 20° isotherm

40   60   80   100   120   140   160   180   160   140   120   100   80   60   40   20

THE DARWIN POINT

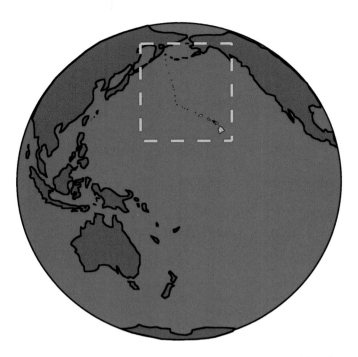

As tropical volcanic islands slowly sink beneath the surface (due to erosional processes and subsidence), coral reefs often arise around their edges, eventually forming atolls after the island disappears. Yet if one continues to follow the trail of hot spot islands formed over the Hawaiian Hotspot one soon notices that there are no further living reefs after Kure, only submerged flat-topped guyots and seamounts. Why should this be the case? As the Pacific Plate carries Hawaiian reefs towards the northwest (at a blistering rate of 10 cm/year), the growth rate of the dominant reef-building corals decreases to a point where reef accretion (growth) can't keep up with the sinking and erosional rates. This point is presently thought to occur roughly around 29° North of the equator for the Hawaiian Archipelago and has been named the Darwin Point after Charles Darwin who first described atoll formation back in 1836.

The Darwin Point is thought to occur roughly where Kure Atoll (*right*) currently sits. The growth rate of corals on the atoll is so slow (roughly 0.2 mm/yr for *Porites lobata*), reefs are beginning to "drown".

A coral reef (or atoll) is said to be "drowned" when the level of reef growth is less than the sinking and erosional rates. This low growth rate comes about due to insufficient light and/or the surface water being too cool. This leads to the surface growth rate being insufficient to match the change in sea level, with the end result being the death of the entire reef and the eventual formation of a guyot or seamount.

Richard Grigg

CNIDOQUESTION: Which country is closest to the first Hawaiian island?

THE LIFE AND DEATH OF A HAWAIIAN CORAL REEF:

The time line below goes back 250 million years and traces the origins of the Hawaiian islands. Archipelago; and it shows what happens to those reefs over time. Also note that it places the age of

Planula larvae begin to settle on new lava flow

Reef-building corals die-off

Fringing Reef
Apron Reef

Barrier Reef

Atoll

0	100	1000	1,000,000	5,000,000	10,000,000	

Hawai'i   Mau'i   Moloka'i   O'ahu   Kaua'i   French Frigate Shoals   Kure

Average Human Lifespan   Origin of Humans (Note: Only 1/10 of 1% the age of the origin of corals)   Origin of the Great Apes

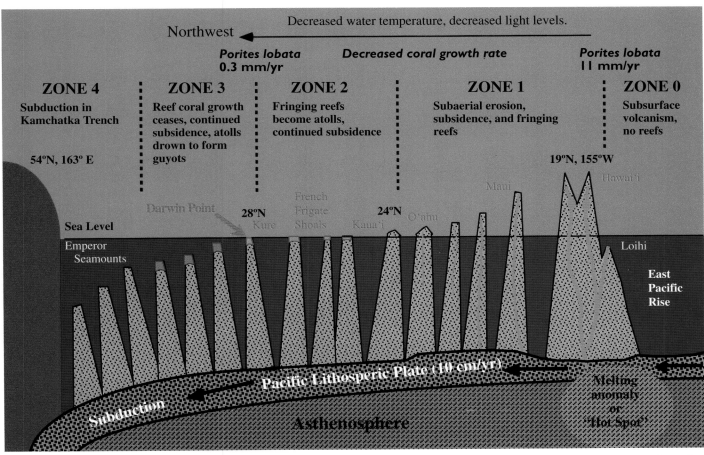

Decreased water temperature, decreased light levels.

Northwest ←

Porites lobata
0.3 mm/yr   *Decreased coral growth rate*   *Porites lobata*
                                                           11 mm/yr

ZONE 4   **ZONE 3**   **ZONE 2**   **ZONE 1**   **ZONE 0**

Subduction in   Reef coral growth   Fringing reefs   Subaerial erosion, Subsurface
Kamchatka Trench   ceases, continued   become atolls,   subsidence, and   volcanism,
                   subsidence, atolls continued subsidence fringing   no reefs
                   drown to form   reefs
54°N, 163° E   guyots   19°N, 155°W

Darwin Point   French   24°N   Maui   Hawai'i
                28°N   Frigate   O'ahu
Sea Level   Kure   Shoals   Kaua'i   Loihi
Emperor
Seamounts   East
                                                                               Pacific
                                                                               Rise

Pacific Lithosperic Plate (10 cm/yr) ←

Subduction   Melting
                                                                           anomaly
                        Asthenosphere   or
                                                                           "Hot Spot"

The above diagram depicts the island and reef history of the Hawaiian Archipelego as it moves along with the Pacific Plate towards the Northwest and the subduction area near the Kamchatka Trench. Each zone represents a stage in a volcanic island's existence; the light green color represents reef growth. Note the location of the Darwin Point separating zones 2 & 3; from this point southeast to French Frigate Shoals most of the islands and shoals are calcareous (composed primarily of reef-derived materials). If it weren't for living corals, the Hawaiian Archipelago would be about half of its current length of 2,450 km, due to erosion and submergence (Diagram modified after Grigg, 1982, copyright Springer-Verlag. Used with permission).

Roughly 20 other hotspot "trails" (chains of emerged or submerged islands, guyots and seamounts) have been identified in the world's oceans; Samoa, Tahiti and the Cook Islands all are thought to have arisen from separate hotspot anomalies.

The Hawaiian Archipelago, because of its active volcanism, isolation and linear progression, represents a near perfect textbook example of the life and times of both islands and reefs.

> **CNIDOQUESTION:** Some of the Emperor Seamounts have no evidence of coral reefs on them, any ideas why?

It shows how many years scientists think it takes for various types of reefs to form in the Hawaiian reefs and corals in context with that of humans.

Drowned Atoll   Guyot   Subduction

50,000,000   100,000,000   250,000,000
                                                              Oldest
                                                              Known
                                                              Coral Reefs

Time (years)

SUCCESSION, DISTURBANCE AND DIVERSITY

Like most ecosystems, coral reefs change naturally over time. Scientists who study natural processes on reefs have come up with a number of theories concerning processes that may contribute to the complexity and stability of a reef ecosystem:

Succession:

In new environments (such as a recent underwater lava flow) one does not immediately see a coral reef start to emerge; instead a number of colonizing species establish footholds. Over time, the community that they form starts to be replaced as other organisms are able to settle and survive among the cover that the original settlers created. This replacement of one community of organisms by another is termed **ecological succession**. In Hawai'i, examples of colonizing species of coral include many of the *Pocillopora* species and *Porites lobata*. **Successionist species** would be those that can only survive on developed reefs (not bare substrates), and include many of the other non-dominantcorals in Hawai'i.

> We have no examples of what a climax stage of reef development would look like.

New Lava Flow

New Reef Substrate

Old Lava Flow

Old Reef Substrate

Time

Colonizing Stage **Successionist Stage** **Climax Stage**

So which factors govern change? As time goes on, the colonizing species alter the environment making it more favorable for settlement by successionist species. In turn, as resources change, the colonizing species are out-competed and replaced by other species and the emerging reef becomes more complex; presumably at some point, a state of equilibrium will be reached where very little change occurs (the climax stage) and the ecosystem is stable (that is, the chance of extinction is low). At least that was the theory, and to some extent it seemed to hold up; new substrates were colonized and **diversity** (the number of species within a set area) increased as reefs became more complex. Yet as these systems become more complex, competition would increase and scientists began to question where among the various stages would diversity be the highest (many people view a diverse ecosystem as being healthier and more desirable then a less diverse one; though this may not always be the case).

LOW DIVERSITY OF FISHES **HIGH DIVERSITY OF FISHES**

What soon became apparent was that in the absence of **disturbance** (an event in time that brings about change to an ecosystem) a few species of coral would often come to dominate the ecosystem as a result of competition between coral species for resources. With lack of disturbance, those coral species that became dominant within an ecosystem were often the ones that could best out-compete other species for the limited resources available.

Disturbances can be either long-term or short-term, direct or indirect, continuous or rare. With the exception of short-term, rare disturbances, one often sees dominant coral species emerging even in the presence of disturbances. In this case the dominant corals are often those species that can best deal with the stresses brought on by the disturbance.

"Whew, this is getting confusing..."

"Here, let's look on the next page for some examples"

Case 1: No Disturbance
[Competitive Exclusion Model]:

As time goes on following initial settlement on a new substrate, organisms replace each other and the emerging reef becomes more complex; often the colonial species are replaced or eliminated by successionist species. Lacking environmental change, both direct and indirect competition between corals (and between corals and other sessile organisms such as algae and sponges) soon results in a few dominant species that make up the majority of the coral cover. Obviously such a situation will eventually result in lower species diversity. Examples of reefs in this situation are rare but conceivably would include highly protected patch reefs within lagoons or unusually protected bays. Note that this view entails an idea of **scale** (that is, the length of time involved between disturbances - i.e., is it on a daily, monthly-, yearly-, decade-long or century-long scale? No disturbance in this case would mean lack of a major disturbance to the ecosystem is on a scale greater than that for robust reef growth - often on a time frame of decades to centuries).

Case 2: Occasional Strong Disturbance
[Intermediate Disturbance Model]:

Hurricanes and strong storm surge occur infrequently enough in many areas to allow reefs to flourish; yet when they do occur they appear to be devastating, wiping out large sections of reef that may take hundreds of years to return. Hurricane Iwa in 1986 wiped out a number of reefs along the Wai'anae Coast of O'ahu and around Kaua'i. A number of scientists feel that such storms may be important for coral reefs in the same way that natural forest fires are important for certain types of forests. The storms wipe out large sections of the reef, and with it the dominant corals: In essence, resetting the playing field and opening up settlement space for corals that normally would not be able to survive amongst the dominant species.

Such storms have their greatest effects on exposed fringing and barrier reefs; but even in protected bays they can have an impact, breaking up dominant branching corals and creating open space for non-dominant corals to gain a foothold. This reshuffling of the species' deck of cards often provides for the highest number of species, since under such circumstances diversity would be enhanced by occasional disturbances; that is, dominant species would not be allowed to reach competitive exclusion. Note that after each disturbance there will be a recovery period during which larval recruitment will play a major role (along with competition) in determining the new make-up of the reef.

Case 3: Constant Strong Disturbance
[Colonial Model]:

Some reefs are constantly exposed to recurring disturbance creating continuous forms of environmental stress. Certain coral species (due to their morphology, physiology, behavior, etc.) are better adapted to survive within these forms of environmental stress. Curiously, these frequently are represented by the colonizing species (such species are often characterized by having high numbers of larvae, fast growth rates, and are often very plastic in their morphology). The end result is a reef with low diversity (though low diversity does not necessarily mean low coral cover; a reef may have only one or two species of coral but those species could cover 95% of the available substrate).

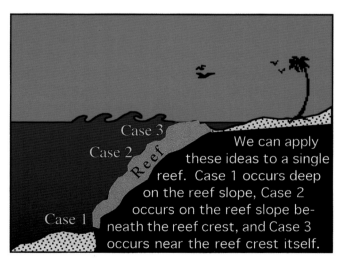

We can apply these ideas to a single reef. Case 1 occurs deep on the reef slope, Case 2 occurs on the reef slope beneath the reef crest, and Case 3 occurs near the reef crest itself.

Deep portions of a reef would be exposed very rarely to environmental disturbance; which, combined with low-light, results in very few coral species present. The reef slope receives occasional disturbance (storm waves & surge) resulting in high species diversity. The reef crest receives continuous disturbance resulting in low diversity of corals adapted to this high-energy zone.

CORAL REEF GROWTH AND SUCCESSIONAL DEVELOPMENT:
CASE STUDY: THE BIG ISLAND

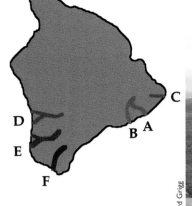

The Hawaiian Islands erupted out of the middle of the Pacific atop volcanoes which created new substrate for organisms to colonize...from these fiery beginnings arose the variety of reefs that surround the Hawaiian Islands today.

Back in the early 1970's, two scientists from the University of Hawai'i, Richard Grigg and James Maragos, set out to describe the development and succession of Hawaiian reefs. Up to that point, studies of these events had primarily been done with terrestrial and coastal species whose habitats could be easily manipulated, but how do you work with organisms such as corals whose life histories span multiple human generations? The answer lay on the developing island of Hawai'i where well-dated lava flows allowed "snapshots" in time of the succession of corals involved in Hawaiian reef development.

3 month old lava flow

A. Three month old lava flow. No visible coral colonies present, primarily diatomaceous slime.

10 year old lava flow

B. Ten year old lava flow supporting a coral colony roughly ten years old.

15 year old lava flow

C. Fifteen year old lava flow. Coral cover is almost entirely *Pocillopora meandrina*; a fugitive species often found colonizing such flows.

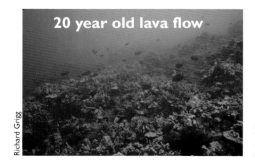
20 year old lava flow

D. Twenty year old lava flow. Reef is made up of 12 species of corals, almost 100% coral cover.

40 year old lava flow

E. Forty-four year old lava flow. At this point coverage is primarily *Porites compressa* and *Porites lobata*.

100 year old lava flow

F. A hundred year old lava flow in a relatively undisturbed area. This very developed reef is almost 100% *Porites compressa*.

Since most reefs in the Hawaiian Islands are over a 100 years old, why don't you see primarily *Porites compressa* reefs throughout the chain?

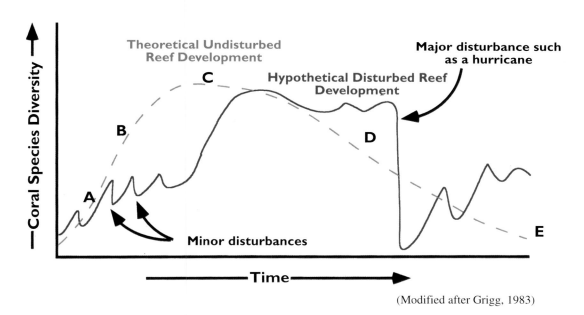

(Modified after Grigg, 1983)

Because of occasional large scale disturbances such as major hurricanes and smaller disturbances such as seasonal storms, Hawaiian reefs are constantly being reset to various earlier stages of development. The diagram above was developed by Dr. Grigg to show these concepts. Compare the Theoretical Undisturbed Reef Development graph (red dashed line) with the Hypothetical Disturbed Reef Development graph (blue solid line), what do they tell you in terms of time to development of a climax stage? What about levels of diversity? What might the letters **A** and **B** represent? How about **C**? At what point on these graphs might a situation of competitive exclusion occur (say of a reef made-up almost entirely of *Porites compressa*)? Where on these graphs do you see examples of intermediate disturbance occurring? If

you were to look at your favorite snorkeling or diving reef, where would it occur on these graphs?

By extending these ideas further, we can look at the ages of the islands to get some idea as to how long it took to form different types of reefs in Hawai'i. Apron reefs such as those found off the island of Hawai'i take only a 100 years or so to form. Fringing reefs (such as those seen off Kawaihae on the island of Hawai'i) can take anywhere from 100 to 1000 years to form. The youngest true Barrier Reef is found off the island of Kaua'i which is 5 - 7 million years old; while the first atoll (French Frigate Shoals) is 11.7 million years old. Obviously, well-developed coral reefs are truly ancient structures.

THE RAINFOREST
CORAL REEFS AND RAINFORESTS ARE SIMILAR IN MANY WAYS:

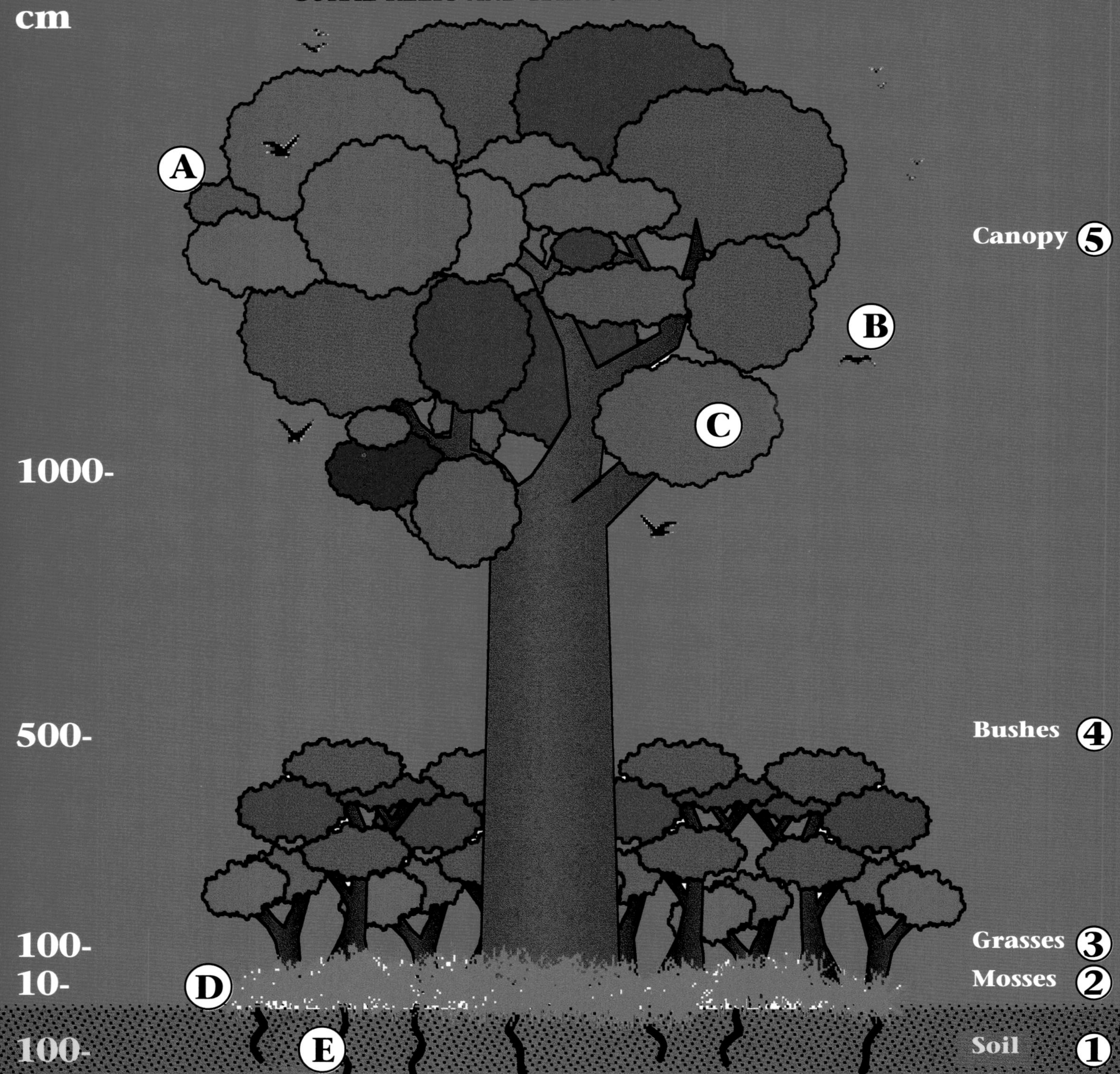

cm

A

Canopy 5

B

C

1000-

500-

Bushes 4

D

100-
10-

Grasses 3

Mosses 2

E

Soil 1

Both rainforests and coral reefs can be divided into discrete layers (1 - 5) which often serve similar functions and vary primarily in scale; with a coral reef being roughly 1/10th the vertical scale of a rainforest. Both are characterized by warm, moist environments (ok, the reefs take the moisture angle to an extreme...). The soil layer 1 of the rainforest, like the hard carbonate substrate of the reef, supports a vast array of boring and bioeroding organisms. The moss layer, like the encrusting algal layer 2 of the reef, tends to be very thin (a few cm) but is very important in providing initial substrate for settlement of larger plants and corals. Grasses in a rainforest 3 are analogous to a great variety of small coral heads, mushroom corals, seaweeds and bryozoans seen on the reef. The bushes and small trees create a dense undergrowth much like

the massive and small branching coral colonies seen on the reef 4. Just as in a forest, all layers of a coral reef are infested with a variety of boring and bioeroding organisms. In addition, like the obligate ant mutualists seen with certain species of *Acacia* trees, branching corals tend to have a variety of crabs and shrimps which are thought to be mutualistic symbionts.

Both ecosystems are full of highly complex three dimensional structures. In both cases, most of the energy/nutrients reside not in the soil or substrate, but in and around the three-dimensional structures themselves; this in turn supports a great diversity of organisms in a relatively small amount of space, making these systems the most ecologically complex on the planet.

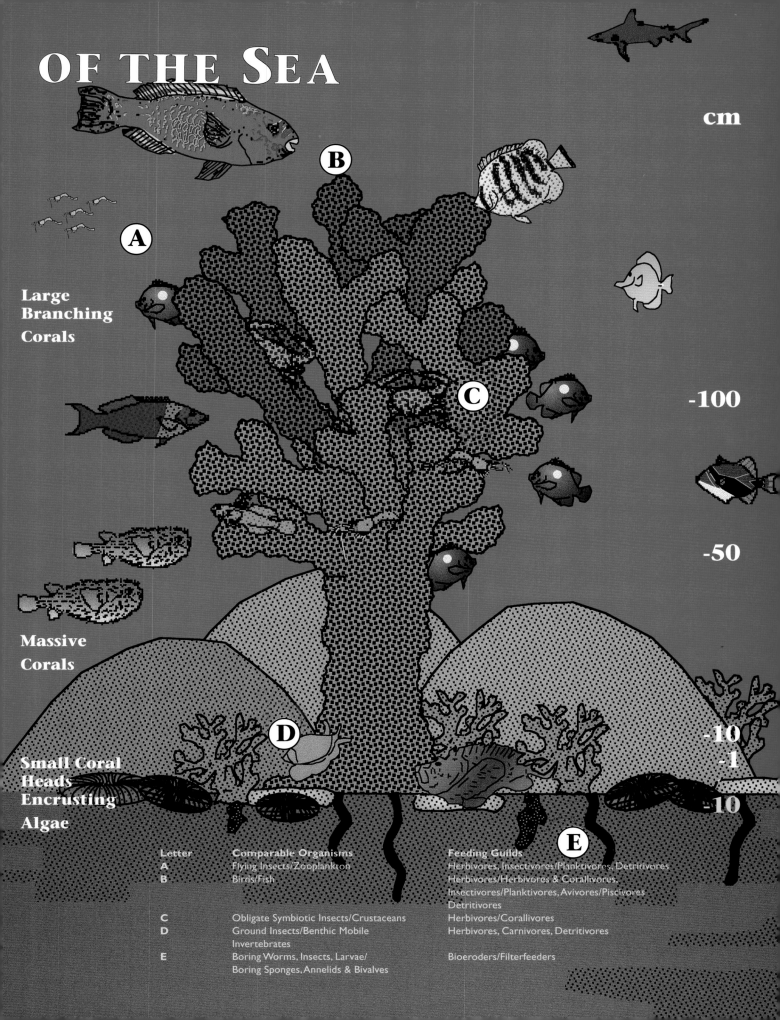

OF THE SEA

cm

Large
Branching
Corals

-100

-50

Massive
Corals

-10
-1
-10

Small Coral
Heads
Encrusting
Algae

Letter	Comparable Organisms	Feeding Guilds
A	Flying Insects/Zooplankton	Herbivores, Insectivores/Planktivores, Detritivores
B	Birds/Fish	Herbivores/Herbivores & Corallivores, Insectivores/Planktivores, Avivores/Piscivores Detritivores
C	Obligate Symbiotic Insects/Crustaceans	Herbivores/Corallivores
D	Ground Insects/Benthic Mobile Invertebrates	Herbivores, Carnivores, Detritivores
E	Boring Worms, Insects, Larvae/ Boring Sponges, Annelids & Bivalves	Bioeroders/Filterfeeders

CORAL IMPOSTERS!

Heinz-Gert deCouet

Coral reefs are made-up of a variety of clonal organisms that are attached to the substrate. Many of these organisms resemble corals to some extent; all of them are important contributors to providing three-dimensional habitat within the reef ecosystem.

The phylum Bryozoa ("Moss animals") contains a large number of colonial species which can lay down calcareous skeletons similar to corals. Lacking symbiotic zooxanthellae they are usually found in areas where they are not competing for space with reef-building corals. Bryozoans are suspension feeders, gathering their food through a retractable structure termed a **lophophore**. The lophophore consists of a horseshoe-shaped group of cilia-bearing tentacles which capture and transport food to the mouth and gut.

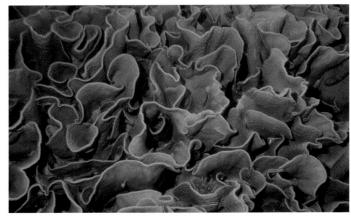

A healthy rugose-shaped coral colony and a similar-shaped bryozoan colony, both in the South Pacific (can you tell which is which?).

Below: A Lace Bryozoan colony (*Reteporellina denticulata*). This bryozoan is frequently found growing underneath ledges or in caves protected from heavy water flow. It is extremely fragile and easily breaks apart.

Deborah Gochfeld

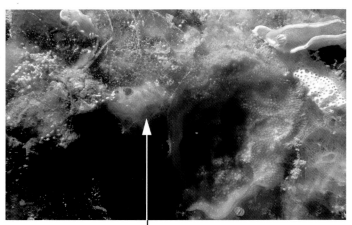

Above: An encrusting bryozoan common to ledges. As elsewhere on the reef, space is at a premium and is often filled with an assortment of sponges, tunicates and bryozoans. Certain dorid nudibranchs specialize on feeding on bryozoan colonies.

Calcareous Algae

It's a plant!!!

Keoki Stender

Above: What appears to be a small coral colony is in fact a calcareous alga called *Porolithon gardineri.* Note the lack of calices and polyps. The same factors that help to shape the form of a coral colony may function in a similar way with calcareous algae.

Calcareous algae serve an important role in cementing together loose rubble and reef material.

Right: Many calcareous algae serve as important food sources for a number of grazing/scraping herbivores (animals that feed on plant material) such as urchins and fish (see pp. 161-162).

Marc Rice

Keoki Stender

Keoki Stender

Above: The stuff that looks like purple or pink cement painted atop the reef and rubble is actually a type of alga that, similar to a coral, has a very hard, calcareous structure. The flat, plate-like forms are also calcareous algae (based on what you've learned about corals, where would you expect to find such algae growing?).

Left: Halimeda is an important component of sand in many reef areas. Sometime, take a look at sand particles under a hand lens. You may be amazed and surprised!

Sponges come in a variety of

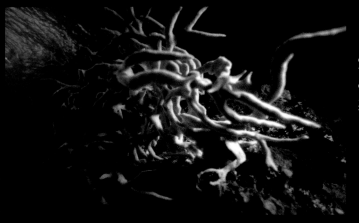

Lisa Privitera

Heinz-Gert deCouet

Shapes,

Heinz- Gert deCouet

Heinz-Gert deCouet

Colors,

and
Sizes.

Heinz-Gert deCouet

All are important
components of the reef...

Even dead sponges add to the
framework of the reef (right)

Heinz-Gert deCouet

Sponges

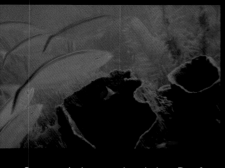

Unlike the South Pacific or the Caribbean, where sponges can sometimes dwarf corals (both in size and area of coverage), sponges in Hawai'i tend to be primarily cryptic on the reefs. They are most easily seen under overhangs, under rubble and in calm bays where they're frequently seen growing under piers and docks.

Sponges belong to the phylum Porifera and are among the most simply-constructed animals (in terms of tissue-types and body systems) found on coral reefs. Most sponges are filter feeders, taking in water through small holes in their structures, filtering out nutrients and expelling the filtered water through larger openings (called **oscula**). The "spongy" material that makes up their structure is often supported by loose skeletal fragments called **spicules**; these fragments can be made of silica or carbonate. Being loosely embedded in the structure they easily come out and into the fingers of those people commonly termed "foolish sponge squeezers"; the sensation is irritatingly familiar to playing with loose fiberglass. It should be noted that most sponges are extremely fragile and tear easily. Additionally, something as simple as a snorkelor lifting a sponge out of the water to show to a friend will often do irreparable harm to the sponge as its internal cavities collapse under their own weight without the support of an aqueous medium. As with most marine organisms, it's best to observe, not disturb.

(Above and Above Left) Sponges are important competitors for space with sessile cnidarians. Some sponges contain symbiotic single-celled plants (much like zooxanthellae) and must compete for open space with hermatypic corals. Most of the species found in Hawai'i tend to occur in low-light environments, where they would be expected to compete with ahermatypic corals and bryozoans.

(Below & left) One of the primary predators on sponges are dorid nudibranchs which feed on the sponge and often incorporate the sponge's chemical defenses into their own tissues.

Example of a spicule

Because of their complex, three-dimensional structures, sponges often serve as habitats for a wide variety of organisms.

CORAL ODDITIES

Someone once described corals as being very "plastic" in nature; that is, having this amazing ability due to their lack of physiological complexity (basically just a wonderful stomach with a mouth and tentacles), to assume a wide variety of shapes and forms. Such plasticity has allowed many coral species to adapt to a wide variety of environmental situations in which more physiologically complex organisms would not have been able to survive. Plasticity has also brought about some unusual phenomena:

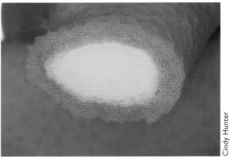 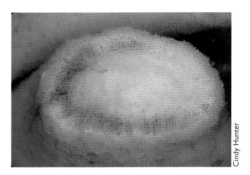

Cross-sections of healthy and "dead" Finger Coral (*Porites compressa*); note that on the "dead" coral living tissue exists beneath the dead exterior.

Multiple Regeneration:

Most coral colonies have the ability to regenerate over areas where polyps have been lost; but *Fungia scutaria*, a solitary free-living coral, has the ability to regenerate from fragments of itself. Occasionally these fragments will form multiple mouths; in essence, becoming a colonial solitary organism! The ability to form new individuals from a fragment of a single parent would be of prime importance to a free-living species exposed to occasional wave- and surge- damage; it possibly could even function as a unusual form of asexual reproduction. Yet what might be the function of a solitary coral with two or more mouths? The fact that these are rare in the field suggests that they are an unusual, occasional byproduct of the ability to regenerate from fragments. Additional research on this phenomena may shed some light on what initiates and controls regeneration of tissues; such knowledge could prove to be invaluable in the medical fields of tissue grafting, burn treatments and wound management.

The Phoenix was a bird from mythology that burned itself to ashes after having lived for 500 years. It then rose up youthfully out of the ashes to live again.

The Phoenix Phenomena:

Often a coral (or coral colony) is thought to be dead when the tissue has sloughed off leaving behind a white skeleton which is quickly grown over by algae. Scientists and researchers use this as a way to gauge mortality both in the lab and on the reef. Finger coral (*Porites compressa*) is a **perforate** coral whose tissue extends deep within the skeleton. Studies have shown that when *Porites compressa* is exposed to extreme stress (exposure to air, heat, freshwater, heavy sediments, etc.) it appears to die off just like most corals; after a short period of time, however, the tissue will start to slough off and leave behind bare skeleton. Yet *Porites* (*above*) and *Fungia* (*left*), like the mythological Phoenix, can sometimes rise from the dead. If the "dead" skeleton is placed back into a clean, normal reef environment, coral will re-appear on its old, bare skeleton just like the Phoenix rising from its ashes. Studies have shown that this tissue is from the original coral, and is not resettlement by coral larvae or from adjacent colonies. Because of its perforate nature, there is often tissue deep within the calcareous skeleton that's still living even when the external surface appears completely dead. Such an adaptation may help to explain both *Porites compressa*'s dominance in certain reef areas around the Hawaiian Islands and also why it was one of the fastest corals to recover in Kāne'ohe Bay after sewage disposal was diverted from the bay (see p. 190).

Corals that rise from the dead...

USE OF NON-LIVING SUBSTRATE

Actually, that's a misnomer, since very little of reef substrate is non-living. What this refers to instead, is how the majority of cracks, crevices and internal space is used for shelter by a wide variety of organisms representing both long- and short-term tenants.

▶ Wave action, lava tubes, bioerosion all contribute to large scale internal spaces within a reef. Often these spaces are used by a variety of sessile organisms that filter feed, and by an assortment of fish seeking shelter. On a smaller scale, vacated calices become home for a variety of micro-inhabitants and bacteria which are increasingly recognized as playing one or more important roles in the cycling and production of nutrients to support the coral reef ecosystem. ▼

Over thirty phyla are known from coral reefs (only four phyla are not represented), making coral reefs the most diverse ecosystem on earth.

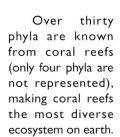

Most of these phyla have representatives that make use of non-living spaces for shelter. How many animals can you think of that shelter in these spaces?

Divers who tend to explore these non-living spaces are often termed "Grub Divers" . While grub diving is extremely rewarding in terms of the many discoveries to be found in many of these holes and crevices, one must be extremely careful not to disturb the wide range of burrows, colonies, mating areas, food sources, sleeping spots, and sheltering areas found there.

The Spiny Lobster

A number of large invertebrates make use of non-living substrate (holes and small caverns) in the reef structure; here we consider just two of them:

Lobsters

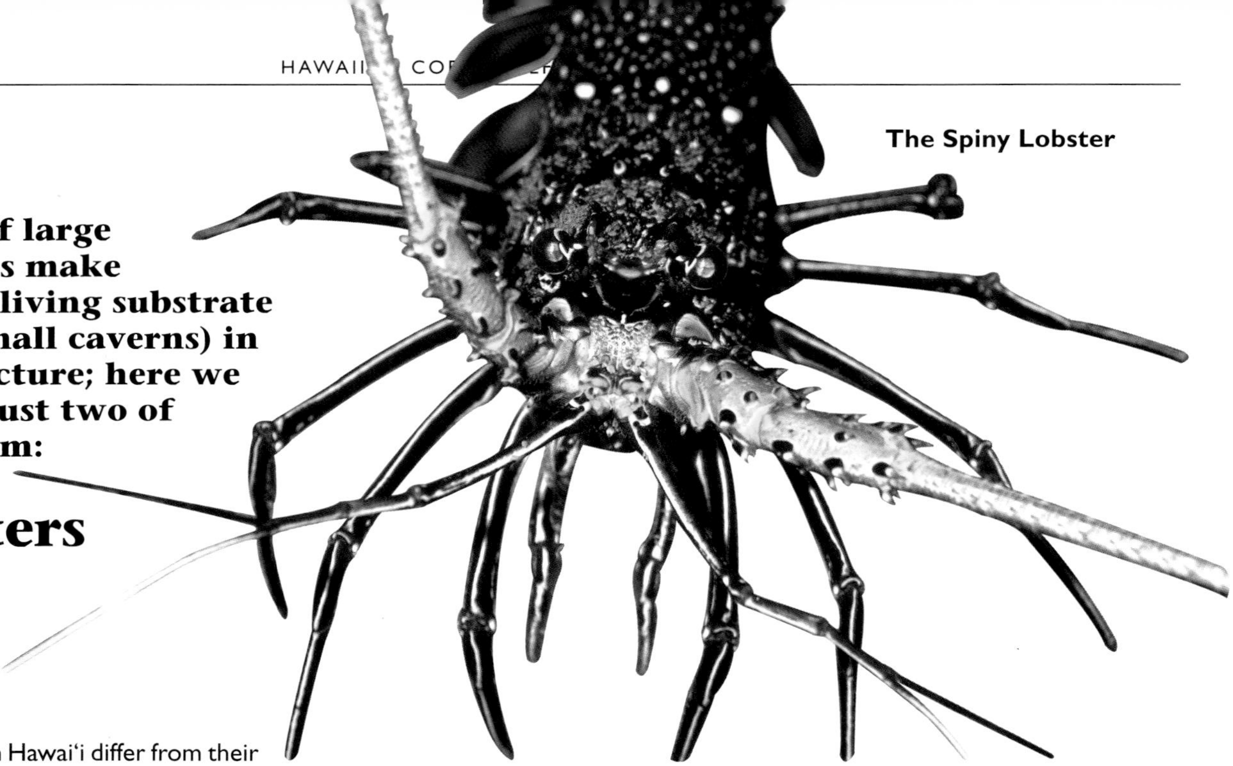

Most lobsters in Hawai'i differ from their Maine cousins by lacking large claws and by possessing a leathery, flexible tail fan.

In Hawai'i we have three basic types of lobster: Spiny Lobsters (3 species), Slipper Lobsters (over 5 species) and the Red Reef Lobster (2 species, see p. 114).

Most lobsters are nocturnal scavengers, spending the daylight hours safely hidden in caves and crevices. Nowadays it's becoming rare to find lobsters in any areas frequented by divers or snorkelors.

In the Caribbean, a species of Spiny Lobster (*Panulirus argus*) is known to form long, single file migratory chains with each lobster using its antennae to keep in contact with the next. Hundreds of lobsters move from shallow to deeper waters every autumn. Scientists aren't sure what causes these mass migrations, but some feel it may be a way of avoiding the effects of winter storms.

Slipper lobsters, because of their shape and coloring, are often difficult to find among the cracks and crevices on the reef. They have strongly reduced antenna and, unlike the Spiny Lobsters, do not seem to congregate in holes during the day.

In general, lobsters will retreat further into their holes when threatened. An exception to this has been noted with some species in the presence of an octopus: the lobsters will often abandon their holes and swim away; unlike most predators, the octopus would presumably have little difficulty reaching the lobster even in the deepest crevice. Interestingly, this has led some to believe that this may help explain why in some areas one can often find spiny lobsters sharing holes with moray eels. An octopus (like certain unfortunate divers) in search of a lobster dinner may find itself getting chomped by the eel. Evidence for such a loose symbiosis between lobster and eel includes observations of moray eels being attracted by the aggitated spiny lobster rubbing its antennae together.

Lobsters have some limited protection in the State of Hawai'i:

- Both Slipper and Spiny Lobsters are not allowed to be collected during their breeding season (May through August).
- Pre-adult lobsters under 3.25" (carapace length) are protected from collection in the main Hawaiian Islands.
- It is illegal to spear or mutilate a lobster; or to collect any bearing eggs. All collected lobsters must be whole.

Even with these restrictions, it's getting harder to find natural concentrations of lobsters in the main Hawaiian Islands. As with a number of other reef organism populations, the problem seems to be primarily with a lack of enforcement of the current laws and too many people collecting too many animals (overfishing).

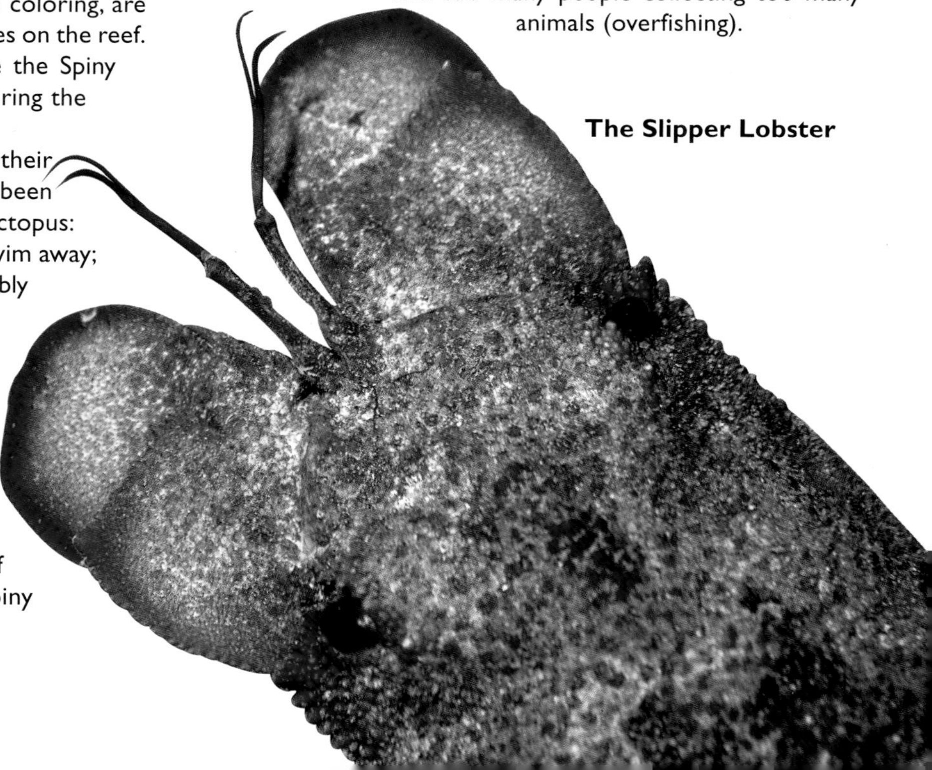

The Slipper Lobster

Octopus

Most people know what an octopus looks like, yet few people see them on the reef, even when they're sitting right in front of them! Octopuses are capable of varying their body coloration, often blending themseleves in with the background substrate.

On the reef an octopus' den can easily be discerned by the numerous shell fragments strewn around the outside; often the resident himself is nearby hunting for a meal. After grabbing its prey, the octopus uses its hard beak to break open mollusc shells and assorted decapods (crabs, shrimps and lobsters).

Octopuses are among the most intelligent of reef animals, showing the ability to learn complex behaviors in the laboratory. These animals, along with their close relatives, have evolved an eye that is considered by many scientists to be more complex then the human eye...hmmm, maybe there's more to these guys then just tako poke, huh?

Above: Surprised by the photographer, this octopus has just turned dark in preparation to flee. Moments after this photo was taken, the photographer was rewarded with a cloud of black ink enveloping him and his camera.

CNIDOQUESTION: Why do octopus often turn dark just prior to releasing their ink?

When threatened, octopus often release a condensed cloud of ink; some of the possible functions of which include:
1. Decoy predator away from octopus.
2. Stick to predator's eyes - blinding.
3. Clog predator's nares (nostrils) and taste buds - can't smell or chemically detect.
4. Clog gills - inhibits chasing ability.

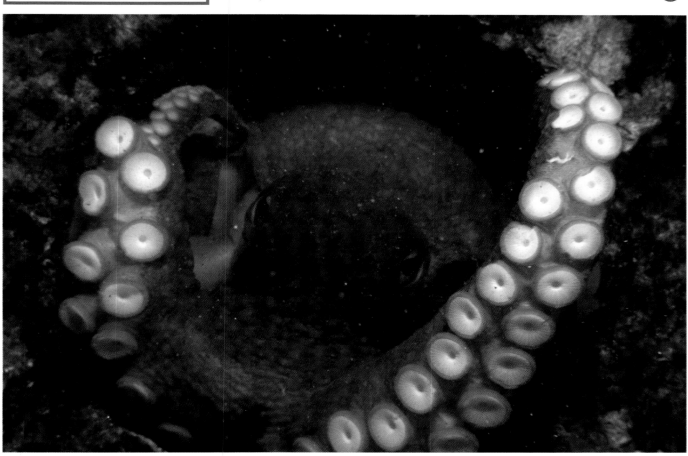

Heinz-Gert deCouet

FEEDING GUILDS ON A CORAL REEF

A feeding guild is a group of organisms (possibly of different families, classes or even phyla) that all exploit the same food resource in a similar way. Organisms can be an **Obligate** member of a feeding guild (in which case they always feed as a member of that guild) or a **Facultative** member (whereby occasionally they will feed as a member of the guild).

CARNIVORES: Feed on animal material. Usually have a short gut.

  BENTHIC ANIMAL FEEDERS: Feed on bottom-living animals.

   AMBUSHERS: Prey are usually quite mobile. Sit and wait for prey then usually grab it with a short lunge. Eyes usually located dorsally; mouth is large and often turned upward.

   Example: Hawkfish, Mantis Shrimp, Scorpionfish.

   FORAGERS: Prey are often immobile or only slightly mobile. Often move or swim slowly over the substrate looking for prey. Well-developed sensory structures.

   Example: Bristleworms, Crustaceans, Eels, Filefish, Goatfish, Hawaiian Hawksbill Sea Turtle, Octopus, Porcupinefish, Snapper, Triggerfish, White-tipped Reef Shark, Wrasses.

   GRAZERS: Prey on large sessile invertebrates. Often spend long periods of time associated with a feeding patch.

   Example: Flatworms, Nudibranchs, Angelfish (*Holocanthus arcuatus*), Butterflyfish, Moorish Idols, Seastars, Trunkfish.

  CORALLIVORES: Prey on reef-building coral colonies.

   Example: Butterflyfish, Crown-of-Thorns Seastar, Cushion Seastar (*Culcita novaeguineae*), Damselfish (*Plectroglyphidodon johnstonianus*), Nudibranchs (*Phestilla* sp.), Shortbodied Blenny.

  MOLLUSCIVORES: Prey on molluscs.

   Example: Drupes, Murex, Octopus, Spotted Eagle Ray, Sting Rays, Spiny Puffer, Wrasses.

 PISCIVORES: Prey on swimming fishes. Mouth is often terminal and large; stomach is large or elastic. Often have short, straight intestines.

   AMBUSHERS: Usually benthic and cryptically colored. Seize prey with a quick lunge.

   Example: Cone Shells, Flatfish, Frogfish, Hawkfish, Lizardfish, Mantis Shrimp, Scorpionfish, Sea Snakes.

   STALKERS: Body is often elongated; swim very slowly, hovering, but capable of short, quick swimming bursts.

   Example: Barracuda, Cornetfish, Trumpetfish, Ringtail Wrasse.

   CHASERS: Usually streamlined and very muscular; strong swimmer. Often pelagic or open water.

   Example: Dolphins, Jacks, Mahi, Marlin, Reef Sharks, Swordfish, Tuna.

DEPOSIT FEEDERS: Feed on particulate organic material that settles on the substrate.

> Example: Angelfish, Blennies, Brittlestars, Sand Dollars, Sea Biscuits, Sea Cucumbers, Spaghetti Worms, Surgeonfish, Vermitid Molluscs.

HERBIVORES: Feed on plant material (usually algae). Usually have a long gut.

> **BROWSERS:** Bite off and ingest algal material only.

> > Example: Angelfish, Blennies, Damselfish, Filefish, Triggerfish, Unicornfish.

> **CROPPERS:** Feed as a school on large areas of benthic algae.

> > Example: Rudderfish, Surgeonfish, Triggerfish.

> **GRAZERS:** Feed on a specific patch of algal growth, often rasping up sections of food.

> > Example: Chitons, Cowries, Limpets, Nerites, Sea Hares, Sea Urchins.

> **GROVELERS:** Feed by ingesting large quantities of bottom sediment (sand or mud) containing plant material or bacteria.

> > Example: Mullet, Sand Dollars, Sea Biscuits, Sea Cucumbers.

> **SCRAPERS:** Ingest pieces of substrate while feeding on algae. Pharyngeal mills often present.

> > Example: Hawaiian Green Sea Turtle, Kole (Ctenochaetus strigosus), Parrotfish, Trunkfish.

OMNIVORES: Feed on both plant and animal material. Often have grinding or crushing plates in the mouth or pharynx.

> Example: Fan-tail Filefish, Halfbeaks, Kupipi (Abudefduf sordidus), Moorish Idols, Pufferfish, Trunkfish, Triggerfish.

PLANKTIVORES: Feed on planktonic organisms suspended in the water column.

> **STRAINERS:** Non-selectively strain plankton from the water column. Often feed on both phytoplankton & zooplankton.

> > Example: Basking Sharks, Barnacles, Bivalves, Humpback Whales, Manta Rays, Silversides, Whale Sharks.

> **PICKERS:** Selectively feed on larger zooplankton which are individually picked out of the water column.

> > Example: Anemones, Bigeyes ('Aweoweo), Butterflyfish, Cardinalfish, Damselfish, Flying Fish, Gilded Triggerfish, Flame Wrasse, Hydroids, Jellyfish, Oceanic Sunfish, Soft & Hard Corals, Spotted Unicornfish, Squirrelfish.

SCAVENGERS: Feed preferentially on dead and dying material.

> Example: Crabs, Lobsters, Sharks, Wrasses.

SUSPENSION/FILTER FEEDERS: Suspension/Filter Feeders: Preferentially feed on particulate organic matter suspended in the water column.

> Example: Barnacles, Bivalves, Brittlestars, Christmas Tree Worms, Featherduster Worms, Sea Cucumbers, Sponges, Vermetid Molluscs.

Though parrotfish and wrasses are very similar, characteristically they belong to different feeding guilds. Wrasses tend to feed on small benthic invertebrates and small fishes; while parrotfish are generally considered to be herbivores.

Grazing Herbivore ▼

Sea urchins are occasionally found out grazing algae during the day on shallow reef flats, but more often they tend to be the primary grazing herbivore on reefs during the evening.

Cropping Herbivores ▲ ▶

CNIDO-QUESTION: If you were a fish, where would you expect the safest position to be in a school?

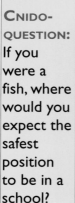

▼ Picking Planktivores

◀ Scraping Herbivore

Foraging Benthic Animal Feeder ▼

Goatfish are uniquely adapted to search for food within the soft sediments and rubble surrounding many coral reefs. Imagine that the primary way for you to find your daily cheeseburger was by dragging your tongue around a table full of stuff until you touched and tasted it...this is what a goatfish does. It basically has two external tongues (called **barbels**) that act as taste buds and probing fingers (*below*) which it uses to search through the sediment (*above*) for small crustaceans, worms and molluscs upon which it feeds.

◀ ▼ Surgeonfish tend to form large schools that roam over reefs and reef flats cropping algae. Often one can find **mixed schools** of different species of surgeonfish moving over the reef (*left*).

◀ ▲ Schooling fish are relatively rare if you look at the number of feeding guilds represented by them. In general, the only feeding guilds that characteristically school on a coral reef are certain types of herbivores and planktivores (such as the surgeonfish shown above or the planktivorous *Chromis* shown on the left).

CNIDOQUESTION: What factors might limit other types of fish from forming schools?

▲ Straining Planktivores

▼ Chasing Piscivore

▲ Jacks are one of the few fish on a coral reef that are well adapted for chasing down their prey. What adaptations can you see that might assist this fish in leading a high-speed eating habit?

▼ Scavenger

▲ Probably one of the best known (and most feared) of all reef creatures; the shark serves an important role as a carnivorous scavenger on reefs.

▼ Ambush Piscivore

▲ Frogfish are one of the most frequently by-passed (by divers) of the Hawaiian reef fish. Having the ability to mimic their surroundings (as adults) they will often remain motionless, out in the open, as a diver comes within inches of them. As juveniles (*above*) they may have a constant yellow coloration; it has been suggested that this serves to mimic yellow sponges. Both juveniles and adults attract their prey close to their mouths through the use of a wiggling fishing lure attached to the top of their heads (just above the eye).

POP QUIZ:

Pictured on the right are five representatives of four different feeding guilds. Can you spot the organisms and correctly name their feeding guilds? (Answer in the back of the book)

HERBIVORY ON CORAL REEFS

Herbivores are animals that feed on the primary producers, the plants. On coral reefs this involves feeding primarily on seaweeds (macroalgae and algal turf) and also microalgae growing atop the sand or suspended in the water column (phytoplankton); some herbivores (such as parrotfish) also feed on the symbiotic zooxanthellae found growing within corals. If not removed by herbivores, seaweeds may competively dominate coral reefs. Most tropical marine herbivores are generalists (they'll feed on a wide range of algae; such a strategy may help to avoid species-specific toxin loading), although there is a group of gastropod molluscs called saccoglossans that selectively feed on certain green seaweeds by piercing the cell wall with their modified radula and sucking up the cell contents. Saccoglossans are able to incorporate the undamaged chloroplasts (photosynthetic structures) of their algal prey into their mantle tissue and derive additional energy from photosynthesis (see p. 32).

Type of Herbivore	Preferred Food
Gastropods, Black Rock Crab	Turf/Macroalgae
Sea Urchins	Turf/Macroalgae
Surgeonfish	Phytoplankton
	Turf/Macroalgae
	Sand/Detritus
Damselfish	Macroalgae
	Microalgae
Parrotfish	Coral Zooxanthellae
	Algae Turf
	Sand/Detritus
Sea Chubs	Turf/Macroalgae
Hawaiian Green Sea Turtle	Turf/Macroalgae

Seaweed Defensive Strategies

- The physical structure of a seaweed may make it difficult to consume. Some are hard & plate-like (*Porolithon*), others are leathery and contain spines (*Turbinaria*).
- Many seaweeds seem to contain chemical compounds which may be distasteful, toxic, growth-inhibiting, etc. in order to be unpalatable.
- Some seaweeds find refuge by occurring within damselfish territories; the damselfish will often exclude herbivores from their territory.
- Some palatable algae gain refuge by growing attached to unpalatable seaweeds (likewise, invertebrates such as Decorator crabs also gain refuge from carnivores and incidental predation by living on unpalatables).
- Small, filamentous and coralline algae may be tolerant of herbivores in order to prevent exclusion by larger macroalgae. A number of filamentous species not only survive passage through the gut of a herbivore, but actually may produce more motile spores (seaweed reproductive cells) as a result of gut passage.

Herbivory on coral reefs can be 10 - 100 times greater than that on tropical forests.

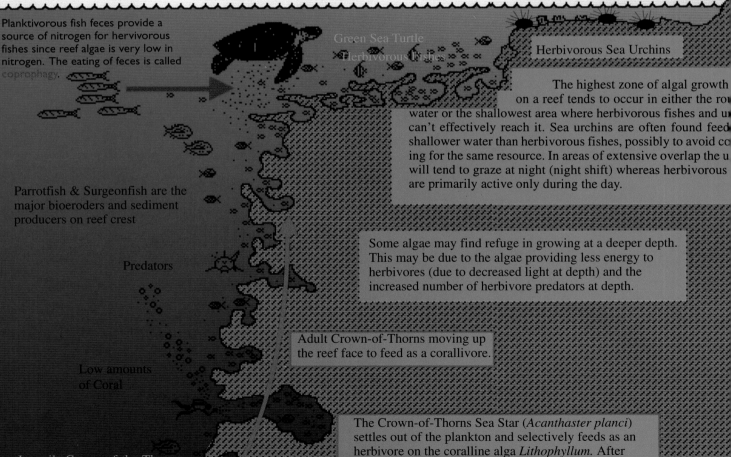

Planktivorous fish feces provide a source of nitrogen for hervivorous fishes since reef algae is very low in nitrogen. The eating of feces is called coprophagy.

High light, High Herbivores — Shallow

Low light, Low Herbivores — Deep

Green Sea Turtle
Herbivorous Fishes

Herbivorous Sea Urchins

The highest zone of algal growth on a reef tends to occur in either the ro... water or the shallowest area where herbivorous fishes and u... can't effectively reach it. Sea urchins are often found feed... shallower water than herbivorous fishes, possibly to avoid co... ing for the same resource. In areas of extensive overlap the u... will tend to graze at night (night shift) whereas herbivorous ... are primarily active only during the day.

Parrotfish & Surgeonfish are the major bioeroders and sediment producers on reef crest

Predators

Some algae may find refuge in growing at a deeper depth. This may be due to the algae providing less energy to herbivores (due to decreased light at depth) and the increased number of herbivore predators at depth.

Adult Crown-of-Thorns moving up the reef face to feed as a corallivore.

Low amounts of Coral

The Crown-of-Thorns Sea Star (*Acanthaster planci*) settles out of the plankton and selectively feeds as an herbivore on the coralline alga *Lithophyllum*. After a certain period of time they are believed to metamorphose into adults which move up the reef face and feed exclusively on corals.

Juvenile Crown-of-the-Thorns Sea Star

Lithophyllum
Coralline Algae

SO, YOU WANT TO BE A PREDATOR, DO YOU???

Richard Pyle

Predators on reefs take many forms and belong to a many different feeding guilds. For now we'll limit our discussion to those animals that prey on mobile macroscopic prey (fish or fast-moving invertebrates such as crabs and squids). Predators generally are of two sorts: those that sneak-up on or ambush prey, and those that chase prey down. Often color and patterning play an important role. Most diurnal (daytime) predators rely to some extent on vision to identify their prey; often this takes the role of a **search image**. Imagine you're at a party with groups of people talking amongst themselves. Your name is Mary and someone in another group says "Next month George and I will marry..." Instantly you start paying attention to their conversation because your brain (which up till now has been filtering out all of these background conversations) has a search image for your own name. Diurnal predators often make use of visual search images to identify their prey.

As a predator you'll also have to capture and consume your prey. Some do it simply by inhaling their prey whole (Trumpetfish, Frogfish, etc.). Others, like the Moray Eel or Lizardfish, have to bite and choke down their food. Lacking grasping appendages (like hands) can cause problems in a liquid environment because even if the prey is dead and can't swim away after the first bite, currents or surge may sweep the meal away. These animals get around this problem by having highly modified teeth (Palatine teeth in Moray Eels, arrowhead-shaped bottom teeth in Lizardfish) that serve to hold the prey while the rest of the mouth orients the food for swallowing. Neat adaptation if you don't have hands, huh???

Predator Profile:

Name: Dragon Moray (*Enchelycore pardalis*)

Primarily nocturnal

Predatory Adaptations:

- Extended nares (nasal openings) allow directional chemical searches ("Taste Vision").

- Palatine teeth (long, spike-like teeth extending down from the roof of the mouth) allow holding of large prey during chewing and breathing.

Nares

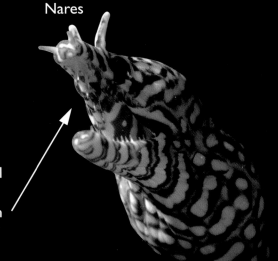

Heinz-Gert deCouet

USES OF COLOR AND PATTERNING

There are a number of theories as to the functions of colors and patterns in reef animals:

Camouflage

A wide variety of animals on reefs use camouflage as a way of either avoiding predation, or as a way of helping to capture prey. Camouflage involves an organism resembling a substrate, and is either passive or active. Passive camouflage involves an organism whose coloration pattern is relatively fixed to resemble a background (ex. hawkfish). Active camouflage is where an organism can change its color pattern (either neurally or hormonally) to match varying substrates (ex. flatfish, frogfish).

Warning

Certain color patterns may serve as a **warning** to potential predators. A number of surgeonfish highlight their caudal spines; the Yellow Tang takes this to extremes - its yellow body and bright white spine make a very strong visual signal.

Advertising

Animals that provide a unique or necessary service to other animals on the reef often use unique color patterns and behaviors to advertise their presence.

The Whitemouth Moray (*above*) at first does not seem to be well camouflaged (light spots on a dark background, while the coral substrate is dark spots on a light background). But at night, when the coral polyps have emerged, the scene changes to one of light spots (coral polyps) on a dark background; thus providing the eel with an excellent background to hide against. The ability to decrease one's visual contrast and visual artifact is very important whether one is the predator or the prey.

Nocturnal

Many nocturnal (night-time) fish have a red coloration (Squirrelfish, Soldierfish, Cardinalfish, etc.) Red is the first wavelength of light to be absorbed underwater. At night, when light levels are already low, being red-colored would make a fish practically invisible.

Many reef fish actually change their color patterning at night in order to decrease their visual signature; note the Ornate Butterflyfish's day coloration (*upper right*) and its less-reflective night coloration (*right*).

Countershading

Found among fish that swim out in the open. Countershading consists of the dorsal (top) side of the fish being darker than the ventral (bottom) side. To an organism above looking down, the countershaded animal will blend in with the darker waters or bottom below; while an organism below will have difficulty picking the animal out against the lighter surface waters above.

Sexual

The exceptionally high-density of similar-shaped fish on the reef mixed with the need to mate with one's own species may have been one of the dominant forces in the evolution of reef fish color patterning. Many of the sex-changing reef fish show strong color pattern differences between males and females. In some reef species the males intensify their color patterning during courting rituals or when protecting nest areas.

BY ORGANISMS ON CORAL REEFS

Lisa Privitera

Misdirection

Often a predator will try to attack its prey from behind in order to maximize the element of surprise. This involves identifying the front from the back of an animal; find the eyes and you've found the front. Some animals take advantage of this by hiding the location of their eyes (eyebars) and/or having false eyespots at the other end of their body (so the predator will think the front is the back and the back is the front; causing it to orient on the front instead of the back and allowing the prey to see it in advance).

Disruptive

Another view is that such patterns break-up the shape of fish (especially in schools) and make it difficult for a predator to orient on a single fish to attack.

Heinz-Gert deCouet

Mimicry

A variety of animals on reefs practice various forms of mimicry. A mimic is an organism that assumes the shape, pattern or behavior of another organism; usually in order to avoid predation or to capture prey. Presented here are three different types of mimicry seen on Hawaiian coral reefs: Batesian Mimicry, Decoy Mimicry, and Shadow Stalking.

Decoy Mimicry

A number of ambush predators make use of "lures" to attract their prey to them. Such decoys can take the shape of small appendages or fins that look like small invertebrates or fish (used by Frogfish and certain Scorpionfish). Some may actually use reflection of light to attract plankton at night which they might consume (Manta Ray) or use as a lure to attract a larger meal (Whitemouth Moray?).

Flash Coloration

One of the things that most people notice about reef fish is that, along with their compressed body shape, these fish often display a bright and broad target for a predator to form a search image on. As the predator closes in, the reef fish pivots such that their appearance is completely changed and to many predators these fish may seem to completely disappear!

Another observation is that many reef fish have vertical barring patterns (like the Convict Tang shown above). Like the zebra, this patterning may actually help the predator to form a search image: food = black & white vertical bars. When the predator attacks, the prey flees and suddenly its search image has disappeared (black & white vertical bars, when moving fast, appear as a solid gray)!

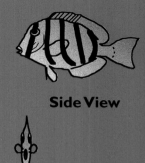

Side View

Front View

Batesian Mimicry

Batesian mimicry involves one species resembling another species that has some defense against predation. The mimic, by resembling the defended organism, gains protection without the cost of maintaining the defensive structure of the animal it is mimicking. The upper right photo shows a Potter's Angelfish; like most angelfish, the Potter's has a defensive opercular spine on the outside of the gill cover. This spine can be flared out in defense. The lower photo shows the mimic, a Shortnosed Wrasse, which lacks the opercular spine but gains protection by resembling the angelfish.

Richard Pyle

Deborah Gochfeld

Shadow Stalking

An unusual behavior called Shadow Stalking is seen in Trumpetfish and Ringtail Wrasses. These fish have the ability to slowly change color as they stalk their prey over a variety of bottom cover. Sometimes they will blend in with a school of herbivorous fish in order to closely approach their smaller prey species of fish hiding amongst the corals. Presumably the prey species would be used to herbivorous schools of fish passing by and would not view such a school as a threat.

WHY SHOULD REEF FISH SCHOOL?

Heinz-Gert deCouet

A number of theories have been put forward to help explain why certain reef fish form and maintain schools:

- Reduced water resistance
- Increased communication, vigilance
- Assurance of finding mates
- Predation avoidance by confusing predator (through disruptive coloration or collective mimicry) and making it difficult for the predator to form a search image. Also the sheer numbers of fish in a school decreases the odds of any one fish being nailed (dilutes the risk amongst all the fish).
- More eyes to search for food (but also more mouths to feed; so tend to a see with fish that feed on a large, non-patchy food sources such as plankton or benthic algae).

Offensive Schooling

Most people think of fish schools existing primarily as a defense against a predator, but schools can also be offensive in order to gang-up against the defenses of a territorial animal. This is often seen with egg predators and the demersal spawners who guard the nests. Sometimes fish of different species will form schools together (**Mixed Schooling**) to overwhelm the defenses of a territorial fish that they could never overcome by themselves.

◄ A mixed school made-up primarily of Raccoon Butterflyfish (*Chaetodon lunula*). The lone male Hawaiian Sergeant (*Abudefduf abdominalis*) cannot defend the nest of eggs (purple mass on the substrate) against all these fish at once.

One's position in a school may be important; traditional theory (The "Selfish Herd" approach) has held that schooling fish continuously jockey for positions within the school, with the center positions thought to be the safest. Another theory proposes that those fish on the periphery are actually the safest because they'll see and respond to the predator sooner; while those in the center won't have accurate information about which direction the threat is coming from.

Single fish may be less likely to see the approach of a predator compared to a school (more lookouts), but a school is much easier for a predator to see compared to a single fish. How do schooling fish minimize this threat?

When a predator does charge a school, the fish often scatter in such a way that it is difficult for the predator to form a search image on any single fish (Imagine someone tossing you a coin; there's a pretty good chance you'll catch it. Now have someone toss you ten identical loose coins at once; it becomes very hard for you to focus on any one single coin to catch).

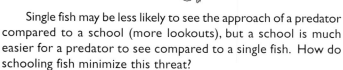

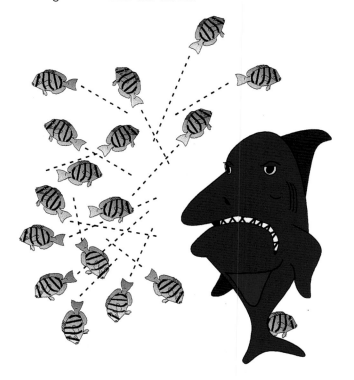

▼▲ Scattering in various directions may serve to limit a predator's ability to form a search image on any one fish.

Heinz-Gert deCouet

Heinz-Gert deCouet

▲
It's becoming more and more rare to see large schools of adult fish (of any species) anywhere around the main Hawaiian islands. Twenty years ago the regulation of such practices as gill netting and seining were not as critical as they are today. With increased population and technology, and decreased protective habitat and adult populations, fish stocks are plummeting.

TERRITORIALITY IN REEF FISHES

A **territory** can be defined as an area guarded by a fish which contains some sort of **limited** resource such as food, shelter, nesting sites or mates; such sites may be defended against members of its own or other species. Some species may have separate territories for separate resources such as feeding and resting. A **home range** occurs when a species tends to roam over the same large area repeatedly. Many species may defend territories within home ranges.

TYPE OF RESOURCE	EXAMPLE
FOOD	
Corallivores	Assorted Butterflyfish
	Blue-eyed Damselfish
	Short-bodied Blenny
Deposit Feeders	Certain Angelfish
	Blennies
Herbivores	Angelfish
	Blennies
	Damselfish
	Certain Surgeonfish
Benthic Animal Feeders	Angelfish
	Butterflyfish
SHELTER	Damselfish
	Blennies
	Gobies
NESTS	Damselfish
	Gobies
	Blennies
	Longnose Hawkfish
MATES	Damselfish
	Wrasses
	Parrotfish
	Groupers & Basslets
	Hawkfish
	Gobies

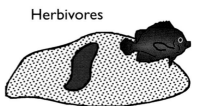

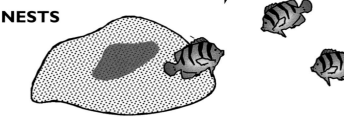

Territory Defense by Herbivorous Damselfish

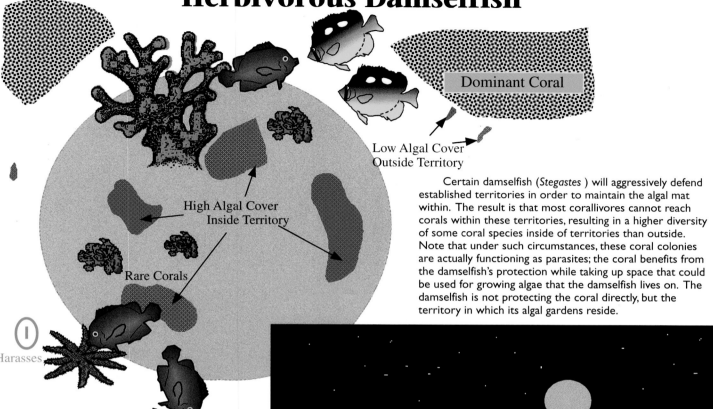

Dominant Coral

Low Algal Cover
Outside Territory

High Algal Cover
Inside Territory

Rare Corals

① Harasses

② Picks up and moves outside of territory

③ Ptooey!!

Certain damselfish (*Stegastes*) will aggressively defend established territories in order to maintain the algal mat within. The result is that most corallivores cannot reach corals within these territories, resulting in a higher diversity of some coral species inside of territories than outside. Note that under such circumstances, these coral colonies are actually functioning as parasites; the coral benefits from the damselfish's protection while taking up space that could be used for growing algae that the damselfish lives on. The damselfish is not protecting the coral directly, but the territory in which its algal gardens reside.

Some damselfish will actually pick up (by biting a spine) and physically remove *Acanthaster planci* from their territories. In areas where *Acanthaster* outbreaks occur, damselfish territories provide refuges for certain coral species, resulting in much more complex assemblages of coral then would otherwise be found. As such, these damselfish function as **keystone species,** since they tend to dramatically shape their environment for the rest of the organisms living in it.

Why protect their gardens so vigorously?

Stegastes fasciolatus grows mostly filamentous algae within its territory. Such "doormats" often trap sediment and organic nutrients which function as a culture medium for small invertebrates and bacteria. These in turn serve as a nitrogen supplement for the damselfish, allowing the damselfish access to a rich, unique source of energy which it protects from other herbivores.

On most evenings there are very few herbivores out grazing on the reef: the dominant fish are planktivores and carnivores. Under such circumstances the damselfish, like most diurnal reef fish, seeks shelter for the evening.

Adult damselfish sheltering for the evening

Juveniles will recruit into territories at night, allowing them to live and grow within coral heads protected by the adult who would have otherwise driven them out.

The Four-spot Butterflyfish *(Chaetodon quadrimaculatus)* can feed at night when the moon is full. Since the damselfish are inactive at night, the butterflyfish can selectively feed by moonlight on the corals within the damselfish's territory.

Damselfish as a Keystone Species

Above: Many territorial damselfish are fiercely protective of their territories, often attacking animals many times their own size (such as the photographer who snapped this picture).

Territorial damselfish, such as the Pacific Gregory (*Stegastes fasciolatus*), that farm filamentous algae are thought to act as **Keystone Species.** The damselfish, a non-carnivore, strongly modifies other herbivore's effects and prevents the monopolization of a section of reef by algal species that would be competitively-dominant if the damselfish were not present. A study by Lassuy (1980) showed this role by the territorial damselfish *Stegastes* (right).

Stegastes

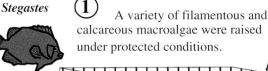

① A variety of filamentous and calcareous macroalgae were raised under protected conditions.

Exclusion cage

Herbivorous fish

② Algae were than placed either inside damselfish territories or outside of these territories, in the open.

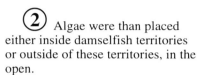

③ Damselfish excluded other herbivorous fish from feeding on the algae, they also weeded-out the calcareous macroalgae allowing the palatable filamentous algae to grow in a protected environment.

④ Filamentous algae were cropped down and eaten by herbivores, the calcareous algae with their chemical and structural defenses were left relatively untouched.

THE EFFECTS ON CORALS:

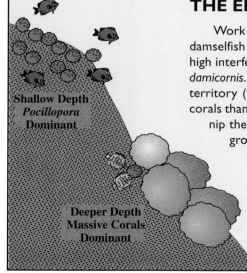

Shallow Depth
Pocillopora
Dominant

**Deeper Depth
Massive Corals
Dominant**

Work done on reefs in Panama (Wellington, 1982), has shown that in shallow depths damselfish shelters are numerous and damselfish densities are high. This is thought to lead to high interference by damselfish with corallivores allowing successful recruitment of *Pocillopora damicornis*. At the same time, nipping behavior by the damselfish on all corals present within its territory (in order to provide open space for algal growth) has a greater effect on massive corals than finely branched corals like *Pocillopora*; this is due to the damselfish only being able to nip the tips of branches versus the entire surface of the massive corals. The result is that growth of massive corals is very limited in these shallow depths, allowing overgrowth by *Pocillopora*.

At deeper depths, damselfish shelters are rare, light levels for farmed algae are lower, and damselfish densities are low. Lack of damselfish interference allows greater activity by corallivores (many of which prefer branching species such as *Pocillopora*), which may account for low success of *Pocillopora damicornis* recruitment. The lack of damselfish nipping behavior may also contribute to a predominance of massive corals in deeper depths.

Sex Change on the Reef

Imagine the most bizarre and kinky sexual antics seen in your average city and they pale in comparison to the strategies seen on the coral reef. Reef fish tend to be either **gonochristic** (same sex throughout life) or **hermaphroditic** (different sexes within a lifecycle). Most reef fish broadcast spawn (watch for interesting courting rituals going on in the water column) or spawn on the bottom (**demersal spawning**), usually around a nest (watch for territorial, courting and parental behaviors around the nest). Some hermaphroditic organisms are simultaneous hermaphrodites (one individual is both a functioning male and female) or sequential hermaphrodites (one individual starts off life as one sex and changes into another later on; this is the type seen in reef fish). There are two basic types of sex change seen on the reef:

Protandry *("First male")* - Whereby animals start off life as males and change into females.

Very rare on the reef, examples include anemonefish and certain species of shrimp.

Protogeny *("First female")* - Whereby some animals start off life as females and change into males.

In fish that show protogeny, one will often times see two types of males:

Initial Phase (IP) Males: Generally small and the same color as females; often spawn in groups of IP males around a single female. Some IP males are **Sneakers** (sneak a mating with a female while the TP [see below] male is busy) or **Streakers** (streaks in and dumps his sperm at the same time, or just prior to, the TP male releasing his sperm on the eggs). Initial phase males do not go through sex change, but start off life as males.

Terminal Phase (TP) Males: Larger and often brightly colored males who defend spawning territories where they mate one-on-one with females. Often have harems of females. These protogenous males started life as females and later sex-changed into TP males.

Examples include species of: Angelfish, Gobies, Groupers, Hawkfish, Parrotfish & Wrasses.

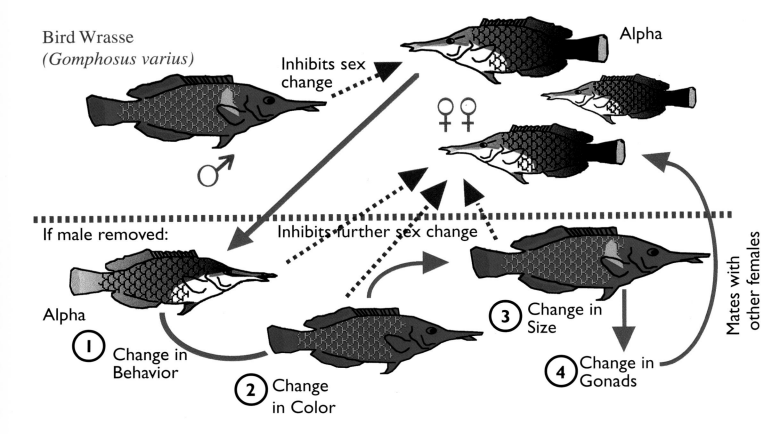

Bird Wrasse
(*Gomphosus varius*)

Inhibits sex change

Alpha

♀♀

Inhibits further sex change

If male removed:

Alpha

① Change in Behavior

② Change in Color

③ Change in Size

④ Change in Gonads

Mates with other females

A good example of how sex change works is seen in the Bird Wrasse, *Gomphosus varius*, where TP males are larger and characteristically green; while females are smaller and gray, white and orange in color. TP males maintain harems of females in which usually resides an 'Alpha' or dominant female. It is thought that the presence of the male inhibits sex change in the females. If the male is removed for some reason the Alpha female will almost immediately start acting like a male ① herding the other females and patrolling the territory. Because she controls the food resource, over the next couple of days she will change her size and start to change her color ② and ③. Finally her gonads will change from producing eggs to producing sperm; at this point she's a terminal phase (TP) male. Though the jury's not in, it is thought that the TP male and possibly the alpha female inhibit sex change through chemical and behavioral means.

Reproductively-active TP males often will display a brightly-colored patch behind the pectoral fin; such a patch (often called a "Badge of Courage") is seen in a variety of wrasse species, the Blue Spotted Grouper, and certain species of triggerfish. If such a bright coloration were used to attract females, wouldn't this also serve to increase the likelihood of predation? One theory is that male fish may be using this brightly colored patch in a way similar to that of many birds; as a way of advertising their fitness to potential mates. The idea here is that a male that can obviously survive in the presence of predators with such a visual handicap must have a greater fitness potential that could be passed on to the female's offspring. Ⓣ

> **CNIDOQUESTION:** What might be the advantage for a territorial fish to start off life as a female?

Terminal male Saddleback Wrasse ▶
(*Thalasoma duperrey*) being
serviced by a cleaner wrasse.
Note the bright white patch
directly behind the pectoral fin.

BIOEROSION

When a coral colony dies, it leaves behind a calcareous substrate upon which other corals can grow; resulting in a coral reef which consists of a carbonate framework with only a thin veneer of living coral atop it. It is upon this massive carbonate structure that certain organisms act, producing additional habitat space within the reef itself and adding to its three-dimensional complexity. Erosion on coral reefs caused by these biological organisms (**bioeroders**) has been estimated to be around 1 kg/m²/yr. Of this amount, roughly half is caused by grazing fish, while about one third is due to the effects of boring sponges. Through their actions, bioeroders may create as much as 40% additional internal space within the reef framework.

Probably the best known of the grazing fish are the parrotfish, so named due to their parrot-like beaks and often brilliant body coloration. Parrotfish are sexually-dimorphic, with primarily greenish males and brown to red females. In Hawai'i, most parrotfish start off their lives as females and eventually change sex into terminal males. This results in small schools of female parrotfish often being seen cruising over reef flats or shallow reefs, and large terminal males, each with a small harem of females, holding limited territories on reef edges and slopes. A common misperception is that parrotfish are corallivores; actually they're more like rabbits, grazing on algae that grows on or within hard substrates (i.e. the zooxanthellae in corals). With their parrot-like mouthparts they can scrape or bite off chunks of substrate (including live coral) and then, using grinding plates in the back of their throats, grind down the substances and extract out the plant material (in their intestines). The end product is clean, newly formed sediment, making the parrotfish the dominant biological (living) sand producer on coral reefs!

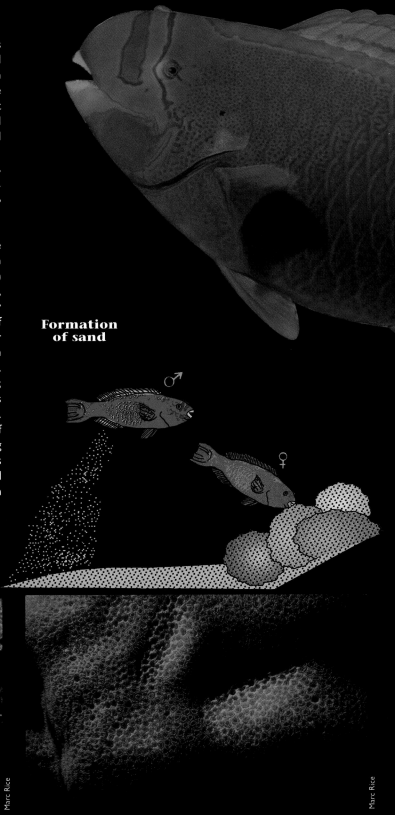

Formation of sand

Bite marks left behind by parrotfish on algae-covered rock (*above left*) and on living coral (*above right*).

Marc Rice

Marc Rice

An urchin (*Echinostrephus acleolatus*) burrowing into the substrate.

Bioerosion is an important process on coral reefs. It opens up settlement space, creates sheltering sites, and helps cement the reef together through the creation of fine sediment trapped within eroded internal spaces.

Sea Urchins

Sea urchins constantly use a highly modified scraping apparatus (called an Aristotle's Lantern) to chew and scrape calcareous and filamentous algae growing atop hard substrates. Some urchins such as the Rock-Boring Urchin (*Echinometra mathaei*) excavate extensive burrows or home cavities, which can modify large sections of intertidal and reef flat areas.

The Collector Urchin (*Tripneustes gratilla*) grazing on algae atop the reef flat. The feeding actions of this animal scrape off portions of the surface substrate along with the algae it feeds on.

Other Bioeroding Fish

With the exception of the parrotfish, most reef fish that act as bioeroders serve primarily to modify existing rubble and sediments into finer sediments. The primary bioeroding fish families include:

The Surgeonfish family - like the Parrotfish, these fish scrape the surface with their teeth.

The Pufferfish family - bite off chunks of substrate.

Other organisms that serve as bioeroders on reefs include bacteria, algae, fungi, various polychaete worms, bivalves, barnacles, and sipunculid worms.

Boring Sponges

Surprisingly, one of the most active of bioeroders on reefs are a group of sponges in the family Clionidae. These sponges are able to burrow into calcareous structures such as those making up corals and mollusc shells. The sponge excavates a series of channels into which it grows. Often the sponge will weaken the structure to the point of collapse, resulting in the decomposition of unused dead shells and coral skeleton.

Zzzz!

Yawn!

A cone shell heavily infested by the boring sponge *Cliona* sp.

The Big Picture:

EFFECTS OF FISHES ON CORALS

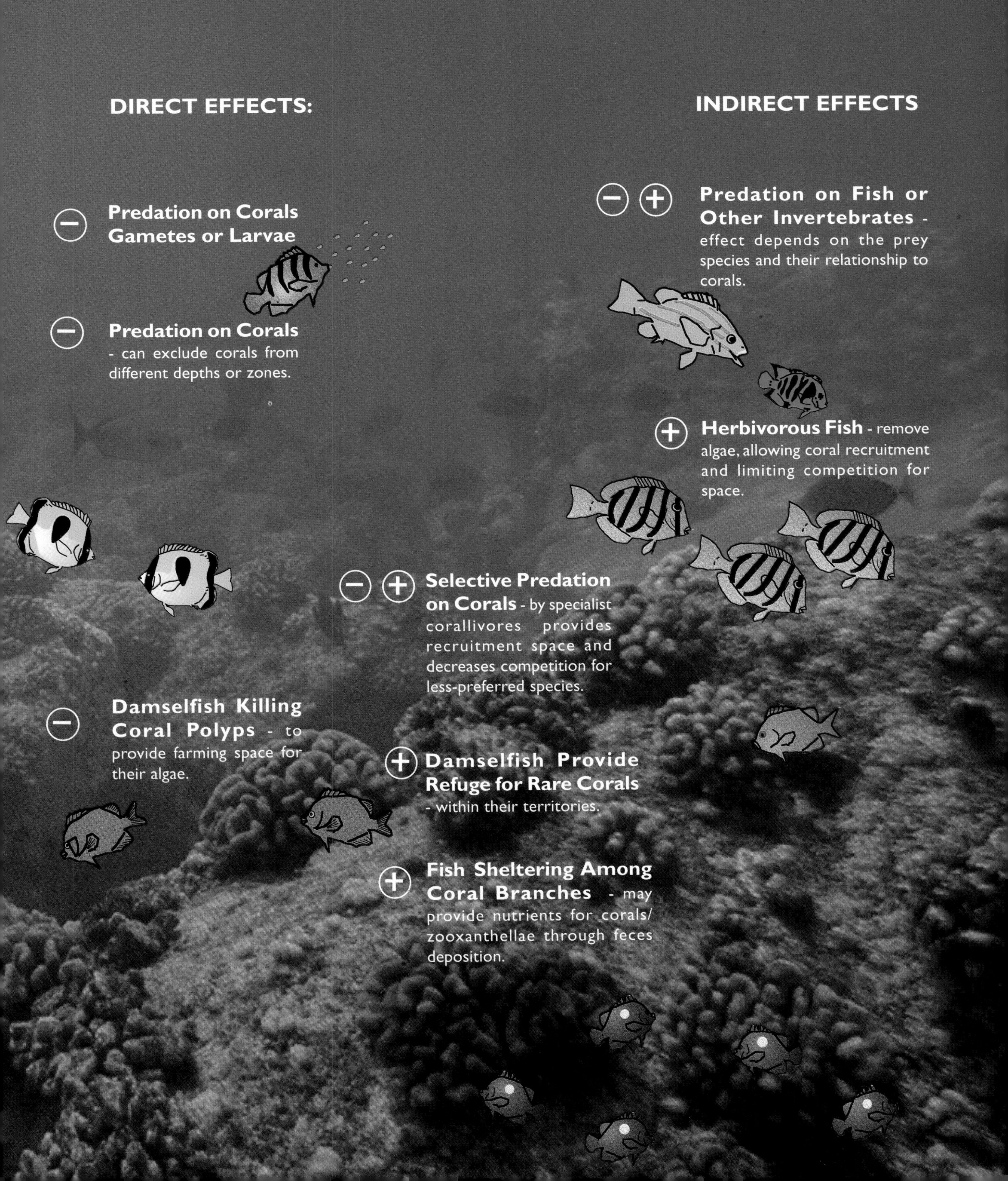

DIRECT EFFECTS:

⊖ **Predation on Corals Gametes or Larvae**

⊖ **Predation on Corals** - can exclude corals from different depths or zones.

⊖ **Damselfish Killing Coral Polyps** - to provide farming space for their algae.

INDIRECT EFFECTS

⊖ ⊕ **Predation on Fish or Other Invertebrates** - effect depends on the prey species and their relationship to corals.

⊕ **Herbivorous Fish** - remove algae, allowing coral recruitment and limiting competition for space.

⊖ ⊕ **Selective Predation on Corals** - by specialist corallivores provides recruitment space and decreases competition for less-preferred species.

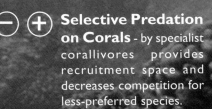

⊕ **Damselfish Provide Refuge for Rare Corals** - within their territories.

⊕ **Fish Sheltering Among Coral Branches** - may provide nutrients for corals/ zooxanthellae through feces deposition.

CLEANING STATIONS ON CORAL REEFS

Cleaning behaviors are fairly common among a variety of marine species. Often this involves either the host soliciting the cleaning behavior by adapting a characteristic motionless 'listing' posture or the symbiont bringing this behavior about by signaling the host that the cleaner is available.

There are a number of shrimp and fish that conduct cleaning behaviors in Hawai'i; probably the best known is the Hawaiian Cleaner Wrasse (*Labroides phthirophagus*). This little wrasse (terminal males rarely exceed 12 cm) sets up cleaning stations on the reef; these stations usually are a well-defined outcropping or other physical feature. The characteristic color and movements of these wrasses are thought to play an important role in elicitation of hosts. Male Cleaner Wrasses maintain harems of females, with each female maintaining separate cleaning stations within the territory of the male.

Cleaner Wrasses tend to pick off external parasites, dead tissue and occasionally, bits of live tissue. Studies in Hawai'i have shown that many Hawaiian reef fishes that visit cleaning stations have relatively low parasite loads and on occasion lose bits of their flesh to the cleaner. If this is the case, why should an animal expose itself to harm through unnecessary cleaning behavior? A study by Dr. George Losey of the Hawai'i Institute of Marine Biology suggests that the host may not be responding to the removal of parasites as much as it is to the tactile stimulus of the cleaner itself; in other words, the host likes to be tickled. A lab study by Dr. Losey found that host fish would posture in front of a moving model of a cleaner wrasse; one day the model fell off the moving wire, yet the host fishes continued to posture and let the wire rub them Such tactile stimulus is common for cleaner wrasses and also for cleaner shrimp such as the Barber Pole Shrimp (*Stenopus hispidus*) which uses its long antennae and long, narrow front claws to stimulate hosts. Because they frequently do remove parasites and dead tissue, the cleaners are providing a necessary service to the fish and as such, predation on cleaners is thought to be relatively low. It is not unusual to see a cleaner wrasse or shrimp cleaning inside the mouth of a piscivore such as an eel; this could be the only way for an animal without appendages to clean its long teeth of pieces of previous meals that have gotten stuck there. The lack of such dental care is important because over time it would affect the ability of the eel to capture its prey.

Yes, the Cleaner Wrasse (*Labroides phthirophagus*) is cleaning the fish, and therefore is a mutualist. But what if this innocent-looking cleaner were to pick a fish scale or some live tissue... and some more, and more, until the fish (who had been quite still and complacent during the cleaning) suddenly darts off to escape the damage being done to it. Shades of Stephen King? This actually happens in the wild!!

Green Sea Turtle Cleaning Stations

Though cleaning stations involving surgeonfish cleaning sea turtles have been noted elsewhere, a unique situation has been recently documented in Kaneʻohe Bay, Hawaiʻi. Here, not only are the turtles cleaned by surgeonfish (herbivores), but also appear to posture for, and be cleaned by, endemic Saddleback Wrasses (carnivores).

Marc Rice

Above: A number of shrimp species serve as cleaners; in this case, the long antennae and long, thin claws serve the same function as the mouth of the Cleaner Wrasse in terms of stimulating the fish.

The Cleaning Staff:

The Saddleback Wrasse

Appears to be feeding on parasitic barnacles (*Platylepas hexastylos*) found primarily on the skin areas of the Green Sea Turtle.

Assorted herbivorous surgeonfish

Feed on a variety of filamentous and small, leafy red and green algae growing on the upper surface of the turtle's shell. It is thought that the turtle gains from this relationship by reducing the drag associated with the presence of the algae on its shell, like a ship having had its hull scraped.

Below: One can often find a number of fish waiting their turn to be serviced at a cleaning station. Look carefully at the wrasse waiting in line below. Note the large chunk of tissue missing from its flank (one of the few examples of incomplete predation that one can occasionally see on the reef). The cleaner will trim away most of the visible tattered dead tissue.

SEA TURTLES

Heinz-Gert deCouet

The Hawaiian Green sea turtle (*Chelonia mydas*) is thought to be a strict herbivore during its sub-adult phase when it frequents reefs around the main Hawaiian Islands. Studies on these animals suggest that they spend the majority of their lives in waters associated with the Hawaiian Islands. An increase in the number of cases of viral tumors (fibropapilloma) in many of the turtles in Hawai'i (see p. 200) has been noted recently. Other major impacts on these animals include getting caught in unattended gill nets, being hit by high-speed watercraft and being harrassed by reef visitors.

Richard Pyle

◄ ▲

A common sight on many Hawaiian reefs are sea turtle resting holes. Care needs to be taken to not disturb the animal while it's resting; repetitive harassment may imprint the animals not to visit reefs where they are commonly seen. These animals are protected by both State and Federal laws.

SEA TURTLE TIDBITS & TRIVIA

Phylum Chordata
Class Reptilia
Order Chelonia
family Cheloniidae (True Sea Turtles)
family Dermochelidae (Leatherback Sea Turtles)

The Leatherback Sea Turtle
(Dermochelys coriacea)
Endangered species

Very rare, primarily a pelagic species. The Leatherback derives its name from the lack of a hard shell covering its body. Its diet consists of primarily sea jellies.

A GIANT AMONG TURTLES
Largest of all living reptiles, Leatherbacks can reach a weight of over 1500 pounds!

Only three (of the seven known) species of sea turtles are usually seen in Hawaiian waters

The Hawaiian Hawksbill Sea Turtle
(Eretmochelys imbricata)
Endangered species

A very rare and rather small sea turtle, the Hawaiian Hawksbill has been heavily impacted by habitat alteration and introduced mammalian predators around beaches on the main Hawaiian Islands where it comes ashore to lay its eggs. Diet consists of a wide variety of invertebrates.

The Hawaiian Green Sea Turtle
(Chelonia mydas)
Threatened species

The most commonly seen sea turtle in Hawaiian waters, the Hawaiian population of Green Sea Turtles is very different from populations seen elsewhere. Like the Hawaiian Hawksbill it is thought that Green Sea Turtles in Hawai'i stay associated with the Hawaiian Islands for the majority of their lives. Additionally, Hawai'i lacks large amounts of sea grasses resulting in both subadults and adults grazing on mostly small, filamentous seaweeds; this may account for the very long time it takes for these animals to reach sexual maturity (about thirty years!). Hawaiian Green Sea Turtles also show **basking behavior**, where both sexes tend to haul up onto beaches and just lie there like tourists. Basking may serve as a way to elevate body temperatures or may act as a way of avoiding predation by tiger sharks.

Adults can weigh upwards of 400 pounds, of which a considerable portion may consist of a green-colored fat from which this turtle derives its name. It's very difficult to externally tell sexes apart with these animals before they reach adulthood. As adults, males have larger and more elongate tails and a single mating claw on the trailing edge of the fore flippers.

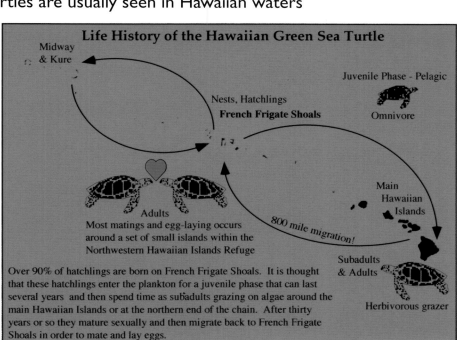

Life History of the Hawaiian Green Sea Turtle

Over 90% of hatchlings are born on French Frigate Shoals. It is thought that these hatchlings enter the plankton for a juvenile phase that can last several years and then spend time as subadults grazing on algae around the main Hawaiian Islands or at the northern end of the chain. After thirty years or so they mature sexually and then migrate back to French Frigate Shoals in order to mate and lay eggs.

WHAT'S UP DOC???
Scientists and physicians have been studying the Green Sea Turtle's ability to slow down its brain activity during long periods underwater. At such times the turtle's brain is receiving far less oxygen then normal. When a human undergoes a stroke there is a loss of oxygen to the brain; by studying the sea turtle, scientists hope to develop ways to mimic its ability to deal with this situation.

USE OF REEF HABITAT

One of the wonders of a coral reef is the great diversity of organisms that can inhabit it. The large amount of three dimensional substrate and space caused by reef-building corals and plants provide both refuge and food sources for a variety of different organisms. Maximum use of this habitat is provided by organisms having different activity patterns, organisms that are active during the daylight hours (**Diurnal**) occupy a "Day Shift" while those that are active at night (**Nocturnal**) occupy a "Night Shift".

The Day Shift is full of organisms that depend on light to some degree; hermatypic corals (actually, their symbiotic zooxanthellae) and seaweeds are busy with photosynthesis. Many diurnal animals hunt their prey, often through the use of vision.

At night, most of the diurnal animals have sought shelter, often occupying the spaces used by the nocturnal animals during the day. Often fish that are too large to shelter within protected spaces will go through a nightly color change whereby large patches of lightly colored tissue will darken. Other fish have adapted different means to create their own shelter. Many species of wrasse bury themselves at night; while parrotfish and the Hawaiian Cleaner Wrasse may construct mucus cocoons for the evening. Many scientists believe that these cocoons serve to block the detection of these animals by nocturnal predators that would normally find them by "scent". Since light levels are low in the evening, many of the active predators hunt by other senses such as smell and taste. Many animals take advantage of the large amount of zooplankton in the water at night.

Finally, some animals are most active around dawn and dusk. Such **crepuscular** hunters take advantage of the increased activity of fishes at this time; with the diurnal fishes looking for a place to shelter while the nocturnal fish are just starting to come out for the evening. Add to this the large amount of mating that goes on with many reef fishes during this period and one finds this time of day to be one of the most exciting times to observe interactions on the reef.

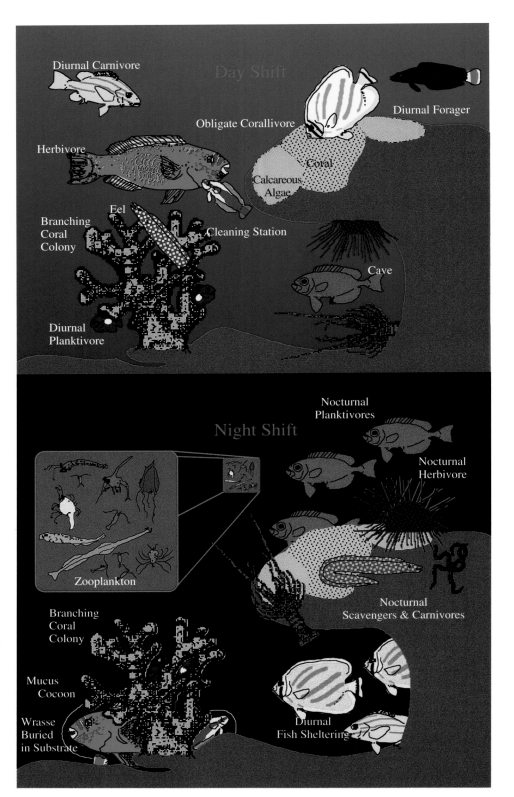

The Reef During the Day

During the day the reef is bustling with photosynthetic activity; this in turn results in a series of behaviors by reef organisms.

Above: Daytime planktivores actively patrol drop-offs and reef crests, but rarely venture beyond the protective cover of the reef itself. These fish, along with the myriad of filter-feeders that make up the coral reef, create a "wall of mouths" along the edges of most reefs.

Above: Corallivorous butterflyfish such as the Multiband Butterflyfish (*Chaetodon multicinctus*) are thought to make use of keen eyesight to selectively pluck and consume coral polyps.

Below and *below right*: Both active and passive hunters prey on a variety of animals moving about the reef during the day.

Above: A great variety of herbivorous fish graze atop the reef during the day. If you were a herbivorous fish, what time of day would be best for feeding and why?

The reef during the day is a scene of primarily planktivorous and herbivorous fish swimming atop the coral ridge with few mobile invertebrates roaming about in the open. The opposite occurs at night.

Left: Based on what you've read elsewhere in this book, what can you say about other behaviors this Peacock Grouper (*Cephalopholis argus*) might be engaged in?

The Crepuscular Period

As daylight changes into night there exists a short period of time when light levels are low and both diurnal and nocturnal organisms are active. Experienced divers know that it is during this **crepuscular period** that they are most likely to see the greatest range of behaviors on the reef.

Above: Dusk finds a flurry of activity taking place on the reef. Daytime reef fish often go through a variety of behaviors; one sees feeding, sex, and hunting for shelter all occurring within a short period of time. At the same time, roving piscivores tend to be most active at this time, taking advantage of low light levels to prey on both diurnal and emerging nocturnal fishes. As a result, one often sees a characteristic "quiet period" (*left*) where most diurnal fish have taken shelter and most nocturnal fish haven't emerged yet. It's no surprise that this short "quiet period" tends to occur during the time when light levels would most benefit active roving piscivores.

Right: Many diurnal reef fish go through intense courting and spawning behaviors shortly before seeking shelter for the evening.

Keoki Stender

The Reef at Night

   Night-time often sees an increase in activity on the reef by a wide variety of organisms, including most corals. It is at this time that the smallest members of the reef community often emerge to safely search for food.

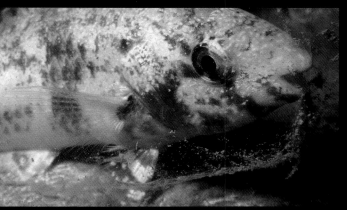

Above: The mucus cocoon produced by resting parrotfish at night is secreted by a gland within the buccal cavity. Some scientists believe that these mucus bags are just a result of mucus build-up by normally slimy parrotfish being inactive at night, others suggest that the cocoon prevents predators from "sniffing-out" the odors of resting parrotfish.

Above and *below*: A number of planktivorous species become active at night, feeding on increased concentrations of plankton both on, and adjacent to, the reef.

Left: Night-time is frequently the best time to observe coral animals as the individual polyps are emerged and active. A good observer can see a myriad of torrid images of sex, feeding, and brutal battles over territory - all within an area encompassing a few centimeters!

Right: While rare in most reef fish, late night spawning is a common occurrence among the invertebrates. Shown here is the annual spawning of the Palolo worm, a type of polycheate worm that engages in massive orgies of inter-twining bodies which allow the hermaphroditic worms to fertilize each other. On some South Pacific islands, the reproductive section (about a third of the body length) is collected during these spawning events and eaten as a delicacy (Hey, stop making faces, most people eat the
reproductive product of fowl pre-sex, i.e. chicken eggs...)

Above and *below*: A number of species emerge from protected areas at night to roam the reef in search of food. With the darkness of evening one is aware of other senses in addition to vision being used by these organisms.

Marc Rice

Deborah Gochfeld

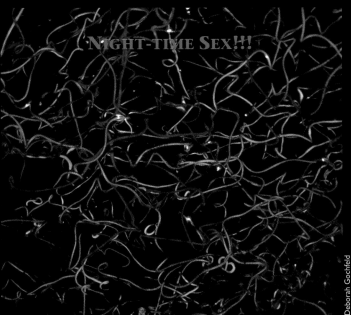

NIGHT-TIME SEX!!!

Deborah Gochfeld

ASSOCIATED HABITATS

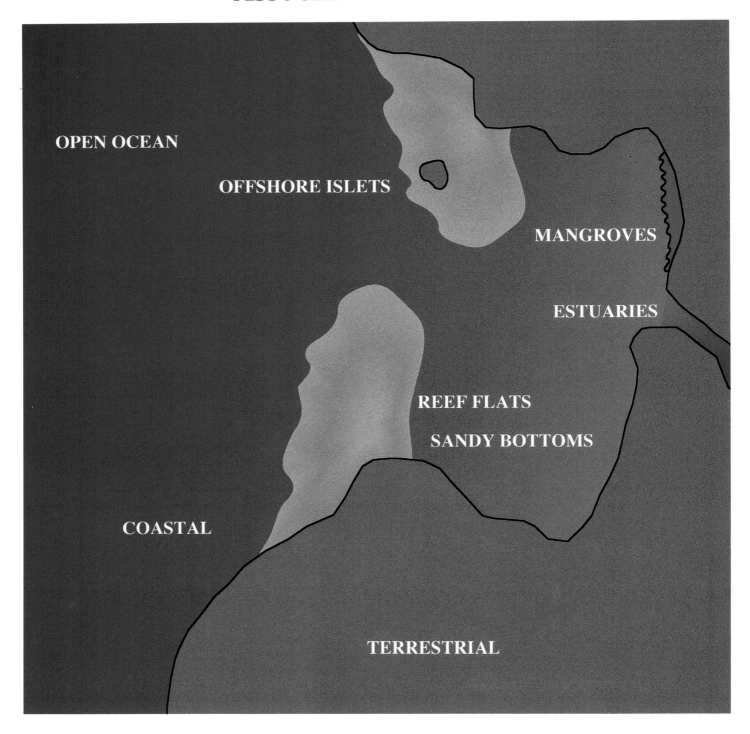

Coral reefs in Hawai'i are not isolated little entities unto themselves. As ecosystems they exist in both direct and indirect contact with a variety of other ecosystems surrounding them. The open ocean has numerous influences on Hawaiian reefs, serving as both a source and a sink for such things as nutrients and plankton (including the larvae of a large proportion of reef organisms). The island, with its wide variety of ecosystems, provides inputs that affect coral reefs. For now, we'll turn our attention to a few of the more unique coastal ecosystems which interact with coral reefs in a variety of ways; often these areas serve as sources of nutrients, barriers to sedimentation (notice any above?), or as refuges for recruiting larval forms that will later live as adults on the reef.

Mangroves

Comprising 60% - 75% of all tropical shorelines, mangroves were absent from the Hawaiian flora until 1902 when the Red Mangrove (*Rhizophora mangle*) was introduced. It has become the dominant plant within a number of large, protected bays and coastlines on both Oʻahu and Molokaʻi. Though it radically alters coastal environments and often displaces native vegetation,

the large amount of three dimensional space it produces can serve as an important shallow water nursery for a variety of marine species. It should be noted that as mangroves continue to grow and trap sediment, the amount of space on the reef flat will decrease as the mangrove forest grows outward over time.

Since mangroves grow in such close proximity to the ocean, they have evolved a number of mechanisms that allow them to flourish where few plants can survive. The leaves and stems are waxy to prevent desiccation in the salt air. Using seawater as a source of H_2O, many mangroves have the ability to shed salt by way of special pores, much like sea turtles do with their tears. The tree itself is supported by a series of prop roots which form an intertwining mesh beneath it. Not only do these roots trap sediment, but they efficiently become a decaying ground for leaf litter and a variety of organisms occasionally swept into them from the reef; this decomposing marine mulch is then absorbed by the roots. As might be expected from such activity, the waters directly surrounding the roots are low in oxygen; aerial roots and un-submerged sections of the prop roots can supplement this need.

Paul Jokiel

Mangrove forests are one of the few biological processes that can increase the size of an island. This is accomplished by the prop roots of the mangrove trapping sediments, which over time creates new land where before stood shoreline.

Sara Peck

Once the aerial root grows down into the water (developing into a prop root) it becomes a new source of settlement space for a wide variety of sessile organisms. These in turn are used as food for a variety of other organisms.

Like the branches of a coral, the prop roots and channels surrounding mangroves provide important three-dimensional sheltering space for a variety of animals, many of which will move onto the reef when they are mature. Note that even juvenile predators (such as this barracuda) can use the mangroves as a hunting ground and shelter from larger predators.

Sandy Bottoms

When people think of tropical environments they often think of expansive beaches; few realize that a beach exists as an ecosystem, with a wide array of organisms that live on, in, and around it. Now think about the extension of the beach underwater (perhaps a better way of phrasing this would be 'the extension of the beach above water', since far more sandy habitat occurs beneath the waves then above them), here exists a world adjacent to the coral reef where the upper layers of the substrate is often in some form of motion depending on both the surge and the organisms moving through it. Animals that live in such an environment are often adapted to burrowing into the substrate as little three-dimensional cover exists above the substrate such as that found on the reef.

Sandy habitats tend to occur from the shoreline beach out to the edge of the reef flat, and then extend down from the bottom edge of the reef depending on the slope. The sands that make up such substrates are formed by a variety of processes. **Terrigenous** sediments are often formed from land sources such as runoff or volcanism, while **Biogenous** sediments arise from broken down skeletal material from organisms such as corals, shells and even calcareous algae (such as *Halimeda*).

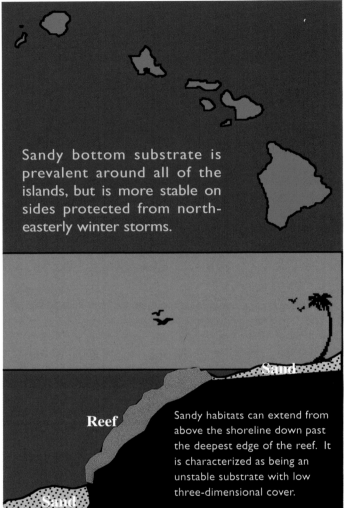

Sandy bottom substrate is prevalent around all of the islands, but is more stable on sides protected from north-easterly winter storms.

Reef

Sand

Sand

Sandy habitats can extend from above the shoreline down past the deepest edge of the reef. It is characterized as being an unstable substrate with low three-dimensional cover.

Heinz-Gert deCouet

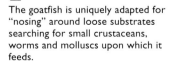

▲

The goatfish is uniquely adapted for "nosing" around loose substrates searching for small crustaceans, worms and molluscs upon which it feeds.

▲

The Ghost Crab (*Ocypode ceratopthala*). One of the most common beach inhabitants, the Ghost Crab is primarily active at night.

◄ At the base of certain leeward reefs, where the sandy habitat starts and extends out, one can occasionally find beds of garden eels swaying in the currents found at these depths. In Hawai'i, the endemic Hawaiian Garden Eel (*Gorgasia hawaiiensis*) can be seen at numerous beds off of the Kona and Kohala coasts of the Big Island. These animals selectively pick plankton out of the water column, yet usually keep a portion of their long body in the tip of their burrows allowing them a quick escape in the event a predator appears.

Reef Flats

Above: From above, many reef flats appear to have little life, don't be fooled so easily...

Above: Gobies are plentiful on reef flats. Some species in the South Pacific, such as *Amblyeleotris guttata*, live in burrows inhabited by alpheid shrimp. The shrimp lives within the burrow and maintains contact with the goby through its antenna. The goby serves as a sentry, warning the shrimp of approaching danger by a simple flicking of its tail. The goby can then retreat into the burrow until the danger passes.

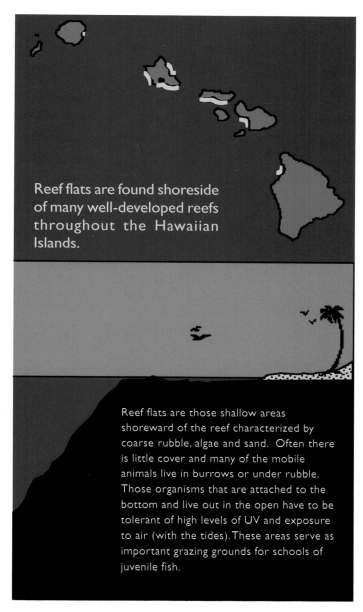

Reef flats are found shoreside of many well-developed reefs throughout the Hawaiian Islands.

Reef flats are those shallow areas shoreward of the reef characterized by coarse rubble, algae and sand. Often there is little cover and many of the mobile animals live in burrows or under rubble. Those organisms that are attached to the bottom and live out in the open have to be tolerant of high levels of UV and exposure to air (with the tides). These areas serve as important grazing grounds for schools of juvenile fish.

Above: The mantis shrimp is one of the top predators on reef flats. Like its namesake, the Preying Mantis, mantis shrimp use a cocked-back front appendage to capture prey (using an action similar to snapping a towel...). There are two types of mantis shrimps seen on reef flats; 'Smashers' have club-like front claws and smash open small invertebrates, while 'Spearers' tend to impale their prey (including small fishes). The speed and force with which these animals use their front appendages is truly amazing. Small mantis shrimp have been observed to break the glass of aquariums; another common name used for these guys by unwary, reef probing people are 'Thumbsplitters'.

Right: Some reef flats in wave-protected areas (such as Kāne'ohe Bay) contain rich assemblages of coral colonies.

The Big Picture:

FOOD WEBS WITHIN THE CORAL REEF COMMUNITY

With so much energy and biomass (the total amount of living material) concentrated within a relatively small area, coral reefs also represent a complex picture of the movement of these materials from one user group to the next within the ecosystem. At its simplest level, this movement can be thought to occur from the primary producers (the marine seaweeds, sea grasses, phytoplankton and zooxanthellae) to the primary consumers (herbivores), then to the secondary consumers (primary carnivores that feed on herbivores) and finally to the tertiary consumers (the secondary carnivores that feed on other carnivores).

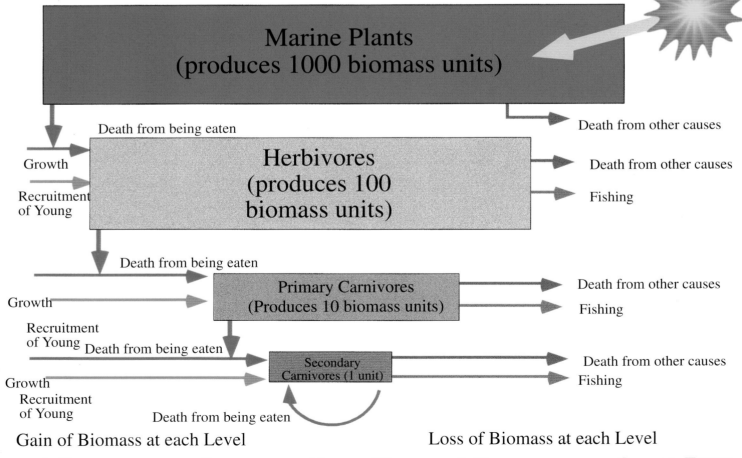

Marine Plants
(produces 1000 biomass units)

Death from other causes

Death from being eaten

Growth

Recruitment of Young

Herbivores
(produces 100 biomass units)

Death from other causes

Fishing

Death from being eaten

Growth

Recruitment of Young

Primary Carnivores
(Produces 10 biomass units)

Death from other causes

Fishing

Death from being eaten

Growth

Recruitment of Young

Secondary Carnivores (1 unit)

Death from other causes

Fishing

Death from being eaten

Gain of Biomass at each Level   Loss of Biomass at each Level

A RIDICULOUSLY-SIMPLIFIED FOOD (BIOMASS) PYRAMID OF A CORAL REEF
(ok, now let's look at it from a different angle)

HAWAIIAN CORAL REEF TROPHIC RELATIONSHIPS

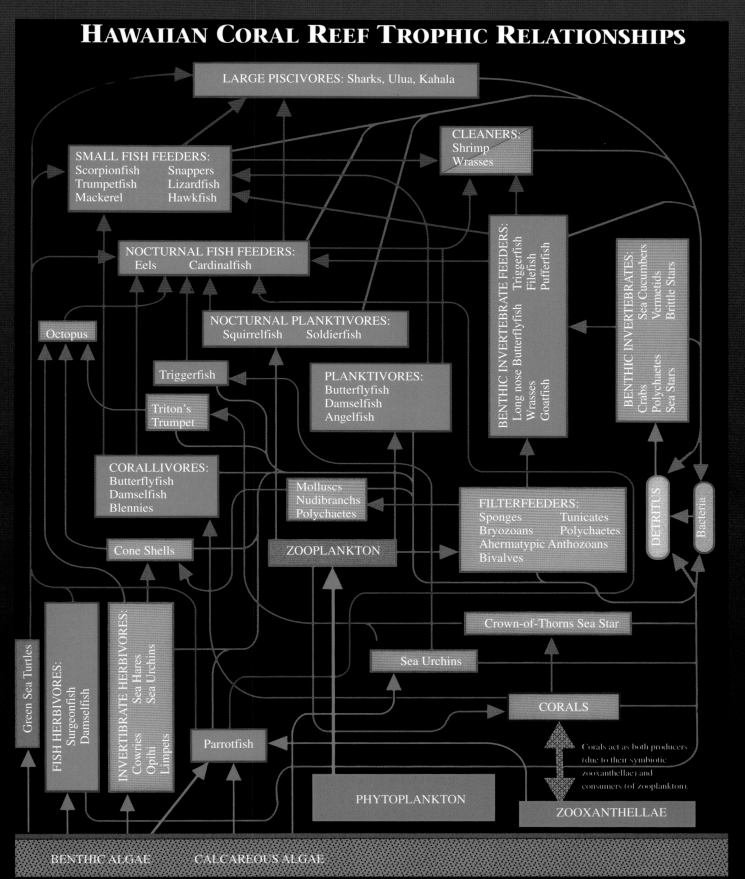

LARGE PISCIVORES: Sharks, Ulua, Kahala

CLEANERS:
Shrimp
Wrasses

SMALL FISH FEEDERS:
Scorpionfish   Snappers
Trumpetfish   Lizardfish
Mackerel   Hawkfish

NOCTURNAL FISH FEEDERS:
Eels   Cardinalfish

BENTHIC INVERTEBRATE FEEDERS:
Long nose Butterflyfish   Triggerfish
Wrasses   Filefish
Goatfish   Pufferfish

BENTHIC INVERTEBRATES:
Crabs   Sea Cucumbers
Polychaetes   Vermetids
Sea Stars   Brittle Stars

NOCTURNAL PLANKTIVORES:
Squirrelfish   Soldierfish

Octopus

Triggerfish

Triton's
Trumpet

PLANKTIVORES:
Butterflyfish
Damselfish
Angelfish

CORALLIVORES:
Butterflyfish
Damselfish
Blennies

Molluscs
Nudibranchs
Polychaetes

FILTERFEEDERS:
Sponges   Tunicates
Bryozoans   Polychaetes
Ahermatypic Anthozoans
Bivalves

DETRITUS

Bacteria

Cone Shells

ZOOPLANKTON

Crown-of-Thorns Sea Star

Green Sea Turtles

FISH HERBIVORES:
Surgeonfish
Damselfish

INVERTIBRATE HERBIVORES:
Cowries   Sea Hares
Opihi   Sea Urchins
Limpets

Sea Urchins

Parrotfish

CORALS

Corals act as both producers
(due to their symbiotic
zooxanthellae) and
consumers (of zooplankton).

PHYTOPLANKTON

ZOOXANTHELLAE

BENTHIC ALGAE   CALCAREOUS ALGAE

Key:

- Primary Producers   - Fish Consumers

NATURAL SOURCES OF STRESS

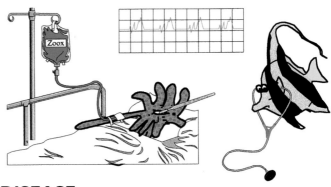

DISEASE

A variety of diseases are known to affect corals (see pp. 185 - 187). It's still unclear how these diseases are transmitted from colony to colony, or area to area.

INTENSE STORMS

Considered by many scientists to be the primary force shaping coral reefs, especially in Hawai'i. The effects are primarily through wave action, but can also include secondary effects caused by the storm's impact on nearby terrestrial environments (such as runoff, etc.)

EL NIÑO

Southern Oscillation Phenomena (termed **El Niño)** occur every couple years and are characterized by increased water temperatures. Such episodes are thought to be responsible for the large coral die-off that occurred in the Galapagos Islands in 1982 -1983. Often the effects of such disturbances are widespread, affecting reefs throughout an area, or even across oceans.

VOLCANIC ERUPTIONS

Though rare in most reef environments, volcanoes do directly affect coral reefs off the coast of the island of Hawai'i, where they can completely cover reefs with lava. Indirectly, volcanoes affect reefs Pacific-wide through earthquakes which can generate tsunamis; upon reaching shallow waters tsunamis can create devastating wave action.

ON CORAL REEFS

PREDATOR POPULATION EXPLOSIONS

There is some evidence that the Crown-of-Thorns Seastar (*Acanthaster planci*) may go through natural blooms where hundreds of these animals can invade a single reef, feeding on the corals (See pp. 101 - 102).

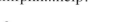

Hmfphh...help!

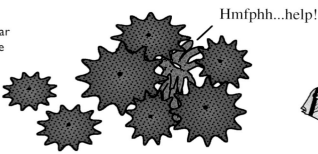

RUNOFF

Well, there goes the neighborhood.

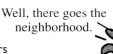

Rain and other erosional factors can cause various forms of runoff to flow over reefs. Often the runoff contains large amounts of sediment (see p. 199) in addition to freshwater.

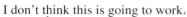

I don't think this is going to work.

Shouldn't the snorkel face the other directon?

Such natural events can have limited or devastating effects on coral reefs depending upon their intensity and duration. Against this is measured the natural recovery rate of the reef itself. It is important to note that many of the above effects can often be increased through the actions of humans; likewise, these natural actions can combine with human-induced actions to drastically impact a reef in ways that would not have occurred if these actions had occurred separately.

EXCEPTIONALLY LOW TIDES

Exceptionally low tides due to solar and lunar rotations can result in short term exposure of corals to air. If this exposure occurs near noon (when ultraviolet radiation levels are often the highest) or during a rainstorm, the negative effects can be greatly enhanced.

LOCAL AND GLOBAL PROBLEMS
(THE HUMAN EFFECT)

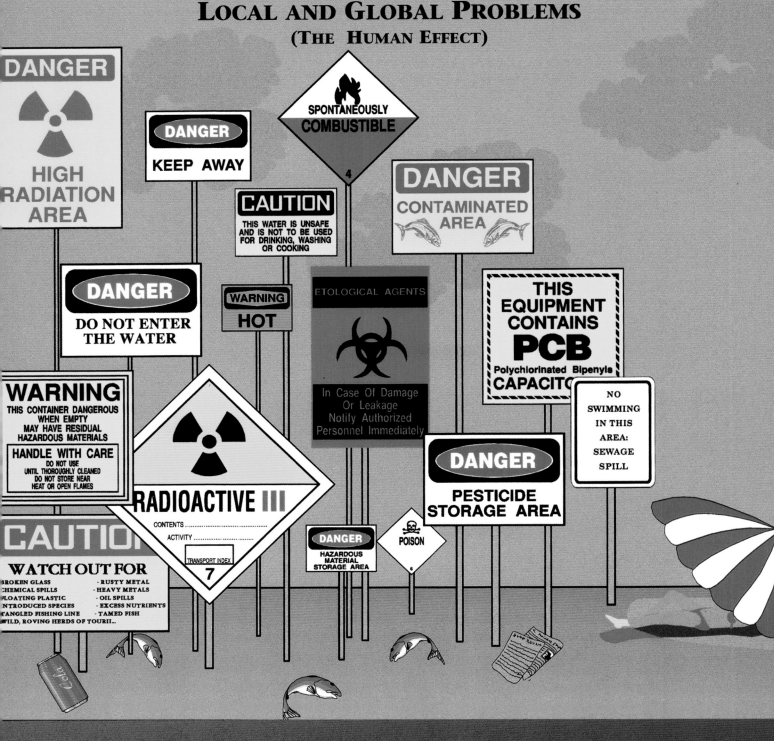

DANGER

HIGH RADIATION AREA

DANGER

KEEP AWAY

SPONTANEOUSLY **COMBUSTIBLE**

4

CAUTION

THIS WATER IS UNSAFE AND IS NOT TO BE USED FOR DRINKING, WASHING OR COOKING

DANGER

CONTAMINATED AREA

DANGER

DO NOT ENTER THE WATER

WARNING

HOT

ETOLOGICAL AGENTS

In Case Of Damage Or Leakage Notify Authorized Personnel Immediately

THIS EQUIPMENT CONTAINS **PCB** Polychlorinated Bipenyls CAPACITO

WARNING

THIS CONTAINER DANGEROUS WHEN EMPTY MAY HAVE RESIDUAL HAZARDOUS MATERIALS

HANDLE WITH CARE
DO NOT USE UNTIL THOROUGHLY CLEANED DO NOT STORE NEAR HEAT OR OPEN FLAMES

NO SWIMMING IN THIS AREA: SEWAGE SPILL

RADIOACTIVE III

CONTENTS ....
ACTIVITY ....

TRANSPORT INDEX

7

DANGER

PESTICIDE STORAGE AREA

CAUTION

WATCH OUT FOR

BROKEN GLASS   - RUSTY METAL
CHEMICAL SPILLS   - HEAVY METALS
FLOATING PLASTIC   - OIL SPILLS
INTRODUCED SPECIES   - EXCESS NUTRIENTS
TANGLED FISHING LINE - TAMED FISH
WILD, ROVING HERDS OF TOURII...

DANGER

HAZARDOUS MATERIAL STORAGE AREA

POISON

6

The nearshore environment of today is in many ways far different from that of thirty years ago. Many of these changes are due to the influence of humans and human activity (**anthropogenic** impacts); which, given the complex nature of reefs, can individually or in combination have devastating effects on the ecology of the reef system.

ANCHOR DAMAGE

Surprisingly, one of the greater direct impacts on coral reefs from the activities of collectors, fisherman, divers, snorkelors or tour boat operators is the effect of anchoring on or near the reef. Usually an anchor is thrown overboard with the intent of hooking it onto something submerged in order to hold the boat in place; often this is part of the reef itself. This action tends to dislodge pieces of the reef; these pieces then cease to function as upright, three-dimensional spaces needed by the wide variety of organisms to live on or around. Instead, they tend to become "smashing objects", breaking up more reef with each heavy storm surge. Heavily used areas often show markings where anchors dragged across reef or the chain from an anchored boat smashed-up branching corals as the boat swung around with the wind. When possible, many people try to anchor in the sand adjacent to the reef; if properly done this can minimize impact, but care has to be taken since the anchor chain itself can heavily damage the substrate. Areas that are continuously and heavily used need special considerations; many commercial operators make use of permanent **moorings** (a "stationary" object that a boat can tie off to) in order to not have to set an anchor every time they visit a site. Moorings can minimize impact but care has to be taken such that the setting of the mooring or the materials used will not themselves impact the reef. Any moorings to be placed in Hawaiian coastal waters have to be approved by both the State of Hawai'i Department of Land and Natural Resources and the Army Corps of Engineers.

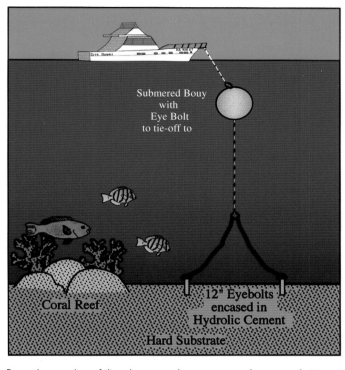

Recently a number of dive shops, tour boat owners and concerned citizens have installed (with the State's backing) a series of day-use permanent moorings. These moorings are located in heavily used diving areas and are designed to minimize physical damage to nearby reefs from visiting boats by having them tie off to the mooring instead of anchoring. These moorings are specially designed to not damage the reef in the way concrete block and other types of loose moorings have in the past.

Reefs can be damaged by the anchor itself or the movement of the chain as the boat swings with the current or swell.

Heinz-Gert deCouet

• Identified as a primary source of Anthropogenic Stress on Hawaiian coral reefs (UNEP/IUCN 1988) •

CORAL BLEACHING

Deborah Gochfeld

When corals lose (or expel) their zooxanthellae in large numbers the result is a living colony of coral that has lost most of its color. This phenomena is referred to as **Coral Bleaching**. First described in the early 1900s as a result of high water temperatures, interest in bleaching phenomena started to occur after a series of major coral bleaching events were documented during the 1980s in both the Atlantic and Pacific oceans. Some of these episodes seemed to be linked to oscillations in atmospheric and oceanic circulation (often referred to as **El Niño**).

When bleaching occurs, corals are sometimes able to slowly re-infect themselves with zooxanthellae, and/or recover through

---

Some of the causes of Bleaching:

• Unusually high or low temperatures
• Unusually high or low salinity
• High amounts of visible or ultraviolet light
• Sedimentation
• High levels of nutrients (sewage, etc.)
• High levels of toxins (pesticides, etc.)

Upper right: Bleaching in the reef coral *Montipora capitata.* The left coral colony is healthy and full of zooxanthellae, while the right colony has bleached due to increased water temperatures.

Right: Examples of normal and bleached colonies of *Pocillopora damicornis.* Note that in the bleached corals you can still see expanded live polyps; they just lack the symbiotic zooxanthellae.

Bottom: Bleaching phenomena are not limited to only corals. The Giant Clam (*Tridacna gigas*) also harbors zooxanthellae and episodes of bleaching, though rare, have been observed in that species.

Deborah Gochfeld

reproduction of the few remaining zooxanthellae left within the colony. Frequently, the loss of large amounts of symbiotic algae results in the colony running up an energy deficit where it is using more energy to exist than it is taking in. If the episode is severe or long-term, the colony dies.

Is this a recent phenomenon? No one's quite sure; SCUBA diving (and therefore an increased number of observers on the reef) has only gained global prominence in the last twenty years or so. Still, many scientists believe that such bleaching events, when they occur together on reefs oceans apart, are evidence of global warming.

As atmospheric temperatures increase due to increased CO_2, surface sea temperatures are expected to increase also. Many bleaching events have been suggested to have resulted from increased water temperatures. Keep in mind that many corals suffer mortality if the temperature is raised just 1 - 2° C; as such, corals may serve as an early warning system for the rest of the planet of the effects of global warming.

Paul Jokiel

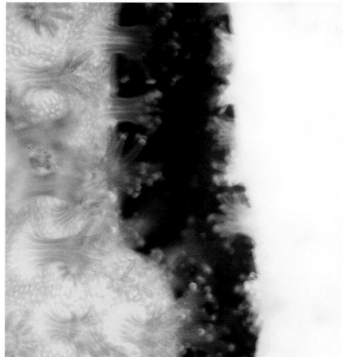

COASTAL DEVELOPMENT

We live in a world where the majority of the people live within a 100 km of the ocean. Here in Hawai'i, most of our population lives within 5 km of the ocean (less than 3 miles)! It is becoming exceedingly rare in Hawai'i to find areas of undeveloped, unimpacted coastline; such areas are crucial buffer zones for nearshore reef systems.

Above: Most of our population is crammed right next to the shoreline; a shoreline filled with high-rise hotels on what used to be wetlands and estuaries that supported the coral reefs offshore.

Above: Development of marinas, seawalls, and new land (by filling in the reef, as was done for the Honolulu Reef Runway, at Honolulu Airport, and Magic Island Park on O'ahu) alter nearshore currents which are crucial for healthy reef development.

Above: Often, nearshore areas are dredged or excavated for fill material, causeways, airport runways, marinas, harbors or to create new land for population expansion. How many examples can you think of for your area? Do you see healthy reefs in the vicinity of these areas, why or why not?

Byproducts of coastal development:

- Loss of habitat through dredging and excavation
- Loss of habitat through landfilling techniques
- Increased harvesting of reef organisms
- Alteration of water circulation patterns
- Increased sedimentation
- High nutrients (sewage, etc.)
- High toxins (pesticides, herbicides, etc.)
- Increased non-point source pollution
- Increased water temperatures (thermal outfalls, etc.)

Above: Most areas where coral reefs occur are often land-poor. As development continues and populations increase, new ways of dealing with the by-products of humans have to be developed.

Above: Not only disposable trash is introduced into our waters; as streams are modified, and upland areas are developed and paved over, numerous toxic chemicals, pesticides, and herbicides are washed into seashore areas. Pretty much everything up to, and including, the kitchen sink makes its way into coastal waters!

• Identified as a primary source of Anthropogenic Stress on Hawaiian coral reefs (UNEP/IUCN 1988) •

AND TOMORROW'S JUST AROUND THE CORNER...

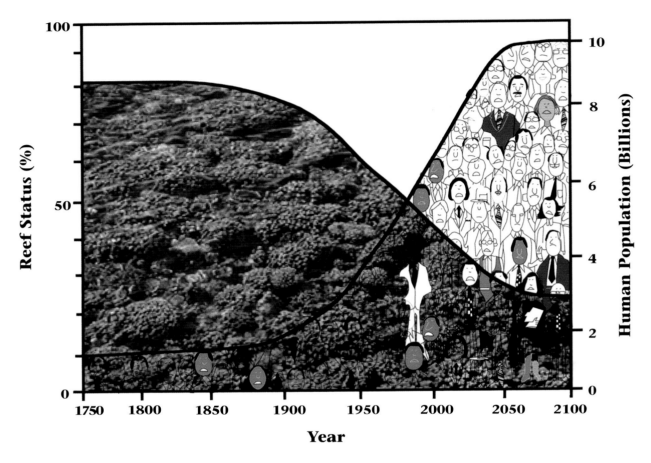

What the future may hold...the increase in global population and the expected amount of coral reef decline based on current rates of reef loss and the status of reefs in areas where data has been taken (Graph adapted from Wilkinson, 1992).

The most critical factor affecting the survival of any organism (be it an endangered, threatened or non-threatened species, or humans themselves) on Earth is the rate of human population growth and its consequences. We may be entering a new age of unparalleled extinctions brought about by our extreme population growth, life longevity and extensive use of non-replaceable natural resources. One way to mediate this is through family planning strategies to limit the number of offspring each of us has. Lacking this, the world-wide loss of coral reefs may just be the warm-up act for our own extinction on this planet.

CORAL DISEASES

Coral diseases of bacterial or viral origin were first described in the Caribbean back in the 1970's. Since that time, similar infestations have been reported from the Red Sea and the Indo-Pacific. Recent studies suggest that disease-like infestations are now occurring in Hawai'i. Since many of these diseases may be bacterial, the possibility exists that they may be spread from colony to colony, reef to reef by corallivorous fish (or even herbivorous fish such as parrotfish). Such fish could easily harbor these bacteria in their mouths and spread the disease as they move over the reef nibbling on their favorite morsels.

Many of these diseases are thought to gain a foothold during periods of extended environmental stress. Additionally, it appears that physical damage (either through wave action, fish bites or wild herds of tourists roaming over a reef breaking off branches and scratching up colonies) may facilitate introduction of the pathogen into the coral tissues.

Four of the different disease-like conditions that have been described for corals:

Bacterial Infections

Various species of bacteria.

Bacteria can grow on mucus secreted from a coral. Under conditions of environmental stress, the bacteria may multiply to a point where they use up much of the available oxygen immediately surrounding the coral, bringing about the coral's demise.

Black Band Disease

Phormidium corallyticum

An infestation of a cyanobacterium which grows as tight, intermeshed filaments which can cover over a coral colony. This disease is seen most often in massive corals and gorgonians.

White Band Disease

Pathogen unknown, but suggested to be a Gram-negative, oval-shaped bacteria.
Often seen with branching corals, this disease is frequently associated with bleaching phenomena.

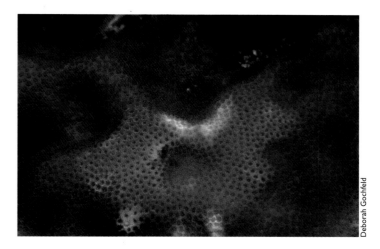

Above: Characteristic stress response caused by bacterial infection, possibly introduced by the adjacent fish bites in the colony.

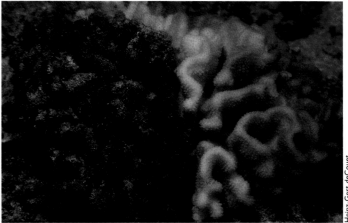

Above: Often it's difficult to differentiate visually between bleaching associated with partial colony mortality and that which occurs with White Band Disease.

Left: White Band Disease in *Montipora*. As the affected tissue peels off the coral skeleton, it forms the characteristic white bands associated with the disease.

Coral Neoplasms (Tumors)

Pathogen unknown.

Brings about uncontrolled growth in a section of a coral colony resulting in a tumor-like protuberance from the colony's surface. Seen in a variety of species of corals in Hawai'i.

Porites lobata

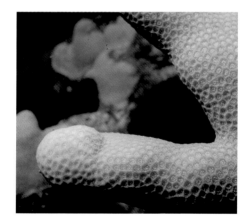

Porites compressa

Montipora flabellata

Montipora patula

Note that these neoplasms seem to occur on a variety of species occurring in Hawaiian waters.

Algal Infestations

Though not a true disease, infestations of filamentous algae are often seen as an after-effect of other impacts.

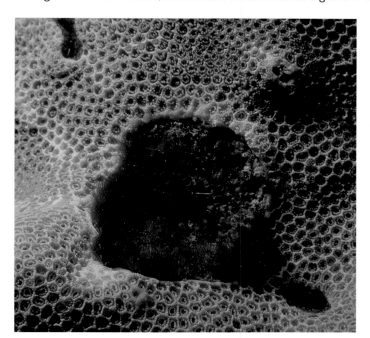

POP QUIZ:

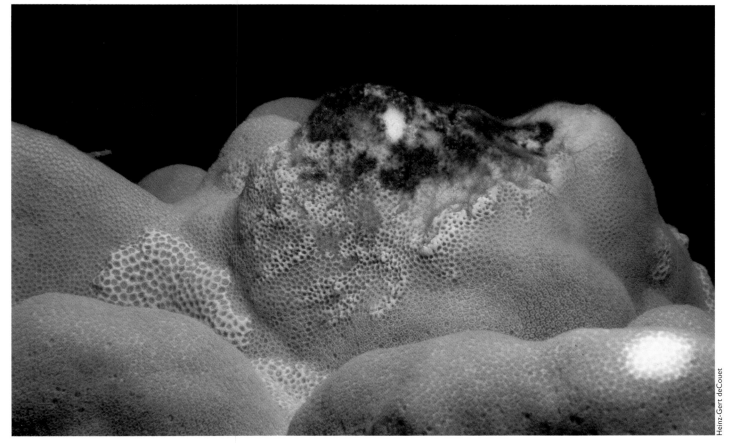

Heinz-Gert deCouet

Look closely at the above coral colony; based on visual evidence can you identify five (5) different biological impacts upon this colony?

(Answer in the back of the book)

FISH FEEDING

Hey Mom, The fish is eating out of my han- Ow!!!

Heinz-Gert deCouet

If fish feeding has to occur, perhaps it would be better to limit it to artificial environments such as artificial reefs or large scale public aquariums. Areas such as Marine Life Conservation Districts (Hanauma Bay, Kealakekua Bay, etc.) should be kept as pristine as possible.

undisturbed reef Ⓐ is made up of a wide variety of different animals whose life histories are often intertwined (see p. 177). Such interactions help to maintain diversity since few organisms can overwhelm the others and most of the organisms are to some extent specialists.

In areas of intense fish-feeding (as described above), generalist fish greatly multiply in number Ⓑ . Eventually, many of the specialist fish are driven away or die-off as the ecology of the reef itself changes due to the large influx of generalists.

In such a scenario, the corals themselves could be affected as herbivorous fish leave or switch over to fish food, allowing the corals to be overgrown by algae and bacteria thriving on the increased nutrients. The resulting loss of three-dimensional cover decreases successful recruitment of both fish and invertebrates leading to a very low diversity habitat.

Why is it that humans have a need to treat certain wild marine animals as if they were personal pets? The animal does not live in the safety of somebody's home aquarium, but in the natural world. Habituating an animal to a different food source can affect that animal's ability to gather necessary nutrients, hold a territory or successfully mate. These changes can in turn eventually affect the whole ecosystem. On the other hand, in areas where fish feeding is abundant many fish learn to recognize the presence of divers or snorkelors as a sort of dinner bell, and gather in preparation for a feeding frenzy. Such gatherings tend to consist of only a few species of generalists and on a number of occasions unwary snorkelors have been seriously bitten.

A number of scientists have hypothesized that intensive fish feeding, using non-specialized feeds (such as dog food) may contribute to a loss of diversity on a reef. The idea here is that a

▼ Impartial Artist's Renditions ▼

Ⓐ **Undisturbed Reef**　　Ⓑ **Altered Reef**

EFFECTS OF FISHING

Richard Pyle

"When I was a kid, there were so many more reef fish then there are today..." Although there are many causes for the decline of nearshore fisheries in Hawai'i, a prominent one is simply overfishing. Our population has steadily grown and more and more people want to fish. This, along with an increased ability to catch fish and a decrease in habitat space for recruitment, has lead to a dramatic decrease in fish populations. When was the last time you saw a really large school of anything?

Heinz-Gert deCouet

Above: Hawai'i's nearshore waters are littered with remnants of monofilament fishing line. While this may pose a danger to divers, it is far more lethal for a wide variety of sea life; from fish to urchins to sea turtles (who can have limbs or their heads choked off by self-tightening strands of loose fishing line).

Ghost Nets: Often times large pieces of fishing nets either break lose or are cut free, drifting away with the current. Such nets continue to trap marine organisms (fish, turtles, mammals) even without human handlers. Eventually the weight from all of the dead animals caught causes the net to sink. After a while the dead organisms decay or are picked off and the net rises back up into shallow water where the cycle begins all over again.

• Identified as a primary source of Anthropogenic Stress on Hawaiian coral reefs (UNEP/IUCN 1988) •

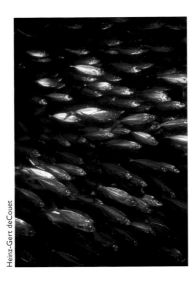

Coral reefs often function as a closed system, most of the energy is tied-up in **biomass**. This results in unfished reefs having lots of fish.

At the same time, coral reefs are situated in relatively nutrient-poor waters, leaving the impression of coral reefs acting as a sort of oasis. This can only occur if reefs have efficient mechanisms to re-circulate nutrients (in other words: it's this efficient recycling of energy that results in the high biomass seen on reefs, not some limitless input of energy from outside).

Within a given trophic level, predation is very high. Such predation is an intricate part of this efficient recycling of energy mechanism (see p. 177).

The complexity of trophic levels on coral reefs leads to energy passing through a number of trophic levels. At each level there is a substantial loss of energy stored in a given organism due to the process of living within its ecosystem (see p. 176). This means that with a large amount of energy loss at each level, very little energy is stored in the higher trophic levels (e.g., the fish that most humans consume).

Therefore, very little energy (fish) is available for human consumption if the desire is to maintain the coral reef system in a pristine state. Even low levels of fishing can drastically alter the coral reef community and maintain the lack of fish within it.

THIS CAN HAVE GREAT EFFECTS ON THE REEF ITSELF:

A study by R. E. Brock (1979) showed that corals and coralline algae (the two major building blocks of reefs) were significantly greater (in terms of growth) on unfished reefs. Why might this be the case?

Planula Larvae

High numbers of herbivorous fishes

= Decreased algae growth
= Decreased competition with coral for space and increased open space for coral and coralline algae settlement.
= Increased corals & coralline algae.

Low numbers of herbivorous fishes

= Increased algae growth
= Increased competition with coral for space and decreased open space for coral and coralline algae settlement.
= Decreased corals & coralline algae.

TROPICAL FISH COLLECTING

Many people believe that tropical fish collecting has minimal impact on reef fish populations because there are far more fish larvae than there is space on the reef. While this may be true for schooling species, the jury's still out for rare and individual species (which often are the ones that bring the higher prices). Additionally, it doesn't take a brain surgeon to realize that if collecting is widespread and you collect the majority of pre-reproductive fish (often collectors go for the smaller fish), over time there will be an impact on the number of larvae that are produced and available for recruitment.

Between 1968 - 1982 the number of commercial tropical fish collecting permits in Hawai'i increased by 1200%!!!

While tropical fish collecting is not the only factor responsible for reductions in nearshore reef fish populations around the main Hawaiian Islands, it is an additional pressure that over a wide scale can contribute to the decline that has been observed.

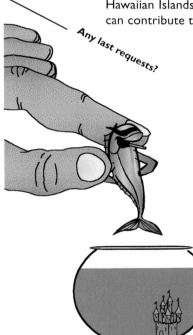

Any last requests?

How Reefs Are Damaged by Collecting Practices

1. Barrier nets - can become entangled in reefs; branching corals can be damaged during setting and retrieving of nets.

2. Damage from the fins of divers chasing fish with hand nets, dip nets or slurp guns.

3. Many fish will hide within branching corals when chased; collectors will sometimes break-up these colonies to get at these fish. Collection of attached reef invertebrates (such as the Featherduster Worm, *Sabellastarte sanctijosephi*) often results in the destruction of bottom substrate.

4. If traps are left untended the fish inside can die. Strong surge can turn a loose trap into a bulldozer which smashes-up sections of reef as it rolls about.

5. Removal of rare or solitary species can quickly lower diversity on a reef. Often such species have slower replacement rates.

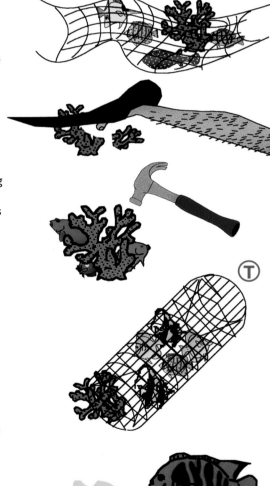

What Can Be Done?

- More oversight of what's being collected and from where is needed in order to determine impacts.
- Rare species need to be protected from commercial exploitation.
- New technologies need to be critically reviewed before they are allowed to be used to assist in collecting in order to prevent over-exploitation.
- Mariculture of rare/ endangered species should be encouraged in order to decrease effects of collecting on reef ecosystems.

While still used in other parts of the Pacific, collecting fish through use of explosives and chemicals (bleach, cyanide, etc.) is illegal in the state of Hawaii (HI Rev. Statutes §188-23).

• Identified as a primary source of Anthropogenic Stress on Hawaiian coral reefs (UNEP/IUCN 1988) •

INTRODUCED SPECIES ON HAWAIIAN CORAL REEFS

The Blue-striped snapper (*Lutjanus kasmira* or Ta'ape) was first introduced to Hawai'i in 1955 and has successfully spread throughout the islands. A commercially valuable species, Ta'ape may have become too abundant and may be replacing deeper water native snappers.

Hawai'i is the most isolated group of islands in the world. Such isolation is thought to be primarily responsible for the high rate of endemism seen in Hawaiian environments (including coral reefs). Recently a worldwide problem has started to increasingly affect Hawaiian waters: the outside introduction of marine organisms. Such introductions can be of two types:

- Accidental Introductions. These tend to occur as a result of organisms hitching a ride on barges and ships (either in the bilge or attached to the hull). Usually these organisms first take hold in harbors and bays.

- Commercial Introductions. In most cases these involved the State of Hawai'i (or the prior Territorial Government) purposely releasing commercially-valuable species. In a number of instances introductions have occurred by non-governmental parties illegally. As a result of many of these introductions, Hawaiian nearshore ecosystems are being altered at increasingly fast rates. Organisms and relationships that have evolved over millions of years in relative isolation are often wiped out by these newcomer organisms that usually have evolved in highly competitive ecosystems. Coral reefs exist as highly complicated

INTRODUCED ORGANISM	DATE	TYPE	COMMENTS
Algae			
Acanthophora spicifera	1950	Accidental	Came on a barge from Guam into Pearl Harbor, by 1960 it was found on Lana'i & Kaua'i. Today it is commonly found throughout Hawai'i.
Eucheuma sp. and *Kappophycus* sp.	1975	Commercial	Introduced from the Philippines by a scientist onto a reef flat at Coconut Island. It has now spread throughout Kāne'ohe Bay.
Hypnea musciformis	1975	Commercial	Introduced from Florida.
Ulva reticulata	pre-1933	Commercial	
Invertebrates			
Upside-down Jelly (*Cassieopea medusa*)	1940's	Accidental	Introduced to Pearl Harbor. Also found in Kāne'ohe Bay.
Phyllorhiza punctata	1940's	Accidental	Introduced to Pearl Harbor.
Snowflake Coral (*Carijoa riisei*)	1972	Accidental	First appeared in Pearl Harbor. Thought to have come from the Caribbean on the hull of a ship. Common on O'ahu, it has now been sighted on the Neighbor Islands.
Black Abalone (*Haliotis cracherochi*)	1958 - 1959	Commercial	Not successful.
Trochus niloticus	1963	Commercial	Introduced from Guam.
Barnacle (*Chthamalus porteus*)	1995	Accidental	Now one of the most abundant intertidal invertebrates on O'ahu, Maui and Kaua'i.
Mangrove Crab (*Scylla serrata*)	1926 - 1935	Commercial	98 crabs introduced during a 9-year period. 26 were introduced to Hilo Bay, the rest were released around O'ahu.
Fish			
Ta'ape (*Lutjanus kasmira*)	1955	Commercial	Introduced from French Polynesia; has spread rapidly and is now found all the way up and into the Northwest Hawaiian Islands.
To'au (*Lutjanus fulvus*)	1955	Commercial	Introduced from French Polynesia
Roi (*Cephalophalus argus*)	1956	Commercial	Common everywhere, but most abundant on the Big Island
Goatfish (*Upeneus vittatus*)	1955	Accidental	

Richard Pyle

Richard Pyle

Above: The Lemonpeel Angelfish (*Centropyge flavissimus*) has been sighted on at least two patch reefs within Kāne'ohe Bay, O'ahu.

Keoki Stender

Above: Tilapia sp. were introduced to Hawai'i a number of times since the early 1950's. Able to breed in seawater, *Tilapia* have become very abundant around O'ahu. There has been some concern that these fish may be feeding heavily on nehu, a baitfish used extensively by tuna fishermen.

ecosystems where trophic interactions can be seriously affected by the introduction of such organisms. Displacement of competitors, symbionts, predators and/or prey species can occur, which in turn could affect a wide range of other organisms within the reef and adjacent ecosystems. Examples such as the spread of *Eucheuma/Kapophycus* seaweed over the patch reefs of Kāne'ohe Bay, or the introduction of schooling snappers into reef environments that had evolved without such predators, serve to warn us of the long range impacts such introductions can have.

Recently non-Hawaiian reef fish have started to appear in a number of isolated reef areas. Presumably these are aquarium fish that have either purposely or accidentally been released. Though nice in an aquarium, such animals pose an extreme risk to native Hawaiian fish and reef ecosystems. Introduced diseases, niche loss, displacement or even extinction of native species have been observed with similar introductions in terrestrial and freshwater systems and are possible in reef ecosystems.

Above: A number of species of anemonefish have been sighted around the island of O'ahu. The host anemones of most of these species do not exist in Hawai'i.

Unwanted non-native aquarium fish should be dropped off at participating pet stores.

A number of years ago a University of Hawai'i scientist was looking into commercially valuable seaweeds. Research specimens of the alga *Eucheuma* sp. somehow were released onto the reef flat at Coconut Island in Kāne'ohe Bay, O'ahu. Over the ensuing years this alga has dramatically increased its coverage in the bay, often growing atop and killing off the corals that make-up the patch reefs found there.

Paul Jokiel

Above: Introduced species of *Acanthophora spicifera, Eucheuma* sp., and *Gracillaria salicornia* overgrowing reef corals in Kāne'ohe Bay, O'ahu. Once they establish a foothold, these alien algae are very difficult to eradicate.

Marine Tourism

TOURIST SUBMARINES
SNORKEL TOURS
THRILL CRAFT   DIVING TOURS
ADVENTURE TOURS   BEACHES
                KAYAKING
TOUR BOATS   WATER SKIING
SNUBA   SAILING
WIND SURFING   SURFING
PARASAILING   WHALE WATCHING
                        FISHING

> 85% of visitors to Hawai'i participate in some form of ocean recreation. In 1990, the marine recreation industry brought $700 million dollars into the State of Hawai'i.

How Reefs Are Damaged by Marine Tourism

– Destruction of coastal and reef-associated habitat (anchialine ponds, mangrove forests, seagrass beds and estuaries) in order to build resorts along the shoreline.

– Pollution of reef areas through sewage, pesticides and nutrients from coastal resorts.

– Alteration of coastlines to create beaches, mining of sand to enhance beaches.

– Direct destruction and disturbance of reef habitat and organisms through actions of improperly-guided visitors, overuse, and operation of thrill craft and other machinery near/on shallow reef areas.

Protection for most reef areas in Hawai'i is by a concept called a Marine Life Conservation District (MLCD). Hanauma Bay, Pupukea, Kealakekua Bay are all MLCDs. A primary focus of MLCDs is public access, but given the limited number of MLCDs and the increasing use of them by the public, one has to wonder how any conservation is going to occur in these areas. In fact, one could argue that by having few preserves, and choosing them partially-based on their accessibility to the recreational public, one is not creating conservation areas but marine tourism/recreational parks. Such areas need to exist, but if most of our large pristine reefs are designated MLCDs without any of them being set aside as true marine life preserves (free from the impact of large numbers of humans), large pristine coral reef habitats in the Hawaiian Islands may be only a temporary tourist attraction.

WHAT CAN BE DONE?

- In some parts of the world, tourism operators are required to have a **certified** reef naturalist on-board their vessels in order to operate within protected areas. The naturalist is certified by the local government and is responsible for not only providing a quality educational experience for the paying customers, but also to minimize the impact of the operation on the natural resource being used.

- We need to **zone** our reef systems as is done in Australia in order to set aside areas for specific uses and to create areas which are completely unaffected by most human activities. Such zoning will help to decrease conflicts between different user groups.

- Create a **reef tax** assessed for any operation operating within a protected reef area. Monies collected would be fees used for protection of reef resources and for training of tour operators in reef interpretation and conservation.

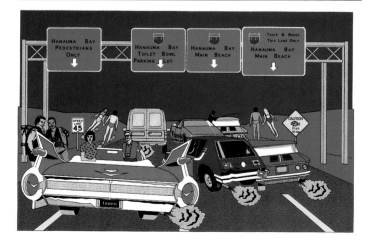

The Hanauma Bay Story

Created in 1967 as Hawaii's first Marine Life Conservation District (MLCD), Hanauma Bay became famous as a preserve where people could go to see live coral reefs and lots of reef fish. The regulations governing the bay prohibit the taking or injuring of any marine life, or the taking or altering of any natural or geological substrate. Hanauma Bay was looked at as the jewel of marine parks, a model for reef conservation efforts elsewhere... and that's where the problems began. You see, Hanauma Bay was the MLCD that was loved to death (literally). The State of Hawai'i views MLCD's as important resources for recreation; and few people realized initially that masses of people within an enclosed, isolated bay would lead to environmental degradation (of the resource that they had set aside for preservation in the first place...). Large numbers of people (upwards of 10,000 people per day!) started to flock to the bay, numerous tour companies would bring in large busloads and run catered events on the beach. Feral cats and pigeons started to multiply as they were continuously fed by the crowds of people. The natural vegetation and the beach sand itself started to become choked with discarded refuse and cigarette butts. The sheer numbers of people wading into the water started to impact the reefs; the oil slicks they left behind from various tanning lotions created a layer on the surface of the water that cut down gas exchange and possibly killed eggs from fish and corals. The park itself was on a septic system and it was conceivable that the large volumes of people using the park overwhelmed the system, allowing large amounts of nutrients and bacteria to enter the enclosed bay ecosystem. By the late 1980's Hanauma Bay was an ecosystem in serious trouble. Since the early 1990's a number of steps have been taken to decrease the impact on the bay's fragile resources; the number of people allowed to visit the bay per day has been cut back, fish feeding is discouraged (though still allowed), a new system that pumps the sewage into the city's sewer system was installed recently, and an environmental education group (The Friends of Hanauma Bay) provides on-site interpretation and guidance that serves to help lessen the impact of visitors. Still, it's one of the "only games in town"; as long as O'ahu lacks more well-managed marine parks and continues to encourage the active use of marine conservation areas as recreation spots for the masses, those few in existence will continue to be impacted. The dire consequences of limiting the conservation that occurs within those few declared refuges could have devastating impacts on marine life throughout the State.

Lots of live coral

Very little live coral

NUTRIENTS (SEWAGE & EUTROPHICATION)

Sewage, non-point source run-off and other forms of eutrophication (the pollution caused by excessive nutrient enrichment) often leads to increased production and biomass of plant material (the equivalent of adding fertilizer to a plot of land).

Cindy Hunter

Bubble Algae (*Dictyosphaeria cavernosa*) was used in Kaneʻohe Bay as an "Indicator Species" for the presence of high nutrients. Even twenty years after sewage diversion outside the bay (and presumably lower nutrient levels) Bubble Algae is still a problem in some parts of the Bay where it is outcompeting, overgrowing and smothering coral colonies (as shown above).

HOW DOES EUTROPHICATION AFFECT A CORAL REEF:

- High nutrients (especially nitrogenous and phosphorus compounds) leads to high phytoplankton populations.

- Slow growth rates of corals (cm/yr) can't compete with phytoplankton growth rates (population doubles in a number of hours) or seaweed growth rates under high nutrient conditions.

- High phytoplankton densities leads to increased turbidity which decreases light available for coral's zooxanthellae.

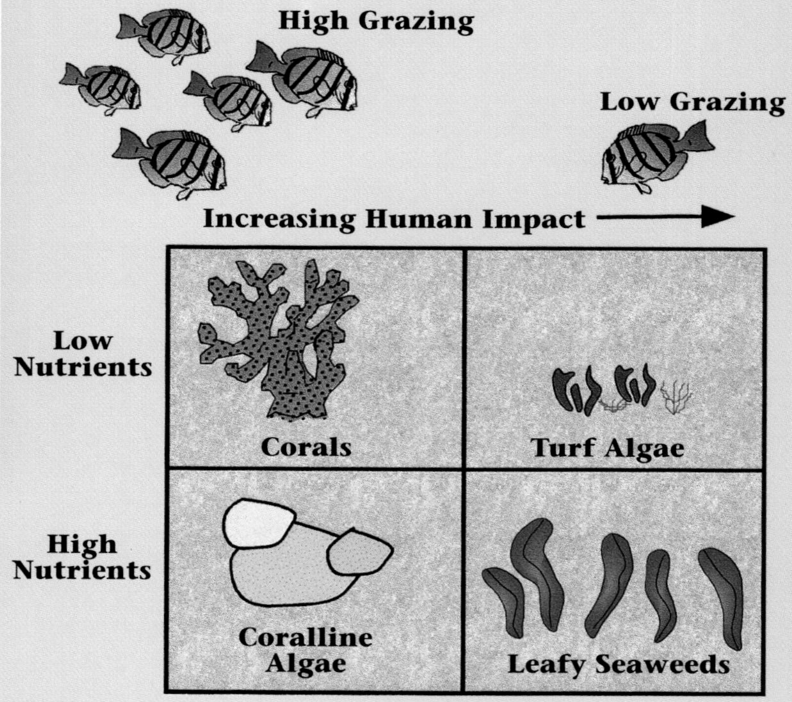

High Grazing

Low Grazing

Increasing Human Impact ➜

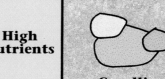

Low Nutrients — Corals | Turf Algae

High Nutrients — Coralline Algae | Leafy Seaweeds

(After Lapointe *et al.*, 1997)

Sewage and other forms of eutrophication can upset the delicate balance seen on coral reefs. High amounts of available nutrients leads to an increase in specific species (usually fleshy algae) and a decrease in the diversity. When combined with other human effects (such as overfishing), the slow growth rate of corals quickly leads to their demise.

• Identified as a primary source of Anthropogenic Stress on Hawaiian coral reefs (UNEP/IUCN 1988) •

The Kāneʻohe Bay Story

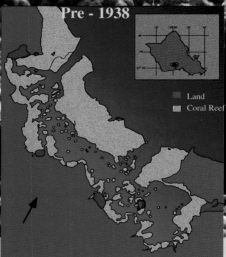

Pre - 1938

Land
Coral Reef

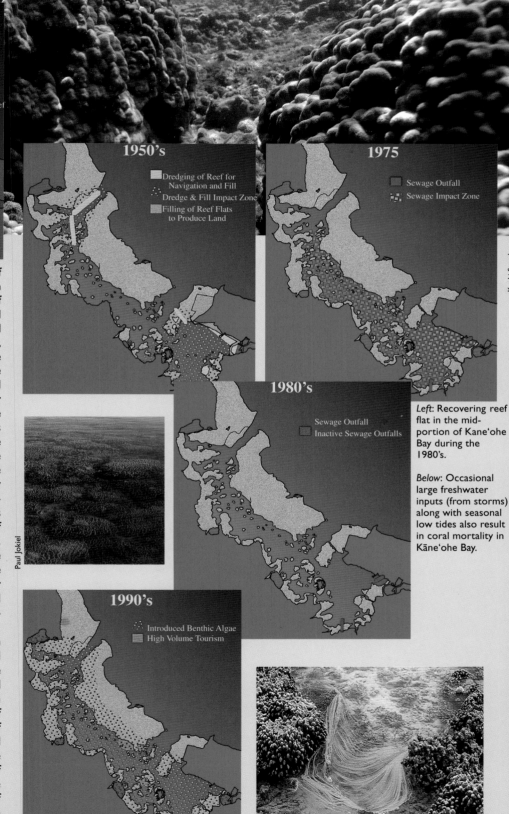

1950's

Dredging of Reef for
Navigation and Fill
Dredge & Fill Impact Zone
Filling of Reef Flats
to Produce Land

1975

Sewage Outfall
Sewage Impact Zone

Keoki Stender

1980's

Sewage Outfall
Inactive Sewage Outfalls

1990's

Introduced Benthic Algae
High Volume Tourism

Paul Jokiel

Paul Jokiel

Left: Recovering reef flat in the mid-portion of Kāneʻohe Bay during the 1980's.

Below: Occasional large freshwater inputs (from storms) along with seasonal low tides also result in coral mortality in Kāneʻohe Bay.

Probably the best-studied example of the effects of sewage and nutrification on coral reefs is Kāneʻohe Bay on the island of Oʻahu. Prior to World War II and up until 1950, Kāneʻohe Bay was dredged and filled in areas to create shipping channels, seaplane lanes and land for expansion of the Kāneʻohe Marine Corps Air Station. At the time Kāneʻohe was sparsely populated and the bay relatively non-impacted except for the southern-most portion. Up until the 1950's, Kāneʻohe Bay was renowned for its lush coral gardens; it was around this time that the population on the Windward Side of Oʻahu started to take off. The increase in population brought with it heavy modification of the shoreline, increased run-off from development, and sewage outfalls emptying up to 5 million gallons per day of high-nutrient sewage directly into the bay. Along with increased sedimentation, the sewage acted as fertilizer for Green Bubble Algae (*Dictyosphaeria cavernosa*) and other seaweeds which grew over and smothered corals throughout the southern and mid-portions of the bay.

Replacement of the outfalls with an ocean outfall in the 1980's resulted in partial to complete coral recovery throughout the bay. Benthic algae numbers decreased dramatically. Still, Kāneʻohe Bay has been severely impacted, and large amounts of sediments are occasionally re-suspended off the bottom. When added to the occasional heavy run-offs from coastal areas and the limited circulation in the southern part of the bay, recovery has been very slow. The introduction of a number of species of benthic algae and concentrated tourism activities directly atop reefs add to the slow recovery.

EFFECTS OF OIL SPILLS & HEAVY METALS ON CORAL REEFS

OIL SPILLS

Oil spills on coral reefs have been relatively rare; mo[...]
the data on effects comes from laboratory work. In a revie[...]
the effects of 16 oil spills that did occur near coral reefs[...]
National Research Council (1985) found no specific repor[...]
adverse impacts on the corals themselves. One reason for[...]
could be that the oil floats on the surface and would ra[...]
come into contact with corals except under exceptionally[...]
tide conditions. If such conditions occurred, coverage of c[...]
and substrate would affect organisms throughout the reef[...]
web. A more probable form of impact would be upor[...]
released gametes and larvae of coral reef organisms. Cor[...]
near the surface could inhibit fertilization, growth[...]
metamorphosis. Coating of bottom substrate or larvae c[...]
inhibit the ability of these larvae to successfully settle.

Often it may not be the oil itself that has the greatest im[...]
studies on certain chemicals given off by various forms c[...]
show lethal effects on corals and larvae. Interestingly, the u[...]
emulsifiers and detergents to break-up and dissolve oil[...]
often has a greater effect on the corals then the oil itself.[...]
suggests that great care must be taken in trying to clean-u[...]
spills near reefs.

HEAVY METALS

A number of metals are present in seawater; their levels can
be elevated by a variety of anthropogenic (human) influences:
- Sediments from runoff (caused by coastal development or mining)
- Sewage Discharge
- Thermal Effluent (often from power plants)
- Certain Desalination Plants' Effluent (primarily copper and nickel)

Copper levels as small as 0.1 mg/l (which is slightly above levels found in Hawaiian nearshore waters) were noted to kill *Pocillopora damicornis* and *Montipora capitata* within six days.

Particulate Metals

Plankton

Heavy Metals (2 forms)

Coral Tissue

Dissolved Metals

Coral Skeleton

Zooxanthellae

after Howard & Brown (1984).

• Identified as a primary source of Anthropogenic Stress on Hawaiian coral reefs (UNEP/IUCN 1988) •

EFFECTS OF SEDIMENTATION ON CORAL REEFS

Sediments can be introduced into the marine environment from terrestrial sources through both natural and human-enhanced processes. Often the effects of such episodes are increased by activities such as on-shore development, deforestation, agriculture, etc.

Effects of sedimentation include:

- Physical smothering/burial. Smothering decreases available oxygen and nutrients, in effect, suffocating the coral (and other reef organisms).

- Decreased light levels. Sedimentation decreases the passage of light through the water column, thus decreasing the amount of light that reaches the zooxanthellae and resulting in decreased energy available for the coral.

- Decreased recruitment. Siltation creates a soft bottom substrate which effectively blocks planula from successfully settling out of the plankton.

- Chemical effects. Sediments can act as miniature substrates to carry a wide variety of chemicals which may have secondary effects on coral colonies, planula larvae, other plankton and other reef organisms. More research needs to be done in this area.

SEDIMEN

Normal

After a Heavy Rain

Above: A reef flat at Coconut Island in the middle of Kāne'ohe Bay, O'ahu before, and after a heavy rain. Much of this sediment is due to increased development on this side of the island of O'ahu.

"Ptoo!"

Most corals can tolerate limited amounts of sedimentation; tides, waves and currents can all help wash away the effects of a short-term bout. Many corals even have mechanisms to help take care of the muddy experience. Examples include production of copious amounts of mucus to shed the silt off and exceptionally large polyps that can adeptly clean themselves. Still, unnatural increases in the amounts of sedimentation can even overcome the best-adapted corals.

Worldwide, a major source of reef sedimentation is deforestation of rainforests, sometimes from areas far away from any coastline. The topsoils that are quickly washed away not only prevent the return of the rainforests but also contribute to the destruction of the reef. Hmm, perhaps these two ecosystems have more in common then we thought...

• Identified as a primary source of Anthropogenic Stress on Hawaiian coral reefs (UNEP/IUCN 1988) •

TURTLE TUMORS

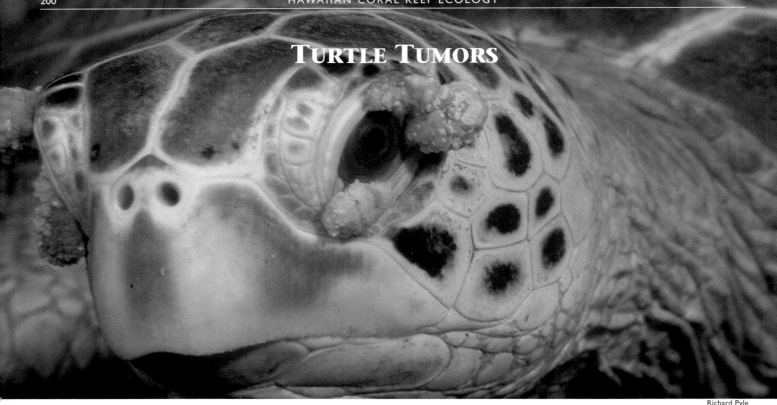

Richard Pyle

Prior to 1985, sea turtle tumors (a condition called **fibropapillomatosis**) were rarely reported in Hawai'i, Florida, and the Caribbean. During the last ten years the number of sea turtles showing this disease has increased dramatically. The exact cause has not been firmly established, though sea turtles associated with areas highly impacted by human activities in Hawai'i seem to have a higher incidence of the disease. Possible sources or initiators include pollutants (from run-off or other sources), blood parasites or habitat change. Preliminary studies have found high numbers of a parasitic trematode's (that's a type of flatworm) eggs within biopsied tumors. It's suspected that the turtle's tissue responds to the presence of these eggs by forming excess fibrous tissue that eventually forms a tumor.

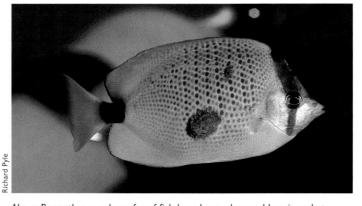

Above: Recently a number of reef fish have been observed bearing what appears to be a form of tumor. While it's unlikely that these are also fibropapillomas, it's interesting that they occur on fish from areas where sea turtles also have tumors. Perhaps an environmental factor or change is occurring that is facilitating the outbreak of these tumors in various reef animals.

Above: This turtle has a large tumor growing off of the right side of its head. Such tumors eventually affect the turtle's ability to feed, see, move about or breath, decreasing their fitness and eventually leading them to an early death. It's been estimated that up to 60% of the sea turtles in Kane'ohe Bay are infected.

Above: This perfectly healthy sea turtle doesn't have tumors attached to it. Those are commensal barnacles.

EFFECTS OF ULTRAVIOLET RADIATION ON CORALS

"I'VE HEARD IT'S BAD, BUT JUST WHAT IS ULTRAVIOLET RADIATION?"

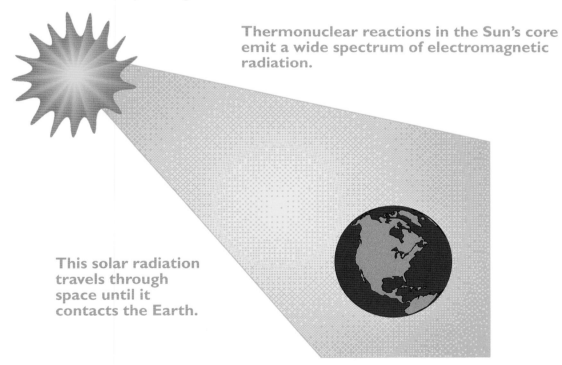

Thermonuclear reactions in the Sun's core emit a wide spectrum of electromagnetic radiation.

This solar radiation travels through space until it contacts the Earth.

This energy striking the Earth can be broken down into discrete wavelengths of radiation, measured metrically using nanometers (nm). What we see as visable light are those wavelengths between 420 nm & 680 nm; ultraviolet radiation (UV) is made up of shorter wavelengths less than 420 nm.

EFFECTS OF UV ON THE
CORAL - ALGAL SYMBIOSIS

Light is necessary for photosynthesis to occur; but certain wavelengths of light can be harmful. Most cnidarians have evolved mechanisms to protect themselves and their symbiotic zooxanthellae from the harmful effects of UV in shallow waters.

Light Energy:
made-up of
Photosynthetically-Active Radiation
(PAR = mostly visible light)
and
Ultraviolet Radiation (UV)

PAR + UV

Some corals (Rose Coral, Blue Rice Coral, Bright Yellow Lobe Coral, etc.) have pigments which may absorb UV light, exciting certain molecules, which in turn emit lower frequency light. Such fluorescence gives these corals a bright coloration; this additional light might also be available for additional photosynthesis by the coral's zooxanthellae.

Harmful UV light can be filtered by coral pigments or special UV absorbing chemicals (Mycosporine-like Amino Acids (MAA's); some MAAs are thought to have a Sun Protection Factor of 50 or more (SPF 50))

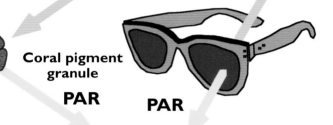

Coral pigment granule

PAR   **PAR**

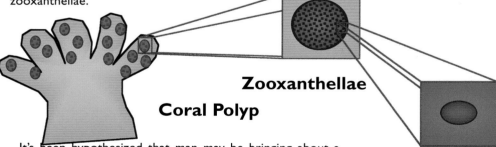

Zooxanthellae

Coral Polyp

Chloroplast

It's been hypothesized that man may be bringing about a decrease in the thickness of the ozone layer which filters the amount of UV reaching the surface of the Earth. What happens when the coral is exposed to increased amounts of UV, or exposed for extended periods of time? High UV can directly affect the animal's cells by acting on nucleic acids such as DNA and RNA (affecting everything from enzyme function to reproduction). Indirectly, the animal is affected by the UV effect on the zooxanthellae. Long-term exposure can cause breakdown of the photosynthetic mechanism; this results in decreased photosynthate being translocated to the host coral and may ultimately lead to expulsion of the zooxanthellae (bleaching). Conversely, high UV and PAR can lead to increased photosynthesis which produces an overabundance of oxygen which can lead to oxygen toxicity. It's thought that the expense of dealing with the effects of high levels of oxygen might lead to the coral expelling the zooxanthellae (bleaching). Notice that in both cases the end result is the expulsion of the zooxanthellae; the mutualist has turned into a parasite and perhaps the coral is cutting its losses...

As scientists take a closer look at how reef animals deal with ultraviolet radiation, they're discovering a wide diversity of mechanisms to help shield the organisms:

ORGANISMS	MECHANISM TO DEAL WITH UV
Sponges, Bryozoans, Tunicates	Avoidance (occur in low-light regimes)
Sea Cucumbers	Some have MAA's, Avoidance
Certain Sea Anemones, Sea Cucumbers & Urchins, Zoanthids	Incorporate sand & other shielding materials into their outer coverings
Crabs, Lobsters, Gastropods	Exoskeleton
Certain Corals, Octacorals, Soft Corals, Zoanthids	MAA's, Fluorescing pigments
Fish, Sharks	Scales, Pigments

In general, those organisms with fewer tissue layers or that tend to be transparent, or that tend to occur in very shallow water are most at risk.

EFFECTS OF
DIVERS ON CORAL REEFS

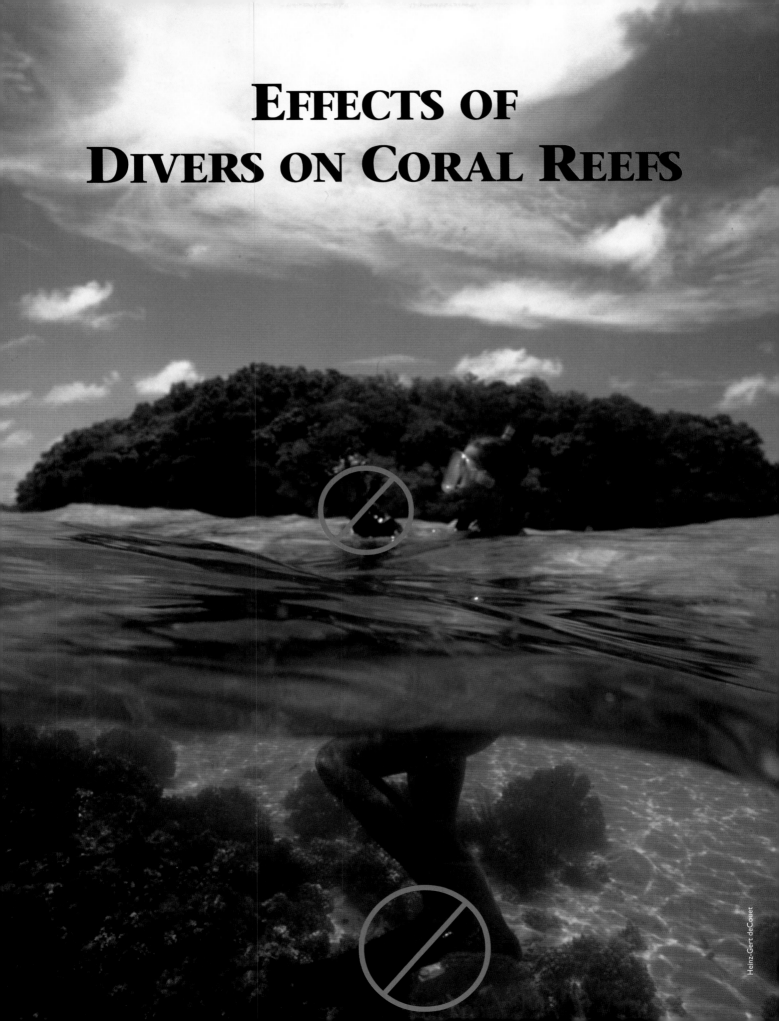

Heinz-Gerr deCaıet

THINK about the impact of your actions underwater on both the organisms and the community as a whole BEFORE you interact with any of the residents of the reef.

OK, I admit it; underwater photographers can be among the most destructive of underwater visitors. Often in search of that one famous magazine cover shot we'll manipulate the environment, placing organisms outside of their natural homes. Many photographers often lie atop or hold onto the reef in order to get the picture.

◀ Snorkelors (and often divers) will sometimes stand or hold onto living coral colonies for support in shallow water. Often branches are broken off or whole colonies become dislodged. Also note that removing this shell from the water is similar to someone forcibly holding your head underwater...both result in severe stress.

Don't even think about it. The behavior shown below would constitute a "taking" under both federal and state laws. There is absolutely no excuse for such behavior by divers today. The stress caused to the animal by such activities as this can be devastating; resulting in avoidance of an area (which may have been a prime area for feeding, reproduction or avoidance of predators), decreased growth rate, etc.

Hand-feeding/taming of wild reef animals is very controversial. While some feel it provides for an interesting experience, the reality is that you are altering a very complex food web by altering natural feeding behaviors and diets.

Author's note: All of these photos were taken over 15 years ago and outside of the United States. Their purpose in this book is to distinctly show what is now considered to be inappropriate diver behavior.

WHAT YOU CAN DO:
AN E.I.S.* FOR YOUR DIVES

As an environmentally aware diver you have to gauge the potential impact of you and your dive group on the reef resource in order to maintain that resource for future use by yourself and others.

Kicking sand up clogs gills, destroys fragile burrows and exposes animals to predation. Standing on, or inadvertent kicking of coral heads can destroy formations that took over twenty years or more to create; in addition you also destroy the food source, recruiting ground and protective cover for a whole community of organisms.

Bubbles inside of caves and overhangs destroy fragile sessile organisms like bryozoans, and stress slow moving animals like nudibranchs. Unsecured gauges and consoles can act like miniature wrecking balls as you move through a coral reef.

Feeding and/or training of organisms modifies natural behaviors and causes the proliferation of generalists, often displacing specialist feeders and therefore changing the whole ecology of the reef.

The use of gloves encourages holding onto living coral for support and touching of fragile organisms. For this reason, they are not allowed to be used for recreational diving in some parts of the world.

Probing with knives or fins often destroys the very structures and organisms that you wish to look at.

Always place organisms back in their original habitats, in their original position and in their original condition. Whereas it may appear that you are only affecting one single organism (and "who's gonna miss just one animal, right?"), you may be separating reproductive mates (in an environment where mates may be far and few between), leaving nests unguarded, displacing essential symbionts, or destroying critical cover for a large number of animals.

Chasing organisms stresses them and may imprint them against visiting an area.

PROPER BUOYANCY!!!

Remember: to many animals quick, jerky movements or a lot of large shapes signals danger. You are likely to see more in small groups that move slowly and smoothly with minimum disruption (once one animal bolts, other species will also react and become more cryptic or leave the area).

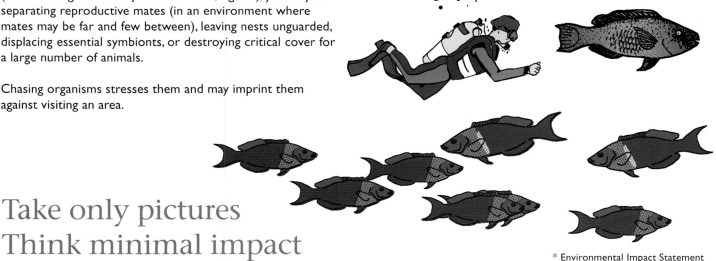

Take only pictures
Think minimal impact

* Environmental Impact Statement

The Big Picture:

POTENTIAL EFFECTS OF HUMANS ON CORAL REEFS

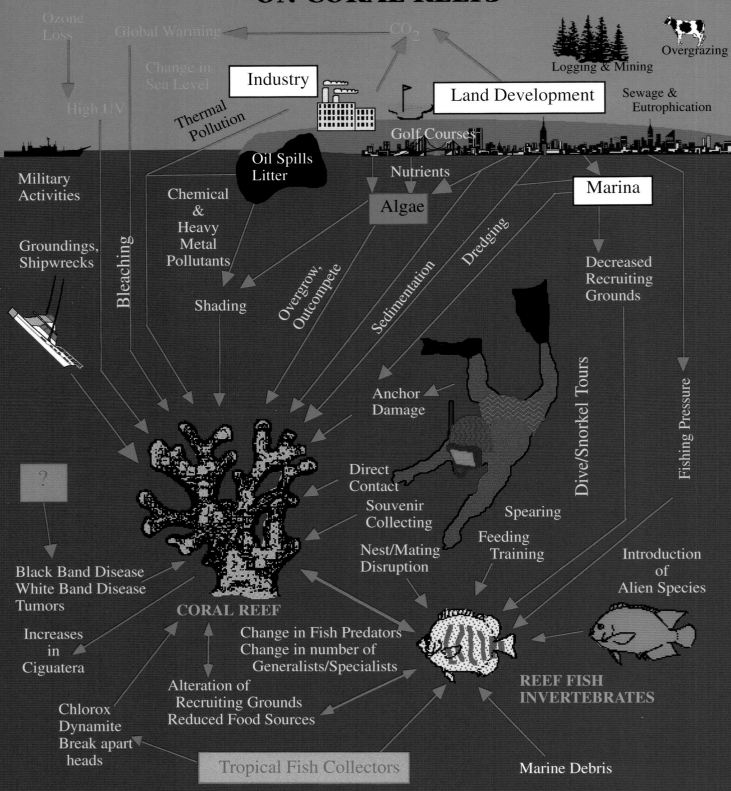

HUMAN USES OF CORALS & CORAL REEFS

It's amazing how few of Hawaii's people recognize the full range of products, income and protection that our corals and coral reefs provide for us. Culturally, coral reefs in Hawai'i have strong ties to the ancient Polynesians who first settled these islands. For today's island residents, the reefs shelter our shoreline from the effects of storms and excessive wave damage. Reefs help provide for a healthy marine tourism industry which brings in excess of $700 million a year into the State. Reefs nourish and support nearshore fisheries, which not only provide food for people's table, but also generate over $20 million a year in landings. As a habitat, Hawai'i's coral reefs shelter over 700 species of fish, 400 species of algae and over 2000 species of invertebrates; many of these organisms have evolved unique chemical and biological defenses which may be of use to pharmaceutical companies to produce the medicines and treatments our children will need in the not-so-distant future.

For a State where no point of land is more than 29 miles from the sea and whose reef ecosystems directly abut our shorelines, the survival of Hawaii's coral reefs are tied directly to the actions or inactions of our residents. Keep in mind that our reefs represent only the thinnest of living veneers covering old foundations; given our geographic position, no real increase in reef coverage is taking place - our reefs are dying as fast as they're being replaced. As such, we have <u>no</u> margin of safety for increasing reef loss due to human effects; without a more active effort on all of our parts, the benefits our reefs currently bring to the Islands may be lost for future generations...

CORALS & CORAL REEFS IN OLD HAWAI'I

Hanau ka 'Uku-ko 'ako 'a
Hanau kana, he Ako 'ako 'a,

**"Born the coral polyp
Born of him a coral colony emerged"**

from the Kumulipo, the Hawaiian Hymn of Creation.

Right and Below: The coral polyp was the first creature to emerge during creation according to Hawaiian mythology. The importance of these animals and the reefs they produced was not lost upon the ancient Hawaiians; in fact, corals often were presented as offerings during religious ceremonies.

The Hawaiians recognized the value of coral reefs and incorporated a respect for the ecosystem into their collection practices.

Above: O'opu and *Hinalea Hina'i* (or fishtrap).

Left: A *Ko'a* (or fishing shrine) dedicated to the god *Ku'ula*. Interestingly, the same word *Ko'a* is used to describe many corals in Hawaiian.

Sara Peck

Corals and their relatives had a variety of everyday uses in old Hawai'i.

Above: The skeletons of corals such as the Mushroom Coral (*Fungia scutaria*) could be used for scraping bristles off of pigs or the scales off of fish. Other coral skeletons could be used for sanding of wood products.

Above: Dead corals were often bleached in the sun and then stacked up, or placed atop rock cairns, along trails over lava fields. The bright white skeletons could be easily seen by people traveling the trail during the day or by moonlight.

Papamu or *konane* board, Bishop Museum

Above: For recreation, Hawaiians would play a game called *Konane*, which was similar to games such as Go, Othello or Chinese Checkers. The players used similar sized chunks of black lava rock and white coral rubble as game pieces.

The ancient Hawaiians used a zoanthid that they called '*Limu make O Hana*' (*Palythoa toxica*) to coat the tips of their spears. The palytoxin contained within this zoanthid's mucus is one of the most potent toxins known in the animal kingdom. Recent studies suggest that the zoanthid may not be secreting this toxin but instead deriving it from a symbiotic bacterium.

In Samoa, an anemone called '*mata malu*' is boiled and eaten as a holiday dish. This same anemone eaten raw can cause death, and was used traditionally to commit suicide.

A number of reef invertebrates were used medicinally, including spaghetti worms, black coral and marine molluscs.

Times have changed. In old Hawai'i 60 - 70 species of *limu*, or seaweeds, were used by the Hawaiian people. Today that number is around 20, of which at least two are recent introductions.

Left and Above: In the late 1700's and early 1800's, mining of coral blocks off of the reef was used for building construction (hundreds of years earlier chunks of coral colonies were used in the construction of fish ponds around the islands). Note the pieces of *Porites compressa* in the bricks above.

CORAL REEFS AS SUPERMARKETS

Reefs in Hawai'i and the Central Pacific provide a tremendous wealth of products to both the local and international markets. Traditional, cultural and new food sources are often present in a variety of different reef animals. Many marine curio, industrial building supplies (important on small islands with limited terrestrial resources) and modern biochemicals are possible as a result of products harvested from coral reefs. In Hawai'i today, many of these reef-related items are in ever-decreasing supply due to **overharvesting** and **poor management** techniques. Often, as in the case of fish collecting, the reef is looked upon as an endless source of material for those few who make a lot of money removing resources from it. Lack of knowledge about the complex ecology of the reef and ever increasing impacts from a wide range of human activities has made it very difficult to harvest many products from Hawaiian reefs in a low impact, sustainable manner. Ignorance by the public, and the all-to-pervasive view that "if I don't take it, somebody else will..." have created a situation where many of the products shown below are in decreasing supply. On a small group of islands such as Hawai'i, that is quickly approaching carrying 1.5 million people (plus tourists), the view that coral reefs are open resources available to all to harvest would be laughable if not for how critical today's situation is. As a result, an increasing number of small island states in the Pacific are looking at Hawai'i as a model for how <u>not</u> to manage their coastal resources; often turning instead to places like Australia, which have successfully commercially zoned their reefs. Hopefully more places (and maybe, just maybe, some of us here) will learn from our mistakes before it's too late.

Obviously, if a market exists for these materials then steps have to be taken to protect resources from overharvesting. One way to do this which would work for almost all of the materials shown below is sustainable mariculture. This approach has been used for years for food products (like mullet, shrimp, etc.) and has only recently been applied to the raising of *limu* (edible seaweed), aquarium fish, and live rock. Such an approach, if carefully monitored and regulated, allows sustainable use of reef resources with minimal impact on the reef ecosystem (the reef serves as a source of larvae as opposed to a harvesting site, thus encouraging protection of the resource). Also encouraging is the use of marine organisms as templates to develop new biotechnologies and medicines.

> If you combined all of the income in Hawai'i from harvesting all of these materials, it still wouldn't equal the amount of money being made from low-impact marine tourism...

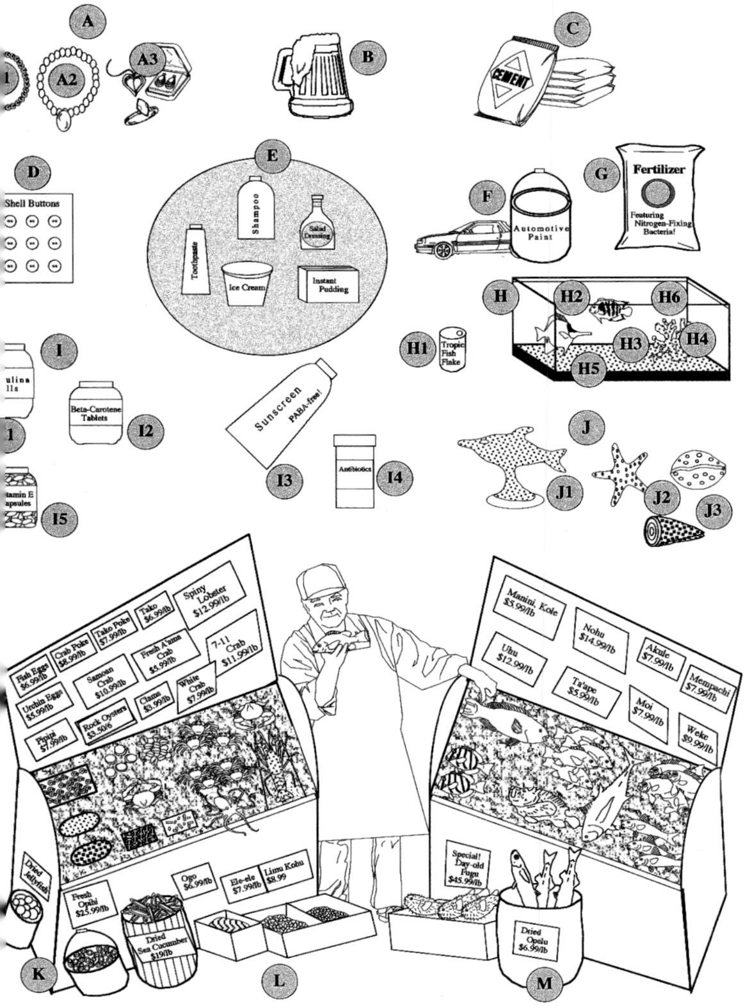

#	Object	Phytoplankton	Zooplankton	Seaweeds	Sponges	Sea Jellies	Soft Corals	Precious Corals	Stony Corals	Marine Worms	Marine Molluscs	Crustaceans	Echinoderms	Tunicates	Fish	Comments
A	Jewelery							●	●		●		●			
	Niihau Shell Leis															Becoming rare
	Black coral							✓								Regulated
	Gold/Pink coral							✓✓								Very deep
	Shell jewelry										✓					Often over collected
B	Beer			●												Stays frothy due to algin from seaweeds
C	Cement/Concrete								●							Sand or calcareous substrate, not living reef
D	Shell Buttons										●					Often from *Trochus*
E	Binding Agents/ Emulsifiers			●												Also used in a lot of processed/fast foods
F	Automotive Paint								●		●					Use crushed shells for reflective effect
G	Fertilizer	●	●												●	Fish byproducts, Cyanobacteria
H	Aquarium Trade	●	●	●	●		●			●	●	●	●	●	●	
H1	Fish Food	✓	✓	✓						✓		✓			✓	Processed Fish/Inverts
H2	Tropical Fish														✓	Possible mariculture?
H3	Tropical Inverts				✓		✓			✓	✓	✓	✓			Possible mariculture?
H4	Corals/Live Rock			✓	✓				✓	✓	✓	✓	✓			Regulated; fake corals; Possible mariculture?
H5	Aquarium sand															Regulated
H6	Aquarium seawater															
I	Health & Medicine	●	●	●	●	●	●	●	●	●	●	●	●	●	●	Lot of organisms still haven't been looked at
I1	*Spirulina* pills	✓														From cyanobacteria
I2	Beta Carotene	✓	✓													From cyanobacteria
I3	Sunscreen															Now synthesized
I4	Antibiotics			✓					✓				✓			
I5	Vitamin E capsules													✓		Now synthesized
J	Ornamental Trade			●	●		●	●			●	●	●		●	Regulated in Hawaii
J1	Sculptures from processed coral							✓								
J2	Dried/dead organisms			✓	✓		✓	✓		✓	✓	✓			✓	Often imported from
J3	Collectable shells															South Pacific (high impact)
K	Food - Inverts				●						●	●	●			Overharvested
L	Food - Seaweed			●												Often incorrectly harvested
M	Food - Fish														●	Overharvested

Shell Buttons
Shampoo
Toothpaste
Salad Dressing
Ice Cream
Instant Pudding
Automotive Paint
Fertilizer — Featuring Nitrogen-Fixing Bacteria!
CEMENT
Tropical Fish Flake
Sunscreen PABA-free!
Beta-Carotene Tablets
Antibiotics
Spirulina pills
Vitamin E capsules

Spiny Lobster $12.99/lb
Tako Poki $7.99/lb
Tako $6.99/lb
Fish Eggs $6.99/lb
Crab Poke
Samoan Crab $10.99/lb
Fresh Anaa $6.99/lb
7-11 Crab $11.99/lb
Urchin Eggs $5.99/lb
Rock Oysters $3.99/lb
Chana $9.99/lb
White Crab $7.99/lb
Pipi $7.99/lb
Manini, Kole $8.99/lb
Nohu $14.99/lb
Akule $7.99/lb
Uhu $12.99/lb
Ta'ape $5.99/lb
Menpachi $7.99/lb
Moi $7.99/lb
Weke $9.99/lb
Fresh Coral $11.99/lb
Dried Sea Cucumber $19/lb
Opihi $6.99/lb
Ele-ele $7.99/lb
Limu Kohu $8.99
Special! Day-old Opae $45.99/lb
Dried Opihi $6.99/lb

MAN'S USE OF CORAL IN THE MEDICAL WORLD

Paul Jokiel

Since the use of PABA as the active sunblock in sunscreens has decreased, a lot of work has gone into synthesizing the Mycosporine-like Amino Acid (MAA) sunblock compounds produced naturally by many cnidarians as a substitute. Currently these synthesized MAA compounds are being used in stabilizing paint and plastics against UV effects from the Sun.

Cytabarine Ara-C is a prescription anitcoagulent, anti-cancer agent originally synthesized from a marine oraganism and used in some forms of chemotherapy.

Various cnidarians have been used medicinally by numerous cultures over the ages. Europeans during the 1500's used powdered corals to cure various diseases and to assist with fertility and deliveries of babies. The ancient Hawaiians used black coral to treat cold sores and for various lung disorders. During modern times, a great deal of research has gone into toxicity and bioactive substances associated with sponges and cnidarians; some of this has resulted in new treatments for cancer and other debilitative diseases. Recent research has looked at pseudopterosins, antiflammatory compounds found in the gorgonian *Pseudopterogorgia elisabethae*. Other sea fans have been looked at for chemicals to assist in birth control. This represents yet another argument for preservation of habitats containing these organisms, since it is only the live organisms that will contain these compounds and only a small portion of cnidarians have been looked at so far.

Coral as a Bone Substitute:

Since the early 1990's doctors have shaped pieces of cleaned, sterilized coral skeleton to use as implants for chipped and missing fragments of human bone. Certain corals (such as *Porites*)

have many similar properties to that of bone, including similar strengths, density and porosity. These corals can be easily shaped to fit the place of missing pieces of bone and often does not result in rejection by the body's natural defenses. Perhaps most important, coral skeleton contains many closed-off, interconnected chambers which allow in bone cells and blood vessel vascularization. Recently, a manufacturer has started to produce a toothpaste-like substance which can be spackled into place to do the same thing. The paste is formed by converting calcium carbonate coral skeleton into calcium phosphate or calcium hydroxyapatite.

CORAL SERVES AS A GOOD BONE REPLACEMENT BECAUSE:

• Similar Ca-based minerals as real bone
• Easy to shape to fit as implant
• Porous to allow real bone & blood vessels to grow into it
• Lacks antigens that might cause rejection

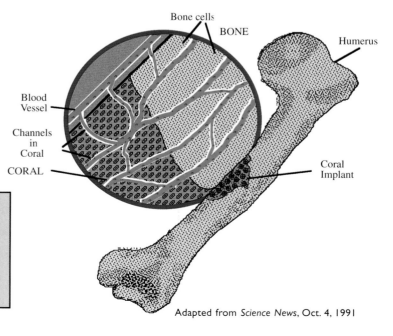

Adapted from *Science News*, Oct. 4, 1991

MAN'S USE OF CORAL:
FOSSIL CORAL REEFS

A close inspection of certain geological features on land can turn up some interesting and perplexing things; for instance, how does one explain the presence of fossil coral reefs on the upper slopes of a mountain on the island of Lanaʻi? Those of us who tend to snoop in the "dirt" that makes up roadcuts in many parts of Hawaiʻi have noticed what appears to be old coral skeletons. More detailed inspections reveal an abundance of well-preserved fossil coral reefs on a number of the Hawaiian islands - well above sea level! Such raised reefs can be very important classrooms for the study of ancient sea conditions, weather patterns, and ecological interactions.

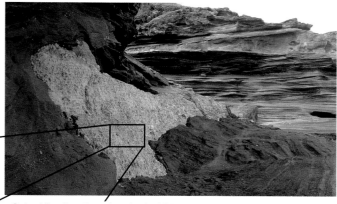

Raised fossil reef on the island of Oʻahu.

Close-up showing the fossil skeleton of an unidentified ancient coral.

For the coral reef biologist, these same fossil reefs raise interesting questions concerning changes in species distributions in Hawaiʻi over time. Coral genera such as *Favia, Galaxea, Platygyra, Seriatopora,* and *Stylophora* all occurred commonly on Hawaiian reefs at one time or another in the geologic past. Yet today those corals are not seen in Hawaiʻi - what changed? Was it climatic? Competition? Was there some major biological event comparable to the Crown-of-Thorns Seastar infestations seen in the South Pacific? The clues to the answer may be staring us in the face in the sides of a roadcut somewhere in the islands. The past can be a pretty interesting place - even in the present...

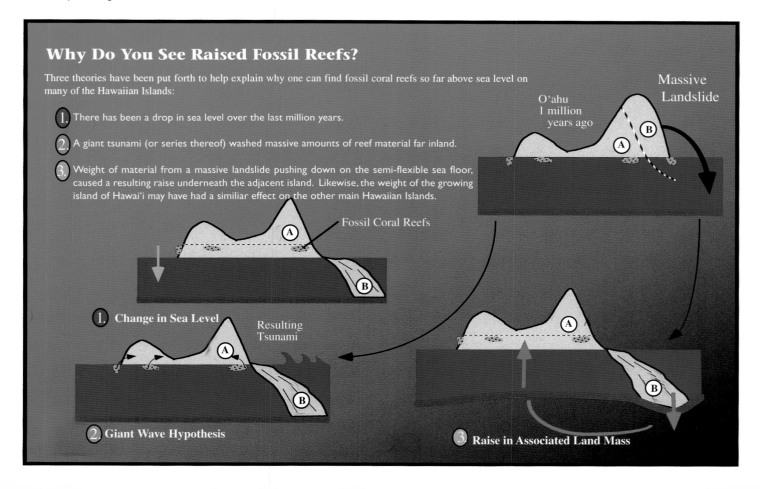

Why Do You See Raised Fossil Reefs?

Three theories have been put forth to help explain why one can find fossil coral reefs so far above sea level on many of the Hawaiian Islands:

1. There has been a drop in sea level over the last million years.

2. A giant tsunami (or series thereof) washed massive amounts of reef material far inland.

3. Weight of material from a massive landslide pushing down on the semi-flexible sea floor, caused a resulting raise underneath the adjacent island. Likewise, the weight of the growing island of Hawaiʻi may have had a similiar effect on the other main Hawaiian Islands.

Massive Landslide

Oʻahu 1 million years ago

Fossil Coral Reefs

1. Change in Sea Level

Resulting Tsunami

2 Giant Wave Hypothesis

3 Raise in Associated Land Mass

THE SCIENCE OF STUDYING CORAL REEFS

Sara Peck

Above: A major interest of scientists all over the globe is the long-term monitoring of reef systems. Given their complexity and growth rates, important changes will tend to be seen on yearly or decade-long scales, and require the need for repetitive **transects** along subsections of a reef. This allows scientists to formulate a picture of the state of the reef without studying every single aspect. Such formulations rely heavily on the use of **statistics** to establish their validity (and you thought that calculus would never be important...).

Paul Jokiel

Above: Sometimes scientific instruments are placed in the field to gather data. The researcher shown above is collecting information about the amounts of sediment that are settling out of the water and onto the reef. This is accomplished through the use of sediment traps which collect the settling sediment for measurement. Laboratory analysis of the collected sediments may provide important clues as to where it originated from and its effects on the corals.

Left: Often one has to place organisms into a controlled laboratory setting in order to isolate the specific effects being studied; this is frequently impossible to do in the field because of the complexity of reefs, the number of organismal interactions and the wide range of environmental parameters to be controlled in order to isolate the effect of interest. The researchers on the left are collecting **gametes** (eggs and sperm) from isolated Mushroom Corals (*Fungia scutaria*) for study; each bowl contains a tagged individual in filtered (relatively pure) seawater. Hawai'i is one of the premier sites in the world for the in-depth study of coral reproduction and physiology. In fact, the Hawai'i Institute of Marine Biology located on Coconut Island in the middle of Kane'ohe Bay has been a center of coral reef research for the last 40 years.

Right: With strong interest in the aquarium field to keep corals in captivity for long periods of time, researchers at the Waikiki Aquarium have developed ways of **culturing** corals and maintaining them under artifical life support. The implications of this breakthrough are far ranging and could go a long way towards decreasing the impact of collection on natural reefs. In addition, it could provide "seed" populations for re-establashing or enhancing reefs in areas where they've been hard hit by natural and anthropogenic influences.

Below: As man continues to modify coastal habitats and directly affect ecosystems, new means of preserving reefs will have to be found. One method being developed at a number of sites in Hawai'i is the transplantation of whole or fragmented colonies to different areas, in order to "jump start" new reefs or preserve remnants of old ones. Often this involves short-term mechanisms of binding coral colonies in close proximity to create stable platforms. Over time, these will become cemented together and grow in such a way that one would never know they were once manipulated systems.

Sara Peck

Paul Jokiel

Left: Recent global issues involving greenhouse gasses, ozone depletion and global warming have refocused attention on corals and other possible species as early warning systems: a "canary in a coal mine" so to speak. Given their range of sensitivities, corals sitting in shallow marine habitats may be able to tell us about changes in our atmosphere; and because of their excellent fossil record, we may be able to look at long-term trends (hundreds, to thousands, to millions of years) in addition to short term (our lifetimes) effects.

The Mushroom Corals (*Fungia scutaria*) on the left have undergone different levels of temperature exposure under laboratory conditions, resulting in differential levels of bleaching (loss of their symbiotic zooxanthellae). Laboratory experiments such as these provide us with crucial information to explain phenomena that we see in the field and serve as a mechanism of validating our explanations.

WHAT IS THE ROLE OF CORAL REEF MONITORING?

Coral reefs are monitored for a variety of reasons, over a variety of scales, and by a variety of groups. In general, such monitoring can be broken down into one of three forms:

Diagnosis

Sometimes the ability to detect an impact on a reef ecosystem can only occur by comparing it with a pre-existing state, or through comparisons with similar reef habitat elsewhere. To do so requires the use of monitoring programs to either establish a baseline, or to provide for wider scale comparisons over time.

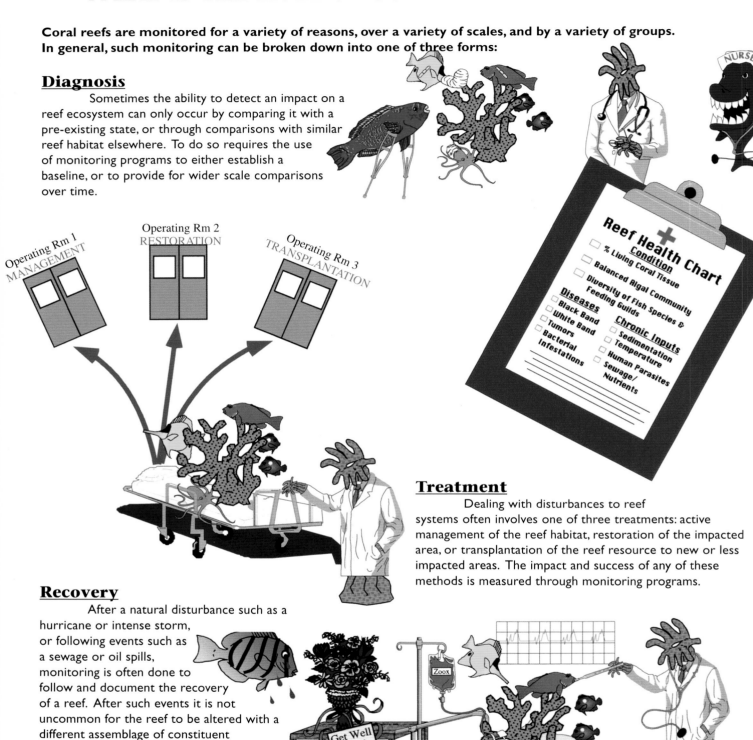

Treatment

Dealing with disturbances to reef systems often involves one of three treatments: active management of the reef habitat, restoration of the impacted area, or transplantation of the reef resource to new or less impacted areas. The impact and success of any of these methods is measured through monitoring programs.

Recovery

After a natural disturbance such as a hurricane or intense storm, or following events such as a sewage or oil spills, monitoring is often done to follow and document the recovery of a reef. After such events it is not uncommon for the reef to be altered with a different assemblage of constituent organisms (or even some invasive ones!). Likewise, the recovery rate may vary considerably based upon the rate of various disturbances to the reef and the availability of essential components that promote reef growth and diversity.

The State of Hawai'i Department of Land & Natural Resources provides guidelines for monitoring programs to assist in management of reef resources.

CORAL REEF SUSTAINABILITY HOT SPOTS

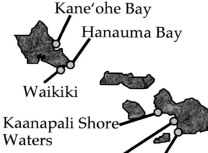

The State of Hawai'i's Department of Land & Natural Resources is charged with the vital mission of sustaining our precious and fragile marine resources for the benefit of future generations.

DLNR has identified 25 natural resource hotspots (including the 9 shown above which contain coral reefs) throughout the State where, in spite of community awareness, there is resource degradation, conflicts among users, public welfare is compromised, and there may be illegal activity.

To address these problems, DLNR has assembled inter-divisional "sustainability" teams for each hotspot. In conjunction with the local community, researchers, and educators, they aim to arrest the misuse and decline of a hotspot and, hopefully, place it on the road to recovery.

We have addressed a number of coral reef impacts below and referenced them against related management concerns along with a listing of possible, applicable hotspot sites.

IMPACT	MANAGEMENT CONCERNS	1° HOTSPOT SITES
ALIEN SPP.	Introduction, Overgrowth of Substrate	Kāne'ohe Bay, South Maui Shoreline, Waikiki
AQUARIUM FISH COLLECTION	Overcollection, Collection of Rare Spp., Collection of Anthozoans, Habitat Destuction, Conflicts with Other Users	Kona Coast, Kāne'ohe Bay
BOATING	Thrillcraft Use & Refueling Near Reefs, Conflicts with Other Users, Impacts of Kayaks & Commercial Ops., Illegal Moorings, Anchor Damage	Kāne'ohe Bay, Na Pali Coast, Hanalei, Waikiki, 'Ahīhi-Kinau, Kona Coast
COASTAL DEVELOPMENT	Runoff, Habitat Destruction, Congestion with Mixed Uses, Loss of Nursery Grounds Shoreline, Kona Coast	Kāne'ohe, Waikiki, Ka'anapali Shore Waters, South Maui
DIVER DAMAGE	Physical Damage, Overuse, Fish Feeding, Trampling	Kāne'ohe Bay, Hanauma Bay, 'Ahīhi-Kinau, Kona Coast
EUTROPHICATION	Introduction of Foreign Substances Runoff, Disease Effects, Algae Blooms	Hanalei, Kāne'ohe Bay, Waikiki, Ka'anapali, South Maui, Kona Coast
OVERFISHING & ILLEGAL FISHING	Gillnetting, Ghost Nets, Fishing in MPAs, Use of Poisons, Fisheries Collapse	All Marine Hotspots
POLLUTION & SEDIMENTATION	Heavy Metals, Disease Effects, Loss of Habitat, Watershed Mgmt	All Marine Hotspots

16 Things You Can Do To Help
Protect Hawai'i's Coral Reefs

- **S**UPPORT REEF-FRIENDLY BUSINESSES. Ask what your dive shop, fishing store, boating and tour operators, hotels and other businesses are doing to save Hawaii's coral reefs. Insure that their operations do not damage our reefs. Let businesses know you are an informed consumer who cares about reef protection, invite them to put something of themselves back into our unique ecosystem. Encourage businesses to sponsor and donate a share of their profits to reef management and education activities.

- **D**ON'T POLLUTE. Plastics in the water can damage and kill a wide variety of marine life (including fish, sea turtles, sea birds and marine mammals). Garbage and human wastes introduce chemicals and nutrient levels not naturally found on reefs and can result in a decrease of coral cover (and a decrease in the diversity of marine life associated with coral cover). Understand that the pollution released on our islands eventually winds its way into the ocean and our reefs.

- **L**EARN MORE ABOUT OUR REEFS. Volunteer your time for an environmental organization/agency, participate in a reef or beach clean-up, participate in reef education programs, become a member of a local aquarium, zoo, or environmental center. Participate in training or educational programs that focus on the ecology of reef systems. When you further your own education, you can help others understand the fragility, value and wonder of Hawaii's coral reefs.

- **R**EPORT DUMPING, POACHING OR OTHER ILLEGAL ACTIVITIES. Environmental enforcement officials cannot be everywhere. While it is important to not directly confront possible violators, you can take down as much detailed information about the activity as possible and contact the appropriate authorities.

- **N**EVER ANCHOR DIRECTLY ON REEFS. Make use of the State's Day-use Mooring System where available; otherwise anchor in sand away from reefs whenever possible.

- **T**AKE STEPS TO DECREASE OVERFISHING. Depletion of our near-shore & coastal fisheries are occurring at alarming rates, some fear many of them are close to collapse. Long-time, local residents often remark how there are fewer fish then when they were kids. Given our population and technological increases, methods of fishing that were acceptable just a few years ago may be detrimental in today's world. Without protection, there may be no fish for your own children or grandchildren to catch in the near future.

- **I**F YOU SCUBA DIVE OR SNORKEL, DON'T TOUCH. Observe the marine environment, don't alter it. In the water, your fins, hands and diving equipment can be lethal weapons that damage the delicate, tiny animals that build the reef substrate. Take care that the use of your fins does not stir up sediments that can smother the corals. Take a moment to think about your other actions in the water; activities which affect the natural behavior of the reef's inhabitants affect the entire ecology of the reef.

- **G**ET INVOLVED IN THE LEGISLATIVE PROCESS. Contact your elected officials and encourage them to support legislation that will protect Hawaii's reefs. Track upcoming legislation, attend public hearings, submit testimony and write letters of support. Support the Department of Land and Natural Resources efforts to increase marine enforcement, increase funding for marine resource protection and education (Did you know that while Hawai'i has the fourth longest coastline in the U.S., we rank 48th in overall funding for fish and wildlife protection, and last in overall State spending on environmental protection! The result is that less than one cent of every State dollar is spent on natural

resource management in the State of Hawai'i). Vote for elected government officials whose records confirm their support for environmental issues, including Hawaii's coral reefs.

- **B**E AN INFORMED CONSUMER & RESPONSIBLE AQUARIUM HOBBYIST. Consider carefully the impact on the ecosystem of purchasing preserved coral (note: such corals by law have to come from outside the State of Hawai'i; still their removal causes negative impact on the reefs of the country they're from) or aquarium fish. How were these organisms collected? Is there a management plan in place to minimize impact from their collection on the reef environment? Exotic aquarium species should never be released into Hawaiian waters. Hawai'i is a very unique place containing marine organisms found nowhere else in the world; introduction of non-native marine life can severely effect the ability of our native species to survive.

- **S**UPPORT CONSERVATION ORGANIZATIONS, AGENCIES & PROGRAMS. Your much-needed support not only allows you to share in their programs and opportunities but enhances their ability to educate and inform others. Your support, whether it be monetary or of your own time, makes a big difference.

- **B**E A WASTEWATER CRUSADER! Get involved in monitoring and preventing marine water pollution (sewage and runoff). Make sure that such inputs have been properly treated to minimize nutrients and harmful chemicals (such as pesticides and fertilizers). Conserve freshwater; the less you use, the less runoff and wastewater that will eventually be dumped onto our reefs.

- **S**UPPORT THE CREATION & MAINTENANCE OF MARINE PARKS & PRESERVES. Most of Hawaii's marine resources are overfished and disappearing at alarming rates. Setting aside and protecting habitat is often the most cost-effective and productive way to not only preserve a wide variety of species, but over time will result in enhancement of nearby areas allowing renewed fishing and gathering opportunities. Volunteer your time to get involved in projects to protect special areas.

- **P**ROMOTE RESPONSIBLE DEVELOPMENT. Uncontrolled coastal development and population increases may have profound impacts on adjacent marine ecosystems. As we develop more and more of our undeveloped coastal (and inland) areas, we place greater and greater pressures on the natural ecosystem to adapt. Most of our native Island species depend on precious few undeveloped natural habitats and have nowhere else to go. Overdevelopment can lead to species extinction and ecosystem collapse.

- **I**NFORM YOURSELF. Find out about existing and proposed laws, programs, and projects that could affect Hawaii's reefs.

- **P**RACTICE RESOURCE STEWARDSHIP. Learn the rules and regulations about fishing, gathering, and use of our marine resources. Follow them in ways that minimize your impact. The use of reef resources is a privilege not a right. Learn more about the ecosystems of the State of Hawai'i and what you can do to protect them. Buy into the idea that these resources are unique to Hawai'i and require an active role on our part to protect them. Encourage others to do the same.

- **S**PREAD THE WORD, HELP TO PROMOTE AWARENESS OF THE IMPORTANCE OF OUR REEFS. Remember your own excitement at learning how important Hawaii's reefs are to us and how intricate the ecology of the reef is. Sharing this excitement with others gets everyone you speak with involved.

THE BIG ENDING, GRAND FINALE, MEANING OF LIFE, ETC.*
* For corals that is...

• Weather

• Terrestrial Inputs

REEF ECOSYSTEMS ARE IMPACTED BY

• Oceanic Inputs

• Human Inputs

• Ecological interactions within and between reefs and adjacent ecosystems

COMMUNITY STRUCTURE IS CONTROLLED BY

• Predation

• Competition

• Primary & Secondary Production

• Energy Flow

• Trophic Structure

POPULATION STRUCTURE IS CONTROLLED BY

• Recruitment

• Survival

• Mortality

ORGANISM STRUCTURE IS CONTROLLED BY

• Growth

• Calcification

APPENDICES

APPENDIX I
HAWAIIAN CORAL SYMBIONTS BY SPECIES

Type of Coral Host	Symbiont	Type of Relationship	Gain From Coral Host	
Fungia scutaria Mushroom Coral	Staircase Shell (*Epitonium ulu*)	Parasitic Pinches off pieces of tentacles & tissues	Food, Substrate for eggs	**Obligate Symbiont**
	Internal Coral Shell (*Magilopsis lamarckii*)	Commensalism	Shelter/Substrate	**Obligate Symbiont**
Montipora capitata Rice Coral	Alpheid Shrimp (*Alpheus deuteropus*) = Forms burrows that can be seen as black fissures on the colony; farms filamentous algae and cyanobacteria within these crevices. Often have a male burrow and a female burrow associated with a set of fissures. Some evidence that shrimp is able to chemically dissolve away coral skeleton to maintain fissures and burrows.	Commensalism	Shelter/Substrate	**Obligate Symbiont**
	Christmas Tree Worm (*Spirobranchus* sp.)	Mutualism	Shelter/Substrate	
	Flatworm (*Prosthiostomium montiporae*)	Parasitism	Food, Shelter	**Obligate Symbiont**
	Vermetid Mollusc	Commensalism	Substrate/Shelter	
Montipora flabellata/patula Blue Rice Coral	Alpheid Shrimp (*Alpheus deuteropus*) = See above for description.	Commensalism	Shelter/Substrate	**Obligate Symbiont**
	Christmas Tree Worm (*Spirobranchus* sp.)	Mutualism	Shelter/Substrate	
	Vermetid Mollusc	Commensalism	Substrate/Shelter	
Pavona duerdeni Flat Lobe Coral	Burrowing Gall Crab (*Pseudocryptochirus crescentus*)	Commensalism	Substrate/Shelter	**Obligate Symbiont**
Pavona varians Corrugated Coral	Alpheid Shrimp (*Alpheus deuteropus*) = See above for description.	Commensalism	Shelter/Substrate	**Obligate Symbiont**
Pocillopora damicornis Lace Coral	Alpheid shrimp (*Alpheus lottini, Synalpheus charon*)	Mutualism (?)	Shelter, Food - tips(?)	**Obligate Symbiont**
	Scaly Drupe (*Drupa elata*)	Parasitism	Food	**Obligate Symbiont**
	Coral Shell (*Coralliophila violacea*)	Parasitism	Food - coral tissue	**Obligate Symbiont**
	Gall Crab (*Hapalocarcinus marsupialis*)	Commensalism	Shelter	**Obligate Symbiont**
	Juvenile Fish	Commensalism	Shelter	
	Coral Guard Crabs (*Trapezia intermedia*)	Mutualism (?)	Shelter, Food - tips(?)	**Obligate Symbiont**
Pocillopora eydouxi Antler Coral	Alpheid Shrimp	Mutualism (?)	Shelter, Food - tips(?)	**Obligate Symbiont**
	Scaly Drupe (*Drupa elata*)	Parasitism	Food	**Obligate Symbiont**
	Burrowing Gall Crab (*Pseudocryptochirus crescentus*)	Commensalism	Shelter	**Obligate Symbiont**
	Coral Shell (*Coralliophila violacea*)	Parasitism	Food - coral tissue	**Obligate Symbiont**
	Hawaiian Domino Damselfish (*D. albisella*)	Commensalism	Shelter	
	Hawkfish (*Paracirrhites arcuatus, Cirrhitops fasciatus,* and *Amblycirrhites bimacula*)	Commensalism	Hunting Substrate	
	Juvenile Fish	Commensalism	Shelter	
	Hawaiian Swimming Crab (*Charybdis hawaiiensis*)	Commensalism	Shelter	**Obligate Symbiont**
	Small Scorpionfish	Commensalism	Hunting Substrate, Shelter	
	Trapezid Crab	Mutualism (?)	Shelter, Food - tips(?)	**Obligate Symbiont**
Pocillopora meandrina Cauliflower Coral	Alpheid Shrimp (*Alpheus lottini, Synalpheus charon*) (*Alpheid clypeatus*) = Often found at the bases of *P. meandrina* heads where it constructs tubes in mats of filamentous algae.	Mutualism (?)	Shelter, Food - tips(?)	**Obligate Symbiont**
	Scaly Drupe(*Drupa elata*)	Parasitism	Food	**Obligate Symbiont**
	Brittlestars	Commensalism	Shelter	
	Coral Shell (*Coralliophila violacea*)	Parasitism	Food - coral tissue	**Obligate Symbiont**
	Gall Crabs (*Hapalocarcinus marsupialis*) (*Pseudocryptochirus kahe*) = Burrowing gall crab whose burrows have openings on the sides of the coral branches, marked by violet rings.	Commensalism	Shelter, Food	**Obligate Symbiont**
	Hawaiian Domino Damselfish (*D. albisella*)	Commensalism	Shelter	
	Hawkfish (*Paracirrhites arcuatus, Cirrhitops fasciatus,* and *Amblycirrhites bimacula*)	Commensalism	Hunting Substrate	
	Juvenile Fish	Commensalism	Shelter	
	Small Scorpionfish	Commensalism	Hunting Substrate, Shelter	
	Trapezid Crab	Mutualism (?)	Shelter, Food - tips(?)	**Obligate Symbiont**
	Other Xanthid Crabs (*Domecia hispida*)	Commensalism	Shelter, Food	

Porites compressa Finger Coral	Boring Bivalve (*Gastrochaena cuneiformis*)	Commensalism	Shelter/Substrate	**Obligate Symbiont**
	Coral Barnacle	Commensalism	Substrate	
	Coral Goby (*Pleurosicya micheli*)	Commensalism, Parasitism (?) May feed on mucus and live coral tissue.	Shelter, Food (?)	**Obligate Symbiont**
	Coral-eating Nudibranch (*Phestilla lugunris*)	Predatory	Food, Substrate for eggs	**Obligate Symbiont**
	Coral Shell (*Coralliophila violacea*)	Parasitism	Food - coral tissue	**Obligate Symbiont**
	Coral Shell (*Drupa cornutus*)	Parasitism	Food - coral tissue	**Obligate Symbiont**
	Scaly Drupe Shell (*Drupella elata*)	Parasitism	Food - coral tissue	**Obligate Symbiont**
	Spits proteolytic (protein-dissolving) saliva on tissues and rasps/sucks partially-digested flesh.			
Porites lobata Lobe Coral	Alpheid Shrimp (*Alpheus deuteropus*) = See *M. capitata* for description.	Commensalism	Shelter/Substrate	**Obligate Symbiont**
	Boring Bivalve (*Gastrochaena cuneiformis*)	Commensalism	Shelter/Substrate	**Obligate Symbiont**
	Boring Sponge	Parasitism (?)	Shelter/Substrate	
	Christmas Tree Worm (*Spirobranchus* sp.)	Mutualism	Shelter/Substrate	
	Coral Barnacle	Commensalism	Shelter/Substrate	
	Coral Shell (*Coralliophila violacea*)	Parasitism	Food - coral tissue	**Obligate Symbiont**
	Internal Shell (*Magilopsis* sp.)	Commensalism (?)	Shelter (?)	**Obligate Symbiont**
	Sundial Shell (*Phillipia radiata*)	Parasitism	Food - coral tissue	**Obligate Symbiont**
	Vermetid Mollusc	Commensalism	Substrate/Shelter	
	Xanthid Crabs (*Maldivia triunguiculata*)	Commensalism	Shelter	
Tubastraea coccina Orange Flower Coral	Nudibranch (*Phestilla melanobranchia*)	Predatory	Food	**Obligate Symbiont**
	Shrimp (*Periclimenes* sp.)	Commensalism	Shelter	
	Staircase Shell (*Epitonium* sp.)	Parasitism	Food	
Others: *Antipathes grandis* Black Coral	Barnacle	Commensalism	Shelter, Substrate	
	Black Coral Goby (*Bryaninops* sp.)	Commensalism	Shelter, Substrate for eggs	**Obligate Symbiont**
	Brittlestar (*Astrobrachion* sp.)	Commensalism	Food, Shelter Feed on mucus sheets & epithelial cells	
	Long Nose Hawkfish (*Oxycirrhites typus*)	Commensalism	Substrate/Shelter	
	Majid Crab	Commensalism	Food, Shelter	
	Ovulid Shell (*Phenacovolva lahainaensis*)	Parasitism	Food - coral tissue	**Obligate Symbiont**
	Oyster (*Dendrostraea* sp.)	Commensalism	Shelter, Substrate	
	Shrimp (*Periclimenes* sp.)	Commensalism	Shelter	
Cirrhipathes anguina Wire Coral	Shrimp (*Dasycaris* sp., *Pontonides* sp.)	Commensalism	Food, Shelter	**Obligate Symbiont**
	Yonges Goby (*Bryaninops yongei*)	Commensalism	Shelter	**Obligate Symbiont**
Anthelia edmondsoni Blue Octacoral	Aeolid nudibranch (*Tritonia hawaiiensis*)	Predatory	Food	
Sinularia abrupta Soft Finger coral	Benthic Ctenophore (*Coeloplana*)	Commensalism	Substrate	
	Copepods	Parasitism	Food	**Obligate Symbiont**
Zoanthus & *Palythoa* sp. Zoanthids	Staircase Shell (*Epitonium millecostatum*)	Parasitic	Food, Substrate for eggs	**Obligate Symbiont**
	Heliacus Shell (*Heliacus variegatus*)	Parasitic	Food, Substrate for eggs	**Obligate Symbiont**
Aiptasia pulchella Common Anemone	Aeolid nudibranch (*Berghia major*)	Predatory	Food	**Obligate Symbiont**
	Staircase Shell (*Epitonium kanemoe*)	Parasitic	Food, Substrate for eggs	**Obligate Symbiont**
Boloceroides sp. Swimming Anemone	Aeolid nudibranch (*Berghia major*)	Predatory	Food	**Obligate Symbiont**
	Staircase Shell (*Epitonium hyalinum*)	Parasitic	Food, Substrate for eggs	**Obligate Symbiont**

APPENDIX II
LAWS GOVERNING CORALS & CORAL REEFS

As of 1998 there existed a number of laws and regulations concerning uses and impacts on corals and coral reefs. As stated earlier, the main problem seems to be one of enforcement of existing laws. Also note that while a number of laws concern coral reefs or impacts on them, there are few that directly deal with the protection of reef ecosystems.

STATE LEVEL:

- HAWAI'I REVISED STATUTES §171-58.5: Sand, dead coral or coral rubble may be removed if it is seaward of the shoreline, does not exceed one gallon per person per day, and is taken only for personal, noncommercial purposes.

- HAWAI'I REVISED STATUTES §188-68: Prohibits the taking of any **live** stony corals from the waters of Hawai'i, including any live reef or mushroom coral. It is also unlawful to take any rock to which marine life of any type is visably attached or affixed. This statute also prohibits the sale in Hawai'i of the following species (regardless of origin):
  - Cauliflower Coral (*Pocillopora meandrina*)
  - Lace Coral (*Pocillopora damicornis*)
  - Elkhorn Corn (*Pocillopora eydouxi*)
  - Rice Coral (*Montipora capitata* (*verrucosa*))
  - Lobe Coral (*Porites lobata*)
  - Finger Coral (*Porites compressa*)
  - Mushroom Coral (*Fungia scuteria*)
  - Orange Flower Coral (*Tubastraea coccinea*)

- HAWAI'I REVISED STATUTES §205A: Restricts anchoring on coral reefs.

- HAWAI'I STATE CONSTITUTION Article XI - Section 1 Conservation & Development of Resources: For the benefit of present and future generations, the State and its political subdivisions shall conserve and protect Hawaii's natural beauty and all natural resources, including land, water, air, mineral and energy sources, and shall promote the development and utilization of these resources in a manner consistent with their conservation and in furtherence of the self-sufficiency of the State. All public natural resources are held in trust by the State for the benefit of the people.

- HAWAI'I STATE CONSTITUTION Article XII - Section 9 Environmental Rights: Each person has the right to a clean and healthful environment, as defined by laws relating to environmental quality, including control of pollution and conservation, protection and enhancement on natural resources. Any person may enforce this right against any party, public or private, through appropriate legal proceedings, subject to reasonable limitations and regulation as provided by law.

- STATE OF HAWAI'I ADMINISTRATIVE RULES 11 -54: Mandates conservation of coral reefs in class AA waters.

- STATE OF HAWAI'I DEPARTMENT OF LAND & NATURAL RESOURCES (DLNR): Responsible for enforcing State conservation and resource laws through the Division of Conservation and Resources Enforcement (DOCARE). DLNR also manages Marine Life Conservation Districts (MLCDs) and Fisheries Management Areas (FMAs) such as:

  Hawai'i Island:
Kealakekua Bay MLCD	Lapakahi State Historical Park MLCD
Waialea Bay MLCD	Old Kona Airport MLCD
Kailua Bay FMA	Hilo Bay FMA
Puako Bay & Reef FMA	Kiholo Bay FMA
Keauhou Bay FMA	Kona Coast FMA

  Maui:
Honolua & Mokule'ia Bay MLCD	Molokini Shoal MLCD
Kahului Harbor FMA	'Ahihi - Kina'u Natural Area Reserve (NAR)

  Kaho'olawe:
  Managed by the Kaho'olawe Island Reserve Commision (KIRC)

  Lana'i:
Hulopo'e - Manele Bay MLCD	Manele Boat Harbor FMA

  O'ahu:
Hanauma Bay MLCD	Pupukea Beach Park MLCD
Waikiki - Diamond Head FMA	Coconut Island Marine Refuge
Paiko Lagoon Wildlife Sanctuary (under Division of Forestry & Wildlife, DLNR)	

  Kaua'i:
Waimea Bay FMA	Hanamaula Bay & Ahukini FMA

• STATE OF HAWAI'I DEPARTMENT OF HEALTH (DOH): Responsible for issuing National Pollution Discharge Elimination System (NPDES) Permits regulating the disharge of materials into nearshore waters. Applications reviewed by the Department of Land and Natural Resources (DLNR) as to their impact on aquatic ecosystems.

FEDERAL LEVEL:

• THE CLEAN WATER ACT (CWA): Provides regulations for the introduction of materials into waters (marine and freshwater). Contains provisions governing the filling or draining of wetlands (which include seagrass beds, mangroves and salt marshes).

• THE COASTAL ZONE MANAGEMENT ACT (CZMA): Provides for controlled management and development of shoreline areas through interactions between federal and state agencies.

• THE ENDANGERED SPECIES ACT OF 1973(ESA): Provides for monitoring and limited protection of species listed as either Endangered or Threatened as it relates to the use of federal monies or institutions. An Endangered Species is any "species, subspecies, or distinct population of fish, or wildlife, or plant which is in danger of extinction throughout all or a significant porion of its range. A Threatened Species is "any species, subspecies, or distinct population which is likely to become an endangered species within the foreseeable future throughout all or a significant portion of its range". Currently there are no marine fish or invertebrates listed as either Endangered or Threatened Species; although this act may provide some protection for reef ecosystems through the designation of Critical Habitat for the endangered Hawksbill Sea Turtle (*Eretmochelys imbricata*) and the threatened Green Sea Turtle (*Chelonia mydas*).

• THE NATIONAL ENVIRONMENTAL POLICY ACT OF 1969 (NEPA): The portion of this act that primarily affects coral reefs concerns the need to conduct Environmental Impact Assessments (E.I.A.'s) when projects occur that involve federal monies or institutions.

• NATIONAL WILDLIFE REFUGES: All of the islands and reefs within the Northwest Hawaiian Islands (NWHI) are designated as National Wildlife Refuges under the jurisdiction of the State of Hawai'i and the U. S. Department of the Interior (DOI). Exceptions to this are Kure Atoll which is managed by DLNR, and Midway, Pearl & Hermes, and Nihoa which are managed solely by DOI. No commercial or recreational fishing is allowed in any of the refuges (except for Midway where limited recreational fishing is allowed).

INTERNATIONAL:

• CONVENTION AGAINST INTERNATIONAL TRADE IN ENDANGERED SPECIES (CITES) 1975: Controls international trade in species listed as endangered or threatened either by the country of origin, the importing country or any country that the species (or product from the species) passes through on its way to the importing country. Ratified by over 104 countries.

• INTERNATIONAL CONVENTION FOR THE PREVENTION OF POLLUTION FROM SHIPS (MARPOL) 1973, 1978: Controls five types of pollution caused by ships: oil and oil products, noxious liquids carried in bulk, harmful packaged substances, sewage, and garbage.

GLOSSARY

Abiotic: The non-living component (either physical or chemical) of an environment.

Aboral: In radially symmetric organisms, the end opposite from the mouth.

Acontia: Thread-like structures containing nematocysts.

Aegism: Symbiotic relationship for protection.

Ahermatypic: A coral that does not build reefs.

Algae: A number of groups of organisms that function as autotrophs but lack the structural characteristics of plants.

Amino Acid: A type of nitrogen-containing molecule that makes up proteins.

Anchialine: Specialized brackish habitat that shows tidal fluctuation, but has no direct connection to the ocean.

Anthozoa: A class of cnidarians that exist as only complex polyps in their life cycle.

Anthropogenic: Influenced by humans or human-related.

Aolid: A type of nudibranch whose external gills (cerata) are arranged in rows along its dorsal side. Usually preys on Cnidarians, often incorporating **kleptocnidae.**

Aquaculture: Farming of marine and freshwater organisms.

Asexual Reproduction: Reproduction without exchange of sperm and eggs. much like how our skin grows.

Atoll: A roughly circular coral reef that encloses a lagoon.

Autotrophs: Make their own food from inorganic chemistry and energy.

Avivores: Animals that feed on birds.

Barnacles: A type of crustacean that lives attached to surfaces.

Barrier Reef: A coral reef that develops far offshore.

Basal Disc: Site of attachment of the polyp to the substrate (sometimes referred to as the **Pedal Disc**).

Basalt: A dark-colored volcanic rock which forms the oceanic crust and charecterizes Hawaiian lavas.

Benthic: Associated with the bottom substrate.

Bioerosion: The process by which organisms breakdown the physical/ geological environment.

Biogenous Sediments: Sediments made up of skeletal material from organisms.

Bioluminescence: The production of light by living organisms.

Bleaching: The decrease of zooxanthellae density within a coral.

Broadcast Spawning: The release of gametes (eggs and sperm) directly into the water column where fertilization takes place externally of the parents.

Budding: The asexual formation of a new polyp outside the parental ring of tentacles.

Calcareous: Made-up of calcium carbonate ($CaCO_3$)

Calyx (pl. Calices): Cup-like skeletal depression which houses the anemone-like polyp.

Carbohydrate: An **organic** compound made-up of carbon, hydrogen and oxygen in set arrangements.

Carnivores: Animals that consume other animals.

Cay: See Motu.

Cerata: Long, frilly projections of the mantle used for respiration in certain molluscs. Some nudibranchs are able to store unfired nematocysts in their cerata to use in their own defense.

Chitin: A complex carbohydrate that is a major component of many invertebrate skeletons.

Chlorophyll: A green photosynthetic pigment.

Chloroplasts: The functional site of photosynthesis in a plant; analogous to a photosynthetic 'organ'.

Clone: A series of identical cells or individuals that have all developed from a single cell or individual.

Cnidaria: A phylum of invertebrates whose major characteristics include radial symmetry and the presence of stinging cells (**cnidocytes**) - Geesh, these are the critters the whole book's about...next thing you know, you're going to want me to define **Coral Reefs**.

Cnidae: Another name for a **nematocyst**(see below).

Cnidocil: Mechanical trigger mechanism on a cnidocyte.

Cnidocyte: Unique type of cell which releases a specialized, harpoon-like structure (called a **nematocyst**) for capturing prey and defense. Unique to the phylum Cnidaria.

Coelenteron: Stomach-like structure seen in cnidarians and ctenophores. Also referred to as a gastrovascular cavity.

Colloblasts: Adhesive structures analogous to cnidocytes seen in the phylum Ctenophora (the Comb Jellies).

Colonizing Species: A species characterized by the ability to live in harsh, undeveloped environments; often fast growing with long dispersal capability.

Commensalism: A symbiotic association where the host neither benefits nor is hurt by the relationship.

Community: Several different species occurring together within a set area.

Competition: An interaction between two or more organisms vying for the same resource that is in limited supply.

Coprophagy: The process of eating fecal material.

Coral Reefs: You're very annoying, do you know that? The massive deposition of calcium carbonate by the action of stony corals and other organisms.

Coralline Algae: Green and red algae that deposit calcium carbonate as part of their structure.

Corallivores: Animals that feed on corals.

Crepuscular: Occurring at times when light levels are low but not dark (dawn and/or dusk).

Cryptic Coloration: A color pattern that blends in with the surroundings.

Dactylozooid: Specialized offensive/defensive polyp seen in hydrozoans.

Decomposers: Organisms that break down dead organic matter or organisms.

Deposit Feeders: Animals that feed on particulate organic matter that settles on the bottom.

Desiccation: The exposure of an marine organism to air and drying out.

Detritivores: Animals that feed on broken down, organic material from other organisms.

Detritus: The dead organic matter that decomposers and **detritivores** live on.

Dimorphic: The occurrence of two visually-different types within a species (usually male & female: sexually dimorphic).

Dinoflagellate: A unicellular, planktonic plant that moves about through the use of two whip-like flagella.

Dioecious: Consisting of separate sexes.

Dispersal: The way in which organisms get from one area to another.

Disturbance: An event in time that brings about change to an ecosystem.

Diurnal: Active during the day.

Diversity: The number of species within a defined area.

Ecology: The study of interactions, interactions between an organism and its environment (both physical and biological).

Ecological Succession: The process of replacing one community with another over time (see **Succession**).

Ecosystem: A biological community or series of communities plus all of the non-living components of an environment.

Ectoderm: The outermost tissue layer.

Endemic: A species unique to a specific area.

Endoderm: The innermost tissue layer.

Endoecism: Symbiotic association where the symbiont shelters in the burrow or defensive shelter of the host.

Endosymbiotic: A symbiotic relationship where the symbiont lives within the tissues of the host.

Ephyra: Medusa-like buds formed off of the scyphistoma stage of sea jellies.

Epidermis: See Ectoderm.

Epizoism: Where a sessile organism lives attached to another organism.

Eutrophication: A form of pollution caused by the introduction of excessive nutrients into an environment.

Evolution: The gradual change in the genetic make-up of a species as a result of natural selection.

Facilitated Predation: Predation that occurs as a result of actions of other organisms.

Facultative: Opportunistic; non-obligate; situational.

Fibropapillomastosis: The tumor-like infestation that is affecting Green sea turtles world-wide.

Fission: The formation of a new polyp by an invagination of the oral disc (mouth), inside the parental ring of tentacles.

Flagellum (pl. Flagella): Long, whip-like locomotory structures (Think of the tail on a sperm).

Fluorescence: A process whereby energy of one wavelength is taken in by an object, modified and given off as visible light.

Fore Reef: The outer part of a reef or atoll.

Fringing Reef: A reef that develops adjacent to a shoreline.

Gall: A external chamber in an organism in which a symbiont lives.

Gamete: A reproductive cell containing half the genetic component of the parent organism.

Gastrodermis: This is equivalent to the endodermis in cnidarians; primarily the lining of the coelenteron.

Gastrozooid: Specialized feeding polyp seen in hydrozoans.

Gonochoric: Produces separate eggs and sperm.

Gonochristic: Organisms that remain the same sex throughout their lives.

Gonozooid: Specialized reproductive polyp seen in hydrozoans.

Gulko: The author of this book; relatively nice guy, likes ice cream (Hey, I didn't think anybody would actually read the glossary...).

Habitat: The place where an organism lives.

Herbivores: Animals that consume only plants.

Hermaphrodite: An organism which is produces both male and female gametes at some point in its life; can be either sequential or simultaneous.

Hermatypic: A reef-building coral, usually contains symbiotic zooxanthellae.

Heterotrophs: Consume other organisms in order to derive their needed nutrients and energy.

Hydroskeleton: A type of skeletal support that uses internal water pressure to maintain body shape.

Imperforate: Corals whose skeleton structure is more solid than porous.

Inbreeding: The exchange of genetic material through sexual reproduction between two closely-related individuals.

Inquilism: Symbiotic association where the symbiont shelters on or inside the host.

Intercalical Tissue: The tissue that connects polyps to each other.

Interspecific: Between different species.

Intraspecific: Between genetically different members of the same species.

Island Arcs: Island chains that are formed along submergence zones; usually associated with trenches.

Kleptocnidae: The taking of stinging cells by another organism for its own use and defense.

Larval Stage: Self-sustaining, independent embryonic stage of an organism.

Lithospheric Plate: Sections of the earth's crust which move about atop the mantle.

MAA's: Mycosporine-like Amino Acids. Chemical compounds thought to act like a sunscreen to decrease the affects of ultraviolet radiation on an organism.

Mantle: (Geological) The semi-liquid layer of the earth between the crust and the core.
(Biological) The outer layer of tissue in most molluscs that is responsible for such things as shell secretion.

Medusa: Bell-shaped, free-living body form typified by scyphozoans.

Mesenchyme: The middle tissue layer of cnidarians (sometimes called **Mesogloea**)

Mesenterial Filaments: Tentacle-like structures within the gastrovascular cavity used for digestion. In some species these tentacles can be extruded outside the organism to digest the tissue of neighboring organisms.

Mesoglea: See **Mesenchyme**.

Metamorphose: To change into a wholly different form or appearance; transform.

Monogamous: Tend to remain in the same mating pairs each mating season.

Motu: A non-volcanic, flat island formed by rubble being washed atop a reef flat.

Mutualism: Symbiotic relationship where both the host and symbiont benefit from the association.

Necrosis: Tissue death.

Nematocysts: Unique stinging structures fired out of a stinging cell (cnidocyte).

Neoplasm: Fancy name for a **Tumor**, which is just an abnormal growth.

Niche: An ecological niche represents the unique role of a species within a community.

Nocturnal: Active during the night.

Oceanic Islands: Volcanic islands usually formed through the action of stationary hot spots or mid-ocean ridges.

Omnivores: Consume both plants and animals.

Operculum: A covering; often used to protect an opening or to keep something inside of a structure.

Oral Arms: Tentacle-like structures around the mouths of sea jellies used primarily for food manipulation.

Organic: Material composed of carbon, hydrogen and oxygen, usually produced through biological processes.

Oscula: External opening on sponges used to dispose of filtered water.

Palatability: How tasty/distasteful something is.

PAR: Photosynthetically-Active Radiation. Those wavelengths of light(radiation) used by primary producers to conduct photosynthesis. Roughly equal to visible light.

Parasitism: Symbiotic relationship where the host's fitness suffers as a result of the association.

Perforate: Corals whose skeleton structure is highly porous.

Pedicellaria: Small protective pinchers located on the surface of sea stars & sea urchins thought to function in protecting the skin gills from small scavengers.

Phoresis: Symbiotic relationship where the symbiont uses the host for transportation.

Photosynthate: The organic energy product produced by the process of photosynthesis.

Photosynthesis: The production of organic energy (carbohydrates) from CO_2 and H_2O in the presence of chlorophyll by using inorganic light energy and releasing O_2.

Phyllosoma: Larval stage of lobster.

Phylum: The initial way of grouping organisms within a kingdom.

Phytoplankton: Plant members of the plankton

Piscivores: Animals that feed on fishes.

Planula (*pl.* Planulae): The planktonic larval stage of most Cnidarians.

Plankton: A wide ranging group of drifting or free-floating organisms which have little (if any) control over their movement in the open ocean.

Planktivores: Animals that feed on plankton.

Planulation: The release of brooded planula larvae from the adult colony or organism.

Pneumatophore: Specialized gas-filled float seen in Portuguese Man-O-War.

Polygamous: Tend to mate in pairs, but the pairs may vary with each mating.

Polymorphism: The retention of morphologically-distinct members of a colony.

Polyp: Cylindrical, usually sessile body form typically seen in anthozoans and hydrozoans.

Population: All of the individuals of a set species within a set area.

Porosity: How porous something is.

Primary Producers: Organisms that convert inorganic energy such as light into organic energy.

Promiscuous: Tend to mate together as a group; often seen with schooling fish.

Protandry: Sex change where an animal starts as a male and then changes into a female.

Protogeny: Sex change where an animal starts as a female and then changes into a male.

Radial Symmetry: The regular arrangement of similar body parts around a central axis, such that they can be equally divided in along an axis.

Recruitment: The process of leaving the plankton in order to settle into another habitat.

Rhopalia: Sensory structures on sea jellies and box jellies.

Scale: A way of looking at something as it varies in either time or space.

Sclerites: Skeletal fragments that serve as a loose skeleton; seen in some octocorals.

Scyphistoma: A sessile polyp-like stage seen with most sea jellies.

Septum (pl. Septa): Thin, vertical skeletal partitions fused to the walls of the calyx. Usually project towards the center of the calyx.

Sessile: Attached to the substrate.

Sexual Reproduction: Didn't they teach you anything in school (see **Asexual Reproduction** and reverse it)???

Species: A natural group of organisms that can interbreed.

Spicules: Skeletal fragments that serve as a loose skeleton as in sponges.

Statocysts: Balance structures on sea jellies and box jellies.

Stolon: Membranous tissue expansion from which polyps arise.

Strobilation: The release of free-living medusae from the sessile stage of sea jellies.

Stylets: Barb-like structures on the sides of nematocysts, used for slicing into a prey item to facilitate the stinging structure entering the organism.

Submergence: A geological process where one plate slides underneath another.

Substrate: The base upon which an organism lives.

Succession: The process of replacing one species with another over time (see **Ecological Succession**).

Suspension Feeders: Animals that feed on particulate organic matter suspended in the water column.

Symbiont: Usually the smaller of the two partners in a symbiotic relationship.

Symbiosis: A close relationship between two organisms, usually the smaller organism is the symbiont and the larger organism is the host.

Terrigenous Sediments: Sediments composed of materials from land.

Theca: The walls of the calyx which encloses the aboral end of the polyp. Epitheca are elevated extensions of the theca that surround individual calices.

Tissue: A group of cells all specialized for a single function.

Translocation: Movement of material from the endosymbiont to the host and vice-versa.

Trophic Level: Each of the steps in a food chain.

Tsunami: A seismic sea wave; what used to be called a 'tidal wave', until someone pointed out that it had nothing to do with tides.

Ultraviolet Radiation: Electromagnetic radiation of shorter wavelength than visible light but longer than X rays.

Verrucae: Small, nipple-like projections arising from the skeleton of specific corals (example: *Pocillopora*).

Vivipary: Development of an egg inside the female where the developing embryo derives nourishment from the mother.

Zooplankton: Animal members of the plankton.

Zooxanthellae: Single-celled plants (Dinoflagellates) that live symbiotically within the tissue of certain Cnidarians (notably the stony corals).

APPENDIX IV:
SUBJECT BIBLIOGRAPHY

CORAL BIOLOGY & ECOLOGY:

 Life and Death of Coral Reefs
by C. Birkeland (1997). Chapman & Hill; 536 pp.

 Coral Reefs
by H. Breidahl (1994). MacMillian Education Australia Pty, Ltd.; Melbourne, Australia. 40 pp.

 A Guide to the Identification of the Living Corals (Scleractinia) of Southern California
by J. C. Bythelle (1986). San Diego Society of Natural History; San Diego, CA. 40 pp. Field guide to corals (primarily ahermatypic) found along the southwestern coast of the United States.

  Reef and Shore Fauna of Hawaii - Section I: Protozoa - Ctenophora
edited by D. M. Deveney & L. G. Eldredge (1977). Bishop Museum Press; Honolulu, HI. 278 pp. The only major reference guide out on Hawaiian reef corals. Also great for information on other cnidarians, ctenophores, sponges and foraminiferans.

 Ecosystems of the World 25: Coral Reefs
edited by Z. E. Dubinsky (1990). Elsevier; Amsterdam. 525 pp. One of the most thorough volumes available, with contributions by all the big names who work on corals and coral reef systems. Each chapter is written by an expert in the field.

Corals and Coral Reefs of the Galapogos Islands
by P. W. Glynn & G. M. Wellington (1983). University of California Press; Berkeley, CA. 330 pp.

Coral Reefs & Islands
by W. Gray (1993). David & Charles; Cambridge. 192 pp. Interesting reading, lots of info on coral reef and island natural history. Oriented towards the Great Barrier Reef and the Central Indo-Pacific.

 "The Annual Coral Spawning Event on the Great Barrier Reef"
IN: Reef Notes, July '86. Great Barrier Reef Marine Park Authority; Townsville, Australia. ISSN 0814-9453. Nicely produced and informative newsletter published a couple of times a year with articles about coral reef ecology on the Great Barrier Reef.

 Hawaii's Precious Corals
by R. W. Grigg (1977). Island Heritage; Norfolk Island, Australia. 64 pp. Could have more info on biology/ecology, but still a great resource on man's interactions and marketing of precious corals.

Coral Reefs
by L. Holiday (1989). Tetra Press; Morris Plains, NJ. 204 pp. Interesting guide to diving coral reefs around the world; some good natural history information.

 Reef Coral Identification: Florida - Caribbean - Bahamas
by P. Humann (1993). New World Publications; Jacksonville, FL. 239 pp. Probably the best picture guide book currently available for Caribbean waters. Accurate, very thorough and well-documented. Also includes information on sea grasses and seaweeds.

 Coral Reefs
by S. A. Johnson (1984). A Lerner Natural Science Book, Lerner Publications; Minneapolis, MN.

 Coral Reef Population Biology
edited by P. Jokiel, R. H. Richmond, & R. Rogers (1984). Hawai'i Institute of Marine Biology Technical Report #37; Sea Grant Cooperative Report UNIHI-SEAGRANT-CR-86-01. 498 pp. Great collection of papers concerning coral reef ecology, mostly in terms of Kane'ohe Bay, Hawai'i.

 Biology and Geology of Coral Reefs (Volumes I-IV)
edited by O. A. Jones & R. Endean (1976). Academic Press; NY, NY. ~430 pp. each. In-depth series consisting of two volumes dealing with the geology and two volumes dealing with the biology of coral reefs.

 Peterson Field Guides: Coral Reefs
E. H. Kaplan (1982). Houghton Mifflin Company; Boston, MA. 288 pp. Great field guide to all aspects of Caribbean coral reefs including corals and other invertebrates, and fish.

 Coral Reefs in the South Pacific
by M. King (1988). South Pacific Regional Environment Programme Regal Press; Launceton, Australia. 40 pp. Very short, cartoon-like booklet written as an introductory guide for peoples of the South Pacific.

 Living Coral Reefs of the World
by D. Kühlman (1985). Arco Publishing, Inc.; NY, NY. 185 pp. Excellent resource for all aspects of coral reef ecology.

 The World Heritage: Coral Reefs
by A. R. de Larramendi (1993). UNESCO, Chidren's Press; Chicago. 33 pp. Very short guide to the two World Heritage sites that are coral reefs: the Great Barrier Reef in Australia and Aldabra Atoll in the Seychelles.

The Coral Reef at Night
by J. S. Levine (1993). Harry N. Abrams, Inc.; NY, NY. 192 pp. Beautiful coffee table book showing the reef and many of its inhabitants during their nocturnal phase.

 Coelenterate Biology: Review and Perspectives
edited by L. Muscatine & H. M. Lenhoff (1974). Academic Press; NY, NY. 501 pp. Collection of cnidarian physiology papers; good chapter on nematocysts.

 The Hawaiian Coral Reef Coloring Book
by K. Orr (1992). Stemmer House Publishers, Inc.; Owing Mills, MD. 48 pp. Amazing amount of quality information in a short, well-written and illustrated coloring book.

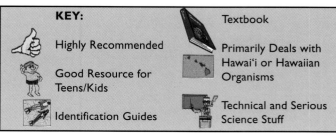

KEY:

Highly Recommended

Good Resource for Teens/Kids

Identification Guides

Textbook

Primarily Deals with Hawai'i or Hawaiian Organisms

Technical and Serious Science Stuff

CORAL BIOLOGY & ECOLOGY (CONT.):

Guide to the Coastal Resources of Guam:
Vol. 2 The Corals
by R. H. Randall & R. F. Myers (1983). University of Guam
Press; Guam. 128 pp.

Living Corals
by B. Robins (1980). Les Editions De Pacifique; Papeepe, Tahiti.
144 pp. Very good, inexpensive guide to tropical Pacific corals,
their physiology and ecology.

A Natural History of the Coral Reef
by C. R. Shepard (1983). Blanford Books, Ltd.; Britain. 153 pp.

Dive to the Coral Reefs
by E. Tayntor, P. Erickson & L. Kaufman (1986). A New England
Aquarium Book, Crown Publishers, Inc.; NY, NY.

Corals of Australia and the Indo-Pacific
by J. E. N. Veron (1993). University of Hawai'i Press; Honolulu, HI.
644 pp.The ultimate in coffee table books for the affectionate coral
"groupie". A phenomenal piece of work - great information on reef
formation and species accounts on every known Pacific coral.

A Biogeographic Database of Hermatypic Corals
by J. E. N. Veron (1993). Australian Institute of Marine Science;
Townsville, Australia 433 pp. Database of coral families, genera
and species gives distribution and taxonomic references
information. Excellent genera distribution maps at the end.

Corals in Space & Time
by J. E. N. Veron (1995). Cornell University Press; Ithaca, NY.
321 pp. Amazing book covering everything you ever wanted to
know about the evolution , biogeography and paleontology of
corals. Highly theoretical and intriguing reading.

The Greenpeace Book of Coral Reefs
by S. Wells & N. Hanna (1992). Sterling Publishing Co., Inc.; NY.
160 pp. A great resource guide for man's effects on coral reefs.

Coral Reefs of the World Volumes 1, 2 & 3
edited by S. Wells (1988). The United Nations Environment
Programme & The International Union for the Conservation of
Nature and Natural Resources; Cambridge, England. ~380 pp
each. A three volume set (one for each of the major tropical ocean
areas) consisting of compilations of information on coral reefs of
international importance. Contains a wealth of information. Vol.
3 contains info about Pacific reefs including Hawai'i.

Corals and Coral Reefs in the Caribbean: A Manual for
Students, 2nd ed.
by E. Williams & A. Edwards (1993). Caribbean Conservation
Association. 70 pp. Excellent introductory guide with in-book
and follow-up activities.

Corals of the World
by E. M. Wood (1983). T. F. H. Publications, Inc.; Neptune City, NJ.
256 pp. ID guide to major genera of corals; divided into Atlantic and
Pacific Ocean groupingss. Appendix of distributional maps.

Corals Reefs
by J. Wood (1987).
Scholastic Inc.; NY, NY. 31pp
Well written introductory guide for young children.

CORAL REEFS & CONSERVATION BIOLOGY:

Coastal Environments in the South Pacific
by M. King (1989). South Pacific Regional Environment
Programme Regal Press; Launceston, Australia. 40 pp. Very
short, cartoon-like booklet written as an introductory guide for
peoples of the South Pacific.

Save Our Coral Reefs
by D. E. Miller & A. Ansula (1993). Ocean Voice International;
Ottawa, Canada. 126 pp. Excellent manual on human impacts,
cultural effects, and conservation actions. Written for the
Phillipines. Great reference section and appendix of environmental organizations.

Global Marine Biological Diversity
edited by E. A. Norse (1993). Center for Marine Conservation,
Island Press; Washington, D.C. 383 pp. Great resource volume
for information and views concerning various aspects of marine
conservation and threats to biological diversity.

Our Coral Reefs
by S. Soule (1994). ICLARM; Manila, Phillipines.

Rescue the Reef, Coloring Activities Book
by R. Stec (1993). RMS Publishing for the Nature Company;
Birmingham, MI.

Conservation Biology in Hawai'i
edited by C. P. Stone & D. B. Stone (1989). Cooperative National
Park Resource Studies Unit, University of Hawai'i; Honolulu, HI.
252pp. Includes sections on island formation, endangered species,
anchialine ponds, etc. Heavy terrestrial focus.

The Marine Curio Trade: Conservation Guidelines and
Legislation
edited by S. Wells & E. Wood (1991). Marine Conservation
Society, Herefordshire, UK. 23 pp. Great little booklet detailing
the laws concerning trade in dead marine organisms.

CORAL REEF PLANTS AND SEAWEEDS:

The Limu Eater
by H. J. Fortner (1978). University of Hawai'i Sea Grant College
Program, Honolulu, HI. UNIHI-SEAGRANT-MR-79-01 102 pp.
First section of the book is dedicated to hawaiiana about seaweeds and
their natural history. Second half is filled with recipes.

Phycology
by R. E. Lee (1980). Cambridge University Press; Cambridge,
England. 478 pp. Standard textbook on microalgae (diatoms,
dinoflagellates) and macroalgae.

Seaweeds of Hawaii
by W. H. Magruder & J. W. Hunt (1979). Oriental Publishing Co.;
Honolulu, HI. 116 pp. Excellent picture guide to Hawaiian
marine macroalgae.

Field Keys to Common Hawaiian Marine Animals and Plants
State of Hawai'i, Dep't of Education, Office of Instructional
Services (1983). Dep't of Education, RS 83-4549; Honolulu, HI.
447 pp. Includes dichotomous keys and graphics for Hawaiian
seaweeds, corals, sea cucumbers, sea urchins, polychaetes and
hermit crabs.

CORAL REEF INVERTEBRATES:

Indo-Pacific Coral Reef Field Guide
by G. R. Allen & R. Steene (1994). Tropical Reef Research; Singapore

Invertebrate Zoology, 6th ed.
by R. D. Barnes & E. E. Rupert (1994). Saunders College; Philadelphia, PA. 1089 pp. Considered by many to be the "Bible" of invertebrate textbooks.

Hawaiian Nudibranchs
by H. Bertsch & S. Johnson (1981). Oriental Publishing Co.; Honolulu, HI. 112 pp. Nice picture guide to Hawaiian nudibranchs, sea hares and bubble shells. Not alot of information.

The Living Shores of South Africa
by G. Branch & M. Branch (1981). C. Struik (Pty) Ltd.; Cape Town, South Africa 272 pp. Excellent book on coastal ecosystems found in southern Africa. The descriptions of adaptations and physiology of inverts and fish are applicable to many Hawaiian organisms. Excellent diagrams.

Invertebrates
by R. C. Brusca & G. J. Brusca (1990). Sinaur Associates, Inc.; Sunderland, MA. 922 pp. Extensive textbook on invertebrates; excellent chapters on arthropods.

A Guide to the World of the Jellyfish
by E. Campbell (1992). The Monterey Bay Aquarium Foundation; Monterey, CA. 16 pp. Short booklet on sea jellies; limited information but very nice photos.

Tropical Pacific Invertebrates
by P. L. Colin & C. Arneson (1994). Coral Reef Press; Beverley Hills, CA. 296 pp. Extensive photo field guide geared towards the central Indo-Pacific region.

Armoured Knights of the Sea
by H. Debelius (1983). Zweigniederlassung der Reimar hubbing GmbH; Esse, Germany. 120 pp. Contains a lot of information about ecological aspects of shrimps and crabs.

Sand to Sea: Marine Life of Hawaii
by S. Feeney & A. Fielding (1989). University of Hawai'i Press; Honolulu, HI.

Hawaiian Reefs and Tidepools
by A. Fielding (1985). Oriental Publishing Co.; Honolulu, HI. 103 pp. An inexpensive, well-written guide to Hawaiian shallow-water invertebrates.

An Underwater Guide to Hawai'i
by A. Fielding & E. Robinson (1987). University of Hawai'i Press; Honolulu, HI. 156pp. An expanded follow-up to Fielding's previous work; this work deals extensively with reef fish but has a good section on inverts.

Coral Reef Animals of the Indo-Pacific
by T. Gosliner, D. Behrens & G. Williams (1996). Sea Challengers; Monterey, CA. 314pp. Extensive photo field guide geared towards the central Indo-Pacific region.

The Crown-of-Thorns Starfish
The Great Barrier Reef Marine Park Authority (1987). Australia Science Magazine; Townsville, Australia. 54 pp. Short, but highly informative guide to *Acanthaster planci.*

All About Lobsters, Crabs, Shrimps and Their Relatives
by R. Headstrom (1979). Dover Publications; NY, NY. 143 pp. A lot of information, but mostly concerning species that are not found in Hawai'i.

The Wierd and the Beautiful: The Story of the Portuguese Man-of-War, the Sailors-by-the-Wind, and Their Exotic Relatives of the Deep.
by R. Headstrom (1984). Cornwall Books; NY, NY. 194 pp. Interesting book detailing hydrozoans and other cnidarians.

Hawaiian Reef Animals, 2nd ed.
by E. Hobson & E. H. Chave (1990). University of Hawai'i Press; Honolulu, HI. 136 pp. Contains a lot of good information about organisms (mostly fish but with a fair amount of inverts) on Hawaiian coral reefs.

Hawaii's Sea Creatures: A Guide to Hawaii's Marine Invertebrates
by J. Hoover (1998). Mutual Publishing, LLC., Honolulu, HI. 376 pp. The only complete guide to the wide range of marine invertebrates found on Hawaiian reefs.

Reef Creature Identification: Florida - Caribbean - Bahamas
by P. Humann (1992). New World Publications; Jacksonville, FL. 320 pp. Probably the best picture guide available for the Caribbean region. Accurate, very thorough and well-documented.

Living Seashells
by S. Johnson (1981). Oriental Publishing; Honolulu, HI. 116 pp. Inexpensive, nicely photographed book showing LIVE molluscs (as opposed to the dead shells usually seen in ID books).

Shells of Hawai'i
by E. A. Kay & O. Schoenberg-Dole (1991). University of Hawai'i Press; Honolulu, HI. 89 pp. Interesting short book on Hawaiian marine shells, contains information on natural history.

Hawaiian Marine Shells
by E. A. Kay (1979). Bishop Museum Press; Honolulu, HI. 654 pp. Second in the Bishop Museum series on Hawaiian reef and shore fauna. Extensive accounts on the vast majority of Hawaiian marine molluscs. Great for ID use - though not a picture guide.

A Coral Reef Handbook, 3rd ed.
edited by P. Mather & I. Bennett (1979). Surrey, Beatty & Sons Pty, Ltd; Chipping Norton, NSW, Australia. 264 pp. Extensive field guide for coral reef and cay animals. Geared primarily for the Great Barrier Reef.

Partnerships in the Sea: Hong Kong's Marine Symbioses
by B. Morton (1987). Hong Kong University Press; Hong Kong. 120 pp. Excellent guide defining different types of symbiotic relationships.

Hawaiian Reefs: A Natural History Guide
by R. Russo (1994). Wavecrest Publications; San Leandro, CA. 173 pp. Good guide to Hawaiian inverts and fish. Limited natural history information.

The Invertebrates: Function and Form, A Laboratory Guide
by I. Sherman (1976). Macmillan Publishing Co., Inc.; NY, NY. 334 pp. Excellent pictorial guide; goes into a lot of detail about morphology and physiology of major invertebrate groups.

Nudibranchs
by T. E. Taylor (1976). T. F. H. Publications; Neptune City, NJ. 96 pp. Good resource for information on a variety of nudibranchs and their biology.

CORAL REEF INVERTEBRATES (CONT.):

Native Use of Invertebrates in Old Hawaii
by M. Titcomb (1979). University of Hawai'i Press; Honolulu, HI. 61 pp. Excellent resource for Hawaiiana aspects of marine invertebrates, including native uses of cnidarians.

Living Together in the Sea
by L. P. Zann (1980). T. F. H. Publications; Neptune City, NJ. 416pp. The definitive book on all aspects of marine symbiotic relationships.

CHILDREN'S NATURE-BASED FICTION:

Polyp
by G. Carlin (1986). Great Barrier Reef Marine Park Authority; Townsville, Australia.

Ellisella the Coral
by K. Muzik (1986). Mitchiaki Ogawa, Libro Port Publishing Co., Ltd.; Tokyo, Japan.

At Home in the Coral Reef
by K. Muzik (1992). Charlesbridge; Watertown, MA.

The Reef and the Wrasse
by S. Steere & K. M. Ring (1988). Harbinger House, Inc.; Tuscon, AZ.

SEA TURTLES:

Hawaii's Sea Birds , Turtles and Seals
by G. H. Balazs (1976). Worldwide Distributors, Ltd.; Honolulu, HI. 34 pp. Short pictorial guide.

Synopsis of Biological Data on the Green Sea Turtle in the Hawaiian Islands
by G. H. Balazs (1980). U. S. Dept. of Commerce, N.O.A.A., N.M.F.S., Southwest Fisheries Center; Honolulu, HI. NOAA-TM-NMFS-SWFS-7. 34pp.

Manual of Sea Turtle Research and Conservation Techniques, 2nd ed.
Prepared for the Western Atlantic Turtle Symposium; San Jose, Costa Rica (1983). Center for Environmental Education; Washington, D.C. 125 pp.

Hawaiian Reptiles and Amphibians
by S. McKeown (1978). The Oriental Publishing Co.; Honolulu, HI. 34 pp. Some information on sea turtles and sea snakes, but mostly terrestrial.

Draft Hawaiian Sea Turtle Recovery Plan
National Marine Fisheries Service (1989).
U. S. Dept. of Commerce, N.O.A.A., N.M.F.S., Southwest Fisheries Center; Honolulu, HI. 108 pp. Draft recovery plan for the threatened Hawaiian Green Sea Turtle and the endangered Hawaiian Hawksbill Sea Turtle.

Sea Turtles
J. Ripple (1996). Voyageur Press; Stillwater, MN. 84 pp. Great photos, up-to-date information, nice layout.

Sea Turtles of the South Pacific
South Pacific Regional Environment Programme (1993). S.P.R.E.P.; Noumea, New Caledonia. 4 pp. This very short pamphlet is full of information about the major sea turtle species in the area, their life cycles and migration patterns. Short section about human impacts.

Biology and Conservation of Sea Turtles, 2nd ed.
World Conference on Sea Turtle Conservation (1995). Smithsonian Institution; Washington, D. C. 615 pp. Updated training manual for researchers on the biology and natural history of sea turtles.

CORAL REEF MONITORING GUIDES:

Quantitative Ecology and Marine Biology
by G. J. Bakus (1990). Oxford & IBH Publishing Co. Pvt., Ltd.; New Delhi, India. 157 pp. Primarily developed for use in India, this book presents standard surveying techniques in a simple manner for college-level students.

Survey Manual for Tropical Marine Resources, 2nd Ed.
edited by S. English, C. Wilkinson & V. Baker (1997). Australian Institute of Marine Science; Townsville, Australia. 390 pp. Very well written, with information on techniques for surveying coral reefs, mangroves, seagrasses and soft-bottom habitats. Includes information on sampling design and monitoring programs.

The Underwater Catalog: A Guide to Methods in Underwater Research
by J. Coyer & J. Witman (1990). Shoals Marine Laboratory, Cornell University; Ithaca, NY. 72 pp. Short, inexpensive booklet outlining techniques and resources for conducting underwater transects.

Coral Reef Monitoring Manual for Hawai'i'
edited by D. Gulko (1998). Department of Land and National Resources, State of Hawai'i. 110 pp. Handbook designed to assist managers, researchers and community volunteers in designing and conducting a coral reef monitoring program. Based on original manual designed for use in Caribbean (see Rogers 1994 below).

The Ecology of Deep and Shallow Coral Reefs
edited by M. L. Reaka (1983). Symposia Series for Undersea Research, Vol. 1, No. 1. U.S. Dept. of Commerce, NOAA; Washington, D.C. 149 pp. A series of edited papers on coral reef research and technique development.

The Ecology of Coral Reefs
edited by M. L. Reaka (1985). Symposia Series for Undersea Research, Vol. 3, No. 1. U.S. Dept. of Commerce, NOAA; Washington, D.C. 208 pp. A series of edited papers on coral reef research and technique development.

Coral Reef Monitoring Manual for the Caribbean and Western Atlantic
edited by C. Rogers et. al. (1994). National Park Service Virgin Islands National Park.

Coral Reef Monitoring Handbook: Reference Methods for Marine Pollution Studies No. 25, 2nd ed.
South Pacific Commission (1984). United Nations Environment Programme (UNEP) and South Pacific Regional Educational Programme (SPREP); Noumea, New Caledonia. 25 pp. A short booklet outlining basic techniques. Includes sample data sheets.

CORAL REEF FISH:

Fishwatching in Hawaii
by R. B. Carpenter & B. C. Carpenter (1981). Natural World Press; San Mateo, CA. 120 pp. Inexpensive, easy-reading. Contains a wealth of simple information on the natural history of fishes.

Field Guide to Anemonefishes and their Host Anemones
by D. G. Fautin & G. R. Allen (1992). Western Australian Museum; Perth, WA. 160 pp. Complete field guide to the large variety of anemonefish species and their distributions. Good ecological and aquarium information.

Feeding Ecology of Fish
by S. D. Gerking (1994). Academic Press; San Diego, CA. 416 pp. Extensive book exploring the wide diversity of feeding adaptations in marine fish. Details the ecology of each of the major feeding guilds.

Discovering Sharks
by S. H. Gruber (1991). American Littoral Society; Highlands, NJ. 122 pp. Great compilation of short descriptive papers on shark biology and ecology, each written by an expert in the field. Could be used by intermediate and high school students.

Hawaii's Fishes: A Guide for Divers and Snorkelers
by J. P. Hoover (1993). Mutual Publishing; Honolulu, HI. 178 pp. One of the best picture guide book currently available for Hawaiian waters. Accurate, very thorough and well-documented. Excellent photography.

Shore Fishing in Hawaii
by E. Y. Hosaka (1973). Petroglyph Press; Hilo, HI. 175 pp. Originally published in 1944; good source for info on Hawaiian names, use and fishing techniques.

Reef Fish Identification: Florida - Caribbean - Bahamas, 2nd ed.
by P. Humann (1995). New World Publications; Jacksonville, FL. 392 pp. Probably the best picture guide book currently available for Caribbean waters. Accurate, very thorough and well-documented. This book is very interesting in how it groups fish and uses morphological structures for field identification.

Sharks of Polynesia
by R. H. Johnson (1978).Les Editions De Pacifique; Papeepe, Tahiti. 170 pp. Excellent, inexpensive book containing a lot of information on sharks found in the tropical Pacific (including Hawai'i). Identification, native and modern uses, biology.

Reef Sharks & Rays of the World
by S. W. Michael (1993). Sea Challengers; Monterey, CA. 107 pp. Great descriptive field guide to the wide diversity of reef sharks found throughout the world. Interesting appendix on mating behavior.

Mysteries & Marvels of Ocean Life
by R. Morris (1983). Usborne Publishing Ltd,; London, UK. 32 pp. Fun look at marine animal adaptations. Great cartoons and graphics.

The Butterflyfishes: Success on the Coral Reef
edited by P. J. Motta (1989). Kluwer Academic Publishers; The Netherlands. 256 pp. Includes chapters on all aspects of butterflyfish ecology, written by experts in the field.

Micronesian Reef Fishes
by R. F. Myers (1989). Coral Graphics; Barrigada, Guam. 298 pp. Excellent guide to the majority of reef fishes found throughout the central Pacific. Contains a wide variety of information for each group of fish; beginning of the book does a good job of introducing reef fish ecology.

Encyclopedia of Fishes
edited by J. R. Paxton & W. N. Eschmeyer (1995). Academic Press; San Diego, CA. 240 pp. Good general introduction to the evolution and ecology of fishes. Descriptive guide to the wide diversity of fish families found throughout the world.

Shore Fishes of Hawai'i
by J. R. Randall (1996). Natural World Press; Vida, OR. 216 pp. Very complete photo guide to Hawaiian fishes. Male, female and juvenile shots for many species. Good glossary at the end.

Underwater Guide to Hawaiian Reef Fishes
by J. R. Randall (1981). Natural World Press; Vida, OR. 216 pp. Waterproof photo guide to most Hawaiian reef fishes. Non-waterproof version contains species and family descriptions.

The Ecology of Fishes on Coral Reefs
edited by P. F. Sale (1991). Academic Press, Inc.; San Diego, CA. 447 pp. Great compilation by most of the major researchers in coral reef fish ecology. Written for those with some science background; especially those who plan to work in the field.

Butterfly and Angelfishes of the World, Vol. 1 &2
by R. C. Steene (1977). Mergus Publishers Hans A. Baensch; Melle, Germany. 144 pp.

Sharks of Hawai'i: Their Biology and Cultural Significance
by L. Taylor (1994). University of Hawai'i Press; Honolulu, HI. 126 pp. Excellent resource guide for natural history and Hawaiiana concerning the major species of sharks found in Hawai'i.

Reef Fish: Behavior & Ecology on the Reef and in the Aquarium
by R. E. Thresher (1980). The Palmetto Publishing Co.; St. Petersburg, FL. 171 pp. Great species accounts, covering a wide variety of ecological conditions, centered on Atlantic species.

Reproduction in Reef Fishes
by R. E. Thresher (1984). T. F. H. Publications; Neptune City, NJ. 399 pp. Great reference work on reproduction in coral reef fishes though centered almost entirely on Atlantic species.

Native Use of Fish in Hawaii, 2nd ed.
by M. Titcomb (1972). University of Hawai'i Press; Honolulu, HI. 175 pp. Excellent resource for Hawaiiana aspects of reef fish..

Watching Fishes: Life and Behavior on Coral Reefs.
by R. Wilson & J. Q. Wilson (1985). Harper & Row Publishers; NY, NY. 275 pp. Interesting reading on the behavior of reef fish covering a wide breadth of material; centered on Atlantic coral reefs.

WHAT'S THAT? YOU WANT TO KNOW MORE....

Anemones:
Godwin, J. & Fautin, D. G. (1992).
Defense of host actinians by anemonefishes.
Copiea **1992**(3): 902 - 908.

Bioerosion:
Hutchings, P. A. (1986).
Biological destruction of coral reefs: A review. *Coral Reefs* **4**: 239 - 252.

Calcareous Algae:
Littler, M. M. (1973).
The population and community structure of Hawaiian fringing reef crustose Corallinaceae (Rhodophyta, Cryptonemiales). *J. Exp. Mar. Biol. Ecol.* **11**(2): 103 - 120.

Cleaning Behavior:
Losey, G. S. (1979).
Fish cleaning symbiosis: proximate causes of host behavior. *An. Beh.* **27**: 669 - 685.
Losey, G. S., Balazs, G. H. & Privitera, L. A. (1994).
Cleaning symbiosis between the wrasse, *Thalassoma duperry* and the Green Turtle, *Chelonia mydas. Copeia* 1994(3): 684 - 690.

Clonal Cnidarians:
Harvell, C. D. & Grosberg, R. K. (1988).
The timing of sexual maturity in clonal animals. *Ecol.* **69**(6): 1855 - 1864.
Hughes, R. N. & Cancino, J. M. (1985).
An ecological overview of cloning in Metazoa. *In:* 'Population Biology and Evolution of Clonal Organisms', J. B. C. Jackson, L. W. Buss & R. E. Cook (eds.). Yale Univ. Press, New Haven, Conn. Pgs 153 - 186.
Jackson, J. B. C. (1985).
Distribution and ecology of clonal and aclonal benthic invertebrates. *In:* 'Population Biology and Evolution of Clonal Organisms', J. B. C. Jackson, L. W. Buss & R. E. Cook (eds.). Yale Univ. Press, New Haven, Conn. Pgs 297 - 346.

Color & Patterning:
Aronson, R. B. (1983).
Foraging behavior of the west Atlantic trumpetfish, *Aulostomus maculatus*: use of large herbivorous reef fishes as camouflage. *Bull. Mar. Sci.* **33**: 166 - 171.

Coprophagy:
Robertson, D. S. (1982).
Fish feces as fish food on a coral reef. *Mar. Ecol. Progr. Ser.* **7**: 253 - 265.

Coral Bleaching:
Brown, B. E. (1990).
"Coral Bleaching", edited by B. E. Brown. *Coral Reefs* (Special Issue) **8**: 153 - 232.
Glynn, P. W. (1991).
Coral reef bleaching in the 1980's and possible connections with global warming. *T. R. E. E.* **6**: 175 - 179.
Jokiel, P. L. & Coles, S. L. (1977).
Effects of temperature on the mortality and growth of Hawaiian reef corals. *Mar. Biol.* **43**: 201 - 208.

Coral Competition:
Lang, J. C. & Chornesky, E. A. (1990).
Competition between scleractinian reef corals - a review of mechanisms and effects. *In:* 'Ecosystems of the World 25: Coral Reefs'; Z. Dubinsky (ed.). Elsevier, Amsterdam, pp. 209 - 252.
Lang, J. C. (1973).
Interspecific aggression by scleractinian corals: why the race is not only to the swift. *Bull. Mar. Sci.* **23**: 260 - 279.

Coral Diseases:
Antonius, A. (1985).
Coral diseases in the Indo-Pacific: A first record. *Marine Ecology* **6**(3): 197 - 218.
Peters, E. C. (1997).
Diseases of coral-reef organisms. *In:* 'Life and Death of Coral Reefs'. C. Birkeland (ed.). Chapman & Hill Publ. , pp. 114 - 139.
Santary, D. L. & Peters, E. C. (1997).
Microbial pests: Coral diseases in the Western Atlantic. *Proc. 8th Int. Coral Reef Symp.* **1**: 607 - 612.

Coral Feeding:
Fabricus, K. E., Benayahu, Y., & Genin, A. (1995).
Herbivory in asymbiotic soft corals. *Science* **268**: 90 - 92.

Coral Hydromechanics & Locomotion:
Chadwick, N. E. (1988).
Competition and locomotion in a free-living fungiid coral. *J. Exp. Mar. Biol. Ecol.* **123**: 189 -200.
Jokiel, P. L. & Cowdin, H. P. (1976).
Hydromechanical adaptation in the solitary free-living coral *Fungia scutaria. Nature* **262**(5565): 212 - 213.
Hoeksema, B. W. (1988).
Mobility of free-living fungiid corals (Scleractinia), a dispersion mechanism and survival strategy in dynamic reef habitats. *Proc. Sixth Int. Coral Reef Symp.* **2**: 715 - 720.
Sebens, K. P. (1997).
Adaptive responses to water flow: Morphology, energetics and distribution of reef corals. *Proc. 8th Int. Coral Reef Symp.* **2**: 1053 - 1058.

Coral Larval Development:
Babcock, R. C. & Heyward, A. J. (1986).
Larval development of certain gamete-spawning scleractinian corals. *Coral Reefs* **5**: 111 - 116.

Coral Larval Settlement:
Goreau, N. I., Goreau, T. J. & Hayes, R. L. (1981).
Settling, survivorship and spatial aggregation in planulae and juveniles of *Porites porites* (Pallas). *Bull. Mar. Sci.* **31**: 424 - 435.
Maida, M., Sammarco, P. W. & Coll, J. C. (1995).
Effects of soft corals on scleractinian recruitment. I: Directional allelopathy and inhibition of settlement. *Mar. Ecol. Prog. Ser.* **121**: 191 - 202.
Richmond, R. H. (1985).
Reversible metamorphosis in coral planula larvae. *Mar. Ecol. Progr. Ser.* **22**: 181 - 185.

Coral Mucus:
Drollet, J. P., Glaziou, P. & Martin, P. M. V. (1993).
A study of mucus from the solitary coral *Fungia fungites* (Scleractinia: Fungiidae) in relation to photobiological UV adaptation. *Mar. Biol.* **115**: 263 - 266.
Krupp, D. A. (1984).
Mucus production by corals exposed during an extreme low tide. *Pac. Sci.* **38**: 1 - 11.

Coral Parasites:
Aeby, G. S. (1992).
The potential effect the ability of a coral intermediate host to regenerate has had on the evolution of its association witha marine parasite. *Proc. 7th Internat'l Coral Reef Symp.* **2**: 809 - 815.

Coral Propagation:
Yates, K. R. & Carlson, B. A. (1992).
Corals in aquariums: how to use selective collecting and innovative husbandry to promote reef conservation. *Proc.7th Internat'l Coral Reef Symp.* **2**: 1091 - 1095.

Coral Reefs Evolution:
Achituv, Y. & Dubinsky, Z. (1990).
Evolution and zoogeogrphy of coral reefs. *In:* 'Ecosystems of the World 25: Coral Reefs'; Z. Dubinsky (ed.). Elsevier, Amsterdam. Pgs. 1 - 9.
Grigg, R. W. (1988).
Paleoceanography of coral reefs in the Hawaiian - Emperor chain. *Science* **240**: 1737 - 1743.
Grigg, R. W. (1982).
Darwin Point: A threshold for atoll formation. *Coral Reefs* **1**: 29 - 34.
Rotondo, G. (1980).
A reconstruction of linear island chain positions in the Pacific: a case study using the Hawaiian Emperor chain. Masters Thesis, Univ. of Hawai'i, 58 pp.

Coral Reproduction:
Ayre, D. J. & Resing, J. M. (1986).
Sexual and asexual production of planulae in reef corals. *Mar. Biol.* **90**: 379 - 394.
Fadlallah, Y. H. (1983).
Sexual reproduction, development and larval biology in scleractinian corals: a review. *Coral Reefs* **2**: 129 - 150.
Harrison, P. L. & Wallace, C.C. (1990).
Reproduction, dispersal and recruitment of scleractinian corals. *In:* 'Ecosystems of the World 25: Coral Reefs'; Z. Dubinsky (ed.). Elsevier, Amsterdam, pp. 133 - 207.
Richmond, R. H. & Hunter, C. L. (1990).
Reproduction and recruitment of corals: comparisons among the Caribbean, the Tropical Pacific and the Red Sea. *Mar. Ecol. Prog. Ser.* **60**: 185 - 203.

Sammarco, P. W. (1982).
    Polyp bail-out: an escape response to environemntal stress and a new
    means of reproduction in corals.*Mar. Ecol. Prog. Ser.* **10**(1): 57 - 65.
Simpson, C. J., Cary, J. L. & Masini, R. J. (1993).
    Destruction of corals and other reef animals by coral spawn slicks
    on Ningaloo Reef, Western Australia. *Coral Reefs*: **12**: 185 - 192.
Tunnicliffe, V. (1981).
    Breakage and propagation of the stony coral *Acropora cervicornis*.
    Proc. Nat'l Acad. Sci. **78**(9): 2427 - 2431.

Coral Symbionts:
Abelson, A., Galil, B. S. & Loya, Y. (1991).
    Skeletal modifications in stony corals caused by indwelling crabs:
    Hydrodynamical advantages for crab feeding.
    Symbiosis **10**: 233 - 248.
Coles, S. L. (1986).
    A guide to animals symbiotic with reef corals in Hawaiian waters.
    In: 'Coral Reef Population Biology'; P. L. Jokiel, R. H. Richmond
    & R. A. Rogers (eds.). Hawaii Institute of Marine Biology
    Technical Report #37, pp. 308 - 320.
De Vantier, L. M., Rechelt, R. E. & Bradbury, R. H. (1986).
    Does *Spirobranchus giganteus* protect host *Porites* from predation
    by *Acanthaster planci*:: predator pressure as a mechanism of
    coevolution. *Mar. Ecol. Prog. Ser.* **32**: 307 - 310.
Glynn, P. W. (1982).
    Crustacean symbionts and the defense of corals: coevolution on the
    reef? *In:* 'Coevolution: Proceedings of the 5th Ann. Spr.
    Systematics Symposium: Coevolution. Chicago, IL. May 1982'; M.
    H. Nitecki (ed.). University of Chicago Press, Chicago. pp. 111 - 178.
Glynn, P. W. (1980).
    Defense by symbiotic crustacea of host corals elicited by chemical
    cues from predator. *Oecologia* **47**: 287 -290.
Lassig, B. R. (1977).
    Communication and coexistence in a coral community.
    Mar. Biol. **42**: 85 - 92.
Stimson, J. (1990).
    Stimulation of fat-body production in the polyps of the coral
    Pocillopora damicornis by the presence of mutualistic crabs of the
    genus *Trapezia*. *Mar. Biol.* **106**: 211 - 218.

Corallivores:
Branham, J. M., Reed, S. A., Bailey, J. H. & Caperon, J. (1971).
    Coral-eating sea stars *Acanthaster planci* in Hawaii.
    Science **172**: 1155 - 1157.
Carlson, B. A. (1992).
    Life history and reproductive success of *Exalias brevis*.
    PhD Thesis. University of Hawai'i.
Cox, E. F. (1994).
    Resource use by corallivorous butterflyfishes (family
    Chaetodontidae) in Hawaii. *Bull. Mar. Sci.* **54**(2): 535 - 545.
Glynn, P. W. (1988).
    Predation on coral reefs: some key processes, concepts and research
    directions. *Proc.6th Internat'l Coral Reef Symp.* **1**: 51 - 62.
Great Barrier Reef Marine Authority (1987).
    The Crown-of-Thorns Starfish. *Austral. Sci. Mag.* **3**: 14 - 55.
Hadfield, M. G. (1976).
    Molluscs associated with living tropical corals.
    Micronesica **12**: 181 - 185.
Moran, P. J. (1986).
    The *Acanthaster* phenomenon.
    Oceanogr. Mar. Biol. Ann. Rev. **24**: 379 - 480.
Motta, P. J. (1980)
    Functional anatomy of the jaw apparatus and the related feeding
    behavior of the butterflyfishes (Chaetodontidae) including a review
    of jaw protusion in fishes. PhD Dissertation, University of Hawaii,
    Honolulu. 435pp.
Reese, E. S. (1991).
    How behavior influences community structure of butterflyfishes
    (family Chaetodontidae) on Pacific coral reefs.
    Ecol. Internat'l Bull. **19**: 29 - 41.
Special Issue: *Acanthaster planci* (1990).
    Coral Reefs **9** (3).

Damselfish Territories:
Glynn, P. W. & Colgan, M. W. (1988).
    Defense of corals and enhancement of coral diversity by territorial
    damselfishes. *Proc.6th Internat'l Coral Reef Symp.* **2**: 157 - 163.
Hixon, M. A. & Brostoff, W. N. (1983).
    Damselfish as keystone species in reverse: intermediate disturbance
    and diversity of reef algae. *Science* **220**: 511 - 513.
Lassuy, D. R. (1980).
    Effects of "farming" behavior by *Eupomacentrus lividus* and
    Hemiglyphidodon plagiometopen on algal community structure.
    Bull. Mar. Sci. **30**: 304 - 312.

Dispersal:
Hodgson, G. (1985).
    Abundance and distribution of planktonic coral larvae in Kaneohe
    Bay, Oahu, Hawaii. *Mar. Ecol. Progr. Ser.* **26**: 61 - 71.
Jokiel, P. L. (1990).
    Long-distance dispersal by rafting: reemergence of an old
    hypothesis. *Endeavor* **14**(2): 66 - 73.
Richmond, R. H. (1987).
    Energetics, competency and long distance dispersal of planula larvae
    of the coral *Pocillopora damicornis*. *Mar. Biol.* **93**: 527 - 533.

Disturbance:
Dollar, S. J. & Tribble, G. W. (1993).
    Recurrent storm disturbance and recovery: a long term study of
    coral communities in Hawaii. *Coral Reefs*: **12**: 223 - 233.
Hughes, T. (ed.) (1993).
    Disturbance: effects on coral reef dynamics. Special issue.
    Coral Reefs **12**(3/4).
Karlson, R. H. & Hurd, L. E. (1993).
    Disturbance, coral reef communities, and changing ecological
    paradigms. *Coral Reefs*: **12**: 117 - 126.
Rogers, C. S. (1993).
    Hurricanes and coral reefs. *Coral Reefs*: **12**: 127 - 138.

El Niño:
Glynn, P. W. (1984).
    Widespread coral mortality and the 1982-83 El Niño warming
    event. *Environ. Conserv.* **11**: 133 - 146.

Endemism:
Eldredge, L. C. & Miller, S. E. (1995).
    Records of the Hawaii Biological Survey for 1994: How many
    species are there in Hawaii? *Bishop Mus. Occ. Papers* **41**: 1 - 18.
Hourigan, T. F. & Reese, E. S. (1987).
    Mid-ocean isolation and evolution of Hawaiian reef fishes.
    T.R.E.E. **2**(7): 187 - 191.
Kay, E. A. & Palumbi, S. R. (1987).
    Endemism and evolution in Hawaiian marine invertebrates.
    T.R.E.E. **2**(7): 183 - 186.
Randall, J. E. (1992).
    Endemism of fishes in Oceania. *In:* UNEP: Coastal Resources and
    Systems of the Pacific Basin: Investigation and Steps Toward
    Protective Management. UNEP Regional Seas Report 7 Studies
    No. 147, pp 55 - 67.

Fish Effects on Corals (in general):
Brock, R. E. (1979).
    An experimental study on the effects of grazing by parrotfishes and role
    of refuges in benthic community structure. *Mar. Biol.* **51**: 381 - 388.
Cox, E. F. (1986).
    The effects of a selective corallivore on growth rates and
    competition for space between two species of Hawaiian corals.
    J. Exp. Mar. Biol. Ecol. **101**: 161 - 174.
Glynn, P. W. (1988).
    Predation on coral reefs: Some key processes, concepts and
    research directions. *Proc. 6th Int. Coral Reef Symp.* **1**: 51 - 62.
Neudecker, S. (1979).
    Effects of grazing and browsing fishes on the zonation of corals in
    Guam. *Ecology* **60**: 666 - 672.
Sammarco, P. W. & Carleton, J. H. (1981).
    Damselfish territoriality and coral community structure: Reduced
    grazing, coral recruitment, and effects on coral spat.
    Proc. 4th Int. Coral Reef Symp. **2**: 525 - 535.
Westneat, M. W. & Resing, J. M. (1988).
    Predation on coral spawn by planktivorous fishes. *Coral Reefs* **7**: 89 - 92.

Fish Effects on Coral Growth:
Liberman, T., Genin, A. & Loya, A. (1995).
    Effects of growth and reproduction of the coral *Stylophora
    pistillata* by the mutualistic damselfish *Dascyllus marginatus*. *Mar.
    Biol.* **121**: 741 - 746.
Meyer, J. L., Schultz, E. T. & Helfman, G. S. (1983).
    Fish schools: an asset to corals. *Science* **220**: 1047 - 1049.

Hawaiian Corals:
Grigg, R. W. (1981).
    Acropora in Hawaii. Part 2. Zoogeography. *Pac. Sci.* **35**: 15 - 24.
Grigg, R. W., Wells, J. and Wallace, C. (1981).
    Acropora in Hawaii, part I. History of the scientific record,
    systematics and ecology. *Pac. Sci.* **35**: 1 - 13.

Jokiel, P. L. (1987).
  Ecology, biogeography and evolution of corals in Hawaii.
  T. R. E. E. **2**(7): 179 - 182.
Kenyon, J. C. (1992).
  Sexual reproduction in Hawaiian *Acropora*. *Coral Reefs* **11**: 37 - 43.
Maragos, J. E. (1972).
  A study of the ecology of Hawaiian reef corals.
  PhD. Thesis. Univ. of Hawai'i, Honolulu, HI.

Hawaiian's Use of Corals:
Johnson, R. K. (1981).
  Kumulipo - The Hawaiian Hymn of Creation Vol. I. Top Gallant
  Publ. Co., Ltd. Honolulu, HI. Pg 4.
Titcomb, M. (1978).
  Native use of marine invertebrates in old Hawai'i.
  Pac. Sci. **32**(4): 325 - 386.

Herbivory:
Horn, M. H. (1989).
  Biology of marine herbivorous fishes.
  Oceanogr. Mar. Biol. Annu. Rev. **27**: 167 - 272.
Steneck, R. S. (1988).
  Herbivory on coral reefs: A synthesis.
  Proc. 6th Internat'l Coral Reef Symp. **1**: 37 - 49.

Human Impacts:
Grigg, R. W. (1997).
  Hawaii's coral reefs: status and health in 1997. *In:* 'Status of Coral
  Reefs in the Pacific'. R. W. Grigg & C. Birkeland (eds.). Univer-
  sity of Hawai'i Sea Grant Program.
  UNIHI-SEAGRANT-CP-98-01.
Grigg, R. W. (1995).
  Coral reefs in an urban embayment in Hawaii: a complex case history
  controlled by natural and anthropogenic stress. *Coral Reefs* **14**: 253 - 266.
Howard, L. S. & Brown, B. E. (1984).
  Heavy metals and reef corals.
  Oceanogr. Mar. Biol. Annu. Rev. **22**: 195 - 210.
Lapointe, B. E., Littler, M. M. & Littler, D. S. (1997).
  Macroalgal overgrowth of fringing coral reefs Jamaica: Bottom-up
  vs top-down control. *Proc. 8th Int. Coral Reef Symp.* **1**: 927 - 932.
Maragos, J. E. (1993).
  Impact of coastal construction on coral reefs in the U.S. - affiliated
  Pacific islands. *Coast. Mgmt* **21**: 235 - 269.
Maragos, J. E., Crosby, M. P. & McManus, J. W. (1996).
  Coral reefs and biodiversity: a critical and threatened relationship.
  Oceanography **9**(1): 83 - 99.
Richmond, R. H. (1993).
  Coral reefs: present problems and future concerns resulting from
  anthropogenic disturbances. *Amer. Zool.* **33**: 5234 - 536.
Wilkinson, C. P. (1992).
  Coral reefs of the world are facing widespread devestation: can we
  prevent this through sustainable management practices? *Proc.7th
  Internat'l Coral Reef Symp.* **1**: 11 - 21.

Hydrozoans:
Lewis, J. B. (1989).
  The ecology of *Millepora*: a review. *Coral Reefs* **8**: 99 - 107.

Introduced Species:
Carlton, J. T. (1989).
  Man's role in changing the face of the ocean: Biological invasions
  and implications for conservation of near-shore environments.
  Conserv. Biol. **3**(3): 265 - 273.
Randall, J. E. (1987).
  Introductions of marine fishes to the Hawaiian Islands.
  Bull. Mar. Sci. **41**: 490 - 502.

Kane'ohe Bay:
Jokiel, P. L., Hunter, C. L., Taguchi, S. & Waterai, L. (1993).
  Ecological impact of a fresh-water "reef kill" in Kane'ohe Bay,
  O'ahu, Hawai'i. *Coral Reefs* **12**: 177 - 185.

Marine Conservation:
Bohnsack, J. A. (1994).
  Marine reserves: they enhance fisheries, reduce conflicts, and
  protect resources. *NAGA, The ICLARM Quarterly* **17**(3): 4 - 7.

Octacorals:
Fabricius, K. E., Benayahu, Y. & Genin, A. (1995).
  Herbivory in asymbiotic soft corals. *Science* **268**: 90 - 92.

Oil Pollution:
National Research Council (1985).
  Oil in the Sea, Inputs, Fates and Effects. National Academy Press,
  Washington, D. C.

Pfund, R. T. (ed.) (1992).
  Oilspills at sea. Potential impacts on Hawaii. A report prepared for
  the Department of Health, State of Hawai'i by the University of
  Hawai'i Sea Grant College Program. CR - 92 06, 166 pp.
Te, F. T. (1991).
  Effects of two petroleum products on *Pocillopora damicornis*
  planulae. *Pac. Sci.* **45**: 290 - 298.

Recruitment (Chaos/Order Hypotheses):
Sale, P. F. (1975).
  Patterns of use of space in a guild of territorial reefs fishes.
  Mar. Biol. **29**: 89 - 97.
Sale, P. F. (1978).
  Coexistence of coral reef fish - a lottery for living space.
  Envir. Biol. Fishes **3**: 85 - 102.
Smith, C. L. (1978).
  Coral reef fish communities: a compromise view.
  Envir. Biol. Fishes **3**: 109- 128.

Reef at Night/Crepuscular Period:
Byrne, J. E. (1970).
  Mucous envelope formation in two species of Hawaiian parrotfishes
  (genus *Scaridae*). *Pac. Sci.* 24: 490 - 493.
Hobson, E. S. (1972).
  Activity of Hawaiian reef fishes during the evening and morning
  transitions between daylight and darkness. *Fish. Bull.* **70**: 715 -
  740.
McFarland, W. N. (1986).
  Light in the sea - correlations with behaviors of fishes and
  invertebrates. *Am. Zool.* **26**: 389 - 401.

Sewage:
Pastorek, R. A. & Bilyard, G. R. (1985).
  Effects of sewage pollution on coral-reef communities.
  Mar. Ecol. Prog. Ser. **21**: 175 - 189.

Sex Change:
Warner, R. R. (1984).
  Mating behavior and hermaphroditism in coral reef fishes.
  Am. Sci. **72**: 128 - 136.

Skeleton Formation:
Goreau, T. F. (1959).
  The physiology of skeleton formation in corals. *Biol. Bull.* **116:** 59 - 75.

Succession:
Grigg, R. W. (1983).
  Community structure, succession and development of coral reefs in
  Hawaii. *Mar. Ecol. Prog. Ser.* **11**: 1 - 14.
Grigg, R. W. & Maragos, J. E. (1974).
  Recolonization of hermatypic corals on submerged lava flows in
  Hawaii. *Ecology* **55**: 387 - 395.

Symbiosis:
Castro, P. (1986).
  Symbiosis in coral reef communities: a review. *In:* 'Coral Reef
  Population Biology'; P. L. Jokiel, R. H. Richmond & R. A. Rogers
  (eds.). Hawaii Institute of Marine Biology Technical Report #37,
  pp. 292 - 307.

Ultraviolet Radiation Effects:
Jokiel, P. L. (1980).
  Solar ultraviolet radiation and coral reef epifauna.
  Science **207**: 1069 - 1071.
Schick, J. M., Lesser, M. P., & Stochaj, W. R. (1991).
  Ultraviolet radiation and photooxidative stress in zooxanthellate
  Anthozoa: the sea anemone *Phyllodiscus semoni* and the octacoral
  Clavularia sp. *Symbiosis* **10**: 145 - 173.

Zooxanthellae:
Davies, P. S. (1984).
  The role of zooxanthellae in the nutritive energy requirements of
  Pocillopora eydouxi. *Coral Reefs* **2**: 181 - 186.
Muscatine, L., Falkowski, P., Porter, J. & Dubinsky, Z. (1984).
  Fate of photosynthetically-fixed carbon in light and shade-adapted
  colonies of the symbiotic coral *Stylophora pistillata*.
  Proc. R. Soc. London B.I **222**: 181 - 202.

SCIENTIFIC NAME INDEX

GENERAL INDEX

ANSWERS TO CNIDOQUESTIONS

p 15 (Super Stomach)

Remember that the coelenteron is like a bag and the mouth can close to seal that bag. If gas were to be secreted into a closed stomach it would inflate much like a balloon. Once the pedal disc is loose, the anemone could float up into the water column where currents would move it. Release of the gas would result in the cnidarian increasing its density and returning to the substrate below where it could re-attach.

p 19 (Sea Jelly Symbiosis)

In addition to possibly serving as an attractant, the associated fish might also remove parasites (such as the lobster larvae) from the external bell of the sea jelly.

p 20 (Sea Jelly Tidbits)

Bioluminescence could possibly function to attract prey organisms towards the tentacles, serve for mate attraction (remember that sea jellies have photosensory capability) or as a form of countershading to blend in with down-welling light in order to not present a silhouette to predators or prey.

p 32 (Zooxanthellae)

Though we'll never truly know how such a complex symbiosis may have arose, we can hypothesize based on the life histories of those involved. We know that animals such as anemones and clams feed on microscopic plankton. Presumably, at some early point in the evolutionary history of these organisms, certain shallow water individuals who were genetically unable to digest certain single-celled plants and had relatively thin, transparent tissue layers consumed unicellular algae that was genetically predisposed to surviving within the organism's internal tissue environment. The non-digested plants would presumably be able to conduct some photosynthesis allowing them to survive and possibly dumping the extra photosynthate onto their hosts. This additional energy over time would have given these animals a competitive edge and enhanced their own reproduction. With reproduction, the traits that selected for such a symbiosis would be enhanced, eventually resulting in very complex, obligate host/symbiont complexes like those seen with corals and giant clams.

p 68 (Anemone Symbiosis)

The crab is thought to benefit from increased camouflage and protection from certain parasites that might otherwise try to worm their way into its shell. The anemone gains a form of transport, protection, and due to its close proximity to the crab (and the fact that crab are notoriously messy eaters), a source of food as it can capture the scraps formed as the crab macerates its food.

p 79 (Fragmentation)

Possible biological sources of fragmentation include: boring sponges (p 162), sea turtle sleeping behavior (p 166), fish behavior, and the actions of humans on reefs.

p 83 (Coral Reproduction)

Traditionally, corals (and many reef fish) have been thought to spawn at night to avoid predation on their gametes by visual, diurnal predators. Other possible reasons involve tying in dispersal with tidal and lunar cycles, and limiting ultraviolet radiation effects on gametes.

p 103 (Bite Marks)

A - 2, B - 1, C - 4, D - 3.

p 109 (Symbiosis)

Nope, too easy...you're going to have to find these on your own!!!!!!!

p 110 (Crabs)

Atop *Pocillopora* corals on which it usually resides, the dark spots may mimic the retracted polyps during the day (remember that under natural light conditions underwater, the orange and dark red colors will be partially absorbed resulting in a very close matching with the colony).

p 112 (Crab Defense)

Most corallivorous fish remove distinct bites from a coral colony. This is a rather fast and concentrated versus the very slow, wide-spread attack by the seastar. As such, it is unlikely that the shrimp or crabs could be very effective at preventing a corallivorous fish from feeding on a coral, and may in fact be exposing themselves to increased predation from fish predators.

p 112 (Crab Defense)

It might seem counter-productive for the seastar to warn the crab and shrimp of its approach. But by cueing the coral's crabs and shrimp chemically, the Crown-of-Thorns elicits an early warning of the coral being defended. Energetically, it might be more advantageous to know which corals are well defended in order to avoid wasting energy attacking them and concentrate on less-well-defended colonies.

p 113 (Gall Crabs)

The female crab makes a much greater investment in the offspring then does the male. Not only does she invest more of her own energy into the eggs (relative to the male's investment in sperm), but she carries the fertilized eggs with her till they hatch. By living in a gall she, and her eggs, are protected from predation allowing her to focus her energies on feeding and reproduction (Note how, unlike most crabs, she is relatively soft-shelled).

p 130 (Darwin Point)

If one follows the Emperor Seamounts all the way to the northwest, the oldest one is Meiji Seamount (70 million years) which lies close to a portion of Russia called Siberia.

p 131 (Darwin Point)

Many scientists feel that the older seamounts in the chain were near the surface (and the hot spot) at a time when oceanic currents were very different, possibly preventing coral larvae from reaching them and successfully settling.

p 145 (Octopus)

By turning black the octopus may be implanting a search image on a potential predator (i.e. the predator's mind is telling itself that food = black octopus shape); the octopus then orientates its body such that it's tapered towards the predator with the tentacles and mouth facing its attacker. At this point the ink can be released along with an associated color change by the octopus back to a background coloration. The predator meanwhile sees the black "octopus" (which is now the condensed ink blob) heading towards it. Thus the color change by the octopus may facilitate a search image by the attacker which can be passed on to the ink cloud as a distraction before the ink comes into contact with the predator. Yup, the ink serves as a smoke screen, but perhaps in a different way then most people think...

p 148 (Feeding Guilds)

Both are trick questions...see the section on schooling behavior (p 154 - 155).

p 160 (Sex Change)

In the highly complex world of a coral reef where small patches of reef can serve as important resources (and thus often become territories) to be held by the largest and strongest members of a species that uses that resource; this is usually the male (males often put far less energy into reproduction than females ("sperm is cheap!") and thus are thought to have more energy available for growth). In such cases where a large male controls a resource, it would be disadvantageous to allow access to smaller males (which given such access, can grow and contest control of the resource at a later time). Females on the other hand represent an opportunity to pass on one's genes and thus may provide a return for sharing of the limited resource.

A FINAL LOOK AT THE MULTIPLE USE OF HABITAT BY REEF ORGANISMS

One last point: Sometimes it's good to be skeptical about what you read in books like this. Take the time to think about what's being said and then evaluate it for yourself. The picture above is of a scorpionfish resting on the bottom.

POP QUIZ ANSWERS

(p 115) Shrimps

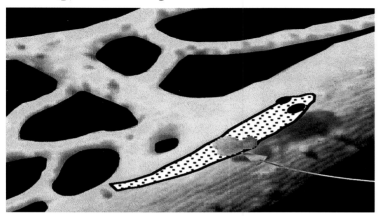

OK, I admit it, this has absolutely nothing to do with shrimp - but I really liked the photo...

Parasitic Copepod attached onto symbiotic goby living atop sea fan.

(p 149) Feeding Guilds

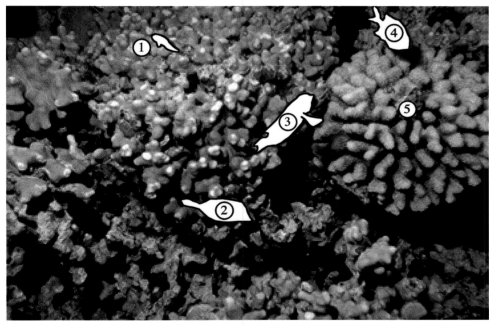

① - Ambush Predator (Hawkfish)

② - Grazing Benthic Invertebrate Feeder (Trunkfish)

③ - Cropping Herbivore (Surgeonfish)

④ - Picking Planktivore (*Chromis* Damselfish)

⑤ - Picking Planktivore (Coral Colony)

(p 187) Biological Impacts on Coral Colony

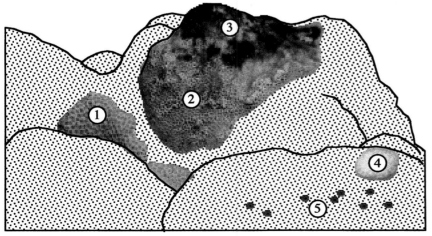

① - Neoplasms (tumors)

② - Stress Response

③ - Algal Infestations

④ - *Exalias brevis* (Shortbodied Blenny) Bite Mark

⑤ - Butterflyfish Bite Marks